HEINEMANN **GEOGRAPHY**

NEW EDITION *FOR EDEXCEL B*

Global Challenges

Series Editor

Bob Digby

Authors

Bob Digby
Jane Ferretti
Ian Flintoff
Andy Owen
Chris Ryan

Heinemann Educational Publishers
Halley Court, Jordan Hill, Oxford, OX2 8EJ
Part of Harcourt Education
Heinemann is the registered trademark of Harcourt
Education Limited

© Bob Digby, Jane Ferretti, Ian Flintoff, Andy Owen,
Chris Ryan, 2001

First published 2001

10-digit ISBN: 0 435352 49 0
13-digit ISBN: 978 0 435352 49 3

08 07 06 05
10 9 8 7 6 5 4

Original illustrations © Heinemann Educational
Publishers 2001

Designed and illustrated by Hardlines, Charlbury,
Oxford OX7 3PS

Printed and bound in Spain by Edelvives

Photographs

P.10: Figure 1.1, Associated Press / Amit Bhargava; P.10: Figure
1.2, Associated Press / Vikram Kumar; P.16: Figure 1.14, USGS;
P.16: Figure 1.15, Associated Press / Victor R Caivano; P.25:
Figure 2.7, NERC; P.26: Figure 2.12, NERC; P.26: Figure 2.13,
NERC; P.33: Figure 2.23, Woodfall Wild Images / David
Woodfall; P.34: Figure 2.25, NERC; P.41: Figure 3.7A, Still
Pictures / Mark Edwards; P.41: Figure 3.7B, Robert Harding
Picture Library; P.41: Figure 3.7C, Still Pictures / William Fautre;
P.42: Figure 3.10, Corbis; P.46: Figure 3.16, Associated Press
NOAA; P.47: Figure 3.17, Still Pictures / Tantyo Bangun; P.47:
Figure 3.18, Reuters / Manuel Llanos; P.48: Figure 3.19, Joanna
B Pinneo; P.49: Figure 4.1, Greenpeace / Beltra; P.56: Figure 4.12,
Popperfoto; P.60: Figure 4.17, Environmental Images / Michael
Dean; P.68: Figure 1, Associated Press / Laura Rauch; P.70:
Figure 3, Neil Fitzgerald and Stephen Dye; P.72: Figure 5.2,
Panos Pictures; P.73: Figure 5.3, Still Pictures; P.77: Figure 5.7,
Panos Pictures / Jean-Leo Dugast; P.83: Figure 6.3, Woodfall
Wild Images / David Woodfall; P.85: Figure 6.6, Oxford
Scientific Films / John Mitchell; P.86: Figure 6.8, Bob Digby; P.89:
Figure 6.11, Bob Digby; P.90: Figure 6.13, Woodfall Wild Images
/ David Woodfall; P.91: Figure 6.15, Bob Digby; P.99: Figure 7.3,
Graham Ranger; P.100: Figure 7.4, BBC; P.101: Figure 7.5, Still
Pictures / Mark Edwards; P.102: Figure 7.6, Still Pictures / Mark
Edwards; P.106: Figure 8.1A, Still Pictures / Fred Dott; P.106:
Figure 8.1B, Still Pictures / Yves Lefevre; P.106: Figure 8.1C, Still
Pictures / Roland Seitre; P.106: Figure 8.1D, Environmental
Images / Rob Visser; P.106: Figure 8.1E, Oxford Scientific Films
/ Colin Monteath / Hedgehog House; P.106: Figure 8.1F, Still
Pictures / Sarvottam Rajkoomar; P.109: Figure 8.4, Still Pictures
/ Jeffrey Rotman; P.113: Figure 8.8, Bob Digby; P.114: Figure
8.10A, Greenpeace / Vaccari; P.114: Figure 8.10B, Woodfall Wild
Images / H Berg; P.114: Figure 8.10C, Woodfall Wild Images /
David Woodfall; P.116: Figure 8.12, Still Pictures / Mark
Edwards; P.120: Figure 9.2, Oxford Scientific Films / Daniel J
Cox; P.121: Figure 9.6, Bruce Coleman Collection / Mark
Carwardine; P.122: Figure 9.7, Environmental Images Steve
Morgan; P.124: Figure 10.2, Woodfall Wild Images / Bob
Gibbons; P.126: Figure 10.8, Bob Digby; P.131: Figure 1, REX /
Ray Tang; P.131: Figure 2, Andy Owen; P.132: Figure 3, Still
Pictures / Mark Edwards; P.133: Figure 11.1, Corbis; P.136:
Figure 11.6, Woodfall Wild Images / N Hicks; P.144: Figure 12.1,
NASA / Science Photo Library; P.145: Figure 12.3, Andy Owen;
P.145: Figure 12.4A, Skyscan Photolibrary; P.145: Figure 12.4B
Popperfoto / Reuters; P.152: Figure 12.16, Jim Wark /
AIRPHOTO; P.153: Figure 12.17, Popperfoto / Reuters; P.156:
Figure 13.2, Panos Pictures / Jean-Leo Dugast; P.156: Figure
13.8, Still Pictures / Mark Edwards; P.159: Figure 13.9, Panos
Pictures / Sean Sprague; P.161: Figure13.14, Still Pictures / John
Issac; P.164: Figure 13.19, Andy Owen; P.167: Figure 14.1A,
Associated Press; P.167: Figure 14.1B, Panos Pictures / Paul
Smith; P.170: Figure 14.7, Andy Owen; P.175: Figure 14.13, Panos
Pictures / J Holmes; P.177: Figure 14.17, Oxford Scientific Films
/ Michael Pitts; P.183: Figure 15.7, Reuters / Pascal Rossignol;
P.183: Figure 15.8, REX / Frenado Cavalcanti; P.188: Figure
15.18, REX / Bengin / Milliyet; P.191: Figure 3, Empics; P.191:
Figure 4, Bob Digby; P.200: Figure 16.8, Bob Digby; P.200: Figure
16.9, Woodfall wild Images / Nigel Hicks; P.204: Figure 17.1,
Bob Digby; P.210: Figure 17.11, Panos Pictures / Jeremy Horner;
P.214: Figure 18.4, Robert Harding / Glyn Genin; P.216: Figure
18.8, Panos Pictures / Chris Stowers; P.220: Figure 19.5, GSK
House Project Team / GlaxoSmithKline; P.235: Figure 20.8A,
Environmental images / Martin Bond; P.235: Figure 20.8B, Ted
Edwards Photography236: Figure 20.9, Shropshire Star; P.236:
Figure 20.10, Aerofilms; P.242: Figure 21.1, Oxford Scientific
Films / Keren Su; P.242: Figure 21.2, Still Pictres / Hartmut
Schwarzbach; P.243: Figure 21/4, Woodfall Wild Images / Nigel
Hicks; P.248: Figure 22.2, Popperfoto / Reuters / Robert Sorbo;
P.249: Figure 22.3, Woodfall Wild Images / Bill Sanderson.

The publishers have made every effort to trace the copyright
holders, but if they have inadvertently overlooked any, they will
be pleased to make the necessary arrangements at the first
opportunity.

Contents

Acknowledgements

The authors and publishers would like to thank the following for permission to use copyright material:

Maps and extracts

p.6 The Perfect Storm © 2000 Warner Bros.; **p.6** Reuters Limited 2000; **p.7** The Boston Globe; p.8 The Yearbook of Australia / Australian Bureau of Statistics; **p.11** The New Internationalist December 1999; **p.13** PJ Das, Monsoons / Fein & Stephens 1987. Reprinted by permission of John Wiley & Sons, Inc.; p.14 T, 15 L Landsea et al, Weather / Royal Meteorological Society; **p.15 R** The Observer; **p.16 M** National Geographic Volume 196 1999 / National Geographic Society; **p.18** Landsea et al, Weather / Royal Meteorological Society; **p.21 T** Greg O'Hare and John Sweeney, Geography Vol. 78, 1 1993 / Geographic Association; **p.21 B** The Guardian; **p.22 L** The Met Office; **p.23** N Law and D Smith, Decision Making Geography / Stanley Thornes 1990; **p.24, 25** The Met Office; **p.29 B** RG Barry and RJ Chorley, Atmosphere, Weather and Climate / Methuen; **p.30** The Daily Mail; **p.31** The Times / News International; **p.32** The Surrey Weather Book – The Physical Environment Series / Frosted Earth; **p.34** The London Evening Standard; **p.36** 'El Nino: Disasters in the Wind,' Geodate, Vol. 11 2 May 1998 / Warringal Publications Australia; **p.42 B** Dr Mike Hulme, 'Causes of climate and variability in the African Sahel / SAGT; **p.43** The Observer; **p.44** Bureau of Meteorology, Australia; **p.45** National Geographic Society; **p.46** The Times / News International; **p.51, 52 T, M** Scientific Assessment of Climate Change / IPCC WMO UNEP; p.52 B WMO Statement of the status of the global climate in 1999 No. 913 / WMO; **p.54** The Guardian; **p.58 M** World Climate News No. 17 June 2000 / WMO; **p.59** The New Scientist; **p.60** Stuart R Gaffin, High Water Blues: Impact of Sea Level Rise on Selected Coasts and Islands / Environmental Defence; **p.63 L** Michael Meacher / The Guardian; **p.63 R** The New Internationalist November 2000; **p.68** www.bbc.co.uk ; **p.71** Greg O'Hare, Soils, Vegetation and Ecosystems / Oliver & Boyd 1998; **p.73** The Independent; **p.76** Friends of the Earth / www.foe.co.uk ; **p.78** Developments 3rd Quarter 1998 / DFID; **p.79** www.panda.org ; **p.79** The Independent; **p.82** www.panda.org ; **p.85** By permission of Greenpeace International; **p.98** Edexcel Exam Board 1991; **p.102** The Kilum Mountain Forrest Project; **p.111** http://coral.aoml.noaa.gov ; **p.114** The New York Times; **p.114** The Independent; **p.114** The Sunday Telegraph; **p.117 B** Sue Cunningham, A Raindrop Cleans the Wetlands / www.changemakers.net/journal/98october/cunningham.cfm ; **p.119, 121 B** By permission of Greenpeace International; **p.121** Japan Times; **p.121 C** High North Alliance / www.highnorth.no ; **p.124** Ben Box, South American Handbook / NTC Publishing 1997; **p.125 M** www.wcmc.org.uk/protected_areas/data/wh/galapago.html ; **p.129** www.unep.ch/seas/mappage1.html ; **p.133** Meadows et al, Beyond the Limits / Earthscan Publications Ltd and Chelsea Green Publishing Co.; **p.134** A Goudie and H Viles, The Earth Transformed / Blackwell Publishers1987; **p.138 T** A Bowen and K Pallister, AS Level Geography / Heinemann 2000; **p.138 B** Population Concern Database / Population Concern 1997; **p.140 T, B** P Sarre and J Blunden, An Overcrowded World / Oxford University Press 1987; **p.141 B** J Cole, Geography of the World's Major Regions / Nippon 1993; **p.142** P Demeny, 'A perspective on long term population growth' Population and Development Review Vol. 10 1 1984 / The Population Council; p.144 CWDE; **p.147** The Washington Post; **p.148 T** Food and Agriculture Organization of the United Nations 1999 ; **p.148 B** Stephen Devereux, IDS Working Paper 105 / IDS 2000. The full text of the working paper can be obtained from the Institute of Development Studies, or downloaded from www.ids.ac.uk ; **p.149 R** Food and Agriculture Organization of the United Nations 1999; **p.150 B** United Nations World Food Programme; p.151 The Daily Mail and Guardian (African Edn); **p.155** www.unicef.org; **p.156 M** B Knapp et al, Challenge of the Human Environment / Longman 1989; **p.156 B** Carol Bellamy, The State of the World's Children – Education / UNICEF; **p.157 T** Common Cause /

Action Aid 1992; **p.159 B** The final programme of Action agreed to in Cairo, VII Reproductive Rights and Reproductive Health, B Family Planning, Basis for Action 7.12 / International Institute for Sustainable Development; **p.160 T, B, 161** Carol Bellamy, The State of the World's Children – Education / UNICEF; **p.162** James Anderson, A Global World? 1995. By permission of Oxford University Press; **p.163 M** The Independent; **p.166** S Raju et al, An Atlas of Women and Men in India / Vedams eBooks Ltd; **p.171 B** J Chrispin and F Jegede, Population Resources and Development / Collins Educational 1996; **p.176 T** The Guardian; **p.176 B, 177** D Drakakis-Smith, The Third World City / Routledge 1987; **p.180 M, B** Social Trends, National Statistics © Crown Copyright; **p.181** AJ Fielding, The Population of England and Wales in 1991 – A Census Atlas / Geographical Association 1993; **p.182** World Population Prospects: The 1998 Revision, Vol. 1 Comprehensive Tables; Vol. II Sex and Age; Vol. III Analytical Report / Population Division of the Department of Economic and Social Affairs of the United Nations Secretariat (1999); **p.183 M, 184 T** www.bbc.co.uk ; **p.184 B** J Chrispin and F Jegede, Population Resources and Development / Collins Educational 1996; **p.185, 186 T** The Times Educational Supplement / News International; **p.186 M** 'Applications for Asylum to the UK 1990-1999,' Home Office Statistical Bulletin 17/00, Asylum Statistics 1999; **p.186 B** 'Asylum applications by area of origin1998 & 1999,' Home Office Statistical Bulletin 17/00, Asylum Statistics 1999; **p.187 T** 'Applications for asylum to the UK by age and gender 1999,' Home Office Statistical Bulletin 17/00, Asylum Statistics 1999; **p.195 M** RJ Cootes, Britain Since 1700 / Longman; **p.195 B** World Bank Atlas 2000; **p.196** The Human Development Report 1999 / United Nations Development Programme; **p.197 T, B, 198 T** World Bank Atlas 2000; **p.198 B** The Human Development Report 1999 / United Nations Development Programme; **p.199** World Development Report 1993; **p.200 B** The World Health Report 1995 / World Health Organization; **p.201, 202 T, M** The Human Development Report 1999 / United Nations Development Programme; **p.205 T** HMSO © Crown Copyright; **p.206 M** Food and Agriculture Organization of the United Nations; p.207 T The New Internationalist; **p.208** Food and Agriculture Organization of the United Nations; **p.215** Council of Labour Affairs, Taipei; **p.216 B** The Money Machine / Delta Electronics Inc. 1994; **p.218 L** Dragons in Distress: Crisis and Conflict in Asia's Miracle Economics / The Ecologist; **p.218 R** W Bello and S Rosenfeld, High Speed Industrialisation and Environmental Devastation in Taiwan / The Ecologist 1990; **p.219 T, 220 M** The Human Development Report 1999 / United Nations Development Programme; **p.221 R** The New Internationalist, July 1999; **p.222, 223** Mattel Inc.; **p.225 B** Population Development Base, Population Concern 12998 / Data World Bank; **p.226** Mattel Inc.; **p.227 T** Eyal Press, Barbie's Betrayal. Reprinted with permission from the December 30, 1996 issue of The Nation; **p.227** Anton Foek, Sweat Shop Barbie: Exploitation of Third World Labour / The Humanist 1997; **p.227 B** www.Mattel.com; **p.228 T** By permission of GreenPeace International; **p.228 B** Reuters Limited 1999; **p.230** The Birmingham Post; **p.230** Electronics Weekly; **p.230** Birmingham Evening Mail, **p.230** Syndication International; **p.230** Labour Market Review Vol. 1 3 1998-99 / Birmingham Economic Centre; **p.232** Birmingham City Council Economic Information Centre; **p.233 T, B** Butt Graham et al, Birmingham: Decisions on Development / Development Education Centre; **p.237 T** The Economist Intelligence Unit Ltd; **p.238** Birmingham City Council Economic Information Centre; **p.240** Birmingham Economic Review October 2000; **p.244, 245 T** World Bank Atlas 2000; **p.245 B** The Human Development Report 1999 / United Nations Development Programme; **p.248 M** The Independent; **p.249 R** Chambers, Challenging the Professions / IT Publications, London 1993; **p.252 R** D Bowden, Mekong River Basin / Australian Association for Environmental Education 1998.

The publishers have made every effort to trace the copyright holders, but if they have inadvertently overlooked any, they will be pleased to make the necessary arrangements at the first opportunity.

How to use this book

This book is written to help you prepare for the A2 examination for Edexcel Geography Specification B. It will also help students who are studying a range of specifications in the UK and overseas.

What is the book about?

The book is about global challenges. It focuses upon issues that concern people and their environments. Geographers study these interactions between people and the physical world in which they live. On one hand, natural processes such as climatic change and global warming pose challenges for people, while on the other human challenges also exist. How can we feed all the people of the world, and provide a decent standard of living for them? What impact is the global economy having on people in the wealthy and the poorest countries of the world? 'Global Challenges' is about some of these changes, and how people are responding to them.

The book is divided into four parts:

- **Part 1 Changing weather and climate**, where you will study climate processes, including those processes that cause weather and climate in the UK and other parts of the world. You will also study how people affect climate through, for instance, emissions of carbon dioxide, which is held to be the main cause of global warming;
- **Part 2 Global Biomes, in which global vegetation zones are studied**, in terms of natural processes (so that you will know and understand how different vegetation zones exist) and the impact that people have upon these. As well as the issues of clearance in areas of rainforest, the section will also consider marine ecosystems and the threats posed by people in the oceans of the world;
- **Part 3 Population**, in which you will study the global population explosion. The section considers where this is happening, who is affected by it, and whether the world can feed and resource so many people. It also considers how the world can sustain increasing numbers of elderly people, as living standards rise and health improves;
- **Part 4 – The Changing Global Economy**, shows how economic change has led to the emergence of a global economy, in which large organisations (such as trans-national companies or international governments such as the EU) create and manage economic change. It considers where the world's wealthiest and poorest countries are, and how the economy of most of the world's poor is driven by demand for goods in the wealthiest parts of the world.

How to use this book

Each part of the book is sub-divided into chapters, which focus on different aspects of issues in different parts of the world. Each chapter is written to enable you to read from beginning to end. You will need to refer to the figures as you read. The following features are threaded into each chapter to help you understand its concepts and content more easily;

a) Theory Boxes, which help to explain geographical processes that are required to understand the issues in each chapter.

b) Technique boxes, to help you to be able to present, interpret and analyse data in each chapter.

c) Student Activities, to help you to interpret data and text, and work with others in understanding different viewpoints on each issue. Some of these are individual, while others are designed for groups.

At the end of each section, a section summary helps you to draw together the concepts and ideas in order to help you reflect upon and revise your learning.

People, weather and climate
Introducing weather and climate

How are people influenced by weather events?

Weather events make startling news. They fill prime time television slots and form the basis of cinema box office hits such as *The Perfect Storm* (Figure 1). In the case of *The Perfect Storm*, the focus of the film is the story of the crew of the swordfishing boat, the *Andrea Gail*, as they encounter the effects of two enormous weather systems which combine unexpectedly over the North Atlantic. The use of computer enhanced imagery enables filmmakers to capture some sense of the awesome nature of severe weather events and the effect that they have on people. For those who fish the seas and lose close colleagues and friends in storms, the terror of the power of the oceans is well understood.

Why is there such interest in severe weather events? For some people it is a fascination with natural processes over which we seem to have no control; for others it raises questions about whether we are altering the nature of weather systems in ways previous generations thought impossible. Figures 2 and 3 give further examples of disruptive and dangerous weather from among a huge range of severe weather events over the course of the year 2000. Is this typical of the Earth's atmosphere or are severe weather events increasing as a result of changing global conditions?

What are our motives in showing an interest in the weather? Urban dwellers do not expect to face

Figure 1 *The Perfect Storm.*

Tornadoes wreak havoc in Fort Worth

FORT WORTH – Overturned cars, shattered glass from high-rise buildings and rain-soaked debris littered streets as the aftermath of destructive tornadoes and severe storms that killed four people paralysed the city on Wednesday.

Power lines were downed and trees were uprooted by the storms that struck the Fort Worth and Dallas areas on Tuesday evening. Rescue crews searched for victims.

'Luckily it was very few and far between as far as victims found in those buildings last night are concerned,' Fort Worth Fire Lt. Kent Wolsey said.

Front-end loaders and dump trucks plied Fort Worth streets as authorities closed the downtown. People were urged to stay away until experts could determine if any buildings sustained structural damage. Authorities also worried about broken glass still dangling from buildings.

Fort Worth is a city of some 500 000 people about 30 miles (48km) west of Dallas. A church lost its roof and the walls of its steeple. Other buildings collapsed and many structures lost all or part of their roofs.

'I've been with the fire department for 23 years and this is the worst damage I've ever seen,' Wolsey said.

'Imagine a large bomb going off,' said Sean Finley, whose restaurant atop a 35-storey building was destroyed by winds that blasted through windows.

Jerry Johns of Southwestern Insurance Information Centre said the early damage estimate was in the hundreds of millions of dollars.

Figure 2 From Reuters News Service, 31 March 2000.

Blistering heat wave in Europe leaves 25 dead, melts roads

ATHENS – A heat wave in southeastern Europe sent temperatures rocketing to 113 degrees in some places yesterday, leaving 25 people dead, melting roads in Turkey, and driving hundreds to seek medical help.

Firefighters battled hundreds of blazes sparked by arid conditions in Bulgaria, Croatia, Greece, Italy, and Romania. In Turkey, the heat killed 5200 chickens and led camel drivers to wet down their animals.

In Athens, sweltering residents snapped up air conditioners and set a record for electric consumption. 'This is the hottest July 6 for some 60 years,' said Turkish meteorologist Seyfullah Celik.

Meteorologists say a high pressure area that has held over the southeast of the continent since the beginning of the week has driven temperatures to record levels. Average daytime temperatures for much of the Balkans normally swing from about 86 to 95 degrees in summer.

The high pressure has trapped hot air masses flowing up from the Sahara desert and the Middle East. Southwestern Iran, for example, had a reported high of 120 degrees. A colder front in central Europe has so far been unable to push through the barrier in the northern Balkans.

'It looks like the situation of Greece, south and east Turkey and also for Cyprus will see high temperatures continuing until the end of the next week. They will be high in the rest of the Balkans,' Greek meteorologist Theodoros Kolidas said.

Figure 3 From the *Boston Globe*, 7 July 2000.

such life threatening events as those in Fort Worth in March 2000 and certainly not in the richest country in the world. But why is it that we appear so out of touch with the threats to our lives and to the economy posed by these natural phenomena? Tornadoes occur annually in Texas – yet city authorities were not prepared! Do wealthy societies really cope better with these natural hazards than poorer countries?

Forecasting weather is now at an advanced stage with a new breed of computer software being developed which will give hour by hour forecasts (renamed 'Nowcasts' by the World Meteorological Organisation!). In September 2000 the UK Met Office used two new programmes called NIMROD and GANDOLF for the first time at the Sydney Olympics to predict with high accuracy the path and pattern of rainstorms and thunderstorms. However, small intensive systems such as tornadoes and thunderstorms and some large systems such as hurricanes still defy even the most sophisticated computer simulation. What comfort would the provision of forecasting be to the people mentioned in Figures 3 and 4? How can new

technology assist the very poorest societies to avoid the life and death conflicts described in Kenya in March 2000 (Figure 4)?

Drought desperation

At least eight monkeys were killed and ten people left injured after a two-hour duel between Kenyans and thirsty monkeys in the Somali Desert. The human population of the area has been forced to exist on relief food and water supplies for six months due to an ongoing drought. *The Daily Nation* reported that the battle took place at a small trading center on the northern border of Kenya when three water tankers arrived at the drought-stricken trading post. When the monkeys saw the water being drawn off the tankers, they attacked the people that had grouped there so ferociously that the humans were forced to flee as the primates quenched their thirst. Members of the group returned with axes and machetes and fought back the monkeys in a lengthy battle.

Figure 4 From the *Boston Globe*, 28 March 2000.

Figures 1–4 show ways in which human activities are influenced by weather events.

1 Study Figures 1–4. With a partner, summarise:
  a) the nature of the weather issue in at least two of the extracts presented
  b) the effects that the weather is having on human activity
  c) why these issues are relevant for geographical study.

2 As a class discuss whether, on the basis of the extracts, you agree with the statement that 'human beings are at the mercy of the weather'. What are your conclusions?

3 Use the web sites at the end of Chapters 1–4 to collect accounts of current weather events. Classify them into categories, such as global or local, short-term or long-term.

Why do geographers study weather and climate issues?

Geographers have always been interested in how different elements of the atmosphere combine to produce particular events such as thunderstorms. These events bring together conditions of temperature, air movement and moisture which are in turn controlled by varying amounts of energy from the sun. These short-term, daily variations in the Earth's atmosphere are known as weather. They may be experienced on a local or micro-scale, such as the tornadoes in Figure 2, or on a wider or mesoscale, such as the depressions which bring wind and rain to large parts of the United Kingdom.

Weather and climate – what's the difference?

When records of weather elements such as rainfall, temperature, wind speed and sunshine are collected for periods of 40 years or more, distinct trends emerge. The averaging of the data produces patterns known as climate. These patterns suggest that:

- there are seasons, characterised by combinations of temperature and rainfall
- particular weather hazards, such as hurricanes, follow regular seasonal patterns.

Climate data enable weather scientists, or climatologists, to draw graphs and maps of average monthly or yearly temperatures, average yearly rainfall and seasonal wind patterns. These are then used to divide up the world into zones of similar climatic conditions. This is known as climatic classification. An example is shown for Australia in Figure 5. This shows a way of dividing a country according to the effects of climate upon people. Figure 6 shows levels of heat discomfort in Australia, which are significant between November and April, with prolonged high temperatures and humidity around the northern coasts and high temperatures in the interior. The cooling system of the human body depends on evaporation of moisture to keep the body temperature from rising to life-threatening levels as temperatures rise. High humidity makes it difficult for the body to release moisture into the air since the air already contains high levels of moisture.

1 a) Study Figures 5 and 6 and suggest what connections there are between levels of heat discomfort and different climatic zones.

b) What other sorts of climatic discomfort might people experience?

2 Study the map of Australian climate zones and world maps of climatic classification in your atlas. On what criteria do classifications like these seem to be based? What problems do you imagine in using averages like these, and in grouping areas together under broad headings?

3 Summarise in 50 words why geographers study weather and climate.

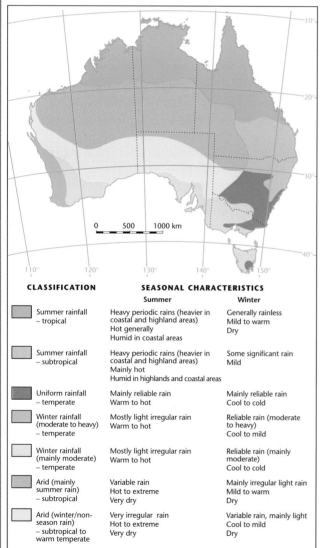

CLASSIFICATION

SEASONAL CHARACTERISTICS

	Classification	Summer	Winter
	Summer rainfall – tropical	Heavy periodic rains (heavier in coastal and highland areas) Hot generally Humid in coastal areas	Generally rainless Mild to warm Dry
	Summer rainfall – subtropical	Heavy periodic rains (heavier in coastal and highland areas) Mainly hot Humid in highlands and coastal areas	Some significant rain Mild
	Uniform rainfall – temperate	Mainly reliable rain Warm to hot	Mainly reliable rain Cool to cold
	Winter rainfall (moderate to heavy) – temperate	Mostly light irregular rain Warm to hot	Reliable rain (moderate to heavy) Cool to mild
	Winter rainfall (mainly moderate) – temperate	Mostly light irregular rain Warm to hot	Reliable rain (mainly moderate) Cool to cold
	Arid (mainly summer rain) – subtropical	Variable rain Hot to extreme Very dry	Mainly irregular light rain Mild to warm Dry
	Arid (winter/non-season rain) – subtropical to warm temperate	Very irregular rain Hot to extreme Very dry	Variable rain, mainly light Cool to mild Dry

Figure 5 A climate classification of Australia.

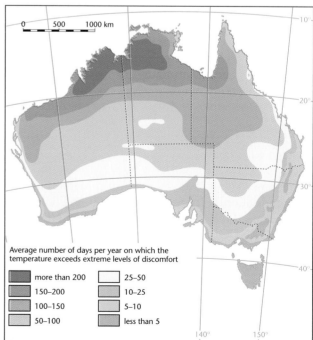

Average number of days per year on which the temperature exceeds extreme levels of discomfort

more than 200	25–50
150–200	10–25
100–150	5–10
50–100	less than 5

Figure 6 Heat discomfort in Australia.

1 Weather and climate: the global challenge

Can we control the climate?

The introductory section has shown that the importance of weather events in our lives cannot be underestimated. People are affected:

- during a weather event, directly as a result of the short-term impact of flood or storm
- after a weather event, indirectly by the longer-term impact on basic services, food supply or livelihoods of those who live in the affected area.

But to what extent are lives fashioned by the yearly rhythm of the seasons, especially where those changes from one time of the year to another are very marked? Is it true that, fundamentally, people have no control over the Earth's atmospheric processes? This chapter explores how seasonality affects human activity.

Determinism and Technological Fix

In the nineteenth century geographers such as Ellsworth Huntington developed theories about the rise and fall of great human civilisations, and claimed that these were based on natural changes in climate. His and other similar theories dominated physical geography for a long time, and showed human beings at the mercy of natural forces. These ideas came to be known as 'environmental deter-minism' – i.e. people and their activities were deter-mined by the environment in which they lived. Huntington's theory was that empires grew in importance in favourable climatic conditions, only to collapse when climatic conditions deteriorated, reducing food supply or spreading disease as a result of drought or flood.

Today, while geographers draw attention to the success of peoples who were able to adapt to climate change in the past and survive, historians such as David Keys still argue that climate change dictated the fate of past civilisations. Keys notes that a massive volcanic eruption in AD 535 in South-East Asia led to global cooling which caused crop failure, famine, migrations of marauding barbarians, the spread of bubonic plague and revolutions that led to the downfall of empires such as the Aztecs in Mexico.

At the other end of the spectrum are those who believe that technology can keep pace with, and find solutions to, environmental problems. This is the notion of Technological Fix and relies on the theory that market forces will create new solutions to environmental changes which threaten economic growth. This theory is becoming more widely quoted as the ozone depletion problem and global warming have made politicians and the general public aware that human populations may indeed have the capacity to change global climates. Dennis Avery, a former advisor to the US Department of State, argues that the world has nothing to fear from global warming caused by human pollution of the planet. 'In the US,' he says, 'malaria and yellow fever once ranged from New Orleans to Chicago. We conquered those diseases, however, and not by changing the climate. We did it by suppressing mosquitoes, creating vaccines and putting screens on doors, windows and porches… Developing countries have had high disease rates because they were poor, not because warm climates cannot be made safe.'

However successful human attempts have been to control the effects of climate through technology (such as air conditioning in homes and cars), experiments aimed at directly controlling the atmosphere (for example, by 'cloud seeding' to either increase or decrease rainfall) are rarely successful. The following two case studies show how different climatic events affect people:

- nationally, exemplified by the Indian monsoon
- regionally, exemplified by Atlantic hurricanes.

The South Asian monsoon – relying on the unreliable

Figure 1.1 Drought in Rajasthan, India.
Soaring temperatures and drought conditions during March to May 2000 caused desperate shortages of cattle fodder and the government started a relief programme for the 20 million people affected.

Figure 1.2 Flooding in West Bengal, India.
Extensive rainfall in August 2000 led to an international relief effort by the British Red Cross as flooding spread to neighbouring Bangladesh, itself no stranger to devastating floods.

Life for the average citizen in India is influenced greatly by the seasonal switch of wind systems known as the 'monsoon'. Human activity reflects the dominant temperature and moisture conditions. Winter's cooler temperatures bring relief and the opportunity to undertake more vigorous physical activity, but drought hits hard especially in the drier north-west regions of Rajasthan and Gujerat. In May and June, temperatures rise to an unbearable 40 °C before the onset or 'burst' of the summer rains. For the majority of Indians who live on and from the land, planning for these seasonal changes and predicting their timing is vital for their survival.

The fight for food

For Chimanbhai Parmar, it has turned out to be an endless wait. More than two months after completing the sowing of the groundnut crop, and hoping for a second bumper harvest in a row, parched and barren fields stare at him. For kilometres in every direction, the absence of the monsoon rains has left behind a picture of devastation and misery.

The outlook this year for Parmar, who has three children to support, is less than promising. With his fields failing to yield anything, he has to look for work elsewhere. Used as he and his fellow farmers are to hardship, the options are, nonetheless, desperate. They could end up as daily-wage labourers for the Public Works Department, which ironically enough is responsible for repairing roads damaged by the monsoon's fury, among other things. A day's toil for the Department would fetch around 30 to 40 rupees (less than a dollar). Or else they could try seeking piecemeal work in local shops and industrial units to tide them over. Each farmer is praying that this lean time is short-lived and that things won't get so unbearable that they have to start selling off their cattle.

Chinambhai Parmar and the other small farmers of Chandroda village in the coastal Saurashtra region of India's Gujarat state are victims of an aberrant weather phenomenon that seems to be becoming more and more established with each passing year. Like thousands of small farmers in the region, Parmar has learned to live with the 'curse' of the rain gods. For more than a decade now the monsoon rains - once regular arrivals in June – have followed their normal trend only every alternate year. This year, hoping against hope, farmers had welcomed the first showers and immediately undertook the sowing of groundnuts, their only cash crop. Within a month of sowing, the plants had paled and withered in the scorching sun – fodder for the cattle to graze on.

Creeping drought

Parmar's village belongs to one of the 11 districts in Gujarat where the rainfall deficiency has been critical, the shortfall exceeding 50 per cent of normal expectations. The long and dry spell has taken a severe toll on crops in Gujarat, the country's biggest groundnut producer, which accounts for about 35 per cent of the total harvest. In the neighbouring state of Madhya Pradesh the lateness of the rains meant that farmers were left with no choice but to forgo the sowing of soya beans and groundnuts. They could not even resort to their usual standby in such situations of sowing coarse millets in the first week of August. When the rains finally did arrive, more than a month after they were due, in late August and early September, farmers were quick to cultivate low-yielding pulses in a desperate effort to make the best use of the available moisture.

Over the years farmers in the rainfed regions of the country – comprising nearly 70 per cent of the land under the plough – have learned to live with the vagaries of the monsoon. With small landholdings, often not exceeding one hectare, and farming entirely at the mercy of the rain gods, the farmers in the drylands of India are a beleaguered lot. Without any official support in the form of subsidies, it is, however, their courage in the face of adversity and endurance at the time of calamities that has enabled them to survive the odds stacked up against them. They rely on an abundant store of existing traditional knowledge to free themselves from the clutches of errant weather.

Among all the factors that influence agriculture the climate is by far the most important. Rapid deforestation, melting of the glaciers, reduced river flows and worsening industrial pollution are all factors in influencing change. In the past eight years the two frontline agricultural states of Punjab and Haryana, forming the food bowl of the country, have been receiving excess rainfall; while Orissa, Madhya Pradesh and Kerala have been receiving less and less of their average share. Last year extremely high summer temperatures, followed by a prolonged dry spell during the monsoon season, brought on severe drought conditions in Orissa. But, soon after, Orissa witnessed flash floods, indicating that such abrupt weather changes were on the rise.

Figure 1.3 The fight for food in India. From *New Internationalist*, December 1999.

The Indian monsoon

The term 'monsoon' refers to the seasonal reversal of wind systems which takes place between winter and summer. The monsoon climate (Figure 1.4) shows a marked seasonal pattern between winter and summer with the rainfall coinciding with summer temperatures. In winter, the Indian subcontinent is dominated by the subtropical jet stream which travels eastwards at high speed over the southern Himalayas. Air descends slowly from the jet stream to form an area of high pressure over northern India. The Inter-Tropical Convergence Zone

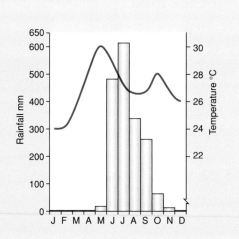

Figure 1.4 Climate graph showing the monsoon in Mumbai, (Bombay).

(ITCZ), described in more detail in Chapter 3 (pages 39–40), is at or south of the Equator. The absence of a strong overhead sun means that airstreams over India are cool and blow outwards from the high pressure over the subcontinent. Since they originate over land, winds are dry. Rainfall during the winter is at a minimum; a glance at climate graphs in an atlas will show that a city like Mumbai receives less than 100mm between October and May.

The overhead sun reaches the Tropic of Cancer on 21 June. As it moves northwards it draws the ITCZ with it and heat becomes intense, rising to well over 40 °C. A number of changes occur in a series of stages. Follow these by referring to Figure 1.6.

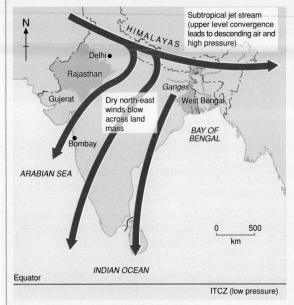

Figure 1.5 The Indian monsoon in winter.

1. Land over northern India is heated quickly by the sun. This causes air to rise and pressure to fall rapidly.
2. The low pressure area over land is intensified by a rapid seasonal jet stream moving eastwards at high altitude. The 'jet' sucks up air to replace that which is flowing out to the east.
3. The result is that moist air from the Indian Ocean is drawn northwards into the low pressure area.
4. As it crosses the Equator, it is deflected to the right by the Coriolis force. This is the effect of the Earth's rotation, which deflects winds into a circular movement as it spins on its axis from west to east. Winds turn from the south to approach India across the Bay of Bengal.
5. As the airstream comes ashore from the Bay of Bengal, it creates terrific downpours of rain at places like Cherrapunji, which is statistically the wettest place in India.

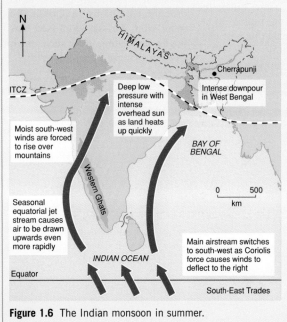

Figure 1.6 The Indian monsoon in summer.

Theory

6 A second main airstream makes its way over the western coast from the Indian Ocean. On the western coast the rainfall is heavier as the airstream is made to rise over the Western Ghats mountain range. This results in 'relief' or 'orographic' rainfall, as well as convectional rainfall brought by unstable south-west winds crossing a warm subcontinent.

Timing of the onset and withdrawal of the monsoon varies every year but the 'typical' pattern is shown in Figures 1.7

and 1.8. After considerable variation during 1998–2000, Indian meteorologists expected a typical pattern of onset in 2001 with average totals of rainfall (789mm) slightly lower than 1999 (840mm). The dry north-west of India, which relies for well over 80 per cent of its annual rainfall on the summer rains, is the most vulnerable to lower totals and farmers are forced to change their planting times and crop types each year to anticipate the timing of the monsoon.

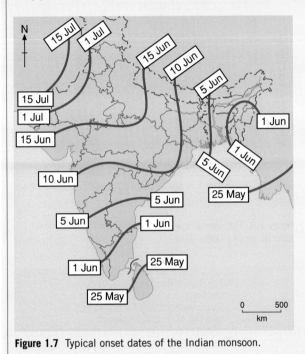

Figure 1.7 Typical onset dates of the Indian monsoon.

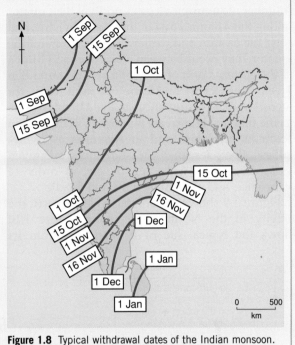

Figure 1.8 Typical withdrawal dates of the Indian monsoon.

Making sense of the monsoon in India

1 Draw an A4-size outline sketch map of India based on Figure 1.5.
   a) Draw annotated arrows to show why there is a dry season across much of India during winter.
   b) Using points 1–6 in the theory box above, rewrite the sequence of events that would lead to drought during the Indian winter. Use Figure 1.5 to help you.

2 Draw an A4-size outline sketch map of India based on Figure 1.6. Include annotated arrows to show why the monsoon affects much of India during summer.

3 Study Figures 1.1, 1.2 and 1.3 which show contrasting hazards caused by the monsoon.
   a) Use Figure 1.3 to explain why the timing of the monsoon is so critical to farmers.
   b) Use web sites on page 19 to construct a brief case study on the contrasting drought and flood hazards in India in 2000.
   c) Research the use of and the value of forecasting the monsoon in India.

4 Consider the theories of environmental determinism and Technological Fix on page 9. Does the Indian monsoon show that people are at the mercy of nature, or is there a technological fix to relieve the problems that it causes?

Regional weather hazards: Atlantic hurricanes

Hurricanes are some of the fiercest weather systems on Earth and produce winds of enormous destructive power. The Saffir/Simpson Hurricane Scale (Figure 1.11), which is used for hurricane measurement, shows just how much stronger these intense areas of low pressure are than any other mid-latitude depression described in Chapter 2. Hurricanes occur between July and October along a number of subtropical coasts north of the Equator – along the Atlantic coast of the southern USA, and along the eastern and western Pacific. South of the Equator, they occur between November and March off the eastern coast of Australia and in the Indian Ocean. The term 'hurricane' is used only for intense tropical disturbances in the Atlantic; in the Pacific they are known as 'typhoons', in the Indian Ocean as 'cyclones' and in Australia as 'willy-willies'. Each season the disturbances are given names beginning with 'A', 'B', etc. in order of occurrence, and alternately male and female.

Figure 1.9 shows the annual cycle of hurricane activity in the North Atlantic and Figure 1.10 shows the typical life of a hurricane, from its beginning as a tropical storm off the West African coast to its development east of the Caribbean into a fully-fledged hurricane as recorded on the Saffir/Simpson Scale. It is extraordinarily difficult to forecast the pace and direction of movement of any hurricane. Pressure and wind speeds can alter within hours leaving scientists and local governments little time to prepare those at risk.

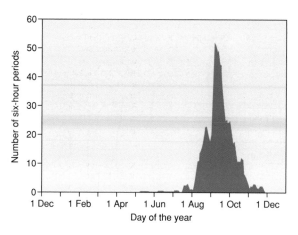

Figure 1.9 The annual cycle of intense hurricanes in the Atlantic basin, 1886–1989.

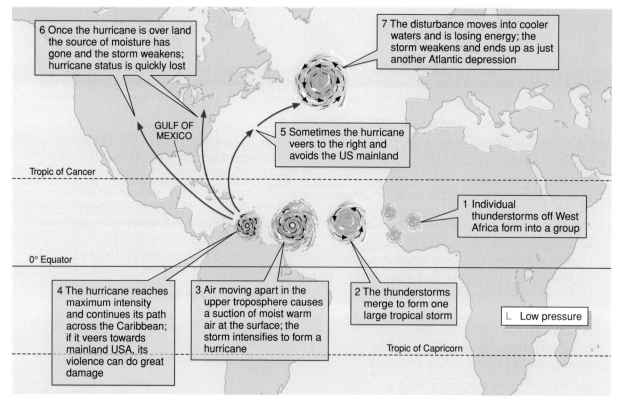

Figure 1.10 The life of a typical hurricane.
Tropical depressions average wind speeds of 24–34 knots (37–63km/h), tropical storms average wind speeds of 34–64 knots (63–118km/h). A disturbance can be classified a hurricane when wind speeds exceed 64 knots (118km/h).

The Saffir/Simpson Hurricane Scale

Category 1
Winds 118–152km/hour (64–82 knots). Damage primarily to shrubbery, trees, poorly constructed signs, and unanchored mobile homes. No significant damage to other structures.

Storm surge 1–1.5m above normal tide. Low-lying coastal roads inundated, minor pier damage, some small craft in exposed anchorages torn from moorings.

Category 2
Winds 154–176km/hour (83–95 knots). Considerable damage to shrubbery and tree foliage; some trees blown down. Extensive damage to poorly constructed signs. Major damage to exposed mobile homes. Some damage to roofing materials of buildings; some window and door damage. No major damage to buildings.

Storm surge 2–2.5m above normal tide. Coastal roads and low-lying escape routes made impassable by rising water 2–4 hours before arrival of hurricane centre. Considerable damage to piers. Marinas flooded. Small craft in unprotected anchorages torn from moorings. Evacuation of some shoreline residences and low-lying island areas required.

Category 3
Winds 178–209km/hour (96–113 knots). Foliage torn from trees; large trees blown down. Practically all poorly constructed signs blown down. Some damage to roofing materials of buildings; some window and door damage. Some structural damage to small buildings. Mobile homes destroyed.

Storm surge 2.5–3.5m above normal tide. Serious flooding at coast and many small structures near coast destroyed; large structures near coast damaged by battering waves and floating debris. Low-lying escape routes made impassable by rising water 3–5 hours before hurricane centre arrives. Flat terrain 1.5m or less above sea-level flooded inland 13km or more. Evacuation of low-lying residences within several blocks of shoreline possibly required.

Category 4
Winds 211–250km/hour (114–135 knots). Shrubs and trees blown down; all signs blown down. Extensive damage to roofing materials, windows and doors. Complete failure of roofs on many smaller residences. Complete destruction of mobile homes.

Storm surge 4–5.5m above normal tide. Flat terrain 3m or less above sea-level flooded inland as far as 11km. Major damage to lower floors of structures near shore due to flooding and battering by waves and floating debris. Low-lying escape routes made impassable by rising waters within 3–5 hours before hurricane centre arrives. Major erosion of beaches. Massive evacuation of all residences within 500m of shore possibly required, and of single-storey residences on low ground within 3km of shore.

Category 5
Winds greater than 250km/hour (135 knots). Shrubs and trees blown down; considerable damage to roofs of buildings; all signs down. Very severe and extensive damage to windows and doors with extensive shattering of glass components. Complete failure of roofs on many residences and industrial buildings. Some complete building failures. Small buildings overturned or blown away. Complete destruction of mobile homes.

Storm surge greater than 5.5m above normal tide. Major damage to lower floors of all structures less than 4.5m above sea-level within 500m of shore. Low-lying escape routes made impassable by rising water 3–5 hours before hurricane centre arrives. Massive evacuation of residential areas on low ground within 8–16km of shore possibly required.

Figure 1.11 The Saffir/Simpson Hurricane Scale.

Hurricanes? Monsoons? Blasé Brits should wake up to the weather threat

It has been a year of living dangerously for tourists. First in the Yemen, later in Uganda, tourists were taken hostage and murdered. Then a terror group declared open season on visitors to Turkish coastal resorts. Now the threat comes from natural phenomena. Earthquakes near Istanbul and in Athens have been followed by hurricanes in the Caribbean – and a charter aircraft split into three while landing during a violent storm in Spain.

The tourists huddling for safety in the basements of their hotels in Nassau and Orlando as Hurricane Floyd swept across the Bahamian islands and along the coast of Florida were probably unaware that hurricanes are becoming more frequent after a 20-year spell of relative calm.

I lived in Nassau, the Bahamian capital, for three years from 1974 without seeing a hint of a hurricane. This marked the beginning of a quiet phase that lasted until 1994. The years 1991–94 were the quietest recorded, with fewer than four hurricanes a year. In contrast there have been 33 hurricanes in the past four years, a number of them causing extreme damage.

Scientists relate hurricane activity cycles to a rise in the surface temperature of the North Atlantic. They are cautious about making predictions but we could be entering several decades of considerable hurricane activity.

There has been a change in the pattern of tourism to Florida and the Caribbean since the last active hurricane period in the 1960s when the main holiday season was from Christmas to Easter. The past decade has seen massive growth in charter flights to the region. Britons have been attracted by low prices in the hot, humid months from May to October when the North Americans tend to stay away. This is the hurricane season and it peaks in mid-September.

BA Holidays, like other tour operators, issues a general warning about hurricanes at the back of its brochure. Tropical storms may be random but perhaps the hurricane season ought to be more prominently highlighted.

Travellers should always take account of weather patterns when planning their journeys. In India, for example, you can be sure of the arrival of the monsoon in June: the best months to travel across most of the subcontinent are from December to February (though prices can be cheaper in other seasons). Remember how the Raj took to the hills during the summer in the plains.

Figure 1.12 From the *Observer*, 19 September 1999.

Understanding hurricanes

1 Work in pairs.

   a) Read Figure 1.12 and explain why British holidaymakers are described as 'blasé'.

   b) To what extent do travel companies alert travellers to potential threats from hurricanes in their brochures? Research the internet or holiday brochures from travel agents. Are any other weather threats highlighted?

2 Imagine you have been asked by a travel company to produce some guidance for travellers intending to fly to the Caribbean during the hurricane season. Use the information from the figures above and your own research to produce a flyer of no more than 350 words.

A case study: coping with Hurricane Mitch, October 1998

Hurricane Mitch is now one of the best-known and best-recorded hurricanes of recent times. Only one hurricane surpassed the destruction of Mitch and that was in 1780 when 22 000 people died in the eastern Caribbean.

The account in Figure 1.13 gives some impression of the terror people felt in one small town on the flanks of Nicaragua's Casita volcano, when a week of rain caused by Hurricane Mitch triggered a massive landslide of mud, rock and uprooted trees. It was just before midday on 30 October 1998; farmers were tending corn, beans and rice in fields, and women were preparing the midday meal. In less than an hour virtually all 176 houses were washed downslope and 455 people had lost their lives. This tragedy was one of thousands across the central American states of Nicaragua, Honduras, El Salvador, Guatemala and Belize in which damage was caused not by strong winds but by intense rainfall as Mitch struck land.

> 'We heard a sound like a plane, and we thought people had come to rescue us because our houses were filling with rain... But 15 minutes later the land began to tremble, and the mud and stones were on top of us. My children and I went rolling with everything that came down, including pieces of our house.'
>
> (Vilma Urritia Martinez, a young mother from the town of Rolando Rodriguez, Nicaragua)

Figure 1.13 Quotation from survivor of Hurricane Mitch.

Figure 1.14 Satellite photograph of the Choluteca River, Honduras.
The river overran its banks by over a kilometre and dumped a huge load of sand, mud and stones on part of the city of Choluteca (see the grid pattern of roads at the bottom left of the photograph). The surging river devastated the valley's bridges and roads. The majority still await permanent repair.

Figure 1.15 Residents cross a temporary bridge on the Bonito River, Honduras. The one-lane bridge will be constructed by US Marines until a more permanent structure can be built. Pedestrians, cyclists and motor cyclists use a rope and plank suspension bridge while cars and trucks drive across the river itself further downstream.

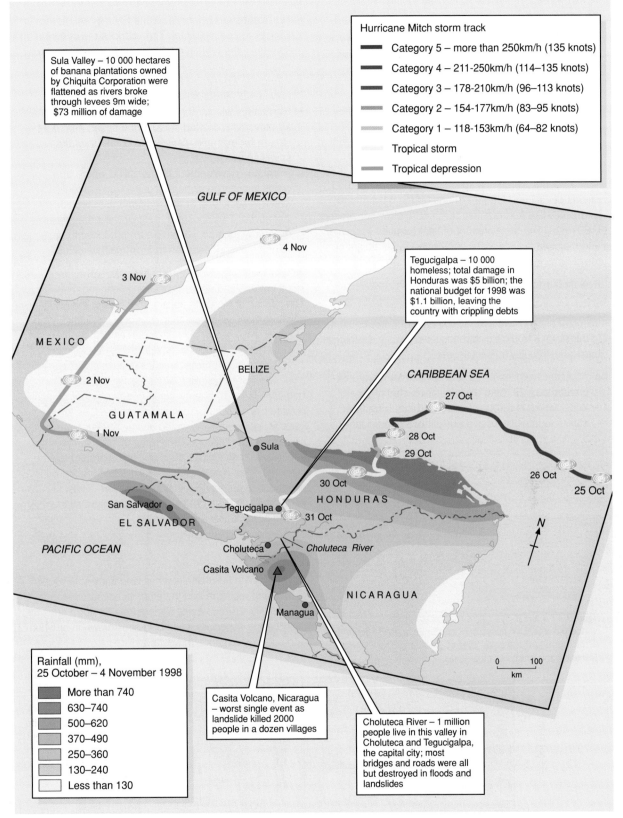

Hurricane Mitch storm track

Category 5 – more than 250km/h (135 knots)
Category 4 – 211-250km/h (114–135 knots)
Category 3 – 178-210km/h (96–113 knots)
Category 2 – 154-177km/h (83–95 knots)
Category 1 – 118-153km/h (64–82 knots)
Tropical storm
Tropical depression

Sula Valley – 10 000 hectares of banana plantations owned by Chiquita Corporation were flattened as rivers broke through levees 9m wide; $73 million of damage

Tegucigalpa – 10 000 homeless; total damage in Honduras was $5 billion; the national budget for 1998 was $1.1 billion, leaving the country with crippling debts

GULF OF MEXICO

4 Nov
3 Nov
2 Nov
1 Nov

MEXICO

BELIZE

CARIBBEAN SEA

27 Oct
28 Oct
29 Oct
26 Oct
25 Oct

GUATAMALA

Sula

30 Oct

San Salvador

Tegucigalpa
31 Oct

HONDURAS

EL SALVADOR

PACIFIC OCEAN

Choluteca
Choluteca River

Casita Volcano

N

NICARAGUA

Managua

0   100
km

Rainfall (mm),
25 October – 4 November 1998

More than 740
630–740
500–620
370–490
250–360
130–240
Less than 130

Casita Volcano, Nicaragua – worst single event as landslide killed 2000 people in a dozen villages

Choluteca River – 1 million people live in this valley in Choluteca and Tegucigalpa, the capital city; most bridges and roads were all but destroyed in floods and landslides

Figure 1.16 Hurricane Mitch storm track.

Hurricane formation and development

Hurricanes, cyclones and typhoons are a major hazard in the tropics. Every year some 80 occurrences claim, on average, 20 000 lives and cause immense damage to property, natural vegetation and shipping.

A hurricane is a large rotating storm around a centre of very low pressure with values of 950mb or lower. The lowest ever recorded pressure was 877mb in Hurricane Ida in the Philippines in 1958. Most systems have a diameter of about 650km, less than half of that of a mid-latitude depression. Wind speeds commonly exceed 33 metres per second (119km/h) and, in the most intense hurricanes like Andrew, may reach 50 metres per second (180km/h). The huge amount of heat required to create and maintain the hurricane is reflected in the height of the clouds near its centre, often up to 12km in total.

How do hurricanes form?

A combination of trigger mechanisms, which rely on intensive rising convection or heat currents, are required to transform a tropical disturbance into a more destructive hurricane. The key influences are:

- An extensive ocean area with surface temperatures greater than 27 °C for a significant period of time. Water which is turbulent or subject to mixing from cooler sources reduces the likelihood of hurricanes.

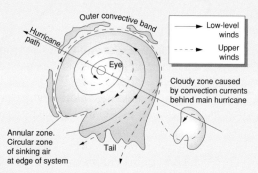

- Hurricanes rarely form near the Equator where the Coriolis force is minimal. This reduces the degree of spin from the Earth's rotation, which is necessary to trigger the vicious spiral in the centre of the hurricane. Hurricane formation is most common between 5° and 30° latitude.
- Hurricanes will not form in zones of strong horizontal air movement or wind shear. Wind shear, near a jet stream for example, causes the break up of the spiralling winds.
- Hurricane development is intensified where upper air winds in the troposphere cause a rapid ascent of air which is sucked in at the sea surface to replace that lost above. This causes a rapid upward draught of moisture-laden air, which in turn produces huge volumes of condensation to form massive clouds.

As trade winds rush into the centre of the storm, they spiral inwards and upwards releasing heat and moisture. The rotation of the Earth adds further twist to the rising columns of air, which come to resemble a whirling cylinder around an eye of still, cloud-free descending air. Towering cumulo-nimbus clouds are typical of this development. At 12–15km in height these fan out into a canopy of cirrus cloud, carried by spiralling winds leaving the core. The hurricane is fed by energy stored in water vapour brought upwards by air from evaporation at sea level. As this air rises, 90 per cent of the stored energy is released as heat as condensation occurs. This heat generates further uplift and instability so long as the rising air is warmer than the surrounding air. The energy released within hurricanes is enormous: a hurricane which hit Galveston, Texas, in September 1900 had sufficient energy to drive all the world's power stations for four years. Such winds could destroy houses in seconds.

Hurricane decay

As soon as the hurricane reaches land it loses its supply of heat and moisture and therefore its energy source. It can quickly return to being a mere tropical storm or disturbance, especially when cold air is drawn in or when upper level divergence moves away.

Figure 1.17 a and b Typical hurricane structure.
Notice the intensive convection and uplift around the centre of the storm and the calm 'eye' of the storm where warm air descends and produces clear skies.

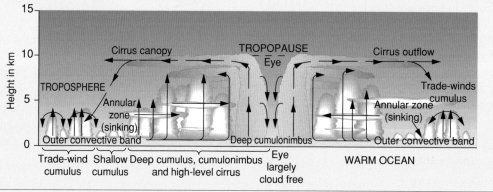

The Mitch story

1 Prepare a report on the growth and development of Mitch in Central America in October 1998.

2 Summarise its social, environmental and economic impacts.

3 Research a contrasting case study from a More Economically Developed Country (MEDC), for example Andrew in Florida in 1992. Compare its growth, development and impacts with those of Mitch. Refer to material contained on the UK Meteorological Office web site, shown below.

4 Research the current state of forecasting with regard to hurricanes. Refer to the web sites below. What makes them so difficult to predict?

Summary

You have learned that:

- Geographical ideas about the effect of climate on human activity focus on two key theories: environmental determinism and Technological Fix.
- The tropical Asian monsoon presents an illustration of the two theories and asks the student to analyse the typical pattern and recent changes to ascertain to what degree natural processes control economic activity.
- Atlantic hurricanes pose a significant challenge to people in their management of extreme weather events and to forecasters in their ability to provide emergency services with sufficient information to allow accurate warning time and contingency planning.

References and further reading

D Keys, *Catastrophe: An investigation into the origins of the Modern World*, Century, 1999
National Geographic, Vol. 196, No. 5, November 1999 (Hurricane Mitch)

Web sites

http://www.heatisonline.org gives huge numbers of examples of current climate events as they occur The UK Meteorological office at http://www.metoffice.com is another excellent source of information, especially on hurricanes World Meteorological Organisation: http://www.wmo.ch has all sorts of data and features on issues in this chapter with an excellent links section

2 Weather and climate in the mid-latitudes

The British Isles – a study in changeability

Stand in any bus or train queue in Britain and it is likely that conversation will turn to the topic of the weather. If you happen to be in a similar queue in southern California or south-west Australia it is less likely that passengers will have the weather on their minds; sunshine is usually the rule in these 'Mediterranean' type climates. For those people who live in the mid-latitude countries such as Britain, variability from day to day affects almost every aspect of life including when, where and how we travel, what we buy and how we may feel on a particular day.

Why does Britain have such varied weather?

In common with many mid-latitude countries found between 40° and 60° north and south of the Equator, the climate of Britain has been classified by climatologists as a 'cool temperate western maritime' type. In brief, the characteristics of such a climate type are:

- cool temperatures throughout the year with average monthly temperatures ranging between 5 °C and 18 °C between January and July
- temperate seasonal weather changes – temperatures and rainfall totals tend to alter gradually, and extremes are rare
- western – this type of climate is found on the western sides of continents facing the ocean
- maritime – the sea plays a very significant role in influencing weather conditions in all seasons, but especially in winter.

This chapter will show that the following play a key role in dictating changes in Britain's weather during the year:

1 Air masses: The regular passage of depressions and anticyclones over Britain link to airflows from regions of settled, relatively uniform temperature and humidity. Some texts will describe these airflows as air masses and the regions they form in as source regions. The climatologist H H Lamb researched these airflow patterns from climate data between 1861 and 1971 and found that certain airflows tend to dominate weather conditions at certain times of the year (Figure 2.1).

2 Prevailing westerly winds: The most common wind direction (the prevailing wind) is from the west or south-west, i.e. from over the Atlantic Ocean, and is characteristically moist and mild. Westerly winds are associated with unsettled windy and wet conditions produced by areas of low pressure known as depressions. Smaller areas of low pressure known as troughs can bring shorter spells of unsettled weather such as the thunderstorms described in Figure 2.2.

3 Ocean currents and the North Atlantic Oscillation: The warm North Atlantic Drift is an ocean current which originates in the sub-tropical waters of the Gulf of Mexico and then flows north-eastwards towards Britain and Scandinavia. The absence of ice in winter in northern Scotland and Norway is largely due to this current; in the same latitudes in eastern Canada and in Siberia ice is common. Water is slower to cool than land so the presence of warm offshore waters reduces the occurrence of frost and subzero temperatures, especially in the south and west of Britain in winter. In recent years weather scientists have identified a switch in the direction and strength of the North Atlantic Drift which happens regularly and may be similar to the regional effects of El Niño in the Pacific described in Chapter 3 (see pages 44–5).

4 Anticyclones: Depressions give way at regular intervals to areas of high pressure or anticyclones which bring settled, sunny weather in both winter and summer. Many of the British summers of the late 1980s through to the mid-1990s were characterised by settled spells of warm summer weather, and 1995 was the warmest and driest year on record. In winter anticyclones can bring frost and fog; in December 1981, Britain's lowest temperature of –25 °C was recorded at Shawbury in Shropshire during a sustained period of high pressure. Temporary areas of high pressure known as ridges can sometimes bring a few hours of settled weather in between depressions.

Airflow type	General weather characteristics	% frequency
1 Westerly	Unsettled weather with variable wind directions as depressions cross the country, giving most rain in northern and western districts, with brighter weather in the south and east. Mild in winter with frequent gales; cool and cloudy in summer (associated with mP, mT airmasses).	27.6
2 Northerly	In winter the weather is cold with snow and sleet showers, especially along the east coast; blizzards may accompany deep polar lows. In summer the weather is cool and showery, especially along the east coast (mA).	8.1
3 North-westerly	In winter, cool, showery, changeable conditions with strong winds. The weather in summer is cool with showers on windward coasts; southern Britain may be bright and dry (mP, mA).	6.1
4 Easterly	Cold in the winter period, sometimes with severe weather in the south and east with snow and sleet, but fine in the west and north-west. Warm in summer with dry weather especially in the west; occasionally thundery (cA, cP).	7.1
5 Southerly	Warm and thundery in summer. In winter it may be associated with a low in the Atlantic giving mild, damp weather especially in the south-west, or with a high over central Europe, in which case the weather is cold and dry (mT or cT in summer; mT or cP in winter).	6.6
6 Cyclonic	Rainy, unsettled conditions over most of the country, often accompanied by gales and thunderstorms. Wind direction and strength are variable. Conditions normally mild in autumn and early winter, cool or cold in spring and summer and cool in late winter (mP, mT).	12.8
7 Anticyclonic	Mainly dry with light winds; warm in summer with occasional thunderstorms; cold often with frosts and fog in winter, especially in the autumn (mT, cT in summer; cP in winter).	17.9

Key: cA = Arctic continental; mA = Arctic maritime; mP = Polar maritime;
cP = Polar continental; mT = Tropical maritime; cT = Tropical continental.

Figure 2.1 Lamb's airflow types and associated characteristics.

Freak winter blast strikes Yorkshire

The man from the met office described the great Yorkshire storm yesterday as 'very exciting weather', a comment which could have caused him to have several inches of hail stuffed down his throat had he made his comment in Hedon, near Hull.

The village was reeling yesterday after it was at the centre of torrential downpours, lightning and hail which turned fields and streets white.

There has been nothing like this since snow stopped play in a cricket match in Buxton, Derbyshire, in June 1975.

The Yorkshire tempest battered an area between York and Hull. York railway station was hit by lightning four times within minutes, knocking out signalling systems and halting all trains for half an hour.

A tornado was spotted off the Humber estuary and amazed coastguards described how it created a spectacular waterspout.

Hedon yesterday was less interested in meteorological phenomena than in how to dry itself out. John Plater, who runs the village's post office, said: 'There is eight inches of hail banked up by the side of the shops – the hailstones were huge.

'The water was above the road and a lot of homes and businesses have been flooded. We've had customers in their 80s saying they've never seen summer weather like this.'

The Hedon HSBC bank shut its doors after water poured in, and the Nutmeg café was forced to shut after it was flooded.

Café owner Kay Bottomley said: 'It started with a leak in the ceiling, then it poured through the door.

'Our back yard is four to five inches deep with hail. We're trying to mop it all up – I can't believe it.'

The met office spokesman said the storm had been caused by a slow-moving trough. 'These troughs let cumulonimbus clouds form at great heights and rain can persist in the places under them for some time,' he said, adding that Norwich had experienced a 15mm deluge in about 40 minutes.

'Some people are calling the hail snow,' he added. 'But it is definitely hail and there have been hail drifts. And you can still make a snowman out of hail.'

Figure 2.2 From the *Guardian*, 22 August 2000.

Location	Average annual rainfall (mm)	Average daily temp. Jan. (°C)	Average daily temp. July (°C)	Average annual sunshine hours
1 Belfast Airport	837	3.5	14.5	1298
2 Douglas	1131	4.8	14.3	1572
3 Ambleside	1865	3.1	15.0	1185
4 Durham	645	2.8	14.7	1300
5 Leeming	617	3.0	15.2	1331
6 Blackpool Airport	847	3.7	15.4	1534
7 Hull	653	3.7	16.1	1380
8 Rhyl	661	4.8	15.6	1475
9 Manchester Airport	806	3.5	15.6	1359
10 Buxton	1289	2.0	13.9	1149
11 Lincoln	593	2.8	15.5	1401
12 Skegness	601	3.4	13.9	1512
13 Shrewsbury	624	3.6	15.9	1349
14 Aberystwyth	959	5.2	15.1	1473
15 Llandrindod Wells	1003	2.8	14.9	1244
16 Stratford-upon-Avon	627	3.2	16.0	1371
17 Cambridge	552	3.5	16.4	1508
18 Cardiff	1064	4.4	16.5	1497
19 Oxford	663	3.8	16.8	1517
20 Heathrow Airport	610	4.0	16.5	1494
21 Clacton-on-Sea	542	3.6	16.7	1635
22 Ilfracombe	1063	6.3	16.2	1631
23 Penzance	1131	6.9	16.1	1738
24 Plymouth	992	5.7	15.9	1687
25 Bournemouth	802	4.6	16.4	1777
26 Shanklin	906	4.8	16.1	1908
27 Eastbourne	811	4.9	16.6	1827
28 Folkestone	727	4.3	16.6	1732

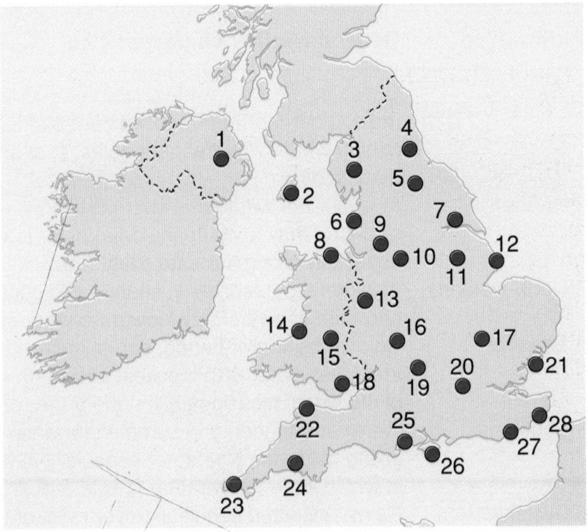

Figure 2.4 Location of places referred to in Figure 2.3.

Figure 2.3 Average climate data for selected places in England, Wales and Northern Ireland, 1961–90.

The whole picture - describing Britain's climate

1 Read about how to draw isoline maps on page 23. Using outline maps of the British Isles and Figures 2.3 and 2.4, produce isoline maps to show variations across the country in:
   a) average annual rainfall
   b) average daily temperatures for summer
   c) average daily temperatures for winter
   d) annual sunshine hours.

You may choose to work as a group on this task.

2 Compare each of the maps you have drawn. Discuss the conclusions you have come to as a group about the variations you observe across the country and produce a summary of these.

3 Use the introduction to this chapter to decide if the generalisations about the reasons for Britain's variable climate seem to explain the patterns on your map. What other factors may be influential? Refer to an atlas and other climate texts to help you.

4 Study Figure 2.2. Is this weather typical of summer in eastern England? You may like to refer to the Met Office web site to help you. What appear to be the reasons for the weather event described? What are the problems of relying on the average climate data you used at the beginning of this task?

5 Now look at the synoptic chart (weather chart) in Figure 2.6 which shows the forecast for Monday 21 August 2000. Use the symbols in Figure 2.11 on page 25 to help you. Produce a two-minute weather summary for England similar to those you have seen on television.

Drawing an isoline map

This is a useful technique for re]vealing patterns when data are presented as a series of points at locations. It is a very effective way of showing spatial variations in weather and climate, for example sunshine or rainfall, which are continuous over a large area. The same technique is used by cartographers when producing contour maps.

Isolines form points of equal value. Isotherms and isohyets are the names given to particular types of isoline which join places of equal temperature and rainfall respectively.

To draw an isoline map, follow these steps:
1 Study your data and its range of figures from highest to lowest.
2 Decide on a suitable set interval between each isoline, for example every 5 °C or every 50mm of rainfall. Remember that too low an interval will make the map too complex, and too broad an interval will mask important detail.
3 Draw isolines as shown in the example below.

Example
Assume that you start with the locations and values shown in Figure 2.5(a). Notice that the lowest value, 3, is in the north-west corner of the map and the highest value, 5.6, is in the south-east. This example will assume that you want to draw isolines at 0.5 intervals, starting with 3, and ending with 5.5.

1 Join up all the points with a value of 3 as shown in Figure 2.5(b). All the values inside the 3 line should be higher than 3, and all the values outside should be lower than 3.
2 Draw the 3.5 line. This can be done by joining all places of value 3.5. Mostly, however, you will have to guess where the line should go. If you have two places, one value 3 and the other value 4, 3.5 will go half-way between. If you have 3.3 and 4.2, you will need to be much closer to 3.3 than to 4.2. It is best to mark it out first in rough as a series of points, and then join them, just as you did with values of 3. You can then join these up as shown in Figure 2.5(c).
3 Study Figure 2.5(d) which has the rest of the lines drawn in. Notice how the 5.5 line has been drawn to show isolated areas.
4 Shade carefully between the lines to show patterns more clearly. Select one colour for this, such as blue, and use different shades, or select a sequence of colours which are closely related, such as yellow-orange-red-brown. Use light shading for low values and darker shading for the higher values. This technique of shading is used for most atlas maps, so look at some examples for suitable colour schemes. One exception is isobar maps which show lines of air pressure; these are never shaded.
5 Include a title and colour coded key.

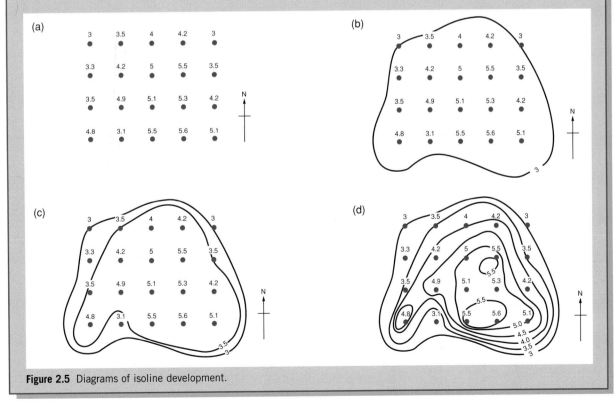

Figure 2.5 Diagrams of isoline development.

What challenges are presented by depressions? The storm of January 1990

The depression of 25 January 1990 was typical of storms which pass over Britain, such as those of October 1987, December 1999 and November 2000. It began as a shallow area of low pressure off the eastern coast of North America on 23 January 1990. Here, warm moist air from the south-west (tropical maritime, mT) meets cold moist air (polar maritime air mP) forcing the warmer air to rise and water vapour to condense into cloud. This is shown by a band of cloud stretching across the mid-Atlantic south of Iceland (Figure 2.7).

At this point, the pressure of the air is not very low. By midnight GMT on 24 January, the depression had started to deepen and air pressure was falling. Pressure falls further as the air passes over the warm North Atlantic Drift causing it to gain energy as more warm air is forced to rise, more cloud forms and air is sucked in at the surface more quickly leading to rising wind speeds.

By midday on 25 January pressure had fallen to 992mb and wind speeds were high. By 1800 hours on 25 January pressure fell to its lowest at 948mb and southern Britain was hit by storm winds. On satellite photographs (Figures 2.7, 2.12 and 2.13) the following features are visible:

- The whole depression is shown by a cloud mass, a hook shape, caused by anticlockwise winds which take moisture and cloud towards the centre of the depression where air is rising fastest.
- The cloud mass coincides with the position of the fronts shown on the weather maps.
- The cloud mass moves from west to east.
- Once it has passed over, Britain is affected by shower clouds shown as white speckling.

In Figure 2.7 Iceland is shown at A, and Greenland at B, in white outline. To the south is a black/grey area at X, which is an area affected by the Azores high pressure; clouds are thin and reflect very little, hence their grey colour. The depression is shown in clear white bands of cloud.

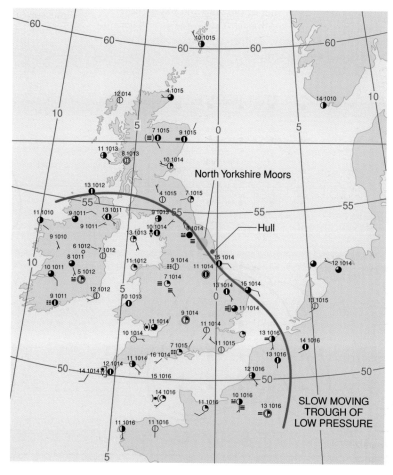

Figure 2.6 Synoptic chart for the British Isles for 21 August 2000. The red lines are lines of latitude and longitude.

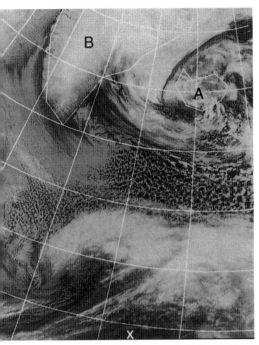

Figure 2.7 Satellite photograph of the North Atlantic at 1517 GMT on 24 January 1990.

CLOUD		WEATHER	
Symbol	*Cloud amount (oktas)*	*Symbol*	*Weather*
○	0	≡	Mist
◑	1 or less	≡	Fog
◕	2	●	Drizzle
◐	3	●	Rain and drizzle
◖	4	•	Rain
◑	5	●	Rain and snow
◕	6	✳	Snow
◑	7 or more	▽	Rain shower
●	8	▽	Rain and snow shower
⊗	Sky obscured	✳▽	Snow shower
⊠	Missing or doubtful data	△	Hail shower
		⚡	Thunderstorm
		⦁	Rain in sight

WIND		
Symbol	*Speed*	
	(knots)	(km/h)
◎	Calm	
	1–2	1–5
	3–7	6–15
	8–12	16–25
	13–17	26–34
	For each additional half-feather add 5 knots or 10 km/h	
	48–52	90–98

Figure 2.8 Synoptic chart weather symbols – these are the symbols used on all weather maps.

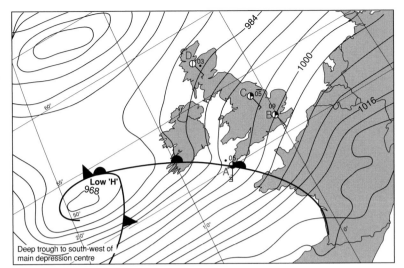

Figure 2.9 Synoptic chart for 00 GMT on 25 January 1990.

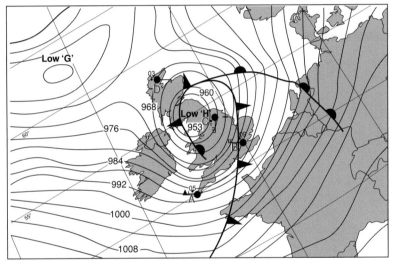

Figure 2.10 Synoptic chart for 1200 GMT on 25 January 1990.

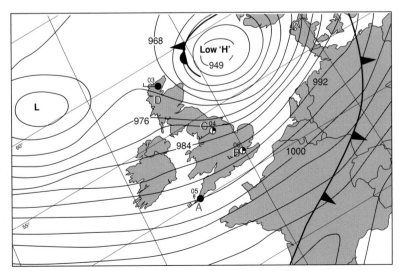

Figure 2.11 Synoptic chart for 2400 GMT on 25 January 1990.

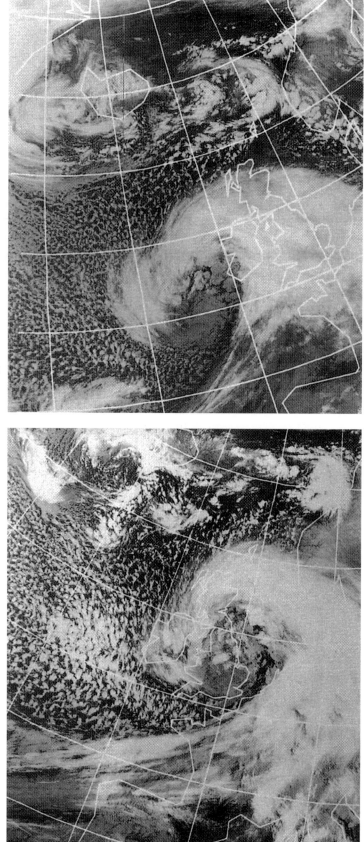

Figure 2.12 Satellite photograph of a depression crossing the British Isles at 0330 GMT on 25 January 1990.

Figure 2.13 Satellite photograph of a depression having passed over the British Isles at 1324 GMT on 25 January 1990.

The diary of a storm

This exercise will help you observe and interpret some of the changes which take place when a depression passes over the British Isles. The pressure system to which it refers is pressure system 'H' on Figures 2.9–2.11, which caused the storm of 25 January 1990. Although it was much stronger than many systems which affect us, the main difference between this and other systems was that it occurred further south. The North Atlantic and northern Scotland frequently experience storms of this kind.

1 On a blank outline map of north-western Europe, sketch the outline of cloud for 0330 GMT on 25 January 1990 (Figure 2.12). Using the synoptic charts for 1200 GMT on 25 January 1990 (Figure 2.10) and 2400 GMT on 25 January 1990 (Figure 2.11) to help you, mark the following features on your map:
   a) the position of the fronts
   b) the position of low pressure area 'H'
   c) the Azores high pressure
   d) the area of showery cloud affecting the North Atlantic
   e) an arrow showing the direction in which the low pressure system seemed to be moving.

2 Copy and complete the following table, and record the air pressure at Lands End (location A), London (location B), Leeds (location C) and northern Scotland (location D) on Figures 2.9–2.11. These show the development of the pressure system over a 24-hour period between midnight on 24/25 January and midnight on 25/26 January.

	00 GMT 25.1.90	1200 GMT 25.1.90	00 GMT 26.1.90
Land's End London Leeds Northern Scotland			

3 Now complete similar tables for each of the following using Figure 2.8 to help you:
   a) wind speed
   b) temperature
   c) cloud cover
   d) precipitation.

4 Radio 4's midnight news each day includes a three–four minute summary of the day's weather over the whole of the UK. It notes such features as changes throughout the UK in temperature, precipitation, wind speed, and tries to link them to the movement of depressions or anticyclones. Write a report of the 24-hour period shown in Figures 2.9–2.11 for the midnight news on 25 January 1990.

5 What was happening to the pressure of the low pressure system by the time it reached northern Europe? What does this suggest about what eventually happens to areas of low pressure?

Theory

Depressions – formation and development

'Depression', or 'cyclone', is a name given to a range of atmospheric disturbances which are characterised by low atmospheric pressure. 'High' and 'low' pressure are relative terms meaning air which is higher pressure or lower pressure than air in the surrounding areas. 'Atmospheric pressure' is a term used to mean the total weight of air molecules in a given column of air. Air pressure is measured in millibars, or mb: 1000mb is about average air pressure, 1050mb is exceptionally high and 950mb very low. Usually most systems lie between these two figures.

Whether air pressure is lower in some places than in others is due to differences in temperature. Air which is being warmed expands and rises, and weighs less, thus reducing the pressure it exerts on the Earth's surface. This is air which is referred to as 'low pressure' and which forms depressions. Air which rises is unstable. It takes with it water vapour into the upper atmosphere which is much colder. On cooling, the vapour condenses and forms water droplets. At high levels, these droplets form clouds. Depressions are therefore associated with cloud and, often, precipitation.

Each time air becomes lighter and rises, or becomes heavier and falls, it allows more air to replace it. In broad terms, depressions are linked to warmer rising air at lower pressure, and anticyclones to sinking air at higher pressures. The movement of air across the Earth's surface from higher pressure towards lower pressure causes air movement, or wind. The force of the wind depends upon the difference between the two pressure systems. If the pressure systems are far apart, and the difference in pressure small, air movement or winds will be slight. This will be characterised by isobars being widely spaced apart on a weather map. If, as happened in the January 1990 storm, the pressure difference is great and the systems are close together, winds will be strong. This will be characterised by isobars being closely grouped on a weather map.

The development of depressions in the northern hemisphere

Most depressions exist for no more than three or four days. They begin their short life in the North Atlantic, along a boundary between warm, tropical maritime air to the south and cold, Arctic maritime air to the north. This boundary is called the 'polar front'. The trigger for a depression is the development of upper air movement ahead of a trough. In general the process can be divided into four stages, shown in Figures 2.14–2.17.

Stage 1: Cyclogenesis

Surface pressures fall rapidly as polar and subtropical air converge and spiral upwards into the upper air. This is known as the 'vacuum cleaner' effect. This brings greater mixing of warm and cold air at the polar front. Air streams begin to change from their normal parallel pattern as air is sucked into the centre of lowest pressure.

Stage 2: The development of a wave depression

The rotation of the Earth produces a force called the Coriolis force. This causes air to blow in an anticlockwise fashion around the centre of the depression, as dense cold air undercuts the less dense, rising warmer air to the west. This is called the 'cold front'. Warm air slides up and over the denser, colder air to the east of the depression centre. This is called the 'warm front'. Pulled along by the upper air jet stream, the cold front moves south-east while the warm front moves north. Satellite photographs show a dense area of cloud to the north of the depression centre with a convex hook shape.

Stage 3: Warm sector depression

As pressures continue to fall, circulation strengthens and wind speeds increase. The cold front rapidly undercuts the warm air which rises even faster. The wedge of warm air, known as the 'warm sector', progressively shrinks in size. This stage is best shown in cross-section (Figure 2.16b). Compare this cross-section with the weather patterns shown in the synoptic chart (Figure 2.10) and satellite photograph (Figure 2.12).

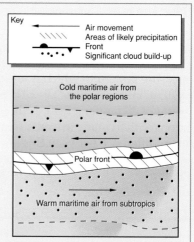

Key
Air movement
Areas of likely precipitation
Front
Significant cloud build-up

Figure 2.14 Stage 1 Cyclogenesis stage.

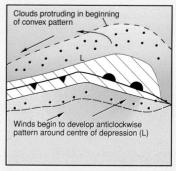

Figure 2.15 Stage 2 Wave depression stage.

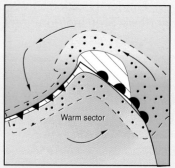

Figure 2.16a Stage 3 Warm sector stage.

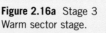

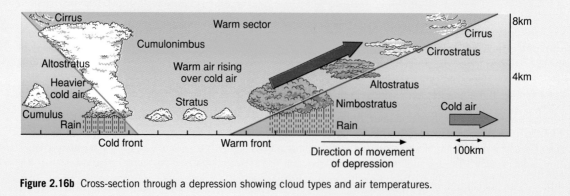

Figure 2.16b Cross-section through a depression showing cloud types and air temperatures.

Stage 4: An occluding depression

The cold front eventually catches up with the slower-moving warm front and the two fronts meet. The warm air which was originally at the surface is now lifted above it, first at the centre, then further away. This is called an occlusion. It occurs after two or three days and may persist for several more as cold air replaces warmer air at surface level. The depression achieves its lowest pressure in this phase and satellite photographs show its characteristic hook shape. As the 1987 and 1990 storms showed, this is the most destructive phase when temperature differences between tropical and polar air are extreme. In 1987, the depression deepened by 50mb in one day and temperatures rose by 9 °C within an hour as the warm sector passed over southern Britain.

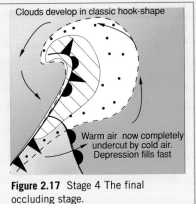

Clouds develop in classic hook-shape

Warm air now completely undercut by cold air. Depression fills fast

Figure 2.17 Stage 4 The final occluding stage.

---

1 Construct a series of annotated diagrams to show how a depression develops from wave, through mature depression to occlusion. Define all your key terms.

2 In a pair, explain to another pair the development of a depression. The other pair should listen and ask questions at the end. Which parts of the explanation were the most difficult to communicate?

3 In the same pairs, read the more recent theory on depressions and upper air movements shown below. This time the pair who listened last should present their understanding of this theory. Again allow time for questions and identify the most difficult aspects of the topic.

4 Compare and contrast the two theories. What are the easiest and most difficult parts to understand?

Theory

Depressions and jet streams

The formation of depressions and anticyclones is linked to air movements in upper levels of the atmosphere, at about 8000–12 000m above sea-level. This is the height at which most commercial passenger aircraft fly. Some idea of this can be gained from British Airways transatlantic flights between London Heathrow and New York's JFK airport. A Boeing 747 is scheduled to take 8 hours for the journey between London and New York; on its return journey, the same aircraft is scheduled to take 6 hours and 45 minutes. Research carried out after 1945, using measurements by high-flying aircraft and balloons with weather sensors, discovered that rapid air currents move from west to east around the Earth in waves. Just like those at the Earth's surface, these fast-moving air currents move between upper air troughs of low pressure and ridges of high pressure.

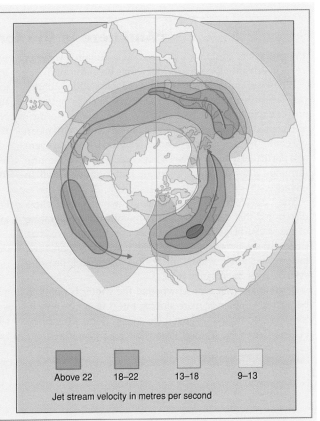

Figure 2.18 Jet streams and their speeds over the northern hemisphere in July.
This map shows the average position of jet streams during July. Notice that the UK is right on the track of these high-velocity winds. These are closely associated with the development of fronts and depressions, and are part of the driving force which directs depressions from west to east across the Atlantic towards Europe.

| Above 22 | 18–22 | 13–18 | 9–13 |

Jet stream velocity in metres per second

Aircraft travelling from North America to London are helped by these tail winds, while those flying in the opposite direction may meet strong headwinds. During periods of fast-moving low pressure systems such as the January 1990 storm, planes may arrive much earlier than scheduled into Heathrow airport, having had a tail wind to help them across the Atlantic.

Above the Earth's surface there are also higher and lower pressure systems. High pressure exists where there is colder stable air, and low pressure where there is unstable warmer air. Movement of air takes place, causing high level winds. Without the rotation of the Earth these winds tend to blow in much more direct paths, and without the Earth's friction they may blow at very high speeds. These are known as jet streams (Figure 2.18). The development of depressions and anticyclones is very closely linked to the speed and position of these jet streams. The continual west-to-east movement of upper air winds causes the regular west-to-east movement of depressions and anticyclones which dominate British weather.

The effects of storms in north-west Europe

In 1987, 1990 and 1999 storms caused significant damage to Britain and the countries of north-west Europe. Loss of life, damage to property and disruption to basic services were common to all three storms, but contrasts emerge when details of their impact are studied. The time of day, the season in which the storm occurred and the path of the storm all create unique patterns of impact. In every case a strong jet stream caused rapid deepening of the low pressure system and dictated the course of the storm. The aftermath of the storms leaves weather scientists and planners to consider a range of issues such as:

- Is the frequency of storms increasing and could this be a result of natural climatic fluctuations (see the new theory on the North Atlantic Oscillation on page 32) or global warming (see Chapter 4)?
- How will local authorities and central government plan for future storm damage to minimise the impact?
- House insurance premiums are rising fast as companies anticipate climatic changes. How will individuals and companies cope with higher taxes and insurance premiums in the future?
- Can weather forecasting develop to assist planning for such events?

And here is the forecast for 2004

TV forecasters could soon be predicting Britain's weather years in advance thanks to a Met Office breakthrough.

A new system, which could be available within months, can determine broad seasonal changes, such as whether any one winter will be particularly wet, windy or stormy.

The predictions – up to five years in advance – will mean we could decide whether to holiday in the UK in the event of a particularly hot summer. They could also revolutionise farming, allowing preparation for bad summers well in advance.

The development came about when researchers discovered that during the winter months the temperature of the sea surface is a major influence on Britain's weather. Crucially, sea temperatures are more predictable than other factors, including winds, air temperatures and pressure systems over the Atlantic.

'It gives an indication of whether the winter is going to be wetter, windier or more stormy, but it won't be able to forecast individual events,' Dr Mark Rodwell, of the Hadley Centre for Climate Prediction, said yesterday.

'It could be very useful for utility companies who need to plan over several years.' The new system, reported in the journal Nature, centres on a weather phenomenon called the North Atlantic Oscillation – a European version of El Nino – which scientists have found is directly controlled by the sea surface temperature of the Atlantic.

The NAO 'flips' the air pressure across the ocean every few years, triggering dramatic changes to the weather for thousands of miles around.

The researchers discovered that when the NAO was said to be high, winters were wet, windy and mild. Winters with a low NAO were dry but extremely cold.

They found that during the 1940s the NAO was low, bringing some of the bitterest winters of the century.

But it was high during the mild wet winters of the late 1980s.

Although the system focuses on winter weather, other seasons could soon follow, say scientists at the Met Office, who only predict the weather a week in advance at present.

Figure 2.19 From the *Daily Mail*, 25 March 1999.

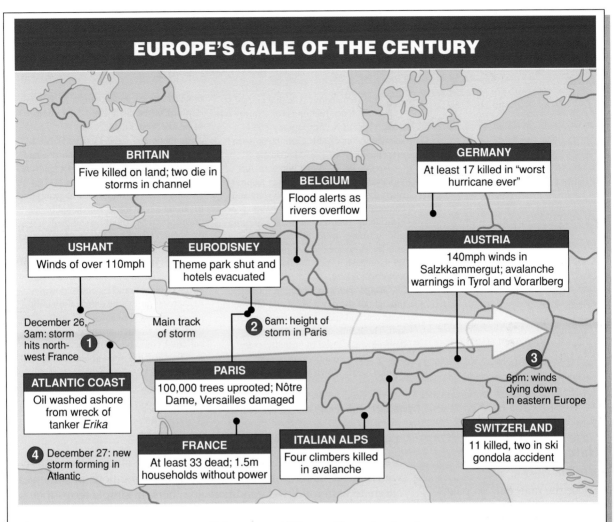

EUROPE'S GALE OF THE CENTURY

BRITAIN
Five killed on land; two die in storms in channel

BELGIUM
Flood alerts as rivers overflow

GERMANY
At least 17 killed in "worst hurricane ever"

USHANT
Winds of over 110mph

EURODISNEY
Theme park shut and hotels evacuated

AUSTRIA
140mph winds in Salzkkammergut; avalanche warnings in Tyrol and Vorarlberg

December 26, 3am: storm hits north-west France **1**

Main track of storm

2 6am: height of storm in Paris

3

ATLANTIC COAST
Oil washed ashore from wreck of tanker *Erika*

PARIS
100,000 trees uprooted; Nôtre Dame, Versailles damaged

6pm: winds dying down in eastern Europe

4 December 27: new storm forming in Atlantic

FRANCE
At least 33 dead; 1.5m households without power

ITALIAN ALPS
Four climbers killed in avalanche

SWITZERLAND
11 killed, two in ski gondola accident

Rivers still on flood alert

FORECASTERS yesterday warned those celebrating Millennium Eve to prepare for a stormy night on Friday.

The severe gales and rain that affected the South of England on Christmas Eve could cause more structural damage and flooding on December 31, some weather experts said. Although the next day or two will be quiet, rain and strong winds will return at the end of the week, a Press Association WeatherCentre forecaster said. He said: 'We are expecting heavy rain and strong winds – it is too early to say whether it will be as bad as Christmas.'

But the Meteorological Office played down the risk of high winds and would say only that Friday night was likely to be mild and overcast with rain.

Yesterday the West Country remained on red flood alert as another band of stormy weather hovered off the coast. Three people were rescued from their cottage in North Curry, Somerset, after being marooned upstairs for hours. The water was rising up the stairs as they were rescued by officers from the Environment Agency. Diana Mallows, who has lived in the cottage for 28 years, said she had never known such bad flooding.

The Environment Agency said that flooding in the area was as bad as in 1994 – the worst year on record – with water 8ft deep in places. Red and amber flood alerts were still in force on several rivers and sandbags were ordered into the area to shore up flood defences.

In East Anglia many rivers were swollen and the ground was said to be at saturation point. The Thames was also expected to continue rising. The Environment Agency gave warning that trees blocking rivers would cause flooding. Almost 48 hours of continuous rain left rivers in Kent and Sussex flowing dangerously fast. Red warnings were in force on the Ouse and Cuckmere in East Sussex.

There were 30 amber warnings on rivers and the coast of Kent and Sussex. Farmland in Romney Marshes was flooded. Red alerts were in force on the River Wye, and on the River Dee, in Wales.

Figure 2.20 From the *Times*, 28 December 1999.

The Great Gale 1990
25th January

The tremendous gale that caused so much destruction across Surrey on Thursday 25th January 1990 seemed inconceivable, coming so soon after the October 1987 'hurricane'.

No one believed that winds of such violence would strike in Surrey again for many a decade. But while foresters and National Trust gardeners were still clearing up after the 'storm of a lifetime', grim warnings were flashed on television as a ferocious area of low pressure looked set to unleash its pent-up fury over wide areas of England.

Savage winds increased in intensity throughout the day and by mid-afternoon, these reached speeds of more than 120 kph. Thousands of pounds' worth of damage was caused in virtually every Surrey street; countless trees were toppled, roofs blown off, many roads blocked and because it struck during the day, unlike the last great gale, a number of people were killed.

A schoolgirl, aged 11 from Banstead, was one of the victims. She was crushed by a tree outside St Philomena's Convent in Carshalton at about 3.45 pm. At Epsom Downs, a 75-year-old man was struggling to put up a rose trellis which had blown down, when he collapsed and died. It was the second tragedy in Epsom. A man died after falling while trying to secure loose roof tiles. In Haslemere, a man was crushed to death by a falling tree while trying to clear branches blown down.

Across Surrey, the damage in public places amounted to at least £5 million, the County Council reported. But while buildings could be reconstructed, the woodlands could not – at least for several decades.

Figure 2.21 The Great Gale 1990, from *Surrey Weather Book.*

Human impact of the storms

1 Use the materials on pages 24–32 and others from the Met Office web site to contrast the 1990 and 1999 storms in terms of wind strength (look up a table with the Beaufort Scale to help you) and social, economic and environmental impact. You may like to present your work in table format.

2 Read the new theory on the North Atlantic Oscillation opposite. What does this tell you about the frequency of such storms?

The North Atlantic Oscillation

Scientists at the UK Meteorological Office have studied the pattern of winters over many years and how cold, dry conditions in some years alternate with mild, wet conditions in others. In simple terms they say that the reason that winters vary is due to the balance between the Azores high pressure (see subtropical high pressure in the General Circulation Model in Chapter 3, page 39) and the Icelandic low pressure (along the polar front in the General Circulation Model). When the Azores high is very strong and the Icelandic low very deep there is a strong pressure gradient with strong westerly winds and a strong jet stream. This tends to be the time when storms are at their strongest and winters are mild and wet. The 1980s and early 1990s in Britain were characteristic of this phase, which is called the 'high phase'.

When pressure is above normal in Iceland and below normal in the Azores, the pressure gradient is weak and westerly wind speed falls by an average of 30km/h over a typical winter. Storms are replaced by cold, dry, settled anticyclonic conditions over Britain. The jet stream is forced to split with one part taking depressions north into northern Scotland and Scandinavia and the other taking weak depressions down into Spain and the western Mediterranean. This is the low phase and was dominant in the 1960s and 1970s when Britain experienced some very cold winters.

What is not clear yet is the extent to which global warming may influence this natural climate fluctuation and whether this will bring more or less high phase periods and therefore more storms. However, the Met Office is now using this research to benefit its forecasting efforts (Figure 2.19).

Anticyclonic weather in Britain – the economic impact of the hot summer and unusual warmth of 1995

The 1995 summer in Britain was the warmest and driest on record, with the July–August average being 3°C above the average for 1961–90. The total rainfall was only 47mm compared to a 1961–90 average of 139mm. The summer followed an exceptionally warm and damp winter. The year was characterised by dominant westerly airstreams in winter and then blocking anticyclonic weather from April to August (see theory box on Anticyclones on page 35). What is significant about the studies of this period is that the human impact is both positive and negative and may have important lessons for planners seeking to anticipate possible effects of future global warming in Britain. Figure 2.22 is a summary of some of the key impacts.

- Energy: When the increases in use of refrigeration and air-conditioning were set against the huge savings in heating bills during the mild winter, the net saving to consumers was £355 million. Shifts to greater use of electricity generated by gas enabled people to respond more easily to changes in climate compared to earlier studies of the 1975 drought year.

- Natural environment: Bird populations grew during the mild winters and forest areas also benefited from higher growth. Britain does not suffer from forest fires and there was little extra damage from the drought, but lowland deciduous trees such as beech did suffer some 'drought stress' in the summer.

- Agriculture: Net losses were £180 million in 1995. This amounted from a surplus of £30 million from certain arable crops (wheat, barley, oilseed rape) set against losses of £210 million in livestock resulting from the need to buy more water and feeds and the decline in the number of pig and poultry births. Farmers had adapted to warmer and drier conditions by making greater use of weather forecasting, irrigation and dry farming techniques designed to conserve water.

- Water: The overall cost to the industry was £100 million, mainly in those areas which were more dependent on surface water supplies such as Yorkshire and North West Water. Co-operation began between water companies to cope with increased demand and reduced supply: Anglian Water signed a co-operation agreement with Severn–Trent Water and has plans to drill permanent groundwater boreholes for use only in drought conditions, while Northumbria Water supplied water by tanker to North West Water to ease its immediate crisis. There was much public criticism of the water companies in their planning for drought and global warming, but by the end of the 1990s most had long-term plans for conservation and innovations such as water metering.

- Retailing: Losses were highest in the clothing sector and in footwear (£383 million) but there were gains in beer, wine and soft drinks (£134 million) and in fruit and vegetables (£25 million). It appears that the retail sector have relied traditionally on the average summer weather profile whereas by the end of the 1990s the industry had started looking to forecast providers like the UK Met Office for more sophisticated data to anticipate demand changes (Figure 2.23).

Figure 2.22 The economic impacts of sustained warm dry weather.

In addition, several other adaptations to the warm weather and drought conditions were made:
- Regulations now state that roads have to have surfaces that can withstand higher temperatures.
- Insurance companies gather information on properties vulnerable to subsidence and damage (for example those built on clay) and may refuse to insure certain properties in the future. There is some evidence of changes in building methods because of this.
- Tourism is expanding its opportunities in outdoor activities, air-conditioning is becoming more common in hotels and on transport, and some cities and towns have adopted the 'café culture' by allowing pavement seating. Many more people took day trips and summer holidays in Britain in 1995 and foreign holiday bookings fell substantially.

Figure 2.23 Dried up waters in a Pennine reservoir. The 1995 drought caught some water companies like Yorkshire Water napping as they miscalculated demand and the impact on their supplies fed largely by surface water rather than groundwater.

The forecast is mixed for salads and fruit

PITY THE POOR British shopkeeper. While Mediterranean rivals stock up on watermelons knowing the summer will be hot to the end of September, the UK retailer is buffeted by the climatic vagaries of the English summer – from tropical beach one day to Siberian chill the next.

The soaring temperatures in July and at the beginning of August sent sales of radishes, hair-removal cream and toilet paper rocketing. Safeway reported a 450% surge in radish sales on sunny salad days, while demand for depilatory cream increased thirteenfold as both the mercury and hemlines rose.

Toilet paper turnover soars in the summer months too as thousands of hay fever sufferers resort to carrying a loo roll to wipe their running noses. Conversely, the recent heavy rain and autumnal chill will have sent cat food sales through the roof as water-hating, house-bound felines fortify themselves with an extra helping of jellied rabbit.

Proving patterns exist between consumers' shopping habits and climatic changes is big business for the country's weathermen, who sell expensive, tailor-made forecasts to the country's biggest retailers. The market is dominated by the Met Office, whose free access to information other companies have to pay for has enabled it to build a commercial division with a turnover of £22 million.

Steve Speck of the Met Office, which claims to supply five of the biggest six supermarkets, says: 'Retailers have got a grip on all the other variables that affect their business, but the weather will always be out of their control. They have to work around it.' Safeway called in the experts following a particularly wet and windy May bank holiday in 1997 after predictions promising heat left the company with a slurry of spoiled barbecue foods, rotten fruit and limp lettuces. It signed a £300 000 three-year contract with the Met Office for 30-day forecasts and short-term updates.

Aylwin says: 'We get payback on that. Realistically, you can lose that sort of money in a week if you get the sales wrong or just through wastage. We are an £8 billion business and 50% of our turnover is fresh produce.'

Weather reports are only useful if supermarkets can cut their lead time with suppliers to around 24 hours. Aylwin adds: 'We had a 30-day forecast telling us the second week of August could see a change in the hot weather. When the three-day report proved that to be accurate we called our suppliers and reduced orders of soft fruit, ice cream and salad.'

Figure 2.24 The value of forecasting to the retail trade. From *Evening Standard*, 26 August 1999.

Theory

Anticyclones

When air is cooled, its volume contracts and becomes heavier. This forces it to sink under gravity. Often, large bodies of cooler air subside and collect as dense air masses. These form large areas of stable air, known as areas of high pressure or anticyclones. Once an anticyclone is established, it often remains for long periods. Because it consists of stable cold air, it contains very little moisture and is therefore dry. Although cold, the clear dry air allows the sun's radiation through to the Earth's surface. In summer, anticyclones are therefore associated with settled, warm, sunny weather. The satellite photograph in Figure 2.25 shows a clear example of this. It was taken on a day when almost all of north-western Europe was visible from space. Some high pressure areas remain as fixed features of the world climate pattern, such as the Azores high of the mid-northern Atlantic.

Winter conditions are somewhat different. In winter, the clarity of the air allows bright sunny days, but the lack of cloud enables heat energy to escape at night. Sometimes the repeated loss of heat during long winter nights results in temperatures dropping further and further. Sustained high pressures become known in winter as 'blocking highs' because of the resistance they offer to encroaching warmer air. Associated weather patterns in the UK during winter include:

Figure 2.25 Satellite photograph of North Atlantic at 1245 GMT on 2 May 1990.

- gradual reductions in temperature overnight as a blocking high establishes itself – during December 1981, a severe cold snap sent temperatures in Shawbury, Shropshire, to as low as −25 °C
- dense fog, particularly in low-lying areas such as the Vale of York and the Thames Valley.

Understanding the impact of weather on the economy

1 Read the account of the 1995 summer weather on Britain and its impact on the economy (Figure 2.22). Draw a summary diagram to show the positive and negative aspects.

2 What conclusions have you reached about the impact of such weather on economic activity in Britain? What other changes might different sectors of the economy have to make if summers of this type become more common in the future?

3 Read Figure 2.24. To what extent do you think there is a direct link between consumer behaviour and weather patterns?

4 What other people might find forecasting useful, and for what reasons? Consider especially those conditions associated with a blocking high in winter, described in the theory box on Anticyclones opposite.

5 Carry out research to find out how weather forecasting is used on a regular basis by other industrial sectors and organisations. Present a short summary for the class.

Summary

You have learned that:
- British weather is typical of a cool temperate western maritime type climate in its changeability from day to day and week to week.
- This changeability is principally related to alternating low pressure and high pressure events as well as to air stream types.
- Recent research shows that a switch in dominant weather systems in the North Atlantic can have significant effects in winter and is now influencing weather forecasting.
- Depressions which form in the North Atlantic develop as a result of air mass and are also explained by new theories which link upper air winds and surface systems.
- Extreme, short-lived weather events continue to be a challenge to planners and weather forecasters in the MEDCs such as Britain.
- Unusual weather conditions which persist over several months can pose equal but different challenges to environmental managers and to weather forecasters.
- Weather events can have widely differing impacts on the economy; some sectors make use of weather forecasting technology to adapt to changing seasonal conditions whereas others are less quick to adjust their activities and planning.

References and further reading

The UK Meteorological Office Education Service provides a number of excellent resources about British weather and its web site www.met-office.gov.uk includes daily weather charts, satellite photographs and forecasts

R Washington and M Palmer, 'The North Atlantic Oscillation', *Geography Review*, November 1999, pp 2–5

The web site of the University of East Anglia www.cru.uea.ac.uk/link includes a massive collection of weather news stories including information on years such as 1995

The challenge of seasonality in the Tropics

The Tropics and the global weather system

If you had studied geography as an A-level student in the 1950s and 1960s it is likely that your course would have included regional geography of the Tropics and some strong assumptions that climate was a predictable element of life for people both in the past and in the future. However, most people are now aware that the weather and climate are changing globally and have become less certain, and that the Tropics have experienced some of the most extreme natural events ever recorded on the planet; Figure 3.1 gives some examples. Rarely does a day go by without reports of another flood, landslide or tropical storm. Given that 75 per cent of the world's population live within the zone between the Tropics of Cancer and Capricorn, and that urbanisation rates are among the highest in the world, it is not surprising that detailed study of the climates in this area is a major focus of organisations like the World Meteorological Organisation.

El Niño misery felt globally

(From the *Age*, 27 February 1998)

Freaky weather to go on for months

(From the *Age*, 27 February 1998)

El Niño wanes in Australia

(From the *Age*, 6 March 1998)

El Niño's trail of destruction

(From *Sydney Morning Herald*, 18 November 1997)

In the early months of 1998,
- torrential downpours and mud slides have hit southern California;
- the north-eastern USA has one of the mildest winters on record;
- droughts have affected Indonesia;
- the UK has enjoyed daytime maximum temperatures of 19 °C in mid-February, when 6 °C is the norm.

(From *Geodate*, July 1998)

Figure 3.1 Reports of weather from different parts of the world.

This chapter will explore some of the processes that lie behind global weather systems. Increasingly, an appreciation of broad global systems such as El Niño or La Niña is helping people throughout the world to understand why climate varies and what causes some of the extraordinary weather events, such as droughts or floods.

How do tropical climates compare with temperate climates?

Any good atlas contains maps showing climate classification. Within these, a broad group of climate types is prefaced with the word 'tropical'. The differences between them are based on the degree to which there are distinct seasons, defined primarily by rainfall totals. In brief there are three key contrasts with temperate climates:

1 Temperatures are much higher throughout the year. In equatorial regions with high cloud cover the average temperature may be 30 °C and the annual range of temperature rarely more than 4° or 5°. In tropical hot deserts with no cloud cover to reflect the intensity of the sun, daytime temperatures may reach 45–50 °C, but at night temperatures plummet to near freezing without the cloud blanket to trap the heat. However, even in cooler seasons, temperatures rarely fall below 20 °C in the Tropics.

2 Daylight length is less variable. Typically, tropical countries receive 11–13 hours all year round because of the high angle of the sun.

3 Rainfall totals and distribution relate directly to the movement of the overhead sun between the Tropics. Peak temperatures also mirror the rainfall pattern. This moving zone of maximum heat and rainfall is known as the heat Equator or ITCZ (see theory box on the ITCZ on pages 39–40). In places north of the Equator the pattern is:
- a single maximum rainfall peak as the sun reaches the Tropic of Cancer on 21 June (called the summer solstice)
- a cooler, dry season for places further away from the Equator which matches the position of the overhead sun at the Tropic of Capricorn on 21 December (called the winter solstice).

For countries around the Equator, a double peak of rainfall is produced by the overhead sun passing twice across the Equator on 21 March and 21 September.

Climatic variations in Africa

The land area of the African continent is enormous and spans the entire Tropics and beyond. Its northern coast fringes the Mediterranean at about 37° north of the Equator, while its southern coast at Cape Agulhas is 35° south. However, there are only five climate types in a typical climate map of the continent; this can be compared to Scandinavia which has four. Does this mean that climate is more uniform than in northern Europe or do the climate types mask variations?

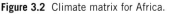

	Rainfall total	No. of peaks in rainfall distribution	No. of months over 50mm of rain	No. of months 10mm of rain or less	Wettest 2–3 months	Temperature range through year	Average diurnal (daily) range of temperature	Average air pressure
Freetown								
Lagos								
Libreville								
Zungeru								
Khartoum								
Timbouctou								
Nairobi								
Harare								

Figure 3.2 Climate matrix for Africa.

1 Study Figure 3.3 on page 38. Make a copy of Figure 3.2 and use it to summarise the similarities and differences between the climates of different places in tropical Africa.

2 Compare your observations with the generalisations shown above about tropical climates and a climatic classification of Africa in your atlas. List the key similarities and differences which you observe.

3 What factors might explain the difference in:
   a) temperature at Libreville and Nairobi
   b) rainfall totals and distribution throughout the year at Freetown and Lagos?

4 What general rules seem to apply:
   a) about rainfall totals, as you move inland from the coast
   b) about temperature variations across the landmass of Africa
   c) about seasonal changes within the different climate zones shown on your atlas map?

5 As a group, collect some travel brochures on a selection of places in tropical Africa which represent at least three of the main climate types. How is the climate described in the brochure details? To what extent are certain features highlighted and others less so? What 'climatic challenges' await the European traveller?

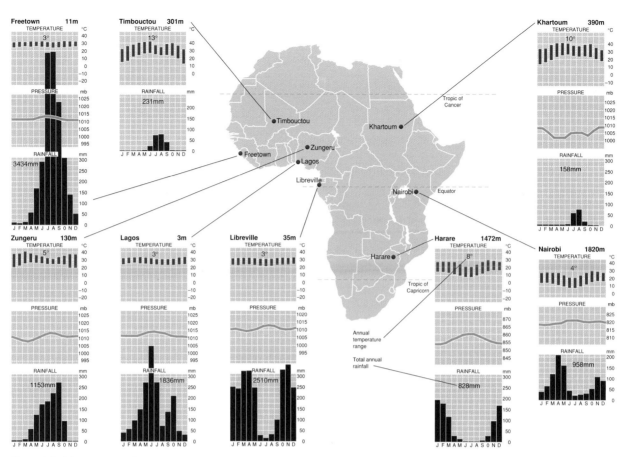

Figure 3.3 Climate graphs for selected stations in Africa.

In continental Africa, seasonality is closely linked to global pressure systems and the migration of the ITCZ described in the theory box opposite. In the continental interior, the landmass is relatively cooler than the surrounding tropical seas during December to February with higher pressure conditions over the Sahara and lower pressure over the Gulf of Guinea. Winds blow into the Gulf of Guinea from the Sahara and these land winds maintain dry conditions over West Africa in winter. Timbouctou and Zungeru in Figure 3.3 illustrate the pattern at this time of the year.

In summer the pattern is reversed. From June to August the landmass north of the Equator is subject to intense heating leading to rapidly rising air, and to low pressure drawing in winds from the Gulf of Guinea. The moist ocean winds from the Gulf of Guinea carry a considerable amount of moisture inland and a look at Timbouctou and Zungeru for summer will reveal heavy seasonal rains.

This pattern of seasonal changes fits into a much broader global system of air circulation. In essence the climates of Africa are determined by two key elements of the global system:

1 the Hadley cell and the movement of the ITCZ
2 periodic climate changes across the whole tropical zone connected with the El Niño/La Niña Oscillation.

The Hadley cell and the Inter-Tropical Convergence Zone

In simple terms the Tropics fit into a global atmospheric system where the Earth seeks to correct the imbalance between excess heat at the Equator and too little heat at the Poles. This imbalance is the result of the different concentrations of solar energy at points on our spherical Earth. Because of its smaller surface area the Equator receives greater concentrations of sunlight but the Poles, because of their much greater surface area, receive much lower concentrations. The result is that the Earth redistributes heat from the Equator towards the Poles by means of:

- vertical and horizontal movements of air (see theory box opposite)
- tropical storms and mid-latitude depressions
- ocean currents which circulate the globe.

General circulation models and Africa – The Hadley cell and the ITCZ

Two climatologists, Ferrel in 1846 and Rossby in 1941, constructed a model of global atmospheric circulation based on three convectional cells. The driving force for the whole model is the central or Hadley cell which develops from intense heating at the Equator. Trade winds blow from this into the low pressure system of the ITCZ which moves northwards and southwards with the overhead sun during the year. The ITCZ, which occurs between the Tropics, is a zone at which two airstreams meet, or converge. Along the ITCZ, the monsoon front brings heavy rains.

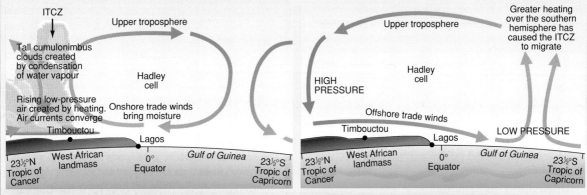

Figure 3.4a The Hadley cell and the ITCZ during the June–August period over the African continent. The diagram shows the on-shore trade winds bringing moisture into the West African landmass, with the position of the ITCZ front over the interior. This front brings rain-bearing trade winds into the interior of West Africa, and produces the rainy season.

Figure 3.4b The Hadley cell and the ITCZ during the December–February period over the African continent. The diagram shows how the ITCZ has migrated south with the passage of the sun. As a result, the trade winds are drawn from the continent into the ITCZ off-shore, thus creating a dry season in the West African landmass.

The trade winds (Figure 3.4) pick up water vapour through the process of evaporation as they cross warm, tropical seas. Inland, they are forced to rise by intense convectional currents which are compounded when heat is released through condensation of water vapour into droplets. This process is often associated with towering cumulonimbus clouds which give rise to frequent afternoon thunderstorms in the equatorial zone. At ground level, winds associated with the ITCZ are light and variable. In the upper atmosphere, however, further cooling causes an increase in air density, and the airflow begins to subside approximately 30° north or south of the ITCZ. This forms the subtropical high pressure belt. Here skies are clear and winds light, and dry stable conditions exist.

Figure 3.5 shows how the Hadley cell is just one of three cells which are formed in similar ways across the northern hemisphere. In terms of its size, the Hadley cell is the largest because of the immense amount of heating which takes place at the Tropics. This is also reflected in the thickness of the troposphere above the Tropics. Where the air is colder and more dense at the northern latitudes, the troposphere is less thick and the polar cell smaller.

Latitude	NORTH POLE	60°N	30°N	0° EQUATOR
Climate/ weather features	Dry anticyclonic	Mid-latitude depressions forming	Sub-tropical high – dry, stable	ITCZ huge convectional clouds
Prevailing winds	North-easterlies	South-westerlies	North-east trade winds	Minimal wind conditions

Figure 3.5 The three-cell model of global atmospheric circulation.

In Figure 3.5, some air returns near the surface into the ITCZ, but some migrates polewards towards the polar front as warm south-westerly winds. These form the basis of the second major cell, the Ferrel cell. These winds collect moisture and meet southward-moving polar air between 50° and 60° north. At this point, the release of latent heat produced by condensation forces the winds to rise, laying the foundation of a new mid-latitude depression. This sequence of depressions is described fully in Chapter 2. The rising limb of the Ferrel cell cools and descends towards the subtropical high. Here it is warmed by compression, making it highly stable.

A final weaker polar cell consists of the diverging, cooling air of the polar front slowly descending over the Pole giving dry, high pressure conditions. A weak movement of cold dense polar air moves south towards the polar front low pressure area. The polar front is formed where this meets the northward-moving subtropical air from the Ferrel cell.

Understanding the General Circulation Model

1 Form groups of two or three. Read together the theory box on the Hadley cell and the ITCZ and discuss how both affect the climates of Africa north of the Equator.

2 Prepare a presentation to show how the theory explains the general climate change from equatorial types to savanna types to tropical hot desert as you move northwards from the Equator in Africa. Base your presentation on labelled diagrams and take no more than seven minutes to give your explanations to the class.

3 Now summarise the key points of the theory, and create a glossary of key terms.

People, environment and climate in Africa

The final part of this section will focus on the impact of climate and climate change on human activity. In general terms, the climate changes gradually from the Equator northwards, and seasonality is a key factor in influencing temperature and rainfall. These changes are also mirrored in the dominant ecosystems and human activity as shown in Figure 3.6, which is a simplified illustration of a transect from the Equator to the Tropic of Cancer.

For some populations, the seasonality of rainfall in particular places enormous stress on their ability to maintain even the most basic aspects of life as water supplies and food resources dwindle in severe drought conditions.

In the 1980s the droughts in Ethiopia and the Sudan shocked the millions of affluent people living in Europe, North America and parts of Asia and relief funds were set up to send emergency aid to these regions. Drought

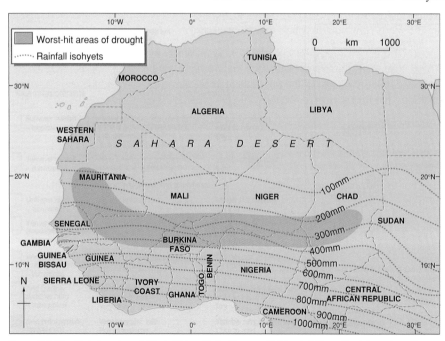

Figure 3.6 The Sahel region of West Africa. Note the very tight rainfall gradient from less than 100mm north of 16° north to over 700mm south of about 10° north.

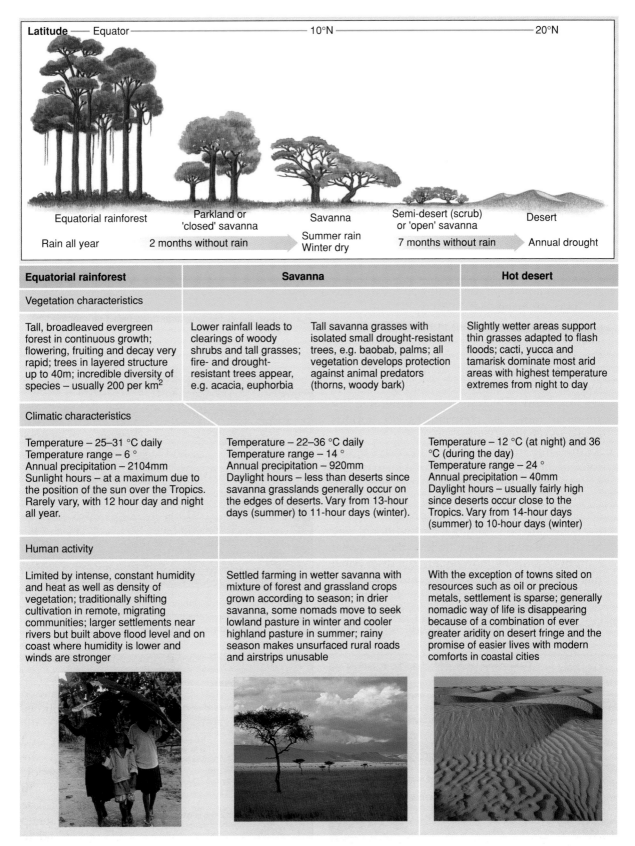

Equatorial rainforest	Savanna		Hot desert
Vegetation characteristics			
Tall, broadleaved evergreen forest in continuous growth; flowering, fruiting and decay very rapid; trees in layered structure up to 40m; incredible diversity of species – usually 200 per km^2	Lower rainfall leads to clearings of woody shrubs and tall grasses; fire- and drought-resistant trees appear, e.g. acacia, euphorbia	Tall savanna grasses with isolated small drought-resistant trees, e.g. baobab, palms; all vegetation develops protection against animal predators (thorns, woody bark)	Slightly wetter areas support thin grasses adapted to flash floods; cacti, yucca and tamarisk dominate most arid areas with highest temperature extremes from night to day
Climatic characteristics			
Temperature – 25–31 °C daily Temperature range – 6 ° Annual precipitation – 2104mm Sunlight hours – at a maximum due to the position of the sun over the Tropics. Rarely vary, with 12 hour day and night all year.	Temperature – 22–36 °C daily Temperature range – 14 ° Annual precipitation – 920mm Daylight hours – less than deserts since savanna grasslands generally occur on the edges of deserts. Vary from 13-hour days (summer) to 11-hour days (winter).		Temperature – 12 °C (at night) and 36 °C (during the day) Temperature range – 24 ° Annual precipitation – 40mm Daylight hours – usually fairly high since deserts occur close to the Tropics. Vary from 14-hour days (summer) to 10-hour days (winter)
Human activity			
Limited by intense, constant humidity and heat as well as density of vegetation; traditionally shifting cultivation in remote, migrating communities; larger settlements near rivers but built above flood level and on coast where humidity is lower and winds are stronger	Settled farming in wetter savanna with mixture of forest and grassland crops grown according to season; in drier savanna, some nomads move to seek lowland pasture in winter and cooler highland pasture in summer; rainy season makes unsurfaced rural roads and airstrips unusable		With the exception of towns sited on resources such as oil or precious metals, settlement is sparse; generally nomadic way of life is disappearing because of a combination of ever greater aridity on desert fringe and the promise of easier lives with modern comforts in coastal cities

Figure 3.7 A simplified transect from the Equator to the Tropic of Cancer to show changes in ecosystems and human activity.

continues into the twenty-first century in these regions as well as in the other countries of the Horn of Africa and in the Sahel, which is a broad fringe of open savanna bordering the Sahara (Figure 3.6 on page 40). This belt of land, which extends for some 3800km from east to west and 700km from north to south, has suffered many years of unreliable rainfall during what should have been the rainy season of June to August. Figure 3.9 illustrates the long-term trend in the Sahel and the very noticeable dryness from the mid-1960s onwards. This persistent drought over many years is taking its toll on both people and the environment.

The causes of the drought are varied; some are likely to be natural, others human.

- Some may have their origin in periodic switches in climatic conditions such as the El Niño/La Niña Oscillation (see theory box on El Niño and La Niña on pages 44) or may be caused by global warming as a result of pollution.
- There may be factors relating to human use of the land which are making matters worse. Overuse of resources, such as collecting fuelwood from rapidly disappearing trees and grazing land which is not regenerated by summer rains, is contributing to serious landscape change (Figure 3.8).
- At the same time populations in Africa record some of the highest rates of natural increase and so land use around settlements becomes more intensive. The few nomadic tribes who have been able to survive years of drought such as the Fulani are now finding their traditional way of life threatened. They follow the seasonal pattern of rains by moving into the drier Sahel highlands in summer to escape mosquitoes and cattle disease and returning to the lowland rivers of the savanna in winter to find pasture. Thousands of nomads now live in towns since

even reliable water holes and pasture have gone and countries are tightening up border controls to prevent incursions into their territories.

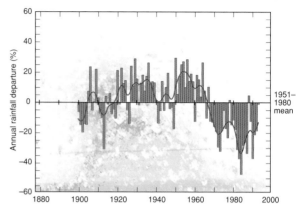

Figure 3.9 This graph shows the annual departure from the mean of the rainfall in the Sahel between 1900 and 1990. The red line shows the long-term trend based on running ten-year averages.

Figure 3.10 Evidence of deforestation of acacia trees in central Sudan. The changing surface characteristics are thought to have a permanent impact on climate.

Figure 3.8 Human use of resources in the Sahel and its link with drought.

Coping with drought in the Sahel

1 Using information from this chapter as well as from atlases, the internet and other sources, create a folder of evidence to show the causes of drought and the impact of drought on the countries of the Sahel. This task will complement your work on ecosystems and pressures on the world's grasslands in particular.

2 Refer to Figures 3.7–3.10. To what extent are the problems of regions like the Sahel and the Horn of Africa the result of:
   a) climate changes
   b) human resource use or destruction caused by war?

The threat of El Niño and La Niña

The dramatic series of extreme weather events in the last few years in the Tropics is illustrated in a single year, 1998 (Figure 3.11). Apart from the devastating loss of life, the economic damage to so many Less Economically Developed Countries (LEDCs) amounts to well over US $20 billion. Poverty in these countries is becoming even more difficult to overcome as countries run up massive debts simply in order to reconstruct the most basic services and the transport infrastructure upon which their fragile economies depend. Weather scientists from around the world have put together enough research for the last 30 years to link the majority of the recent weather extremes to a phenomenon known as the El Niño Southern Oscillation (see theory box on page 44) although detailed records only include the last 13 years.

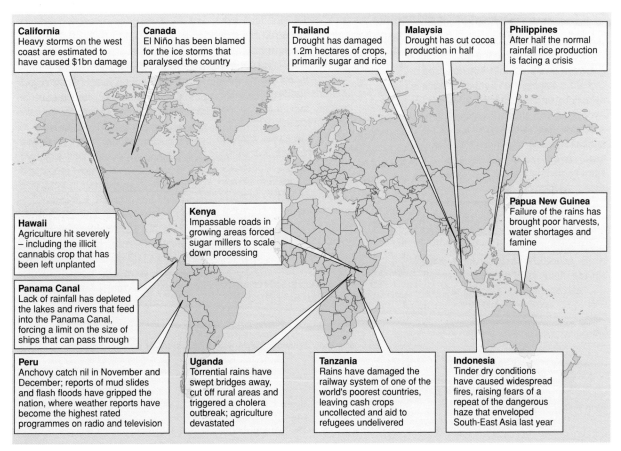

Figure 3.11 Weather extremes in 1998.

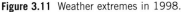

El Niño and La Niña
Why El Niño?

The term 'El Niño' is Spanish for 'boy-child', used by Peruvian anchovy fishermen for a warm ocean current off the South American coast which appears at Christmas every three to eight years. As it replaces the cold Humboldt current, it prevents the upwelling of cold nutrient-rich deep ocean water which provides food for the plankton, which in turn is the food of the anchovy. Anchovy harvests have been ruined by four or five of the most severe El Niño events this century, a blow to the Peruvian fishing industry.

For climatologists, El Niño is linked to sea temperature and air pressure changes in the eastern Pacific and Indonesia when warming is strong.

How it works

In normal years, known as La Niña, the circulation of air in the Pacific is based on the Walker cell which moves east–west (Figure 3.12a). The cold Humboldt current brings cold water from the Southern Ocean north along the west coast of South America. The colder water then flows west along the Equator, where it is heated by the tropical sun. The western part of the Pacific Ocean is 3–8 °C warmer than the eastern part. A low pressure area develops over Indonesia as warm, moist air rises to high levels. Towering columns of cumulonimbus rain clouds are associated with this. It travels east in the upper

atmosphere, and sinks into the subsiding high pressure off the west coast of South America where it gives dry, stable conditions over the eastern Pacific.

During an El Niño event the pressure systems and weather patterns change (Figure 3.12b). Warmer waters develop in the eastern Pacific, with temperatures rising by 2–8 °C. A low pressure forms over this area, drawing in westerly winds. Increased cloudiness results as warm, moist air rises. Around northern Australia and Indonesia, the seas cool and pressure rises leading to lower rainfall. This is thought to be having considerable effects on the Australian economy (Figure 3.13). The change is known as the Southern Oscillation. Its strength and direction and the speed at which change takes place is known as the Southern Oscillation Index (SOI).

The switch from El Niño to La Niña conditions used to occur every seven years. In the past 50 years, El Niño conditions have existed for 31 per cent of the time, and La Niña for 23 per cent. More recently, the switch has occurred more rapidly, with peaks of El Niño in December 1997 and La Niña in December 1998. What is unclear is the possible future effect of global warming upon sea temperatures in the Pacific. Some advisory agencies now attempt to predict the likely chance of an El Niño event to allow governments to prepare for reduced rainfall. In Australia wheat yield has fluctuated closely in line with El Niño events (Figure 3.13), as have bushfire conditions such as those in Sydney in 1993–4.

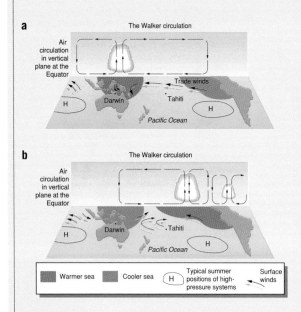

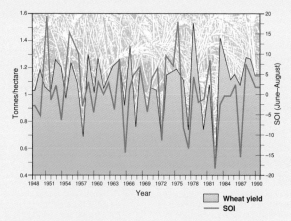
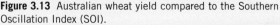

Figure 3.13 Australian wheat yield compared to the Southern Oscillation Index (SOI).
The SOI (rainfall) is shown by the blue line on this graph, and wheat yields are shown in orange. Drier periods are shown when wheat yields fall. In many cases, these coincide with periods of changing pressure systems during El Niño years. Rising air pressure at Darwin, cooling sea-surface temperatures and slackening easterly trade winds are all signals of a possible El Niño event.

Figure 3.12a The normal Walker circulation (La Niña) years.
Figure 3.12b El Niño year circulation.

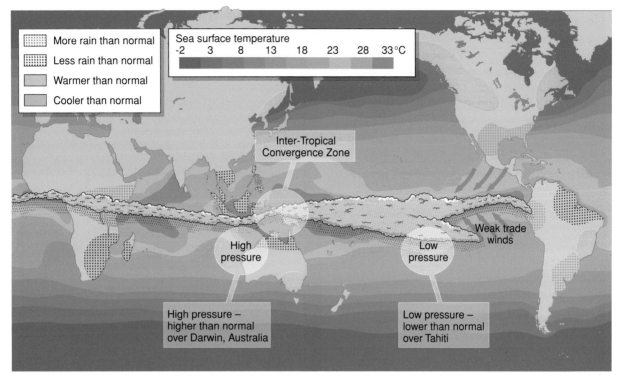

Figure 3.14 El Niño at its peak development in December 1997.

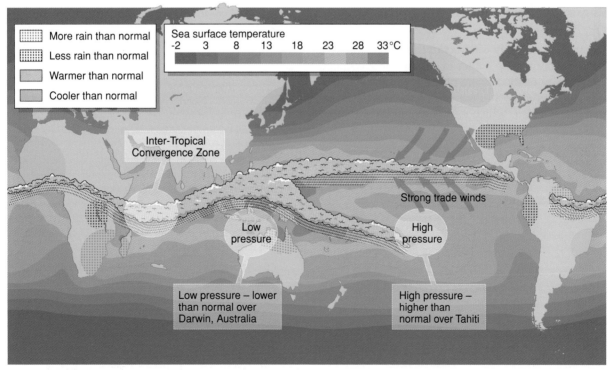

Figure 3.15 La Niña at its peak development in 1998.

The path of El Niño and La Niña

1 Use the theory box on El Niño and La Niña and any other resources you may collect (for example, see web sites on page 48) to give a five-minute summary of the causes of the Southern Oscillation in bullet point format.

2 Study Figures 3.11, 3.14 and 3.15. Use a table to summarise the effects of both El Niño and La Niña on southern Asia, South America and Africa. Which type of year presents people with greater challenges?

3 To what extent does the current research about the Southern Oscillation allow weather scientists to predict global weather conditions in any year? Refer to the World Meteorological Organisation web site or other materials for global weather patterns for the current year – do the patterns suggest a La Niña or El Niño year?

4 What have you learned about the possible implications of the Southern Oscillation for the Sahel?

Regional impact of the Southern Oscillation

The impact on daily life in countries affected by El Niño/La Niña is no longer in any doubt. However, the severity of the impact of the weather switch is also influenced by human use of the environment and the extent to which extremes can be managed

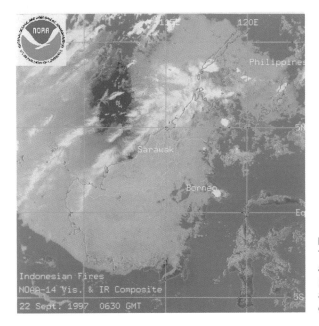

'Even the mild haze is like inhaling hot cotton wool'

The haze over South-East Asia has almost nothing, except poor visibility, in common with the wintry fogs in Britain.

To experience it, even in the relatively mild form that has afflicted Singapore, is unbelievably unpleasant, akin to inhaling hot cotton wool fibres.

A naturally humid climate, where daytime temperatures hover in the mid-30s, adds to the enervating effect of living inside a wet blanket redolent of the refuse tip.

Surgical face masks make no real difference. Eyes sting, even with sunglasses, which are hardly appropriate in the thick murk.

Even for the fit, the haze pollution index needs to reach no higher than the 100-range suffered by Singaporeans to make even walking exhausting, and to pose risks for the very young and those with respiratory problems or weak hearts.

The haze is officially classed as hazardous at between 300 and 500, the top of the scale; and in parts of Malaysia as well as Indonesia the upper end of the scale has now been breached.

As the flight from London approached Singapore last week, the pilot announced that visibility was adequate for landing. The unexplained announcement seemed odd at the time, for mid-afternoon in the dry season.

Stepping from the airport into the semi-darkness, my first reaction was to think that I must have set my watch wrongly; it was clearly much later than I had thought. But for the rest of the week the sun was never to appear. Even in an air-conditioned hotel foyer, you could see the air drifting through doors that were left open for more than a moment. Nearby skyscrapers simply vanished, vehicles had their lights on and shipping had to be curtailed on the Strait of Malacca, one of the world's most congested waterways.

In Singapore criticism of neighbouring Asian countries is discouraged. But Indonesia's failure, year after year, to control the forest fires is breaking down the customary restraints. With Indonesia gripped by drought, these fires could not only be the worst ever but also the most durable.

Foreigners can be evacuated, but South-East Asians are in for a suffocating season.

Figure 3.16 Forest fires cover Indonesia.
The huge spread of the choking haze shown in pink, which affected Indonesia and beyond shocked the world. The impact of people on global climate was recorded by camera and satellite alike. At its worst the smog affected 75 million people in eight countries – an area greater than the size of Europe.

Figure 3.17 The forest is dead. Long live the forest.
Despite a ban by the Indonesian government in 1995 on all large-scale burning, developers openly defy the law. Natural rainforest in Kalimantan is cleared to make way for massive stands of fast growing oil palms for export or acacia trees for quick payoffs in wood pulp. Ironically, the drastic reduction in sunlight caused by the fire haze and the drought resulted in trees wilting, crop failure and food shortage.

on a local, national and regional scale. This enquiry focuses on case studies at either end of the Pacific Ocean during 1997–8: in Peru in the east and in Indonesia to the west. If weather extremes continue to dominate life in such regions then the way in which individual countries, regional organisations such as ASEAN (Association of South East Asian Nations) and the international community respond will be of crucial importance to the survival of all.

Forest fires have been commonplace in Indonesia since 1982 and have caused unprecedented damage to virgin rainforest. Although fire is an illegal practice, it has been used for centuries by traditional 'slash and burn' farmers who clear small areas to plant crops such as cassava and rice before leaving after three or so years to another plot allowing the forest to regenerate naturally. The real damage has been done by large corporations who burn huge areas for commercial plantations of rubber, oil palm and acacia.

There were suspicions in the long drought in 1997 that close friends of the then dictator of Indonesia, President Suharto, were allowed to flout the ban on burning. In the official news media, small farmers were blamed as destroyers of forest since the government claimed it had not agreed to new clearance. Indonesia is the poorest of the ASEAN countries and it is thought that the ruthless use of forest resources is part of an attempt to catch up with its richer neighbours, Singapore, Malaysia and Brunei.

However, some traditional farmers like the Dayak of Kalimantan benefited from the burning which created ready made plots and scrap timber with which to build shacks. Despite rains in February 1998, fires burned out of control as so-called 'hot spots' (where peat and coal burned underground) stoked surface fires and fire fighting equipment proved inadequate.

The core of the fires was in southern Kalimantan and visibility here was virtually zero. In neighbouring countries, where visibility rarely exceeded 200m for several months, ships ran aground, airlines were grounded and respiratory disease was rife. Some 20 million people were treated for asthma, bronchitis, eye, skin and heart disease, and the damage to wildlife and natural vegetation was enormous. Between September 1997 and June 1998, 8–10 million hectares of forest were destroyed in an area which contains 10 per cent of the world's precious remaining rainforest, second only in size to the Amazon.

Figure 3.18 A policeman guides a young girl across a broken bridge in Matucana, east of Lima.
Flash floods triggered huge mudslides in January 1998. Flooding exacted damage similar to that experienced by Honduras during Hurricane Mitch as 300 bridges and 30 000 homes were swept away and the basic fabric of life was destroyed. In this arid part of Peru, people fled the fertile land of the river valleys to live on the desert plateaux above. The mudslides were made much worse by the logging of steep hillsides surrounding villages leaving soil unprotected in the torrential convectional rain.

The severe El Niños of 1982/3 and 1997 triggered a rapid response from the world's weather science community. In 1994 in the USA the National Oceanic and Atmospheric Administration (NOAA) launched the tropical atmosphere/ocean array system where 70 buoys span the Pacific to measure air and wind conditions and the sea temperatures down to 490 metres in order to give warnings of a switch in the Southern Oscillation. Ground data and satellite images enabled scientists to monitor temperature changes away from normal and helped to predict the 1997–8 El Niño using computer models.

Figure 3.20 International tracking of El Niño.

Coping with disaster in Peru and Indonesia

Imagine that you have been asked to produce a report for the British Red Cross web site on the effects of El Niño/La Niña in Peru and Indonesia. The brief for your report states that you must include the following:

- regional sketch maps with clear labelling to show the effects of extreme weather in the two areas
- sufficient detail to show the human cost of the weather events
- a succinct explanation of what caused the weather events and the extent to which human activity influenced their impact
- the work of the scientific community to predict future weather extremes and plan for the future.

You have been asked to limit your report to 1200 words.

References and further reading

Web sites

The following web sites are useful for updates on tropical weather:
www.education.noaa.gov (includes satellite images)
www.worldclimate.com
www.redcross.org/disaster/masters

Summary

You have learned that:

- Tropical weather and climate are more complex than was once thought to be the case and presents strong contrasts to the temperate mid-latitudes in daylight length and seasonality.
- Tropical weather and climate are strongly influenced by the Inter-Tropical Convergence Zone (ITCZ) and, as more recent research shows, by the El Niño/La Niña Oscillation.
- Africa illustrates the seasonal changes and effects on human activity when moving from the Equator to the Tropic of Cancer.
- Some regions like the Sahel suffer extreme seasonal variation in rainfall and the effects have been felt over many years.
- The tropical zone has experienced major weather hazards over the past 15 years. This is now known to have been caused by the El Niño/La Niña Southern Oscillation. The data for this phenomenon is still growing and concern is voiced over the future effects of global warming.

4 Global climatic change

Setting the scene

Rarely does a week pass without broadsheet newspapers publishing something about the ways in which the climate seems to be changing, or about how climatic patterns have somehow been upset. The photograph in Figure 4.1 is typical; a young walrus rests on a rapidly melting fragment of ice in Russia north of the Arctic Circle. The photograph was taken during a scientific study by the crew of the Greenpeace ship *Arctic Sunrise* in July 1999. The Arctic ice pack at this place would have been continuous 20 years earlier; Arctic ice packs have thinned by over 30 per cent since the 1970s and parts of the Arctic fringe were ice free throughout 2000.

There appears to be evidence that increases in global temperature, which we know of as 'global warming', are seriously affecting environments thought previously to be beyond human impact. We know that global temperature has fluctuated over billions of years since the Earth began, including during periods when human populations have been substantial. But it is the pace of recent warming which is now seen as most significant.

This chapter will examine the evidence put forward by both sides of the debate before looking at the consequences for one area of the world and the international action taken to arrive at solutions for a global warming world.

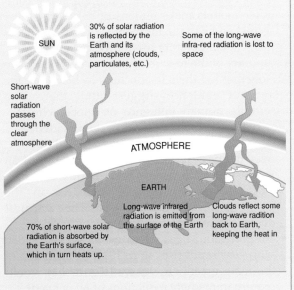

Figure 4.1 Arctic ice heads north!

The greenhouse effect – how it works

The driving force for weather and climate comes from the sun. The Earth intercepts solar radiation in different ways according to surface – oceans, ice, land, living matter, atmosphere. About 30 per cent of this radiation is reflected back into space by clouds, and by reflective land surfaces such as ice and snow. The ability of a surface to reflect back solar radiation is known as 'albedo'. In the long term, energy absorbed from solar radiation is balanced by outgoing radiation from a warming Earth. Crucial to this balance is long-wave infra-red radiation which is partially absorbed and then re-emitted by a number of trace gases in the cooler atmosphere above. These are known as the greenhouse gases. The main natural greenhouse gases are:

- water vapour (the biggest contributor)
- carbon dioxide
- methane
- nitrous oxide
- ozone, which occurs in the troposphere up to 10–15km above the Earth's surface.

30% of solar radiation is reflected by the Earth and its atmosphere (clouds, particulates, etc.)

Some of the long-wave infra-red radiation is lost to space

Short-wave solar radiation passes through the clear atmosphere

ATMOSPHERE

EARTH

Long-wave infrared radiation is emitted from the surface of the Earth

Clouds reflect some long-wave radition back to Earth, keeping the heat in

70% of short-wave solar radiation is absorbed by the Earth's surface, which in turn heats up.

Figure 4.2 How the natural greenhouse effect works.

Without this radiative process, the mean temperature at the Earth's surface would be 33°C cooler and too cold for human habitation. Concentrations of these gases have been found in Antarctic ice cores which go back 160 000 years. These suggest that changes in carbon dioxide and methane, in particular, are linked closely to large global temperature swings such as those which occur during Ice Ages.

An enhanced greenhouse effect?

Many scientists believe that human activities have greatly increased naturally occurring concentrations of greenhouse gases to a point where a major increase of mean annual temperatures will occur. Therefore scientists have used the term 'enhanced', or increased, to describe the effects of this. The greenhouse effect occurs naturally, but recent land use changes, industrialisation and urbanisation have released natural stores of carbon and nitrogen. These increase the net gain of solar radiation from the natural greenhouse effect when they oxidise in the atmosphere.

It is argued that the main greenhouse gas, water vapour, will also increase in quantity because warmer air can hold more moisture than cold air. This will lead to greater condensation and cloud cover, which in turn will create a further heat trap. Other scientists dispute the water vapour theory and question the timing, extent and impact of an enhanced greenhouse effect.

Evidence for an enhanced greenhouse effect

The bulk of the evidence which supports the case for global warming has originated with the Intergovernmental Panel on Climate Change (IPCC) during the 1990s (see theory box on page 51). In brief the case relies on a mixture of:

- direct observation of the atmosphere including remote sensing (satellite photography) to accumulate a huge bank of data
- observation of sea-levels worldwide, ice extent at the Poles and glacier retreat in highland areas
- measurement of greenhouse gas concentrations and the use of massive computers to simulate likely outcomes of global warming; these computer models make billions of calculations per second and will run for months to provide global maps of temperature rise for the current century.

A summary of the research evidence the IPCC have put together led them to conclude in 1995 that 'the balance of evidence suggests that there is a discernible human influence on global climate'. They reiterated the key points of their evidence:

- Global temperatures had risen by up to 1°C over the past 150 years and they predicted an increase for the twenty-first century of up to 3.5°C based on varying increases in the amounts of greenhouse gas. The warmest decade on record was the 1990s.
- All greenhouse gases had increased since 1850 with very rapid rises since 1945. Stabilisation of the main greenhouse gases (Figure 4.4) would require immediate reductions of 60 per cent.
- Some greenhouse gases were more effective at trapping in heat than others. This was termed Global Warming Potential (GWP); gases such as CFCs are 1000 times more effective than carbon dioxide at absorbing heat.
- Sea-levels have been rising by an average of 20cm each century and recent research by The Hadley Centre for Climate Prediction at the UK Meteorological Office indicates a rise of 40cm by 2080 if greenhouse gases rise at the same level.
- Extreme weather events are becoming more common and profound changes in climatic belts could have serious consequences for water supply, food production, ecosystems and human health.
- A number of uncertainties remain as to the response of natural systems to increasing global temperatures (these are points developed to support the case of the sceptics).

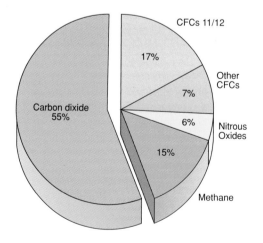

Figure 4.3 Percentage contributions of greenhouse gases to global warming.

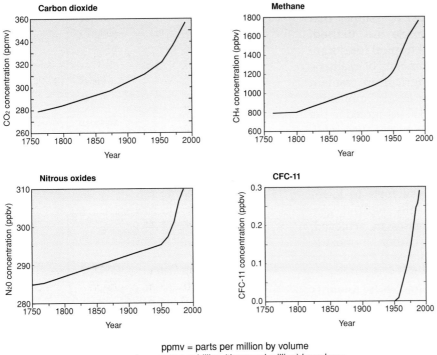

ppmv = parts per million by volume
ppbv = parts per billion (thousand million) by volume

Figure 4.4 Changes in greenhouse gas concentrations, 1750–2000 (based on IPCC reports).

Theory

The Intergovernmental Panel on Climate Change (IPCC)

In 1988 Dr James Hansen, a climate scientist at NASA, warned the United States Congress that global warming was at hand. His speech came at a time when catastrophic drought and blistering heat waves struck the Midwest of the United States and only a year after 50 countries had signed an international agreement to combat ozone depletion, termed the Montreal Protocol. In response to those concerns, the United Nations set up the IPCC to assess the evidence for and the possible impacts of global warming. The IPCC numbers 2500 leading climate scientists from around the world including those from The Hadley Centre for Climate Change at the UK Meteorological Office and from the Centre for Climate Change at the University of East Anglia.

Their first report in 1990 affirmed that the global climate was indeed changing and that increasing greenhouse gases were the main cause. The second report in 1992 formed the basis of the international agreement on climate change at Rio de Janeiro (the Earth Summit) when countries committed to reduce greenhouse gas emissions to 1990 levels by 2000. By the time of the third report in 1995, scientific opinion on global warming was merely confirmed: global warming was here to stay and would overcome temporary cooling from industrial sulphates or volcanic eruptions, and was said to be much stronger than the effects of natural solar cycles. The key points in their evidence base are shown above. IPCC scientific data continues to guide political opinion and was the key evidence considered at the Kyoto climate convention in 1997 (see page 61) and a major conference on global warming impact at The Hague in November 2000.

IPCC scenarios for future climate change

The IPCC was more concerned about future change in the atmosphere and how possible future scenarios seemed to depend upon the increase in greenhouse gases. In Figure 4.4 these increases are shown in graphs of parts per billion by volume until the year 2000.

Figure 4.5 shows four possible predictions of carbon dioxide emissions between 1980 and 2100, and the global temperature rises that could result from each. The four predictions have been made as follows:

1 Scenario A shows 'business-as-usual', with intensive use of coal, and only modest use of

energy efficiency measures in homes, offices, factories and power stations. It assumes that controls on carbon monoxide are limited, deforestation continues until tropical forests are virtually destroyed, and emissions of methane and nitrous oxide from agriculture remain uncontrolled. The reduction in CFC emissions by 50 per cent by the year 2000 (as agreed in the Montreal Protocol in 1987) is partly successful. In this scenario, the world continues to operate as it is now.

2 Scenario B shows an energy supply shifting away from high carbon fossil fuels to lower carbon alternatives, especially natural gas. Large energy efficiency increases are achieved, deforestation is reversed, carbon monoxide strictly controlled and the Montreal Protocol on CFCs fully successful.

3 Scenario C shows a major shift towards renewable energy and nuclear power in the second half of the twenty-first century. CFCs are phased out and agricultural emissions of methane and nitrous oxide are controlled.

4 Scenario D assumes that a move towards renewable energy and nuclear power takes place in the first half of the twenty-first century, leading to a stabilisation of carbon dioxide levels in the developed world. By the middle of the century carbon dioxide levels are reduced to 50 per cent of 1985 levels.

1 What is meant by the term 'scenario'?

2 Work out the approximate rates of change in the graph in Figure 4.5 in units per decade. Describe any trends you notice.

3 What assumptions did the IPCC make in producing their scenarios? Which scenario seems more likely, given your knowledge of present-day patterns of energy use and data in Figure 4.7?

4 Which groups of countries will need to change their energy use and lifestyles most in order to achieve the reductions needed to offset the threat of global warming? What changes might this cause for ordinary citizens and decision-makers?

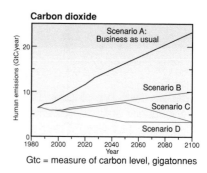

Gtc = measure of carbon level, gigatonnes

Figure 4.5 Simulated increase in carbon dioxide based on the four IPCC scenarios, 1980–2100.

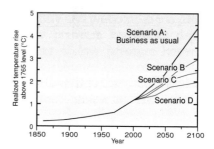

Figure 4.6 The simulated rise in global temperature based on the four IPCC scenarios, 1850–2100.

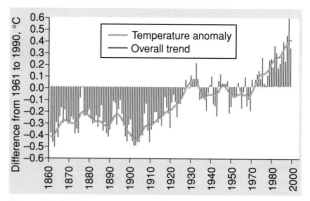

Figure 4.7 World temperature trends 1860–2000, based upon differences from a 1961–90 average.

The main greenhouse gases and their contribution to global warming

Carbon dioxide

Carbon dioxide is one of the major greenhouse gases and is controllable because its emission is caused by human activities, releasing carbon stored in a variety of 'sinks' in the Earth (Figure 4.8). Since 1750, when the British Industrial Revolution began, the concentration of carbon dioxide in the atmosphere has increased by 26 per cent as a result of the burning of fossil fuels in the developed world. In the United Kingdom in 1999, 60 per cent of emissions

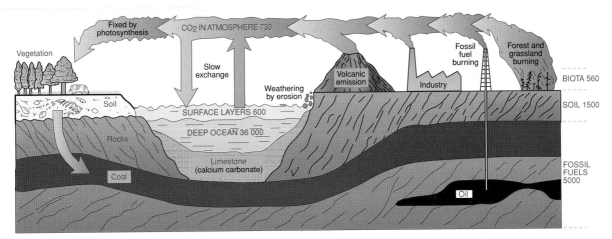

Figure 4.8 Carbon stores, flows and human activity.

came from vehicles alone, with fossil fuel power stations, industry, and domestic and commercial space heating making up the remainder. In the developing world deforestation is contributing most to global warming as cutting and burning releases an estimated 4 billion tonnes of carbon into the atmosphere which would otherwise be taken up by plant growth. The carbon contained in the Amazon basin alone is equivalent to 20 per cent of the entire atmospheric concentration of the gas. It is likely that four-fifths of this could be released into the atmosphere if total deforestation occurred, though half of this would be absorbed by the oceans. In addition, rapid industrialisation in the developing world may more than offset any reduction in carbon emissions in the developed world.

Chlorofluorocarbons

Chlorofluorocarbons (CFCs) were first released in quantity from industries and other uses in the developed world in the 1960s. Their use as propellants in spray cans, blowing agents in foam plastics (for example fast food packaging), refrigerant fluids, and as solvents in the electronics industry soon became widespread. In the 1970s they were thought to be mainly responsible for cooling effects on the atmosphere as a result of their ability to reflect solar radiation, but more recently it has been found that they absorb solar radiation and thus contribute to global warming. The chemical stability of CFCs means that they have a long lifetime in the atmosphere, and their global warming potential outweighs their relatively low concentrations. In the mid-1980s, British scientists discovered an extensive thinning in the ozone layer in the stratosphere 25km above Antarctica. This was attributed to high concentrations of CFCs which had travelled through the upper atmosphere from the northern to the southern hemisphere since the 1960s.

This discovery startled politicians who had believed that pollution would not significantly damage the atmosphere over such a short time span. The result was the first major international agreement on limiting damage to the atmosphere in the Montreal Protocol of 1987, when leading industrial nations agreed to reductions in CFCs and research to introduce substitutes. In 1989 the Protocol was strengthened to reduce CFCs by 50 per cent by the year 2000. In 1992, further amendments sought a phasing out of CFCs and of other chemicals known to destroy ozone by 2000, and the participation of some developing nations in eliminating CFCs altogether. Complete reductions of CFCs were achieved in Europe, the USA, Japan and Australia. However, a lucrative 'black market' is still operating in Russia and parts of Asia.

Methane

Since 1950 the concentrations of methane have risen by 1 per cent per year, four times the rate of increase for carbon dioxide. This could lead to methane becoming the main greenhouse gas within 50 years. The principal reasons for this are increased rice production worldwide, the burning of vegetation, coal mining, leakage of natural gas from distribution systems, and flatulence from livestock as a result of increasingly intensive cattle rearing. Pearce (1989) has estimated that the emission of methane from the world's cattle is close to 100 million tonnes. The trend towards intensive production reflects the demand for cheap mass-produced meat from fast food outlets and supermarket chains.

Nitrous oxide

Human activities which release nitrous oxide into the atmosphere include agricultural fertilisers, fossil fuel combustion (especially from cars), and various industrial processes which involve the production of synthetic chemical substances such as nylon. Nitrous oxide helps to trap infra-red radiation in the lower atmosphere, and changes to nitric oxide in the stratosphere which destroys ozone. Both therefore contribute to global warming.

Ozone in the troposphere

At low levels, ozone is toxic to plants, humans and other organisms and also acts like a greenhouse gas. The most recent research shows that the warming effect of ozone is at its most significant at 12km above ground level, the height at which most aircraft operate and where levels of pollution from nitrogen oxides are at their peak. The total warming effect from ozone is difficult to calculate partly because it is so sensitive to the presence of other gases with which it reacts chemically.

Many scientists now believe that a doubling of carbon dioxide would create a rise in mean annual global temperatures of between 1.5°C and 4.5°C, with an average of 2.5°C. This was supported by the signatories to the World Convention on Climate in 1992. They believed that this rise would offset any cooling trend caused by such events as the Pinatubo eruption in the Philippines in 1991. To support their theory of warming, scientists point to increased storminess in the mid-latitudes and the Tropics, drought in continental interiors and increasing unpredictability in rainfall in arid areas. Globally, 1995 was the warmest year on record and eight of the ten warmest years on record have occurred since 1985 (Figure 4.7).

The evidence against an enhanced greenhouse effect

A vocal but well-informed minority of scientific opinion has produced a series of arguments to support the case that global warming is unlikely; or, that if it does happen, it will not occur with the speed or with the effects that the majority of scientists think likely. The main spokespeople include US scientists, such as Richard Lindzen and Fred Singer, whose work is often supported by the oil companies. In most cases, sceptics comment on IPCC data, rather than generating their own research.

Their arguments against global warming centre around:
- the length of global climatic records and the effects of natural climatic variability
- the slow response of global temperatures so far to a century of greenhouse gas increases and recent carbon dioxide emissions
- the cooling effect of aerosols from volcanic eruptions and human activity
- the role of increasing water vapour levels and cloud formation in reducing solar radiation, and which off-set any warming
- variability in incoming solar radiation
- the role of the oceans in controlling the rate of global warming.
  These are discussed in more detail below.

1 Explain the differences between a natural and enhanced greenhouse effect.

2 Read and summarise the evidence used which supports the arguments for an enhanced greenhouse effect. You can extend your research to include the 1997 Kyoto Summit and data from web pages at the end of this chapter.

The world has experienced that much warming fairly recently. And we loved it. Between 900 AD and 1300 AD, the earth warmed by some 4 to 7 degrees fahrenheit – close to current predictions for the 21st century. Historians call it the Little Climate Optimum…

During this great warming, Europe built the looming castles and soaring cathedrals that even today astonish with their size, beauty, and engineering excellence. These colossal buildings required the investment of millions of man hours, which could be spared from farming because of the higher crop yields.

Europe's population expanded from approximately 40m to 60m, an increase due almost entirely to lower death rates. Trade flourished, in part because there were fewer storms at sea and fewer muddy roads on land. (There was more rainfall, but it evaporated more quickly.)

Figure 4.9 From the *Guardian*, 15 May 1999, by Dennis Avery.

Global climatic records

Records of global temperature only go back to the mid-nineteenth century. Many scientists believe that a rise of 0.5°C over the length of observations may well be within any natural variation of the Earth's climate. In addition, changes in observation methods, improvement in weather recording technology, gaps in the database for several locations and local urban warming effects produce uncertainty in the records by about the same amount – by 0.45°C. Natural changes in climate, such as the El Niño event (see Chapter 3, pages 44–5) and the Little Ice Age in the seventeenth century, are common over several decades and may give a mistaken impression of longer-term warming or cooling. It is possible that they may merely represent temporary patterns of climate change that re-occur at regular intervals. Other authors see the trend to global warming as no more than a worldwide urban 'heat-island' effect, where measurements taken in urban areas reflect the effects of ozone, carbon dioxide and nitrogen oxides in polluted cities.

Responses to carbon dioxide and recent trends in emissions

Some scientists believe that the case for the warming effect of carbon dioxide is exaggerated, and that global temperatures so far do not support IPCC predictions. Richard Lindzen (1993) of the Department of Earth Sciences at the Massachusetts Institute of Technology argues that, if computer models which predict a 4°C warming for a doubling of carbon dioxide are correct, then we might have expected to see a 2°C increase already, rather than the actual 0.5°C figure on the current record. He insists that feedbacks in the atmosphere–ocean system reduce any warming effects from increasing emissions of greenhouse gases. He believes that the small warming effect is nothing more than the natural variability of the global climate. In relation to the Tropics, he states: 'There is ample evidence that the average equatorial sea surface has remained within 1°C of its present temperature for billions of years, yet current models predict average warming of 2–4°C even at the Equator. It should be noted that for much of the Earth's history, the atmosphere had much more carbon dioxide than is currently anticipated for centuries to come.'

Lindzen, like other greenhouse sceptics, feels that global warming supporters ignore the fact that most of the recent warming of the Earth occurred before 1940, which was before the largest emission of greenhouse gases from human activity took place. They are supported by the reduction in the rate of increase in atmospheric carbon dioxide (Figures 4.10 and 4.11), a trend partly related to the reduction in rates of consumption of fossil fuels. It is possible that the atmosphere's ability to absorb more carbon dioxide is slowing down as it reaches saturation point. They believe that plant biomass will increase with more carbon dioxide, and that at higher levels of concentration plants need less moisture to survive. Therefore, increased water vapour levels will produce more heat-reflecting cloud which in turn will produce a net cooling.

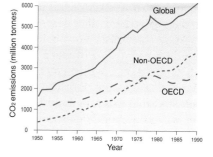

Figure 4.10 Trends in carbon dioxide emissions between 1950 and 1990. OECD (Organisation for Economic Cooperation and Development) countries are in the main those in the economically developed world.

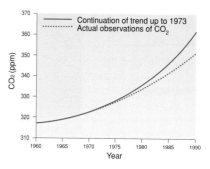

Figure 4.11 Increases in carbon dioxide concentrations at Mauna Loa Observatory, Hawaii.

Note that after 1973 the trend is away from exponential growth which gets faster and faster, to a more linear pattern where increases occur by the same amount in each time period.

The cooling effects of aerosols

The role of aerosols given out by large volcanic eruptions was highlighted by the example of Mount Pinatubo in the Philippines in June 1991. It injected some 20 million tonnes of sulphur dioxide to heights of up to 25km, causing the largest global climatic disturbance of the twentieth century (Figure 4.12). In the stratosphere the sulphur dioxide was dispersed by strong winds and was transformed in sunlight to form sulphuric acid droplets. This helped to scatter incoming solar radiation back to space, while also absorbing re-radiated infra-red energy from the Earth, thus releasing it into the stratosphere and causing a warming of the upper atmosphere and cooling of the lower atmosphere. The overall cooling of global temperatures by 0.4 °C in 1992 is mainly attributed to Pinatubo, although its effect was balanced a little by the El Niño event (see Chapter 3, pages 44–5). Some continental interiors (North America, Asia) experienced a 'year without a summer' in 1992, similar to that of 1816, a year after the historic eruption of Tambora in Indonesia. Both events signal the fact that global climate is highly sensitive to aerosols, but their effect is short lived (two to three years) and may not delay any longer-term warming trends.

Figure 4.12 The eruption of Mount Pinatubo, 1991.
Volcanic eruptions cause short but very large emissions of sulphate aerosols which have a temporary cooling effect on global temperatures. They also discharge volumes of chlorine and fluorine compounds into the stratosphere, which combine with CFCs to deplete the ozone layer further.

The role of sulphate aerosols produced by human activity presents a more continuous impact on global temperatures than volcanic eruptions. Levels of sulphate from human activities tripled over the twentieth century, with greatest concentrations in the northern hemisphere. Sulphate aerosols can prolong the life of clouds by acting as nuclei for condensation, and the increased albedo produces a cooling effect.

Increasing water vapour and cooling effects of clouds

Greenhouse sceptics differ especially from the supporters of a 'warming Earth' over the role of water vapour, the most common greenhouse gas. Too little emphasis, the sceptics feel, is given to the argument that a warmer atmosphere can hold more water vapour than a cooler one, and thus the potential for more condensation and clouds is increased, particularly when combined with the effect of aerosols. Some sources say that increased cloud cover leads to lower daytime temperatures as solar radiation is reflected back to space, while at night higher temperatures are likely as cloud traps heat which would otherwise escape to space. There is some truth in this argument, but the overall impact is difficult to assess. The greatest global warming seems to occur in most northerly latitudes in winter when snowfall is highest, which ought to result in an increasing reflectivity, and therefore cooling!

But the most sobering evidence concerning the influence of the impact of water vapour comes from the planet Venus, where, early in its history, all water vapour rose into the upper atmosphere, releasing the hydrogen content which was lost forever to space. Since then, Venus, without its protective water vapour and cloud layer, has experienced a runaway greenhouse effect and surface temperatures of 470 °C now exist there (Pickering and Owen 1994)!

Variations in solar radiation

Some scientists have argued that cycles of solar activity may account for variations in global temperature. Records of sun-spot activity since 1700 show cycles of roughly 11 and 100 years; while carbon dating of wood fragments has identified a 9000 year cycle. The Little Ice Age of the seventeenth century corresponded to a so-called 'quiet sun' or 'sun-spot minima' of a 100-year cycle, as did the low winter temperatures of the nineteenth century. Twentieth-century warming seems to coincide with a 'sunspot maxima', and some believe that the twenty-first century may return to a 'sun-spot' minima and another Little Ice Age, unless global warming intervenes.

The role of the oceans in controlling the pace of global warming

Oceans transport as much heat around the globe as the atmosphere. They can store as much heat in their top few metres as the entire atmosphere and, when the whole depth of ocean is taken into account, they have a heat capacity which is 1000 times greater. The deepest oceans respond very slowly to atmospheric temperature change compared to land, and may absorb much of the warming currently thought to be taking place. Measurements in the North Atlantic over a 20-year period show some warming at depths of between 500m and 2500m but cooling near the surface (Figure 4.13). More recent research indicated that if melting the ice reduces salinity in the North Atlantic, then the ocean 'conveyor belt' will be slowed down. If water off the coast of Greenland becomes less salty, it sinks less quickly, which in turn slows down the North Atlantic Drift. This would, it is claimed, lead to cooler seas off the coasts of Western Europe.

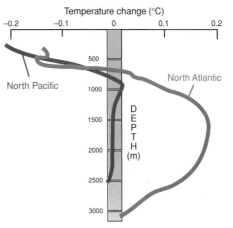

Figure 4.13 Temperature changes at different depths in the North Pacific and North Atlantic over a 20-year period.

1 Read through the evidence against the enhanced greenhouse effect and try to evaluate the strengths and weaknesses of the case. On which side does the evidence seem stronger?

2 Discuss the two cases together in class. Convene a global warming court. You will need lawyers for the prosecution and defence, a judge, witnesses for each side, and the rest of the class as the jury. The charge is that 'global warming is changing the world's climate'. The jury should be asked to reach a majority verdict on the basis of the evidence heard after a summing up by the judge of the key arguments presented. Afterwards, in a debrief, you may like to discuss out of role how a decision was reached. Was additional evidence needed by the jury, by the defence or by the prosecution?

Impact of global warming on a Small Island Developing State – Kiribati, South Pacific

The Small Island Developing States (SIDS) include a range of small countries with relatively low populations (Figure 4.14) but huge lengths of coastline which are already showing signs of damage from global warming. Many island states such as Kiribati, the Maldives and the Marshall Islands are very low-lying and have recently experienced serious flooding and erosion. In the Maldives 65 per cent of the total land area is less than a metre above present sea-level.

Few SIDS could afford to protect themselves; for example, a temporary sea wall for one small island in the Marshall Islands would cost $100 million – more than twice the value of their entire GDP. The SIDS were very vocal at the Kyoto summit, calling for immediate reductions of 20 per cent in greenhouse gases by MEDCs, but their small size and geographical isolation left them with few supporters among the richest nations who were the main decision-makers. The information which follows focuses on the island of Kiribati, pronounced Kiribas, which was the first place on Earth to see in the third millennium.

	Population	Coastline (km)		Population	Coastline (km)
Africa			**Europe**		
Cape Verde	417 000	965	Cyprus	776 000	648
Comoros	672 000	340	Malta	375 000	140
Mauritius	1 154 000	177			
São Tome and Principe	141 000	209	**Latin America and the Caribbean**		
Seychelles	74 000	491	Antigua and Barbuda	67 500	153
			Aruba	79 800	–
Asia and the Pacific			Bahamas	293 000	3 542
Bahrain	594 000	–	Barbados	263 000	97
Cook Islands	19 400	120	Cuba	11 115 000	5 746
Fiji	822 000	1 129	Dominica	83 000	148
Kiribati	81 000	1 143	Dominican Republic	8 232 000	–
Maldives	282 000	644	Grenada	94 500	121
Marshall Islands	59 000	370	Haiti	7 534 000	
Micronesia, Fed. States of	123 000	6 112	Jamaica	2 539 000	1 022
Nauru	11 000	30	Netherlands Antilles and Aruba	204 000	364
Niue	2 300	64	St Kitts and Nevis	41 000	135
Palau	16 700	1 519	St Lucia	156 000	158
Papua New Guinea	4 602 000	5 152	St Vincent and the Grenadines	118 000	84
Samoa	170 000	403	Trinidad and Tobago	1 318 000	–
Singapore	3 491 000	193	US Virgin Islands	97 300	188
Solomon Islands	417 000	5 313			
Tokelau	1 690	–	**Totals**	**46 833 790**	**39 891**
Tonga	105 600	419			
Tuvalu	10 000	24			
Vanuatu	182 000	2 528			

Figure 4.14 The Small Island Developing States.

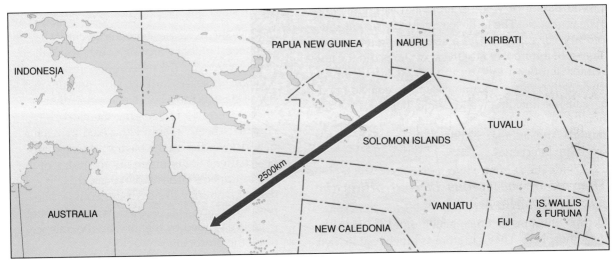

Figure 4.15 Location of Kiribati in the South Pacific.

Turning back the tide

What evidence have you seen of global warming?

We know that the climate is changing. On some islands, we're getting many more cyclones. On others there are more droughts. We are asking, 'why? Is it global warming?' Apart from causing coastal erosion, higher tides are pushing salt water into the fields and into underground freshwater reservoirs. In some places, it just bubbles up from the ground. This is making soils too salty for root crops and is polluting drinking water. We often have to bathe in salt water. You'll know all about coral bleaching in waters which are getting warmer. But for us, this is not just an issue of biodiversity or tourism. The reefs are where we get many of our fish. If the reefs die, so will our food supply. It started in the 1970s. I was working then in the ministry for rural affairs and spent a lot of time in Kiribati's outer islands. Coastal erosion was becoming a problem even then. Villagers living near the sea had to move away as the sea gobbled up their land.

Were you personally affected in any way?

Yes. Eight or nine house plots in the village that my family belongs to have been eroded away. I remember there was a coconut tree where I lived. The beach all around it was eroded, and eventually it disappeared. But erosion is not the only problem. The droughts are much worse than they used to be. We can go more than six months without rain. Our elders say we have never had droughts that last so long. The droughts may be because of El Niño. But if the El Niños are stronger, that must be part of climate change.

This doesn't seem particularly alarming. After all, the disappearance of a few trees and a bit of beach wouldn't matter much in most places...

Kiribati is spread over 3.6 million square kilometres. That's bigger than Western Europe. But more than 99.9 per cent of it is ocean. Our actual land area is 700 square kilometres on 33 islands. We are small, narrow and very vulnerable. The atolls are just rings of narrow islands surrounding a lagoon, with the open ocean on the outside. Some of the islands are only a few metres wide in places.

According to the South Pacific Geoscience Commission, sea levels are now rising by 2.5 millimetres a year. We are losing small islands and strips of land between the larger islands all the time. In Kiribati, the bridges linking Tarawa and Betio were destroyed by tidal surges. And the islet of Tebua Tarawa, which was once a landmark for fishermen, has gone. On some islands, old survey pegs put into the land above the beach have disappeared into the water.

Meteorologists say that a 1.5-metre rise in sea levels is inevitable, even if global warming comes to a halt by 2050. Could your islands survive that?

I don't think our atolls would survive that. Even a rise of 30 centimetres would be very serious. Many of our atolls are no more than 2 metres above sea level at the highest point, and cyclones already raise the water higher than that sometimes. We don't have many options. People are already moving inland. We want to establish mangroves as a first line of protection against cyclones.

What should Western countries do to help?

We think that the industrialised countries should pay part of the costs of sea walls or other options, such as planting mangroves. But so far, developed countries have not committed themselves to any actual projects. Worse, the international climate negotiations that have taken place would allow them to escape curbs on future emissions in return for helping environmentally vulnerable islands. This is unfortunate.

What do you say to those in the West who complain that measures to combat global warming interfere with their quality of life by raising utility bills and the cost of owning a car?

We are suffering from the actions of industrial nations, who are employing delaying tactics rather than trying to help us. We emit very few greenhouse gases ourselves - less than a sixth of the global average per head of population. But there are not very many of us in the South Pacific compared to the population of China or the United States. Perhaps this is why we are being forgotten. But for us, this is not an issue of numbers, it is a question of survival. In the West, you spend millions of dollars a year protecting endangered species. Soon, we will be endangered too.

Figure 4.16 Extract from an interview with Nakibae Teuatabo, Climate Change Coordinator, Kiribati.

Kiribati and global warming

1 In pairs, read the interview with Nakibae Teuatabo. Summarise the evidence he quotes to show that global warming is happening.

2 Divide the evidence into social, economic and environmental impact and then also into present and future impact. What conclusions do you reach about the likely impacts on other SIDS?

3 In groups, write a submission as the elders of Kiribati to support a further reduction of greenhouse gases at the next global climate change summit. Read these to the rest of the class. What is the key evidence? What difficulties might you face in presenting your case to MEDCs?

Figure 4.17 Kiribati, a shrinking paradise? The vulnerability of small islands to flooding and erosion can easily be seen from the air. Every piece of vital infrastructure, such as the airstrip, the main harbour and housing, is barely a metre above sea-level. Without the protection of the fringing reefs around the islands their future is even bleaker; some of the islands in the background have already lost their bridge links in recent storms.

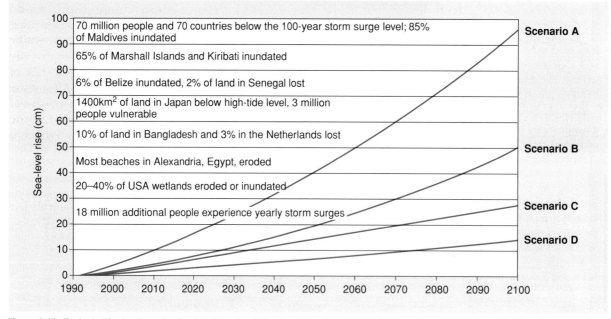

Figure 4.18 Typical effects of varying levels of sea-level rise based on IPCC scenarios. The four scenarios correspond to those presented on pages 51–2.

Action from the international community on global warming

'We are all adrift in the same boat. And there's no way that only half the boat is going to sink'. (Argentine climate negotiator, Raul Estrada Oyuela, Kyoto 1997)

'We need to explain why a transfer of wealth to the developing world – in the form of alternative energy technologies – is in our country's own basic self-interest' (William Ruckleshaus, Head of the US Environmental Protection Agency)

'In the developed world only two people ride in a car and you want us to give up riding the bus' (Zhong Shukong, Chinese negotiator at Kyoto, in response to Canada's insistence than LEDCs cut down on emissions by using bikes)

These quotations summarise the intense political battle waged at global level over decisions to cut greenhouse gases. In a way, actual levels of reduction seem less significant for the LEDCs than who will take a lead, and whether financial help will be available for developing alternative technologies which use little or no fossil fuel. The timeline in Figure 4.19 shows the key events since 1987 in the field of climate change international diplomacy. Key decisions have been made in 1987, 1992 and 1997, but the argument from LEDCs is that targets for greenhouse gas reductions are either too low, are delayed in implementation by governments or in some cases are never implemented at all. As you have seen in Kiribati, feelings run high in small countries without the resources to combat global warming and where the scale of emissions is a fraction of those in MEDCs.

At the Kyoto Summit in December 1997 the following agreement was reached:

- An overall reduction in greenhouse gas levels to 5 per cent below 1990 levels was agreed.
- Some countries agreed to different targets depending on their circumstances. Figure 4.20 shows that Australia was able to agree an increase in its emissions to protect its coal industry, as was Iceland, whose use of geothermal power means that its emissions of any greenhouse gases are very low.
- Targets are to be reached over a five-year period to allow governments to budget for them and alter tax and spend policies and strategies accordingly. The British Climate Levy which

sparked the fuel protests of Autumn 2000 is part of its commitment to Kyoto.

- The agreement included the concept of tradable emissions. Under this, if an MEDC exceeded its quota of oil and coal emissions, it could purchase unused quota amounts from lower-emitting countries thus rewarding the less polluting country and supplying it with funds to spend on alternative energy technology. However, huge problems arose when the actual quotas which countries were to be given had to be decided; LEDCs asked for big quotas on the basis of much lower current emissions and MEDCs found that industrial concerns, especially the fossil fuel sector, would not accept binding quotas on emissions. The future of this part of Kyoto looks decidedly fragile and has been the subject of further debate in Buenos Aires in 1998 and at The Hague in November 2000. Negotiations broke down just before the end of the conference in The Hague. The crucial issue appears to have been that the USA and Canada wished to have modest emission reduction targets and include planting trees as part of their deal. Recent scientific evidence from the IPCC shows that trees only absorb carbon dioxide effectively for a part of their lives. Europe and many LEDCs took exception to the standpoint of the USA and Canada. In March 2001 President Bush withdrew the US commitment to cuts agreed by President Clinton at Kyoto.

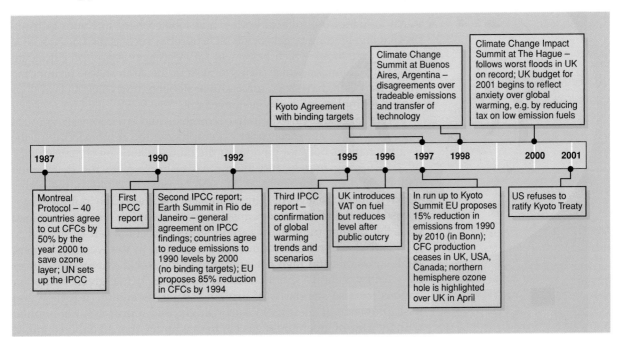

Figure 4.19 Timeline of climate change and international political action, 1987–2000.

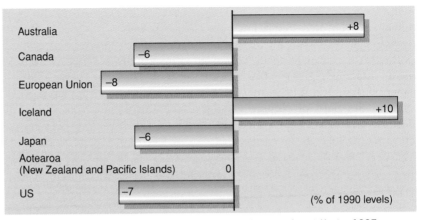

Figure 4.20 Greenhouse gas emission targets for certain countries at Kyoto, 1997.

In essence, the governments have adopted a 'safety first' approach in which very modest reductions in greenhouse gases are combined with some technological changes in energy use away from fossil fuels and energy efficiency, considerable investment in research and changes in taxation and energy policy. Britain is a good example: in the November 2000 pre-budget statement Gordon Brown, the Chancellor of the Exchequer, introduced price cuts in new low sulphur fuels and tax credits for low emission technology on a range of vehicles. This followed the concept of a Climate Change Levy on business to encourage them to adopt more fuel-saving technology and energy efficiency. Figure 4.21 outlines this type of approach from national governments, and emphasises other benefits to human health and welfare of using cleaner technologies.

Greenhouse sceptics adopt a 'wait and see' approach as they believe that the case for an enhanced greenhouse effect is not proven and so changes to energy policy especially are seen as dangerous to continuing economic growth. They believe that the environmentalists have far too much influence on political leaders and lobbied hard in Kyoto to try to prevent any binding targets being set. Countries such as the US, Australia, Canada and those which belong to OPEC (Organisation of Petroleum Exporting Countries which includes most of the Arab states surrounding the Persian Gulf) have been successful in slowing down the practical steps needed to implement the Kyoto agreement.

A very large and varied group of countries and environmental groups support a set of approaches which emphasise the responsibility of the wealthy nations both for paying for the damage done by climate change by transferring money and alternative technology to the developing nations, and for adopting a sustainable approach to life on the planet which reduces the level of human impact. The idea of the 'polluter pays' is based on the much lower emissions of developing nations combined with the greater number of carbon stores present when compared to high emissions and environmental destruction in the wealthy nations. High emissions and high consumption of the world's natural resources by wealthy nations should lead to resources being given to poorer nations to raise standards of drinking water, sanitation, nutrition and basic provision of energy. Not surprisingly, this approach is not popular with the largest greenhouse gas emitters who say that all nations pollute so all should accept emission targets. In the meantime, many developing nations are forging ahead in their use of renewable energy: a southern Indian wind farm with 2000 turbines is the second largest in the world; in Kenya more rural households get their electricity from solar energy than from the national grid; a scheme for supplying mobile solar panels in Mongolia has revolutionised the standard of living for nomadic tribes across the Gobi Desert and high mountain plateaux.

Climate change is not some trendy intellectual scenario for the distant future. It is with us now. It is remarkable that, during the recent fuel crisis, hardly anyone mentioned the environment.

Of course nobody would suggest that Opec's arbitrary ratcheting up of the price of oil is the right way to make an environmental policy for transport. But there is an environmental case to be made. Vehicles are, worldwide, the single fastest rising cause of CO_2 emissions, the main driver of climate change.

The real lesson from the fuel crisis is that we should greatly speed up our shift from fossil fuels to renewable sources of energy. We should cut out our over-dependence on oil by accelerating our research and development of alternative fuels.

That is why we have the tax system to roll out cleaner fuels and are promoting fuel efficient cars. Through the EU, we have persuaded manufacturers to improve fuel efficiency by 25%. Vehicle Excise Duty is now linked to vehicle emissions for the first time. Currently there are around 20,000 cars that can run on gas and over 500 liquid propane gas refuelling sites. Through our Powershift programme we have just made available an additional £9m for converting vehicles to cleaner fuels.

Toyota and Honda are selling hybrid cars that are twice as efficient as conventional models. The Honda Insight does 80 miles per gallon, which would save £400 a year on petrol bills for the average motorist. And hydrogen fuel cell powered cars will offer even more – the prospect of pollution-free motoring.

Biofuels also offer interesting possibilities. Bioethanol can be produced from cellulose biomass, such as agricultural and forestry wastes, and can be blended with petrol and diesel and used in conventional engines. Production costs are expected to fall over time to petrol and diesel levels. The production technology is novel, and the first large-scale plants are only just being constructed in the US. But if these plants are successful, similar plants in the UK could be constructed by 2004.

The potential is there. Renewable energy flows to Earth are roughly three times greater than total global energy consumption.

Figure 4.21 Extract from an article by Michael Meacher, UK Environment Minister. From the *Guardian*, 31 October 2000.

DETERMINING THE 'WISE ACRE'

To arrive at what they dubbed a 'wise acre' Erica and Jim used a mix of science, ethics and intuition.

- How much Earth is there? 125.8 billion acres
- How much bio-productive land and sea? 30.9 billion acres
- Current human population: 6 billion
- How much bio-capacity is there per person leaving nothing for the other species? 5.2 acres
- How much do humans on average use globally? 7 acres
- How much bio-capacity is there per person if we leave 80 per cent wild for the 25 million other species on Earth? 1 acre

With this goal of an acre each they began keeping track of every item they consumed using two powerful tools: ecological footprinting as developed by Bill Rees and Mathis Wackernagel; and the process contained in the book Your Money or Your Life by Joe Dominguez and Vicki Robin, which helps them consider how much of their life is given over to paid work to earn money. At the end of each month they now know how many acres of Earth's surface were appropriated to provide for their monthly consumption. Then they decide if their spending and footprint are in line with their values. To date their footprint is between three and four acres, about that of an average person in China.

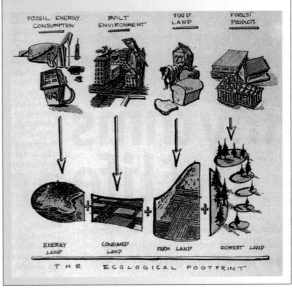

Figure 4.22 Determining the 'Wise Acre'.
A couple called Erica Sherwood and Jim Merkel have set themselves a goal of living off one acre of land to supply all their needs. They share a small, highly insulated strawbale cabin they built for $1600. They use wood and rarely burn fossil fuels, eat a vegan diet, and their entire possessions would only fill one medium-sized van. However, they still live a life in which they consume four times as many resources as the poorest citizen on Earth.

Finding a way out of the greenhouse

1 Refer to Figure 4.19. What are your conclusions about the agreements reached at Kyoto and at the various international conferences since 1997? Discuss your reactions as a class. To what extent do members of the class identify with the various approaches summarised above?

2 Read Figures 4.21 and 4.22. How would you summarise the differences in the two approaches to combating the problem of global warming and human impact on the environment? What do you believe are the strengths and weaknesses of each approach?

3 Work as a group to prepare a presentation to the rest of the class which gives an outline proposal for the UK's policy for responding to global warming for the next 50 years. Keep the presentation to a bullet point or similar format and allow some time to discuss the various approaches taken. You might then like to present them as a class display for others to see.

Drawing together the threads

The prospect of a greenhouse effect has been widely reported in the media. This may give the impression that the link between increasing greenhouse gases and global warming is a cast-iron certainty. In fact, there is much debate about this. Read the quotations in Figure 4.23 and consider some of the ideas contained in them. There is a lot of uncertainty about the cause of any warming, and little agreement among scientists about future climate changes. The process of climate change is complex, and the use of computer models to predict the future is still at an early stage. To complicate matters, every scientist, environmentalist and politician looks at the evidence from a particular viewpoint, so their predictions about the future are affected by their own beliefs and attitudes.

The following activity will remind you to analyse where some of the main players in the debate about global warming stand, and help you to understand why they believe what they do. Then think about people such as the islanders of Kiribati, and their global position. Consider their likely scenarios for the twenty-first century, and the debate that takes place elsewhere.

Shades of green

1 Form groups of two or three. Read carefully the quotations from various speakers and writers on global warming (Figure 4.23). Discuss what each person is saying and what you believe their bias or standpoint is.

2 Study the values spectrum diagram (Figure 4.24) and place the different views on it.

3 Do particular people seem to form groups or clusters on the spectrum? If so, you have probably identified those who may hold similar beliefs or values.

4 Discuss with the rest of the class how helpful you found the spectrum in clarifying and classifying the range of opinions. Do you think that this will change the way you look at the evidence on the causes of the greenhouse effect?

5 How far are political parties in the UK or the USA divided on this issue? Is the spectrum useful in helping you to understand why politicians differ in their opinions?

1

"To capture the public's imagination . . . we have to offer up some scary scenarios, make simplified, dramatic statements, and little mention of any doubts one might have . . . Each of us has to decide the right balance between being effective and being honest. I hope that means being both."

(Dr Stephen Schneider, adviser to US Vice-President Albert Gore Jr, 1989)

2

"Environmental pressure groups have for some years been promoting the apocalyptic vision; so successful have these agents of doom been that by the late 1980s the UN had been persuaded to commission a report on the scientific evidence for climate change – the Intergovernmental Panel on Climate Change (IPCC) report."

(Roger Bate and Julian Morris from the Institute of Economic Affairs Environment Unit, 1994)

3

"The data don't matter . . . Besides we [the UN] are not basing our recommendations [for immediate reductions in carbon dioxide emissions] upon the data; we're basing them upon the climate models."

(Dr Chris Folland, UK Meteorological Office, member of the IPCC)

4

"I promise you that global warming is nonsense, the latest example in a long line of doomsday predictions stretching all the way back to Noah and the Ark."

(Teresa Gorman, Conservative MP, 1992)

5

"If governments do not act to reduce greenhouse gas emissions (a scenario usually described as 'business as usual') global temperatures could rise to levels greater than any experienced over the last 10 000 years."

(Friends of the Earth, Climate Change, 1990)

6

"Uncertainty should make us more rather than less wary of imposing limits on greenhouse gases . . . All energy subsidies and taxes should be eliminated – the market and its supporting institutions will then be able to adapt more readily and rapidly to a changing environment."

(Roger Bate and Julian Morris, IEA Environment Unit, 1994)

7

"There is no longer any significant disagreement in the scientific community that the greenhouse effect is real."

(Senator Albert Gore Jr, later US Vice-President, 1986)

8

"Developed countries should fundamentally change their urban structure, transportation system, and lifestyle from the current industrialized culture aiming only at economic growth for its own sake based on mass production, mass consumption, and mass disposal, to one more environmentally sound."

(Japanese Global Environment Minister, 1992)

9

"Treading gently on the earth becomes the natural way to be. The global must [give way] to the local, since the local exists within nature, while the global exists only in the offices of the World Bank . . . . Any activity with potential impact on the local environment should have the consent of local people."

(Vandana Shiva, Indian environmental activist, 1992)

10

"Several scientists showed . . . that implementing selected policies today versus implementing these policies in 10 years' time makes little difference to future temperatures. They speak of a window of opportunity to get the science right and then make critical policy decisions."

(Dr R. C. Balling Jr, Associate Professor and Director, Office of Climatology, Arizona State University, USA)

▲ **Figure 4.23** A selection of views about global warming.

▼ **Figure 4.24** A values spectrum diagram for analysing environmental issues.

GREEN LABEL

ECOCENTRIC PERSPECTIVE (nature centred)

Holistic[1] world view. Minimal disturbance of natural processes. Integration of spiritual, social, and environmental dimensions. Sustainability[2] for the whole Earth. Devolved, self-reliant communities[3] within a framework of global citizenship. Self-imposed restraint on resource use.

ANTHROPOCENTRIC PERSPECTIVE (people centred)

People as environmental managers of sustainable global systems. Belief in the 'no regrets' principle. Population control given equal weight to resource use. Strong regulation by independent authorities required.

TECHNOCENTRIC PERSPECTIVE (technology centred)

Technology can keep pace with and provide solutions to environmental problems. Resource replacement solves resource depletion. Need to understand natural processes in order to control them. Strong emphasis on scientific analysis and prediction prior to policy-making. Importance of market, and economic growth.

[1]**Holistic** – belief that nature forms 'wholes' of living organisms that are greater than the sum of each part. Change in one part affects every other. Every organism is of equal worth.

[2]**Sustainability** – use of global resources at a rate that allows natural regeneration and reduces damage to the environment to minimal proportions.

[3]**Devolved community** - one that decides how it should progress and has power over decisions which affect it.

Summary

You have learned that:

- Human activity has modified the atmosphere by adding to the concentration of greenhouse gases. These help to maintain life on Earth through the operation of a natural greenhouse effect.

- The majority of the world's leading climatic scientists believe that human activity is causing so much additional emission of greenhouse gases that there is now an enhanced greenhouse effect, which in turn is producing global warming.

- Evidence produced by the IPCC indicates that rising concentrations of CFCs and gases such as carbon dioxide are likely to cause rapidly changing climate across the globe. This is likely in turn to cause rising sea-levels, extensive flooding of tracts of low-lying land, greater extremes of weather, and dramatic impacts on people and the environment.

- Greenhouse sceptics claim that supporters of global warming rely too much on unreliable computer models and underestimate the natural causes of climate change. They believe as well that supporters of global warming ignore the climate record itself, which indicates dramatic change in the past before substantial world population increase and massive industrialisation.

- The implications of global warming are illustrated by the Small Island Developing State of Kiribati in the Pacific where rising sea-levels are already posing significant problems of erosion, flooding and contamination of vital drinking water supplies.

- Climate change agreements at the international level such as at Kyoto in 1997 reflect global concern about the possible implications of global warming for people and the environment. However, progress has been slow and reflects the tensions between greenhouse sceptics and the IPCC, and between the developed and developing worlds' views of who is responsible for global warming.

- How people respond to global warming will determine our ability to manage weather and climate in the future, and could have far reaching effects on people's lifestyles and levels of resource consumption. A variety of options is available from 'wait and see' to more radical approaches which emphasise sustainability and a need to keep individual impact on the Earth to a minimum.

References and further reading

R Gelbspan, *The Heat is on (The climate crisis, the cover up, the prescription)*, Perseus (1998) – a hard hitting account which supports radical action on global warming, but also discusses the claims of the sceptics

R Lindzen, 'Absence of scientific basis' in *Global Warming Debate*, a scholarly publication of The National Geographic Society (spring 1993)

F Pearce, *Turning up the heat: our perilous future in the global green house*, Bodley Head (1989)

K T Pickering and L A Owen, *An Introduction to Global Environmental Issues*, Routledge (1994)

You will also find frequent update articles in magazines such as *New Scientist, Nature, Geography* and *Geographical Review*

Web sites

www.heatisonline.com is based on the book by Gelbspan opposite and is an excellent site to update on all aspects of current thinking about global warming

www.uea.ac.uk is the site for the University of East Anglia where much research on the impact of global warming is done

www.pactok.net.au/cat/cat.htm is a site with hundreds of links on all sorts of environmental issues in the region providing updates on the Pacific and global warming

At times of weather extremes articles on global warming abound; try the archives of a national newspaper such as

http://www.guardianunlimited.co.uk/weather

People, weather and climate: summary

Enquiry questions	Key ideas and concepts	Guidance and possible examples
Why do weather and climate present a global challenge?	• Definitions of weather and climate. The importance of weather and climate for a range of economic activities. Importance of day-to-day, short-term and medium-term forecasts. The need to predict extreme weather events. • Importance of climate as a direct and indirect influence on both the environment and people. Determinism versus Technological Fix. The challenges posed by management of weather and climate.	• Chapter 1 Impact of monsoon on life in India • Chapter 1 Impact of hurricanes on central America and the southern USA • Chapter 2 Impact of storms and depressions on the UK • Chapter 2 Impact of anticyclonic weather and prolonged heat waves on the economy
Why do mid-latitude areas such as the UK experience such changeable weather? What management problems does this changeable weather cause?	• The location of mid-latitudes within the global atmospheric system. The impact of the polar front and polar front jet stream. Contrasting polar and tropical air masses and their impact on the weather. • Formation of depressions and their impact on weather conditions. How depressions can be associated with extreme weather events such as floods and storms. • Development of anticyclones and their associated weather problems of fog, frost and drought. Blocking anticyclones. Summary of the causes of the changing weather – links to the upper atmosphere.	• Chapter 2 The mid-latitudes – weather systems and influences, air masses • Chapter 2 Causes of depression – polar fronts, jet streams and upper air movement; formation of depressions; links to storms and severe weather • Chapter 2 Anticyclonic weather and associated problems
Why do seasonal variations of climate occur? What management problems does the seasonality of climates cause?	• The concept of the migration of the heat equator. Its impact on global pressure systems. Seasonal variations in the position of the Inter-Tropical Convergence Zone (ITCZ). The impact of these processes on seasonal variations of temperature and rainfall. Impact on nature and range of ecosystems – concept of an ecocline. Problems of managing extreme seasonal variations of temperature and rainfall, e.g. short-term drought. • The causes and the problems of management of the El Niño/La Niña cycle both within the Pacific, and globally via tele-connections.	• Chapter 3 ITCZ and the global circulation model • Chapter 3 Impact on the Sahel, drought • Chapter 3 The phenomenon of El Niño and La Niña; causes and effects
What is climatic change? What are its implications for the environment and people?	• The scale of climatic change, spatially and over time. Definition of short-term climatic change to include global warming. Theories for global warming – does it exist? Evidence for and against. Natural/human causes. • Consequences of global warming. Modelling climatic change. Impact on sea levels, meteorology, ecosystems as well as human activities. • Solutions – are they possible? Globally, nationally and locally? Prevention or control?	• Chapter 4 Attitudes towards global warming • Chapter 4 Urban heat islands and pollution; links between pollution and global warming • Chapter 4 Climatic change and global warming; predicted impacts

Global biomes

Introducing global biomes

Figure 1 Forest fires in the western USA in the summer of 2000.

Fighting fires

During July and August 2000 devastating forest fires swept through a large area of western USA, centred on Montana and Idaho. A spate of summer fires set light to over 600 000 hectares and continued to burn for several weeks, fanned by the wind. A particularly dry summer meant the forests were tinder dry and susceptible to lightning. Most of the fires are thought to have started naturally, probably by lightning strikes.

Flourishing forests need fires

Tuesday, 8 August 2000,
by environment correspondent Alex Kirby

The fires raging through eleven western US states are laying waste to human settlements and ravaging wildlife. But the forests will ultimately benefit from the effects of the flames, which are a natural way of clearing old growth. Some experts even criticise the practice of trying to prevent fires at any cost, saying this means bigger problems when the flames take hold. They say policymakers need to accept that they are responsible for this year's devastation, by stopping smaller fires breaking out in the past.

Fires are often blamed for reducing the fertility of the soil and destroying animals and plants, apart from the damage they do to human interests. But, with one important exception, fire is a natural and vital part of forest life. Although people cause most fires worldwide, the most common natural cause is probably lightning. The exception is fires in tropical forests, with their high levels of humidity and moisture. They do not normally burn, and can be very badly damaged by fire. In most other parts of the world, though, the right fire – one that can be controlled – in the right place is a way of letting the forest regenerate itself.

Seeds from fire

Burning causes organic matter to decompose rapidly into mineral components which cause plants to grow fast, and it recycles essential nutrients, especially nitrogen. Some tree species cannot survive without periodic blazes. Lodgepole and jack pines are serotinous species – their cones open and their seeds germinate only after they have been exposed to fire. Forests adapt themselves to relatively small intermittent fires. But when policymakers try to suppress fires altogether, they encourage the accumulation of dead growth and allow new species to establish themselves. When a fire does start, it finds more fuel to sustain itself than would normally be there.

Dr Steve Howard, of WWF's Forests for Life campaign, told BBC News Online: 'Many forests have evolved to burn, and fire plays a key role in maintaining a healthy functioning ecosystem. This is true of the forests in the eleven US states that are burning now. But people have been interfering there for almost a century, preventing the fires which would have broken out naturally every two to seven years.

'The result is plain – fires ten times stronger than they would otherwise have been, with ten times more impact on nature, and ten times harder to control. What we need to do is to get nature back in order by a programme of controlled burning, setting fire to small areas at the start or the end of the growing season. These fires are the result of people. We've inherited a hundred years of fire suppression.'

Figure 2 From BBC Online.

The city burns: Sydney bush fires

Many fires in other parts of the world have attracted media attention in the past. In November 1997, bush fires in New South Wales, Australia, attracted attention, as did those in the summer of 1993–4. In each summer, fires began during long periods of dry warm weather, which have become associated with El Niño (see Chapter 3, pages 44–45). Read this section in Chapter 3 to understand how bush fires in Australia may coincide with El Niño years. However, that is insufficient explanation – dry summers occur in many places, yet do not necessarily create vast fires.

There are many who blame human activity for most fires. True, many fires do occur as a result of either deliberate or accidental intervention by people. But after the fires in Sydney, Australia, in January 1994, only one person was found guilty of causing bush fires by arson. More were the result of carelessness, and were caused by cigarette ends or ignition from fragments of broken glass. The general view of bush fires in Australia is that they occur both naturally, and as a result of increased human pressures on the environment.

The natural cause of fire

Like the fires in the USA (Figure 1), bush fires in Australia are also caused by lightning. Bush fires are a frequent occurrence, for example in the Blue Mountains in New South Wales. In fact, the eucalypt – or gum – forests of Australia are encouraged by fire. Several species of 'gum nut' trees (so called because of the nuts they produce) actually need fire conditions for the nuts to split and be able to germinate later. The outer casing of each seed is resistant to damage that fire may bring.

The increased pressure of human activity on the environment

More likely, fires have been caused by increased urban growth and suburbanisation. Several settlements outside Melbourne have expanded as more and more people seek a place in the rural areas with land attached. Figure 3 shows how houses, often sold with several hectares of land, are being built in the 'bush' rural areas; the example shown is about 70km from the CBD of Melbourne. The house has been built in an area of forest burnt out in the 'Ash Wednesday' fires of 1983, yet planners have given permission to build. The policy is that, every six months, the local Fire Authority will visit to consult with households in order to discuss how prevention measures around their houses can stop the threat of fire. Some measures have already been taken – notice how the area outside the house has been cleared so that there is no leaf litter to act as fuel, and trees have been cut back so that they do not overhang near the house. This strategy has proved so successful that the advice of the Fire Authority is almost always 'stay with the house' in the event of a bush fire.

Yet environmentalists reject this as a policy. They believe that the removal of leaf litter actually destroys the forest because it takes away a source of nutrients, and that the removal of seeds in the process actually prevents the forest from regenerating.

Figure 3 Housing in the Australian 'bush' – a house near Woodend, Victoria, built out of remnants of the forest burnt out in the 'Ash Wednesday' fires of 1983. The owners must keep clearing around the house in case of bush fire.

Fire and regeneration

Although traumatic at the time, it is often the media who express most concern at fire risk. Australian people have lived with the risk of fire for many generations, especially aboriginal groups, who used fire as a means of recycling nutrients and, on a short-term basis, for driving animals out of the undergrowth that they hunted for food. In fact, the vegetation in most forests – the flora – recovers quickly from fire, though animal life – the fauna – takes much longer.

1 Summarise the risks of allowing fire in forested areas as well as any benefits fire might bring. Do the benefits outweigh the risks?

2 Look at Figure 3. What advice should local fire authorities give in order to protect houses such as this from fire?

3 Which side do you believe has the stronger argument:
   a) local authorities in Australia who are happy for people to live in the 'bush' with support from local fire services in managing fire threats
   b) environmentalists who claim that these policies are destroying the forest?

3 Why do you think that the advice in the event of a bush fire is almost always 'stay with the house'?

4 Consider the events of summer 2000 and the Australian bush fires. Should decision makers in Montana and in Australia maintain their present policies of fire prevention? Think about:
   a) the costs and benefits of fire policies in terms of the forest ecosystem
   b) the impact on people living in forested areas of Montana or Victoria, Australia
   c) the possible monetary implications of either preventing or allowing fire.

Threats to global biomes

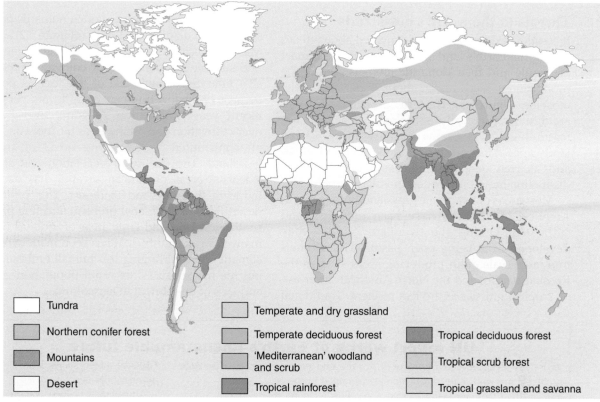

Figure 5.1 Major world biomes.

Tundra

Northern conifer forest

Mountains

Desert

Temperate and dry grassland

Temperate deciduous forest

'Mediterranean' woodland and scrub

Tropical rainforest

Tropical deciduous forest

Tropical scrub forest

Tropical grassland and savanna

This chapter introduces the concept of 'biomes' and some of the pressures that they face. Biomes are large-scale ecosystems identified by their dominant vegetation cover, for example tropical rainforests, temperate grasslands, desert or tundra (Figure 5.1). Usually described in atlases as areas of 'natural vegetation', they cover a wide area and are described in terms of their climate, soils, and plant and animal communities. Large parts of some biomes have been radically altered by human activities such as farming, settlement and industrial development.

The influence of human activities on global biomes

People use the world's biomes in many different ways. The large coniferous and tropical forest biomes are important for their timber resources, while the temperate grassland biomes sustain many of the world's major grain producing areas. Some biomes have been radically altered, for example the temperate deciduous woodland belt has been largely cleared in Europe, North America and Asia and the land used for agriculture and settlement. Even biomes that pose problems for human settlement, such as hot deserts and the tundra, have been exploited in the search for oil and other minerals. Some biomes stand up to human activities better than others. Temperate grassland and woodland biomes seem to be able to tolerate at least some exploitation, whereas tropical grasslands, tropical rainforests and tundra regions are fragile and easily damaged. Increasing pressure from human activities means that very few truly natural ecosystems exist today.

Global pressure is being placed upon biomes. The increasing global population requires space for food and resources, while the expanding global economy fuelled by consumer demand has caused increasingly rapid depletion of the world's forests and natural grasslands. Environments that have never been seriously explored because of their hostility or difficulties are now being opened up for exploitation.

71

Figure 5.2 Fulani herdsman in the African savanna – faced with the threat of over-grazing.

Threats to the world's grasslands

It is estimated that grasslands covered about 40 per cent of the Earth's land surface prior to the impact of people and their domestic animals. Today the proportion is much lower: about 27 per cent at the most (see Figure 5.1). The term 'grassland' is rather ambiguous. Typically grassland areas are not featureless grass plains but are more varied landscapes. Most are mixed woodland and grass, and as tree densities increase there is a fine distinction between wooded grassland and forest.

Most areas of temperate grassland both in North America and Eurasia have been ploughed and cultivated. During the twentieth century they developed from being open pastures for animals into large-scale grain producing areas such as the Russian steppes and the North American prairies.

Tropical grasslands are less resilient. Traditional users of these grasslands are often nomadic peoples such as the Fulani in West Africa (Figure 5.2) and the Masai in East Africa. They travel long distances to find suitable pasture and only cultivate small areas at a time. Sustainable use of this area is possible because of the low numbers of cattle and people. In recent years population pressure, over-grazing, over-cultivation and felling trees for fuelwood have all contributed to damaging areas of tropical grassland. The quality of vegetation and soils in extensive areas of African savanna has declined, reducing the grassland to desert. This process of desertification is a global problem affecting parts of south-west USA and large areas of India as well as many African countries. It has been made worse by climatic change bringing less rainfall to these areas, but the major causes are rapid population growth and lack of investment in agriculture.

UN report warns of Earth's unsustainable future

THE WORLD'S environmental problems are worsening much more quickly than they are being tackled, the head of the United Nations Environment Programme, Klaus Töpfer, warned yesterday.

In a gloomy assessment of the global situation drawn up for the end of the millennium, Dr Töpfer, a former German environment minister, gave a blunt warning that it may already be too late to stop global warming and that the Kyoto protocol, the treaty drawn up to combat climate change, may fail.

There was progress, he said, pointing to the successful agreement to stop the release of chlorofluorocarbons (CFCs), the industrial chemicals which have accumulated in the atmosphere and caused severe damage to the Earth's protective ozone layer.

In Europe there had been real cutbacks on pollutant gases such as sulphur dioxide, which causes acid rain, and on the amount of sewage dumped in rivers.

Furthermore many nations now accepted the importance of environmental problems and taught environmental awareness to their schoolchildren.

'But the gains by better management and technology are still being outpaced by the environmental impacts of population and economic growth', he said. 'We are on an unsustainable course. Time is rapidly running out for a rational, well-planned transition to a sustainable future.'

The two major causes of environmental degradation, he stressed, were the continued poverty of the majority of the planet's inhabitants and excessive consumption by the well-off minority.

'The global environment has never before been under such pressures', he said. 'It is little wonder that it is becoming the worse for wear.

Full-scale emergencies now exist on a number of issues.'

After climate change, water was the most serious. By 2025 as much as two-thirds of the world population would be subject to 'water stress', meaning difficulty of access to water supplies or to clean water.

Already, he said, 20 per cent of the world population lacked access to safe drinking water and half the world lacked access to a safe sanitation system. 'The global water cycle is unlikely to be able to cope with the demands that will be made of it in the coming decades.'

Dr Töpfer also highlighted a new global problem – nitrogen. Put on the land in fertilisers, it is prompting the explosive growth of toxic algae once it is washed down to the sea and making some freshwater supplies unfit for drinking. 'There is mounting evidence that humans are seriously unbalancing the global nitrogen cycle,' he said.

continued on page 73

Action to tackle the problems should focus on four key issues, Dr Töpfer concluded. Gaps in environmental knowledge had to be filled; the root causes of environmental problems – such as overconsumption – had to be tackled; environmental thinking needed to be integrated into mainstream thinking and decision-making; and all those affected by environmental problems should be mobilised together.

'The turn of the century will be a milestone for the Earth,' he said. 'It must be a turning point for the way we treat the environment.'

An algal bloom in the Baltic Sea

After Kyoto: The environment in balance

Getting better

- **Air pollution**
  Air pollution especially by sulphur dioxide from coal-burning power stations, which causes acid rain, is substantially down in Europe

- **Sewage**
  Sewage pollution in European rivers is substantially down thanks to EU directives.

- **Cleaner industry**
  Cleaner and more efficient methods of industrial production have been brought in by many of the rich countries.

- **Ozone layer**
  Release of CFCs, the chemicals that have damaged the Earth's ozone layer, has been cut to a very low level; the ozone layer is recovering.

Getting worse

- **Climate change**
  Getting closer as the amount of carbon dioxide from industry and motor vehicles in the atmosphere continues its inexorable rise.

- **Nitrogen**
  People are putting too much nitrogen as fertiliser on the land and subsequently into water, which is causing toxic algal blooms.

- **Water shortage**
  Severe shortages exist in many parts of the world and about 20% of the human population has no access to safe water. Worsening.

- **Forests**
  Four-fifths of the original forest cover of the Earth has now been cleared, fragmented or degraded, 40% of the remainder threatened.

- **Wildlife**
  Much of the planet's wildlife is threatened with extinction including one-quarter of the mammal species.

- **Coral reefs**
  More than half the world's reefs are threatened by human activities and global warming.

- **Chemicals**
  The widespread use of toxic and hazardous chemicals poses an increasing threat to human health.

- **Fisheries**
  Many marine fisheries have been grossly over-exploited and recovery – if any – will be slow.

- **Natural disasters**
  Increasing in frequency and severity, largely from environmental causes; about 3 million have perished from natural disasters in the last three decades.

Figure 5.3 From the *Independent*, 16 September 1999.

Read the newspaper article in Figure 5.3.

1 Look at the list of nine environmental problems that are getting worse. Work in a small group and identify the three problems that you think most seriously affect ecosystems. Explain briefly what each problem is and state why you think it particularly affects ecosystems. Present your ideas to the rest of the class.

2 In what ways has Europe made particular progress in tackling environmental problems? Find out to what extent the same can be said for other parts of the world, particularly the USA.

3 Suggest reasons why 'The global water cycle is unlikely to cope with the demands that will be made on it in the coming decades.'

4 List the four key issues which need action in order to tackle the global environmental problems. Discuss in a group:

a) which of these key issues is most important

b) which you feel will be most difficult to achieve.

All ecosystems function in two main ways: through energy flow (see theory box below) and nutrient cycling (see theory box in Chapter 6, page 95). However, there are considerable contrasts between these functions in different biomes. The rate of photosynthesis, which controls energy flow, varies greatly between biomes as does the storage of nutrients and the rate of nutrient cycling.

Theory

Energy flow

Energy is essential for all processes within an ecosystem. Virtually all energy is derived from the sun, although a small amount comes from geothermal energy. Solar radiation, or insolation, reaches the ground in varying amounts depending on latitude, altitude, season and time of day. Green plants use some of this light energy in photosynthesis, where inorganic substances of carbon, oxygen and water are converted into organic compounds, particularly sugars. Oxygen is released during this process.

$$6CO_2 + 6H_2O = \text{Energy from sunlight} = C_6H_{12}O_6 + 6O_2\uparrow$$

Globally, this process is vital to the survival of life and as a regulatory mechanism to control the continued increase in carbon dioxide that results from the burning of fossil fuels (see Chapter 4, page 52).

Energy fixed by plants during photosynthesis can be:

- used by the plant for life processes, such as respiration
- stored as plant material or animal tissue, known as biomass
- passed though the ecosystem along food chains or webs.

Plants use energy during respiration, and energy is then released back to the atmosphere. Energy is stored in plant tissue, but may be passed from plants to animals through a food chain. All animals obtain food either directly or indirectly from plants. Primary producers (green plants) are consumed by primary consumers (herbivores). These in turn are consumed by secondary consumers (carnivores) and tertiary consumers (larger carnivores). When plants and animals die, they are decomposed by

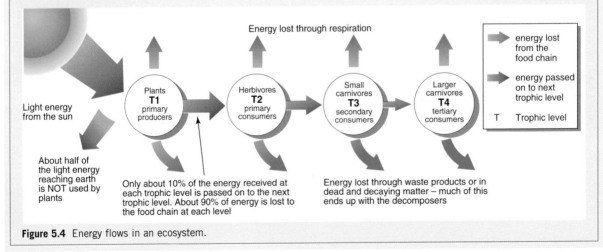

Figure 5.4 Energy flows in an ecosystem.

organisms such as bacteria and fungi, which use the dead tissue for energy. Each stage in the food chain is known as a trophic level. Producers are known as autotrophs and consumers as heterotrophs.

Energy is passed through the ecosystem in this way, but at each trophic level a number of things could occur. Energy could be:

- used by the animal for life processes such as moving, eating and respiring
- lost through animal waste
- stored as body tissue, such as muscle, and become part of the biomass.

In general, smaller numbers of living organisms exist at each successive trophic level, and thus there are larger numbers of primary consumers than secondary. The decrease in numbers in successive trophic levels is marked because there are fewer animal species. The ecological pyramid may also be constructed using biomass, or energy produced by each trophic level.

Whenever energy passes from one trophic level to the next, about 90 per cent is lost and only 10 per cent passed on. This huge loss is common to all ecosystems, and helps to explain why there are rarely more than five trophic levels in any ecosystem. It also explains why many vegetarians point to the inefficient use of world food resources in the production of meat.

Theory

Plant productivity (NPP and GPP)

Green plants use energy from the sun for photosynthesis which allows plants to convert light energy into food energy. The rate at which energy is converted into organic matter by plants is called primary productivity. Gross primary productivity (GPP) is the total amount of energy fixed by plants measured in kilograms per square metre per year. The GPP minus the energy lost through respiration is called the net primary productivity (NPP) of the ecosystem.

Primary productivity varies enormously between biomes because rates of photosynthesis differ. This is largely due to the amount of insolation. Solar radiation reaches the ground in varying amounts depending on latitude, altitude, season and time of day. Soil type and the availability of nutrients also affect the rate of photosynthesis. Different biomes

	NPP per unit area $kg/m^2/y$		World NPP billion tonnes per year
	Range	Mean	
Tropical rainforest	1000–3500	2200	37.4
Cool temperate deciduous forest	600–2500	1200	8.4
Tropical grassland (savanna)	200–2000	900	13.5
Temperate grassland	200–1500	600	5.4
Boreal forest	400–2000	800	9.6
Woodland	250–1200	700	6.0
Tundra and alpine	10–400	140	1.1
Desert and scrub	10–250	90	1.6
Cultivated land	100–3500	650	9.1

Figure 5.5 Mean NPP and the range of NPPs for selected world ecosystems.

have very different NPPs (Figure 5.5) because different amounts of light energy, moisture and nutrients are available for photosynthesis.

The lowest producers are the tundra and desert biomes. This can be explained by lack of moisture in the case of hot deserts. Factors such as cool summer temperatures, a short growing season and infertile, often waterlogged soils, as well as limited precipitation, explain why rates are low in tundra regions.

Forests generally have the highest primary productivity, generating the highest amount of organic matter each year. Trees are large and their many leaves can trap and use a great deal of sunlight. In tropical areas trees are able to grow throughout the year, whereas in temperate zones the cool and sometimes frosty winter period with shorter days means that the growing season is reduced. This explains the lower NPP in both deciduous and boreal forest biomes compared to the tropical rainforest biome.

Grasslands are generally less productive than forests with temperate grasslands growing only about half as fast as temperate deciduous forests. Tropical grasslands are less productive than most forests but do have a higher growth rate than the boreal (coniferous) forest biomes.

Cultivated land has a world average of 650kg/m^2/y. This is greater than the average for deserts and tundra but lower than that for most forests and some grasslands. This relatively low average can be explained as follows:

- the growing season in many areas is limited
- the biomass is small
- many crops are annuals so they are only in the ground for part of the year
- when crops are planted they may be small so there is a lot of open space between them.

All these factors reduce the ability of the crops to make full use of the sunlight whenever it is available.

1 On a world map devise ways to show the information in Figure 5.5. What spatial patterns emerge?

2 Which natural factors determine NPP?

3 Why is it necessary to consider both mean NPP and the range of NPP for different ecosystems?

4 What does the information on your map show about the potential for each biome for food production?

5 How might human activity alter NPP in a forest or grassland ecosystem?

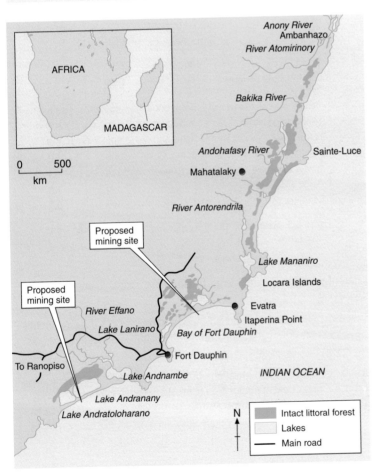

Figure 5.6 South-east Madagascar.

The RTZ mineral sands project in Madagascar

Madagascar is the fourth largest island in the world, nearly two and a half times the size of the UK. Despite its size, it has a population of only 13.9 million with over 80 per cent of people living in rural areas. It is classified as one of the fifteen poorest nations in the world. Yet due to its geographical isolation, its biodiversity is immensely rich in unique flora and fauna with new species being discovered every year. This means its potential for environmental tourism is great. It has four very distinct ecosystems (spiny forest, littoral forest, tropical rainforest and the Indian Ocean) and two established nature reserves.

Rio Tinto Zinc is the British arm of an Anglo-Australian owned mining conglomerate RTZ-CRA, which has large-scale mining operations worldwide. It has particular interests in industrial minerals. In 1986, exploration in south-eastern Madagascar was started, where three areas of heavy mineral sands containing, among other things, ilmenite, an ore rich in titanium dioxide, had been discovered. Titanium dioxide is used as a white pigment in paint, paper, plastics and many other products. Deposits were thought to be sufficient to sustain continuous mining for 40 years, with over 2 billion tonnes of the mineral. RTZ, in collaboration with the Malagasy government, is now developing plans to extract these minerals in what would be the single largest development project ever undertaken on the island.

The mineral sands lie in the Fort Dauphin region (Figure 5.6), beneath the country's last remaining east coast forests. The forests are of global significance because of their unique ecology and biodiversity; they represent a transition between rainforest and dry spiny forest environments. Of the 500 plant species so far identified in the forests, at least 29 are found nowhere else in the world. If mining were to proceed, even RTZ admit that between 66 and 76 per cent of unique forests would be destroyed, and it could lead to the extinction of several species of flora and fauna including the brown collared lemur. Run-off from the mine and changes in drainage would impact on neighbouring forest, freshwater lakes and rivers, and alter the traditional lifestyles of local people.

Figure 5.7 The area where RTZ wish to mine.

What are the alternatives?

Environmental organisations have reacted to the proposal by RTZ. Friends of the Earth is one of many organisations calling on RTZ-CRA to withdraw from the project. It has also asked the Malagasy government to consider alternative sustainable development options for the region. This task, however, is becoming increasingly urgent.

The RTZ project would provide jobs and economic benefit to the region and country as a whole for over 30 years. The project, however, will result in the destruction of the very environment

and coastline that has the potential to provide economic and social benefits to the region for the long-term future. Friends of the Earth believe that there is a need to identify sustainable economic development options that will maintain unique habitats and biodiversity, while placing emphasis on wealth creation for the local population.

Tourism is clearly a sustainable alternative option given the natural habitats of the island. Demand for ecotourism is increasing globally, and would be well suited to Madagascar. At present, tourism is underdeveloped. In 1997–8 only 35 000 international tourists visited the island compared with over 143 000 on the neighbouring island of Mauritius. Nevertheless, tourist investment is increasing and the Malagasy government has set a target to increase tourist arrivals. The south-east of the island, where the proposed mine would be sited, currently attracts between 10 000 and 15 000 visitors per year, and it is estimated that tourism in the region already employs around 1000 people – double the numbers which would be employed by the mine.

Further development of the tourist industry in the region is hindered by lack of infrastructure. This, together with poor access, also explains why the area has been able to retain its rich biodiversity. Any tourist development would therefore have to be planned carefully and controlled so that it had a minimum negative impact.

1 Draw an outline map of south-east Madagascar using Figure 5.6. Annotate it to show:
  a) the location of the proposed mining developments
  b) the impacts that this could have on local people
  c) the impacts that it would have on the environment.

2 Friends of the Earth suggest that the mineral sands project is an unsustainable form of development for this area. Suggest why this is 'unsustainable'.

3 What is 'ecotourism'? In what ways is this a sustainable form of development?

4 Do you think that development of ecotourism would protect the area, and the people who live there, for the future? Put the case for and against the development of ecotourism in south-east Madagascar.

Tourism in Zanzibar

While Madagascar is faced with a threat to its biodiversity, the economic reality means that biodiversity may come second to economic development. Meanwhile, in Zanzibar, off the coast of Tanzania of which it is a part, the threat to biodiversity lies in tourism. Opting for a different approach to the ecotourism that could benefit Madagascar, the island of Zanzibar is keen to benefit from the increase in tourism experienced in recent years by Kenya. However, as Figure 5.8 shows, proposals there could cause significant environmental damage.

Wish you were here?

A row has broken out over British involvement in a massive £2.5 billion tourism development in Zanzibar. Pressure group Tourism Concern fear the development will uproot 20 000 local residents and cause massive environmental damage.

But builders East African Development Company (EADC) have dismissed these claims, pointing out plans to provide utilities to nearby villages and jobs to the workforce. The row goes to the very heart of the argument over what is an appropriate form of development.

Tourism Concern say the plans for the Nungwi peninsula in northern Zanzibar will create East Africa's biggest holiday resort including 14–16 luxury hotels, residential and timeshare villas, a marina and artificial lake for sailing, and a world trade centre complete with hotel, offices, exhibition centre, conference hall and sports facilities, three championship golf courses, two indoor leisure centres and Olympic-size swimming pools.

A spokesperson said: 'The East African Development Company has leased 57 square kilometres at US $1 a year for 49 years… Plans give no indication that there are in fact 20 000 people living in the area.

'Villagers claim they do not know what will happen to them or where they will be resettled. Locals say they read in newspapers of such a project but the government had not informed them.'

Tourism Concern claim locals are terrified of talking critically about the project because of harassment and intimidation. Apart from evictions, locals also fear a development on this scale would deny the local population access to already scarce water supplies. No environmental or social impact assessments have yet been done.

However, a spokesperson for EADC dismissed these fears: 'No work will take place until environmental studies have taken place according to IMF guidelines.

'The fear that [this] development will lead to dislocation of local people is totally misplaced as there are no plans to relocate the existing villages,' he said.

He said EADC had offered to provide proper water, electricity, sewerage, and roads to nearby villages.

Figure 5.8 Tourism in Zanzibar. From *Development*, third quarter 1998.

1 Read the article in Figure 5.8. Outline in ten bullet points the key points in the article.

2 Objections to the proposed tourist development in Zanzibar focus both on environmental damage and on fears that 20 000 people will be relocated. Which of these do you consider to be the greatest threat? Justify your choice.

3 What benefits would a large-scale tourist development bring to the area? Does this, in your view, justify the development taking place?

4 Friends of the Earth suggest that tourist development could be a sustainable form of development for LEDCs such as Madagascar. Figure 5.8 appears to disagree with respect to Zanzibar. Suggest why this is.

The threat to the world's oceans

Biodiversity is not a concept confined to the Earth's land surfaces. The world's oceans are in a state of serious threat (see Chapters 8 and 9). Figure 5.9 shows how the threat is truly global – the cause is said to be global warming, discussed fully in Chapter 4.

The issue of genetically modified seeds

In recent years, genetically modified (GM) seeds have been widely discussed in the world's press. Consider the reactions of different organisations to the issue of GM seeds and products:

- Environmental organisations such as Greenpeace have been prepared to go to court in defence of their actions after destroying a field of GM crops, and have won their case.
- Supermarkets in the UK have withdrawn products that contain GM products or ingredients.
- During 2000, the UK government persisted in its determination to allow trials of GM seeds and to keep the location of the trials secret.

Experts report widespread global warming impacts on world oceans

Rising global temperatures are disrupting life in the oceans from the tropics to the poles and undermining the future survival of a wide variety of species, according to a new report released by the Worldwide Fund for Nature (WWF), the international conservation organisation.

The species affected range from plankton through to polar bears, walruses, seals, sea lions, penguins, various seabird species and coral reefs. The report concludes that global warming could be the knock-out punch for many species which are already under stress from over-fishing and habitat loss. The authors warn, 'the ability of our oceans to support life as it does now may be in the process of being permanently altered.'

If global warming reduces the productivity of the oceans, this will have serious consequences for human communities. Marine life is a vital source of food and medicines, and provides livelihoods for millions of people.

Adam Markham, Director of WWF's Climate Change Campaign, said, 'These findings should set alarm bells ringing in every capital. The global warming threat moves a step closer to home every day. The marine food web could unravel disastrously unless western industrialised countries cut domestic emissions of carbon dioxide.'

Figure 5.9 Adapted from a WWF report, 8 June 1999.

• Environmental groups claimed that GM pollen had been discovered 10 km away from a field in which GM oil-seed rape had been planted.

What is the issue about and why does it cause such strong reactions? The term 'genetically modified' means what it says: that the genetic structure of the plant cell has been altered in some way. Usually, alteration occurs to make the plant less susceptible to either drought or disease. In some cases, alteration prevents the crop from seeding, thereby forcing farmers to purchase seed annually instead of retaining some of a crop for sowing. Environmental groups argue that once genetic alteration is introduced into the environment, it can never be removed. Biodiversity is lost in favour of plants that are likely to outperform others because they have been 'designed' to grow. Natural ecosystems will forever be altered. Research carried out 'in the open' rather than in a laboratory can never leave an environment unaltered.

Figure 5.10 gives the viewpoint of one of the companies involved in the development of GM seeds. For companies such as this, their case rests upon one or more of the following arguments:

• that too much food is lost through consumption by pests, or destroyed by drought
• that faster growing times can be achieved in areas where plant growth is restricted, such as drought-prone areas, or those with a short growing season
• that by devising seed that shows resistance to pests, the need for pesticides is reduced.

Spread of GM seeds cannot be stopped, say firm

THE SEED company at the centre of the GM-contaminated crops scandal, Advanta, has raised serious doubts about attempts to stop genetically modified seeds from contaminating the environment.

Advanta was giving evidence to MPs yesterday after it was made public that 5400 hectares of its allegedly GM-free oil seed rape, which was planted across the UK, had been contaminated by genetically modified crop pollen. All the crops have been destroyed because of the risks of further cross-contamination.

Ministers waited four weeks after being alerted to assess the legal and scientific implications, before making the contamination public.

Earlier, Advanta executives told the committee the seed had become contaminated even though Advanta's Canadian sister company had used a 4km-wide buffer zone between it and GM crops, five times the 800-metre exclusion zone required under Canadian law.

The British Government's existing 50 to 200-metre buffer zones are now under review.

However, Michael Meacher, an Environment minister, said the Canadian Government had yet to prove pollen from 4km away was responsible for the contamination.

Dr David Buckeridge, Advanta's European affairs director, admitted his company had never tested the 'Hyola' hybrid seeds, sold in the UK, France, Germany, Sweden and Finland, for GM contamination because it thought the 4km buffer zone was sufficient.

Dr Buckeridge added, however, that he doubted the reliability of tests used to check that seeds are GM-free. It was impossible, he said, for non-GM crops to be entirely pure because of the scale of GM crop planting, which now stands at 40 million hectares worldwide.

Figure 5.10 From the *Independent*, 19 July 2000.

1 The article in Figure 5.10 suggests that 'It is impossible for non-GM crops to be entirely pure.'
   a) Why is this the case?
   b) What are the implications for natural ecosystems if the scale of GM crop planting increases still further worldwide?

2 Make large a copy of the table below. On it, compare the impacts of the four projects referred to, and suggest ideas about what should be done for each.

Project/Title of article	Brief statement of the issue	Causes of damage or threats to ecosystems	Short-term gains – what and for whom?	Long-term environmental effects	What should be done?
RTZ mineral sands project in Madagascar					
Wish you were here? Tourism in Zanzibar (Figure 5.8)					
Experts report widespread global warming impacts on oceans (Figure 5.9)					
Spread of GM seeds cannot be stopped (Figure 5.10)					

Summary

You have learned that:

- The word 'biomes' refers to large areas or zones of similar vegetation types, such as tropical rainforests. These result from broadly similar climatic conditions. Where variations occur, they result in only minor variations in vegetation. Therefore, biomes show a distinct distribution pattern.
- Biomes can be distinguished as ecosystems, which function on the basis of primary productivity, itself the result of physical conditions such as climate.
- Very few truly natural ecosystems remain as a result of increasing human influence.
- Biomes are vital environmentally, for example they regulate the amount of carbon dioxide and oxygen in the atmosphere. They also play a major role climatically and economically.
- Several threats to biomes are posed by human activities which affect marine and terrestrial ecosystems. The loss of biodiversity is a worldwide issue of concern.

References and further reading

Greg O'Hare, *Soils, vegetation and ecosystems*, Oliver and Boyd (1988)

RSPB, *Ecosystems and human activity*, Collins Educational (1994)

Web sites

Global Dimension web site provides an excellent selection of web site addresses for many environmental issues: www.globaldimension.org.uk
These include:
Friends of the Earth: www.foe.co.uk
Worldwide Fund for Nature: www.panda.org

6 Understanding the world's forests

The world's forests are disappearing. Consider the following statement made in 2000 by Friends of the Earth, who are concerned at the loss of forests across the world:

> Massive global demand for wood and paper is driving destruction of the world's natural forests. Dozens of plant and animal species become extinct each day, while the way of life of millions of forest people is threatened. Global wood and paper consumption in 1990 was 1.7 billion cubic metres. This is predicted to increase by almost 60 per cent by the year 2010! All over the world, forests are being cut down or converted to intensive plantations to meet the demand for newspapers, writing paper, window frames, doors and a host of other everyday items.

Today little over 25 per cent of the world's land surface is forested. Three hundred years ago almost 65 per cent of land was forested, and even as recently as 1950 it was 45 per cent. The reasons for the loss of forest are:
- the need for land for farming and settlement
- the huge increase in demand for timber.

The map in Figure 6.1 shows the extent of forest biomes. Temperate deciduous forests which were once extensive have all but vanished leaving only small woodland areas; tropical rainforests have disappeared from many areas, particularly in South-East Asia; and even the boreal forests of the northern latitudes are far less extensive than they once were.

Figure 6.1 World forest biomes.

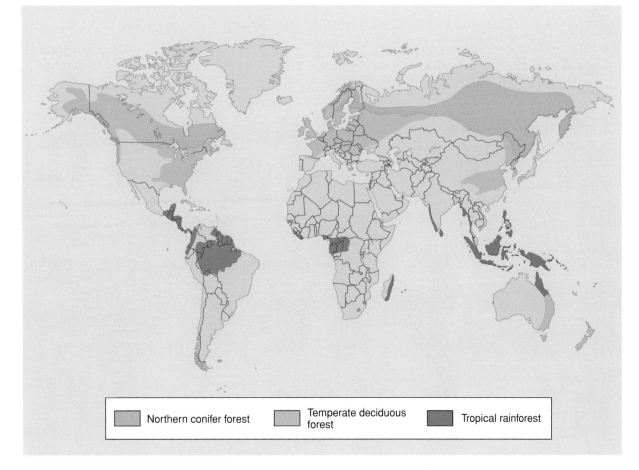

Northern conifer forest   Temperate deciduous forest   Tropical rainforest

1 On a world map, shade world forest biomes. Annotate your map with names of forested areas, and then identify areas where you think that forest

  a) has been removed   **b)** is under threat.

  Give reasons for the deforestation or degradation.

2 Explain why the global demand for wood and forest products is increasing so rapidly.

The boreal forests

The most northerly forest biome is the boreal forest or taiga where coniferous trees predominate (Figure 6.2). This biome lies generally north of latitude 60°N in Europe, Asia and North America. Coniferous forest is also found at high altitudes in more temperate areas such as in the southern Rockies in the USA and in the Andes in Chile. There is no coniferous forest belt in the southern hemisphere because there are no large land masses at the appropriate latitude.

Coniferous trees such as those in Figure 6.3 are the main type of vegetation in boreal forests. There are relatively few different species compared to other forest biomes. Four types of conifer predominate: spruce, pine, fir and larch. In warmer, more southerly locations, some tolerant deciduous cypress and redwoods are found together with

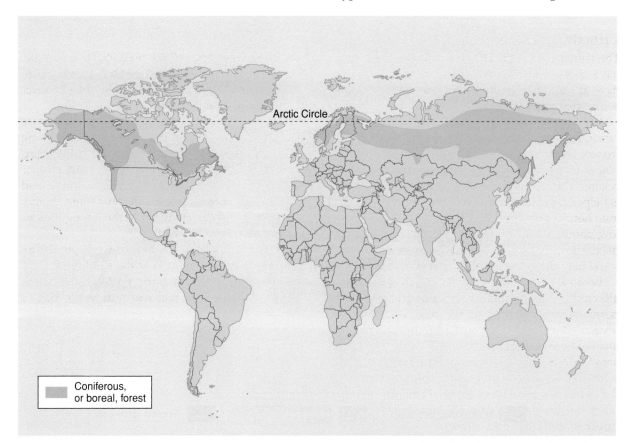

Arctic Circle

Coniferous, or boreal, forest

Figure 6.2 The extent of coniferous, or boreal, forests.

Figure 6.3 Sitka Spruce forest in Canada.

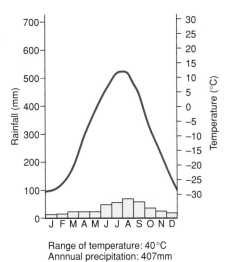

Range of temperature: 40 °C
Annnual precipitation: 407mm

Figure 6.4 The climate of the boreal forest biome – Churchill, Canada (latitude 59°N, altitude 13m).

hardwoods such as alder, birch and poplar. Further north, trees become smaller in size and the distance between them increases. Trees can only grow where average temperatures are over 10 °C for at least one month of the year; beyond this limit lies the tundra.

Climate and soils

The climate graph in Figure 6.4 shows these areas have cool summers and cold winters. Many areas have at least six months with average temperatures below freezing point, sometimes falling as low as −30 °C. Strong winds mean there is a high wind chill factor and any moisture is rapidly evaporated or frozen. The frost-free period is only 50 days in some places in Siberia but up to 250 days nearer to the oceans. The growing season is short, but tree growth is helped by clear skies, warm and sunny days, and long hours of daylight. Precipitation in these areas is low, about 400–500mm a year with a slight summer maximum. In winter, snowfall can be heavy and snow may lie on the ground for weeks at a time.

Because of low temperatures, much of the area is affected by permanently frozen ground called permafrost. However, snow cover does help to insulate the soil keeping surface temperatures only just below freezing point. Soils in coniferous forest areas are usually low quality and acidic podsols, with few worms or organisms able to survive on the hard waxy pine needles. They contain few nutrients and are infertile, but conifers need fewer nutrients than deciduous trees.

Calculate the growing season for Churchill, which begins when the temperature is 6 °C or higher. Why do such areas offer little potential for agriculture?

Coniferous trees are well adapted to a cold climate.
- Trees are mostly evergreen (larch is an exception) which means they can photosynthesise whenever temperatures are high enough.
- Leaves are wax-coated needles which reduce transpiration. This is important because strong winds evaporate moisture and the cold means water is frozen and unavailable in winter.
- The pyramid shape and flexible trunk and branches means trees can withstand heavy snowfall and can stand up to the strong winds.
- Seed cones protect seeds.
- Roots are shallow so they can take moisture from the surface as soon as the soil thaws.
- Thick and resinous bark protects the trunk from extreme cold and can reduce the risk of summer fires.

Canopy layer ⟶ Tall straight conifers often growing very close together

20m

Field or herb layer Few grasses and wild flowers grow where light penetrates, e.g. beside clearing; they must be acid tolerant

Ground layer Thick bed of needles covering ground; these are very slow to decompose

Figure 6.5 Stratification of plants in coniferous forests.

The structure of coniferous forests

Coniferous forests, unlike other forests, have very simple stratification – or layers – of vegetation (Figure 6.5). Conifers form the main tree canopy and a limited understorey consists of low growing shrubs such as blueberry and crowberry. There is little ground cover apart from mosses, lichens, fungi and some wild flowers such as orchids. This is partly the result of lack of sunlight reaching the forest floor, and partly due to the undecomposed acidic pine needles which form a very deep layer on the surface.

Coniferous forests provide a limited number of different habitats because there are few species and little undergrowth. This means there are also relatively small numbers of animals living in this biome. The harsh climate, particularly cold winters, also makes conditions difficult. The most significant herbivores are deer such as caribou, elk, red deer and reindeer. There are plenty of rodents such as wildcat, pine marten and squirrels, and carnivores include foxes, wolves, weasels, mink and bears. Some birds make this area their permanent home but many more migrate here in summer to feed on the vast swarms of insects found here at this time of year.

1 Use Figures 6.3 and 6.5 to draw an annotated diagram showing the structure of vegetation (layers) in a coniferous forest. Give reasons for this structure. Include details of habitats for fauna.

2 Using separate annotations, identify how seasons make a difference to the nature of the habitat.

3 Why should the most significant fauna be herbivores such as rodents? Consider how each survives harsh winters.

Threats to boreal forests

Conifers are extremely important worldwide for the supply of wood for timber and paper. These forests support important timber industries in Scandinavia, Canada and Russia. The trees grow tall – up to about 20m – and straight and the relatively small number of animals makes felling easier. The timber industry, which includes both logging and sawmill operations, is highly mechanised. After felling, the timber is cut into lengths and either transported to nearby roads by tractor or pulled by a cable to a collection point. Sawn logs are loaded onto lorries or taken to a railway line for transport to the saw mill. Technological advances, such as whole tree harvesters and field chippers and highly mechanised saw mills, mean that 99 per cent of each tree can be used.

In most coniferous forests there is careful ecological management and logging is followed by planting, helping the area to regenerate. However, afforestation is usually in the form of plantations where kilometre after kilometre of the same species are planted in straight lines. These plantations or secondary forests, which replace the natural forest, are not natural ecosystems, and support fewer species of animals and plants.

More than one-third of the paper and over 20 per cent of the wood used in the UK comes from forests in Scandinavia, especially Finland and Sweden. Heavy exploitation has left just 5 per cent of the natural or ancient forest in these countries – the rest has been converted to intensively managed secondary forest. These last valuable fragments are being cut down to satisfy demand for timber and paper.

Figure 6.6 Logging operations in coniferous forest, Ontario, Canada

Natural forests are home to a variety of plants, animals and fungi but only a fraction of these can live in the new intensive 'factory forests'. In Scandinavia some species, including the white-backed woodpecker, are nationally endangered, and the traditional way of life of the Sami people in Lapland is threatened by logging in forests where their reindeer graze. In northern Scandinavia, the lives of the nomadic Sami revolve around reindeer, which provide food and clothing. In the past, the reindeer spent the winters sheltering and eating lichens in the forests. Lichens only grow on old trees; as most of Scandinavia's old-growth forests have now been replaced with young plantations, the reindeer sometimes starve. This has led to conflicts between the Sami and loggers.

About one-third of the world's coniferous forests are in Russia, mainly in Siberia. Russia is a leading producer of timber and wood products, mostly from softwoods such as pine, larch and spruce. Timber is used as fuel wood, for telegraph poles, building and wood pulp. During the Soviet period the most accessible forests were heavily harvested and some were removed completely for agriculture. Remaining forests are less accessible and many contain a high proportion of larch, which is difficult to exploit. Technological improvements, foreign investment and demand for wood worldwide are encouraging more exploitation. Russia does have legislation to protect forests and ensure management, but a need to earn foreign currency is putting remaining forests in danger.

GREENPEACE UNCOVERS ILLEGAL LOGGING IN RUSSIA'S FAR EAST

Greenpeace today revealed the results of months of investigative work related to illegal logging activities in Russia.

According to the Greenpeace survey, at least 20 per cent of timber in Russia is either logged illegally or severely violates forest legislation. Illegal logging is primarily logging without permits, with forged permits or by breaking regulations within existing permits. The Greenpeace report includes video evidence of such activities in the Primorsky region in Russia's Far East. Violations documented include logging outside permitted areas, logging in watersheds, prohibited logging of species such as Korean Pine and transportation of illegal logs by truck.

The Primorsky region is a territory where oak, ash and Korean pine are illegally logged for markets in Japan, China and Korea. Most companies do not ask where timber comes from. Greenpeace is calling on buyers of Russian timber products to take responsible action and to ask for proof that the timber does not originate from illegal logging activity.

In Russia, illegal logging has become a common practice because it is profitable and there is no punishment for illegal loggers. This will be further enhanced by President Putin's abolishment of both the State Committee of Environmental Protection and the Federal Forest Service. Presently 200 000 foresters are employed but all of their functions will be transferred to 9000 officials in the Ministry of Natural Resources, according to information sources available to Greenpeace.

Figure 6.7 Adapted from Greenpeace web site, 30 June 2000.

Read Figure 6.7.

1 Most countries involved in timber industries in the boreal forest have clear forest management policies. Explain why environmental groups are worried that forest management in these countries is not always appropriate.

2 a) Draw a diagram to show how the food web in coniferous forests may be broken by logging.

b) How does this threaten indigenous groups such as the Sami (Lapps) of northern Scandinavia.

3 Explain why illegal logging is widespread in Russia and why it may become worse in the future.

Temperate deciduous forests

Deciduous forests once covered large parts of Europe (including Britain), North America, North-East Asia (including Japan) and New Zealand, but today much has been cleared for agriculture and settlement. Today most European countries protect remaining areas of woodland, many of which are used for recreation. Broad-leafed trees such as oak, ash, elm, beech and maple predominate in this biome (see Figure 6.1 on page 81). The trees are deciduous – they lose their leaves in winter – although conifers and evergreen shrubs such as holly are also found. There are often several species per hectare, more than in boreal forests. Deciduous woodlands are usually clearly stratified with four or five layers of vegetation, a response to competition for light.

Climate and soils in deciduous woodland biomes

The climate in this biome typically has mild summers and cool winters, because the maritime influence prevents extremes of temperatures. Summer temperatures average 15–17 °C with sunny spells broken by cloudy or rainy periods. Winter temperatures average 4–6 °C, and although temperatures may fall below freezing snowfall rarely lasts longer than a few days except in more hilly areas. Rainfall varies between 2000mm in exposed western areas and 600mm in more eastern areas. It is evenly distributed throughout the year but with a slight winter maximum.

Deciduous woodland soils are fertile brown earths. They contain leaf litter which is broken down quite quickly by earthworms and other decomposers to make a fertile humus layer.

Woodland vegetation is adapted to the climate.

- Deciduous trees shed their leaves in winter to reduce transpiration during the colder weather. The rate of photosynthesis decreases when there is less sunlight and soil moisture is more difficult to absorb.
- Leaves are broad and thin skinned allowing them to absorb maximum sunlight in summer.
- Most flowers bloom in spring when more light reaches the forest floor. They survive the winters as seeds, bulbs, rhizomes or tubers.

Structure of deciduous woodland

Woodlands alter seasonally, and the structure alters accordingly (Figure 6.9). During spring, before trees are in leaf, many wildflowers appear, such as prim-roses and bluebells, making the most of the available light. As trees come into leaf, less light reaches the forest floor, but warmer temperatures allow grasses and shrubs to grow in gaps in tree

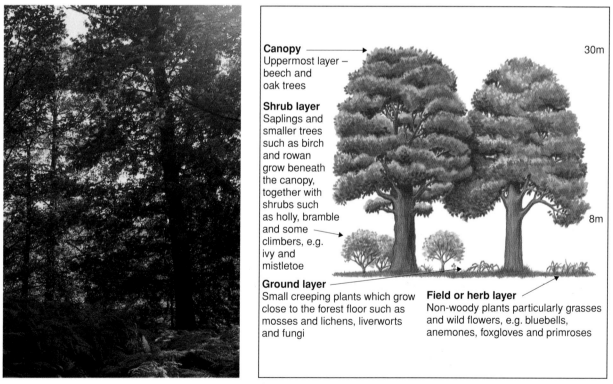

Canopy
Uppermost layer – beech and oak trees

Shrub layer
Saplings and smaller trees such as birch and rowan grow beneath the canopy, together with shrubs such as holly, bramble and some climbers, e.g. ivy and mistletoe

Ground layer
Small creeping plants which grow close to the forest floor such as mosses and lichens, liverworts and fungi

Field or herb layer
Non-woody plants particularly grasses and wild flowers, e.g. bluebells, anemones, foxgloves and primroses

30m

8m

Figure 6.8 Deciduous woodland.

Figure 6.9 The structure of deciduous forest.

cover, or 'glades', where there is more light. In late autumn, trees and shrubs lose their leaves and more light reaches the forest floor. It is too cold for many plants to grow but early autumn produces a large number of fruits and seeds, such as black-berries, acorns and chestnuts (including 'conkers' from horse chestnut trees). Fungi and mosses thrive in the damp conditions at this time of year.

The rich variety of plants in these woodlands also support a variety of animals. There are large numbers of insects, birds and mammals linked through a complex food web. A single oak tree supports hundreds of species of insect including moths, flies, wasps, mites, ants, beetles and butterflies. Herbivores include rabbits, mice, squirrels and hedgehogs and carnivores include weasels, foxes, sparrowhawks and owls. Many animals have developed ways of surviving the cold winter such as hibernation (hedgehogs and doormice); others, particularly birds, migrate, and many insects lie dormant as larvae over winter months.

Use of deciduous woodlands

Most woodlands in Europe are affected by people's activities, either in the past or the present or both. Some of the main ways woodlands are used are:

- stock grazing – sheep may be allowed to graze among the trees which also provide shelter from the weather
- game management – in some areas woodland is managed for fox hunting or let out to syndicates for shooting game birds such as partridge and woodcock
- timber production – a number of products can be harvested such as timber, wood for charcoal, and bark
- recreation – many woodlands are used by the public for walking, pony trekking, off road driving or other activities, especially where woodlands are council owned; private landowners may use woods for their personal recreation or allow access to the public
- habitat for birds and animals – woodland can be managed for conservation to protect and increase the numbers of species of plants and animals.

---

1 Use Figures 6.8 and 6.9 to draw an annotated diagram showing the structure of vegetation (layers) in a deciduous forest. Give reasons for this structure. Include details of habitats for fauna, showing how each layer in the structure supports different fauna.

2 Why should fauna be far more numerous than in coniferous forest? Consider how animals survive during different seasons.

3 Draw a diagram to show a deciduous woodland. Refer to the theory boxes on pages 74–6 and annotate the diagram to show:

   a) how energy is transferred through the ecosystem
   b) how nutrients are cycled
   c) how seasons make a difference to habitat.

4 Explain how using woodlands for sheep grazing and recreation can damage the ecosystem of a deciduous woodland.

Managing woodland – Padley Woods, Derbyshire

Padley Woods are part of the Longshaw estate in Derbyshire, lying within the Peak District National Park less than 16km from central Sheffield. The woodlands are ancient, semi-natural woods, which have been there since before 1600. They are the most important woodlands in the southern Pennines due to their size and variety of species, and have been identified as a Site of Special Scientific Interest (SSSI).

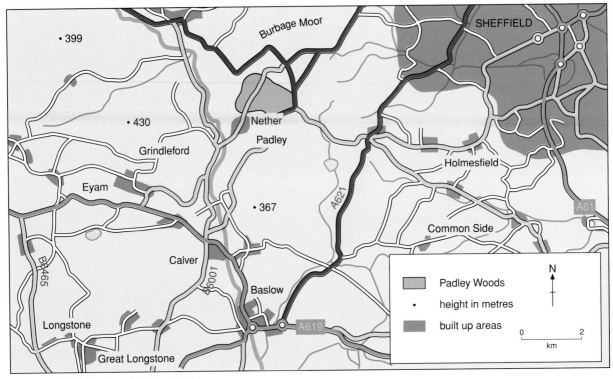

Figure 6.10 The location of Padley Woods.

From 1808 to 1927 the woods were owned by The Duke of Rutland and used as part of a large shooting estate. There was no public access and at this time the woods were natural with native species of oak, hazel, silver birch and holly. The Duke of Rutland changed the woods by planting Scots pine, sycamore and beech to give variety, colour and winter cover. The presence of these non-native species means this is now semi-natural and not natural woodland.

During the nineteenth century, the woods were coppiced – the trees were cut at the base of the trunk, allowed to regrow, then cut again after about twenty years. This was done to supply wood for charcoal (on site) and for fuel in Sheffield's iron smelting industry. Bark was used for tanning leather in Grindleford and Manchester. Coke replaced wood as a fuel in about 1870, and coppicing stopped about this time. Today there are many multi-stemmed trees which have been coppiced in the past. There are few hazel trees, probably because they were felled as the best trees for charcoal. The area was also used for hunting and to graze stock and this prevented many species from regenerating, particularly hazel and silver birch. This explains why there are so few different species. Little variety in types of trees and wild flowers resulted in lack of variety of animal life.

In 1927 the Duke of Rutland sold the estate and six years later it was given to the National Trust who now manage it. Initially the Trust allowed sheep grazing, but between 1975 and 1986 virtually the whole of Padley Woods was enclosed by fences to keep out sheep and prevent them eating smaller plants and saplings. Many young trees have now grown such as silver birch, typically one of the first trees to become established, rowan and oak. There is also a wider variety of shrubs such as heather, bilberry and crowberry and less bracken. The greater variety of plants has encouraged more wildlife into the woods.

The National Trust manage the woods for conservation by selective felling – non-native species such as sycamore and Scots pine are cut to allow light in, encouraging seedlings to grow and regenerate in what is becoming an older woodland. Non-native species do not support the same variety of animals; an oak supports about 400 species of invertebrates and therefore many birds and animals, whereas a sycamore only supports about 100 species of invertebrates and less bird life.

Figure 6.11 Padley Woods.

Visitors are an increasing threat to the area. Padley Woods is well known and easily accessible. Lots of people walk or picnic here, and children paddle in the stream. There are clear footpaths with views, and a cafe and shop. Unfortunately visitors cause damage such as creating new footpaths, widening established paths, damaging grass verges where they park their cars and leaving litter. The National Trust are trying to stop visitors from causing too much damage:

- information boards have been put up to explain to people where they can go and how they should respect the countryside
- car parks and pull-ins have been created so people do not park on the grass verges
- footpaths are well signed and have easy access points such as gates and stiles
- fire beaters have been installed and there are notices warning about fire.

---

1 Draw a timeline from 1800 to 2000 and annotate it to show the different ways Padley Woods has been used and managed. Use one colour to show pressures on the natural woodland and a second to show how they have been managed.

2 Why should the National Trust decide to manage Padley Woods, rather than adopting a non-interventionist strategy (i.e. 'do nothing')?

Tropical rainforests

Tropical rainforest is found within the equatorial climate belt approximately 5° north and south of the Equator. It includes the Amazon basin in South America and the Zaire basin in Africa as well as parts of South-East Asia such as Thailand, Malaysia and parts of India (see Figure 6.1 on page 81).

Tropical rainforest climates

The driving force behind rainforest ecosystems is the rainforest climate. High temperatures are maintained throughout the year, usually over 27°C. Rainfall varies more than temperature, but annual rainfall is usually more than 2000mm and may be over 3000mm. Most months have at least 100mm of rain. A wetter season corresponds with the passage of the overhead sun. In some areas there is a drier season lasting one or two months. This hot and wet climate means that plants can grow throughout the year and a true evergreen, tropical rainforest develops.

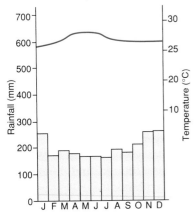

SINGAPORE: Tropical wet rainforest climate

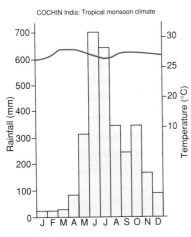

COCHIN India: Tropical monsoon climate

Figure 6.12 Climate graphs.

1 Describe the characteristics of the tropical rainforest climate.

2 What are the key differences between the climates of Cochin and Singapore?

3 How might these differences affect the type of forest vegetation found?

Where rainfall is lower and more seasonal but high temperatures still predominate, different types of tropical forest are found.

- Where rainfall is between 500mm and 2000mm with a dry season lasting up to six months, as in eastern Brazil, Myanmar and Thailand, broad-leaf deciduous forests develop. In this type of forest many trees lose their leaves in the dry season.
- Where rainfall is less than 500mm a year and there is a long dry season a tropical scrub forest will develop, dominated by thorn trees.

In tropical mountain areas, true rainforest dominates on lower slopes, but the character of the forest changes with altitude. Montane, or mountain, forest develops on higher slopes because lower temperatures allow deciduous trees to grow more successfully, and trees are more widely spaced. Higher still, cloud forests develop on slopes covered with damp and heavy cloud. Trees are short and many are deciduous, more open and with more ground vegetation.

Figure 6.13 Tropical rainforest in Amazonia.

Rainforest vegetation and soils

Tropical rainforests contain a huge variety of plants and animals and are home to more than half the world's animal and plant species. This biodiversity exists even within very small areas of rainforest. A high proportion of the world's bird and primate life is found in these areas. One-fifth of all bird species are found in Amazon forests, and 90 per cent of all primates are found only in tropical regions of Latin America, Africa and Asia.

Emergent layer
This is made up of emergent trees which penetrate the canopy. These trees are most exposed, and have to tolerate temperature change and high winds.

Canopy
The canopy consists of interlaced tree crowns which form a dense, almost continuous layer.

Sub-canopy
This is made up of smaller, immature trees. Elongated crowns help trees to use light filtering through the canopy.

Floor
The ground layer is dimly lit and often bare except for a thin layer of dead and decaying vegetation.

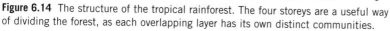

Figure 6.14 The structure of the tropical rainforest. The four storeys are a useful way of dividing the forest, as each overlapping layer has its own distinct communities.

The rainforest has well defined layers. The tallest trees grow to about 50m. These emergents stand well above the main canopy and are home to relatively few animals except birds of prey such as eagles. These forest giants are exposed to full sunlight and strong winds and there is lower humidity than in the rest of the forest. Many of these huge trees are supported by buttress roots, which develop at the base of the trunk up to 9m above ground level.

Below the emergents, the main canopy forms an almost continuous layer about 30-35m above the ground. Trees such as mahogany, rosewood, green-heart, palm and rubber compete for light and space. Their crowns are covered in epiphytes (plants which do not have their roots on the floor – they use trees for support but are not parasites) and are linked together by creepers and lianas. These woody climbers are rooted in the ground but can reach up to 250m in length as they climb into the canopy where their leaves and flowers grow. The canopy is home to a vast number of birds, reptiles, insects and mammals which find this zone much more hospitable than other parts of the forest.

The canopy acts as an umbrella, intercepting most light and rainfall. Below the canopy it is calm, sheltered, shady and very humid. The sub-canopy or understorey consists of younger trees or saplings growing to about 20m (the height of a coniferous tree in Britain). Some of these trees have elongated crowns to help them to obtain sunlight filtering through the canopy. Their trunks are straight and have few branches and they have thin barks because there is no need for protection against the cold. The trunks usually support lianas and other creepers. Few animals live in this zone but many animals use the straight trunks as a means of transport between the forest floor and the canopy.

The forest floor is dank and gloomy. Only about 1 per cent of sunlight reaches the ground even at midday (Figure 6.16). Little grows at this level and the forest floor is covered in leaf litter and fallen logs, though rapid decomposition of dead organic matter means that this may be a relatively thin layer. Where light can penetrate the forest, such as along a river bank or around a clearing, the vegetation is dense with plants growing on the forest floor and forming a layer of shrub.

Figure 6.15 The rainforest canopy.

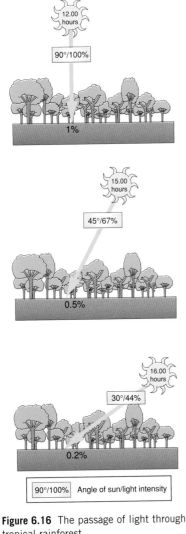

Figure 6.16 The passage of light through tropical rainforest.
Light is absorbed with great effectiveness. If we use noon as a 100 per cent value for light intensity above the canopy, by 1600 hours on a cloudless day only 0.2 per cent of light will reach the forest floor. The light of a full moon is not even perceived here.

Decaying vegetation in rainforests is rapidly consumed and recycled by insects, bacteria, fungi and soil humus. Plants and trees take most of their nutrients from rain and wind-borne dust, rather than through their roots. Many climbing plants use their roots for stabilisation because they have no contact with the soil. Rain falling on the forest canopy has more nutrients than soil moisture on the forest floor. The recycling process is so effective because high temperatures cause rapid evaporation, and fairly continuous annual rainfall allows a wide variety of organisms to survive. When plants or animals die all their biochemicals and components are recycled by decomposers.

Rainforest soils are, perhaps surprisingly, infertile. They contain relatively little organic matter because of very rapid decay. Nutrients are therefore stored in the vegetation (biomass) rather than in the litter or the soils. Heavy rain causes leaching which removes soluble nutrients away from plant roots into deeper layers of the soil.

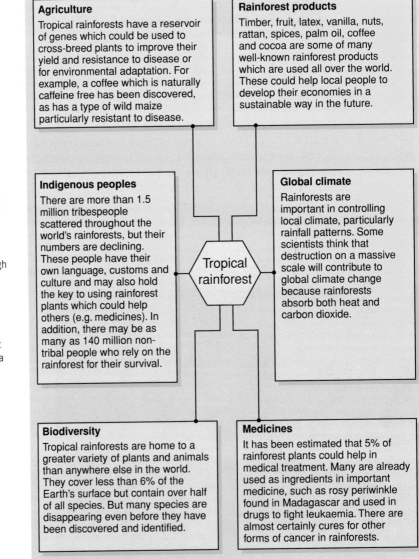

Agriculture
Tropical rainforests have a reservoir of genes which could be used to cross-breed plants to improve their yield and resistance to disease or for environmental adaptation. For example, a coffee which is naturally caffeine free has been discovered, as has a type of wild maize particularly resistant to disease.

Rainforest products
Timber, fruit, latex, vanilla, nuts, rattan, spices, palm oil, coffee and cocoa are some of many well-known rainforest products which are used all over the world. These could help local people to develop their economies in a sustainable way in the future.

Indigenous peoples
There are more than 1.5 million tribespeople scattered throughout the world's rainforests, but their numbers are declining. These people have their own language, customs and culture and may also hold the key to using rainforest plants which could help others (e.g. medicines). In addition, there may be as many as 140 million non-tribal people who rely on the rainforest for their survival.

Tropical rainforest

Global climate
Rainforests are important in controlling local climate, particularly rainfall patterns. Some scientists think that destruction on a massive scale will contribute to global climate change because rainforests absorb both heat and carbon dioxide.

Biodiversity
Tropical rainforests are home to a greater variety of plants and animals than anywhere else in the world. They cover less than 6% of the Earth's surface but contain over half of all species. But many species are disappearing even before they have been discovered and identified.

Medicines
It has been estimated that 5% of rainforest plants could help in medical treatment. Many are already used as ingredients in important medicine, such as rosy periwinkle found in Madagascar and used in drugs to fight leukaemia. There are almost certainly cures for other forms of cancer in rainforests.

Figure 6.17 Why are rainforests so important?

Deforestation of the rainforests

No one really knows how quickly rainforests are disappearing but it is clear that destruction is rapid and probably still increasing. Some estimates suggest about 40 hectares of rainforest are lost every minute and an area equivalent to five times the size of Switzerland is lost every year.

Some rainforest destruction is on a huge scale. The timber industry is responsible for about 40 per cent of destruction, the worst affected areas being in West Africa and South-East Asia. Commercial logging provides important income for many LEDCs and there is a high demand for tropical hardwoods in Japan, the USA and Europe. Mechanisation of the industry has led not only to more rapid felling but also to more widespread destruction of the forest, as vehicles and machinery carve a way through the forest and falling trees bring down surrounding vegetation.

By developing roads and services, logging companies open the way for migrant settlers into the forest. Settlers clear land for agriculture, usually by burning, but infertile soils soon become exhausted and within three or four years land is abandoned and another patch of forest is cleared. This 'slash and burn' is almost as much of a threat to forests as the timber industry. Settlers are not always to blame, for they are often landless labourers forced off their land by wealthy landowners or by development projects. In some places governments have actively encouraged this type of settlement.

Cattle ranching has rightly earned itself a reputation for destroying rainforest, especially in Central America and Amazonia. Forests are cleared for grazing, but pasture is unlikely to last more than ten years as over-grazing and torrential rains turn it into semi-desert. Elsewhere large-scale mining projects, such as at Carajas in Amazonia, or hydroelectric schemes, such as the Tucurui dam in Brazil, also lead to destruction of the rainforest.

1 Make a copy of Figure 6.18 which shows the hydrological cycle in rainforests. Then make a second copy to show how this cycle is altered by deforestation.

2 Look at Figure 6.19. Explain why regeneration of the forest is difficult after large-scale clearance.

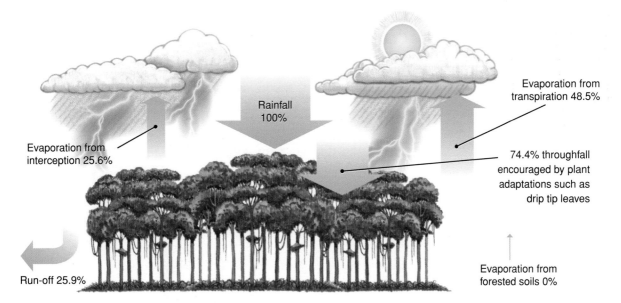

Rainfall 100%

Evaporation from transpiration 48.5%

Evaporation from interception 25.6%

74.4% throughfall encouraged by plant adaptations such as drip tip leaves

Run-off 25.9%

Evaporation from forested soils 0%

Figure 6.18 Hydrological cycle in tropical rainforests.

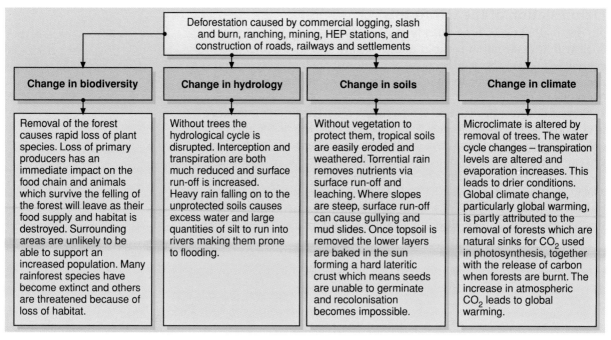

Figure 6.19 Human impact on the rainforest ecosystem.

The consequences of deforestation for rainforests are far reaching, affecting the structure and functioning of the forest ecosystem (Figure 6.19).

The reasons why rainforests are disappearing are largely economic. Most rainforests occur in LEDCs, which need to use forest resources to help economic development. MEDCs for their part often provide the market for minerals, agricultural products and timber. The reasons for protecting the forests are largely environmental and few countries are able or willing to conserve or protect the forests at the expense of their economic growth. The result will inevitably be short-term gain at the expense of long-term environmental disaster.

Comparing forest ecosystems
Energy flows in forest biomes

The NPP for the forest biomes are shown in Figure 6.20.
Read the section about primary productivity in Chapter 5 (pages 75–6).

1 Describe how the NPP of the three forest biomes differs.

2 Explain these differences.

| Forest biome | NPP per unit area (kg/m²/y) | | World NPP (billion tonnes per year) |
	Range	Mean	
Tropical rainforest	1000–3500	2200	37.4
Temperate deciduous forest	600–2500	1200	8.4
Boreal forest	400–2000	800	9.6

Figure 6.20 Primary productivity in forest biomes.

The cycling of nutrients within ecosystems

Nutrients are chemical elements and compounds needed by plants for growth. Unlike energy, which flows through the ecosystem, nutrients are cycled within it. They may be introduced or lost either naturally or by human actions. Essential plant nutrients include carbon, nitrogen, oxygen, hydrogen, calcium, phosphorous and potassium.

Ecosystems obtain nutrients from the atmosphere, lithosphere and hydrosphere. These are the three main nutrient pools. Some nutrients, such as oxygen and carbon dioxide, enter and leave the system as gases, but others, such as nitrogen, are absorbed by plants in solution from

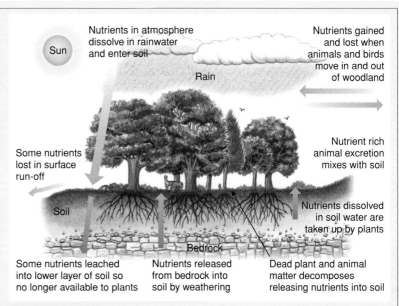

Figure 6.21 Typical nutrient flows in a forest ecosystem.

the soil. The process of obtaining nutrients and recycling them depends entirely on the flow of energy. Nutrients are used by plants to grow and are converted into plant and animal tissue. When organisms die and decompose, nutrients are released and are used again by living things. Thus there is continuous cycling of nutrients in an ecosystem.

Nutrients may be introduced into an ecosystem by visiting birds and animals or by the wind, and may be lost in surface run-off or leaching of soils. Greater changes to the balance can occur as a result of human activities, such as deforestation or the addition of fertiliser which finds its way into water courses.

Nutrient cycling in forest biomes

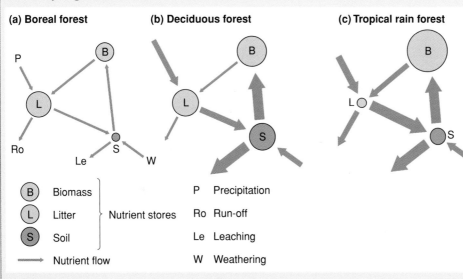

Figure 6.22 Nutrient cycling in forest ecosystems. Nutrients may be stored within the ecosystem in biomass, soil or litter. They are cycled between the stores by means of growth, fall-out and decay, and may be added or removed by weathering, run-off, leaching and precipitation.

Study Figure 6.22.

1 Explain why the proportion of nutrients stored in the biomass is much greater in the tropical rainforest than in the boreal forest.
2 In which of these three forest ecosys-tems would the soils be most fertile? Explain your answer.

3 Why are the nutrient losses from surface run-off greatest in the tropical rainforest?
4 Redraw the diagram to show the likely impact that defor-estation would have on the way nutrients are stored and cycled within the ecosystem. Annotate your diagram to show why the stores and flows have changed.

Summary

You have learned that:

- The distribution of the world's major forest types – coniferous (boreal), deciduous and tropical rainforest – depends upon physical factors, particularly climate and soils.
- Forest types can be compared in terms of structure, functioning, variations in primary productivity and ecological value.
- Each type of forest faces issues of destruction, degradation, management and regeneration.

References and further reading

Bob Digby ed., *Changing Environments*, Heinemann (2000)

Greg O'Hare, *Soils, vegetation and ecosystems*, Oliver and Boyd (1998)

RSPB, *Ecosystems and Human Activity*, Collins Educational (1994)

Web sites

Global Dimension web site provides an excellent selection of web site addresses for many environmental issues: www.globaldimension.org.uk

These include:

Friends of the Earth: www.foe.co.uk

Worldwide Fund for Nature: www.panda.org

Managing tropical forests

Tropical forests once covered 14 per cent of the world's land area; now they cover less than 7 per cent. The rate of tropical forest destruction, or deforestation, has increased by 90 per cent since the mid-1980s. Forests are threatened and destroyed by unsustainable or illegal logging, forest fires and clearance for agriculture, settlement or mining. Currently, 14 million hectares are being destroyed annually and a further 15 million hectares degraded. If these rates continue, tropical forests will have practically vanished in your lifetime.

This chapter will consider how far management can protect forests. Conservation or preservation may protect some forests, but in most cases the solution lies in sustainable development – making use of the forest resources in ways that benefit people now but ensure that they remain for the future. In this type of development the ability of the forest to replace itself must be greater than the level of exploitation.

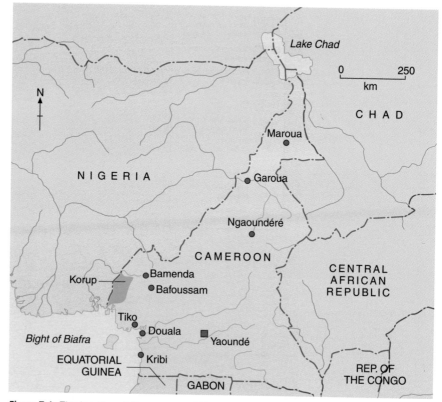

Figure 7.1 The location of Cameroon and Korup in West Africa.

Conservation of tropical rainforest – the Korup Project

The Korup Project in south-west Cameroon is an attempt to conserve an area of pristine rainforest. The area is unusual as a rainforest in that it has no large deposits of minerals. As in most rainforests, soils are poor and rainfall is high, making it unsuitable for crops. The terrain is difficult and inaccessible, making it of little interest to loggers. The forest has been left virtually untouched and is one of the world's oldest and most diverse with the largest number of plant species anywhere in Africa. Animal life is diverse and rare. The forest is home to 25 per cent of Africa's primate species as well as huge numbers of birds and 52 mammal species, including water-shrew, red colobus monkey, chimpanzee, golden cat, forest leopard and forest elephant.

The Cameroon government established Korup as Cameroon's first, and currently only, national park in 1986. They were helped and supported by organisations such as WWF and the Overseas Development Administration (ODA) of the UK government. The main aims are:

- to preserve wildlife, the environment and its biodiversity
- to foster scientific research
- to enhance tourist development
- to educate local people to minimise their impact on the rainforest.

What is the project about?

Figure 7.2 The Korup Project.

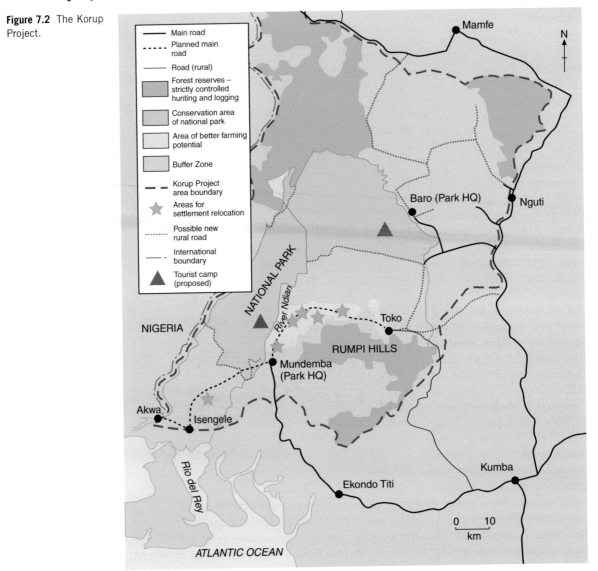

Figure 7.2 shows that the project consists of:
- a central national park
- three forest reserves (Nita-Ali, Rumpi Hills and Ejagham)
- a park buffer zone for agriculture and rural development.

Establishing and delimiting the national park itself was the first step in conserving the rainforest. This included building a fence around the park, creating nature trails, and building camp sites and guard posts. Hunting in the park was controlled quickly as this is the biggest threat to wildlife. Local people are employed as park guards to try to discourage poaching. In order to achieve true national park status people living in six villages inside the boundary had to be resettled.

The second step was to develop a buffer zone around the park where most development would take place. New roads and bridges are being built, schools and health centres have been set up and a resettlement programme has begun. Education is a major part of the project. Villagers are taught how to grow crops and raise livestock in the forest so hunting is no longer necessary, and community farms and tree nurseries have been set up so that replanting can begin. Workshops teach people skills such as carpentry and masonry, and how to make handicrafts such as soap.

The third step is to encourage tourism in order to earn foreign exchange and offer employment and business opportunities. The project insists that local people must benefit from such development, and that tourism must be controlled. Tourists can only experience the rainforest on foot. Most tourists are 'adventurers' wanting a different kind of holiday experience or scientific tourists interested in flora or fauna. Korup has particular appeal to butterfly, bird and botanical groups but is not a good place to see large animals. There are difficulties. Mundemba (Figure 7.2) is the main centre for tourists but it is at the end of a dusty or muddy road, depending on the season, and the park entrance is a further 10km away. Facilities are poor and there is only one way into and out of the park.

Figure 7.3 Village in the Korup, with electrification.

1 Consider the four main aims of the project:
- to preserve wildlife, environment and biodiversity
- to foster scientific research
- to enhance tourism
- to minimise the impact of local people on the forest.

For each one explain how the project has tried to meet this aim, and suggest problems faced in doing so.

2 Draw a simple base map of the Korup area based on Figure 7.2. Annotate it carefully to show how the national park and the buffer zone are being protected and developed.

Korup ... success or failure?

Wildlife in Korup is now protected in a way no other rainforest in the world has yet been able to achieve. There are real hopes that this forest will become an example to other countries. It has attracted funding from international agencies such as the World Bank and support from non-governmental organisations (NGOs) from Britain, the USA and Germany. One of the most exciting achievements has been the discovery of a plant, Ancistrocladus korupensis, found only in Korup. This plant may be useful in the fight against HIV. If the plant proves useful, it could provide a valuable source of income for local farmers as well as contributing significantly to world health.

One of the major problems of the scheme has been establishing the trust and co-operation of local villagers. There are 29 villages in the Korup area. Six were inside the national park and had to be relocated to the buffer zone. There is resentment and unhappiness about these plans, and although some have accepted relocation others very much resent it. The issue of hunting is contentious. For many, hunting is part of tradition and a main source of income, yet now carrying a firearm without a permit is illegal and hunting is discouraged. The park has been enclosed by a fence, and guards are employed at entry points. According to WWF, hunting by villagers in the north has declined and some people have surrendered weapons.

Poverty remains a major problem. The rural development programme to help people to change their methods of farming and learn new skills is still at an early stage. For some, the traditional way of life has been taken away with little to replace it.

1 The Korup Project has been criticised for putting wildlife before people. How far would you agree with this criticism?

2 Imagine you are employed by WWF to work on the Korup Project. How would you try to persuade villagers to stop hunting and to move out of the park to the buffer zone?

3 Write a 400-word evaluation of the project. Assess the benefits and achievements of the project and weigh these up against the problems. Should this project be used as a model for other areas?

The Kilum Mountain Forest Project

Montane, or mountain, forests are different from rainforests. They are found where the tropical climate is altered at higher altitudes, such as the Kilum Mountain forests in north-west Cameroon. Here, the climate is temperate because of the relief of the area. Mount Oku, or Kilum, is the second highest point in mainland West Africa at 3011m and these highlands have a unique but threatened flora and fauna.

This is a highly populated area by Cameroon standards. Over 100 000 people depend on the forest for a variety of products and for their water supply in the dry season. Population growth has placed pressure on the land and communities; the impact on the ecosystem is leading to unsustainable practices, for which action is needed. The Kilum Mountain Forest Project (KMFP) was set up in 1987–8 to help local people to improve management of the forest's resources. It is now funded by the International Council for Bird Preservation (ICBP), WWF and the ODA. The aims of the project are:

- to conserve the mountain forest
- to promote sustainable use of natural resources.

Three ethnic groups hold rights to the forest: the Oku, Nso and Kom peoples. These people depend on the forest for firewood, building materials, honey, medicinal plants and bushmeat. The forest holds cultural significance for people and plays a crucial role in regulating water supply. Fuel consumption in Oku's cool climate is high, and domestic firewood is collected from the forest. Building materials such as rattan, bamboo and thatching grass are harvested from the forest and surrounding grassland. Because of its biodiversity, Oku has become a centre for traditional medicine, using honey as a constituent of herbal remedies.

Figure 7.4 Temperate forest of Mount Kilum, Cameroon.

Figure 7.5 Sustainable activities in Cameroon include honey collection (a) and working with bamboo (b).

What problems face Kilum?

Forest destruction

Between 1963 and 1983, half the montane forest was destroyed or badly degraded. The principal cause of this destruction was 'slash and burn' for farmland. Thousands of goats and sheep have been brought into the forest, preventing regeneration and causing erosion on steep, thinly-soiled slopes. Beehives have been destroyed by fire.

Population pressure

Agriculture is difficult because of the hilly terrain, heavy seasonal rain and poor, easily eroded soils. As population pressures increase, people try to farm steep, marginal land. More and more cash crops are grown to pay for medical and school costs, but over-production has resulted in a price fall. The traditional fallow period has been abandoned so that soil has no chance to recover. Even on steep slopes, most permanent vegetation is cleared. Trees and stumps are burned. As land deteriorates, farmers look to the forest for productive land. Now, the forest has receded, firewood collection is more difficult, dry-season water supplies have dwindled, livestock wander uncontrolled through farmland and landslides are common.

Activities of the KMFP

From the outset this project involved local people in decisions and management. Environmental education is probably the most important activity, aimed at schools, farmers, women's groups, traditional leaders, agricultural staff and the government. Many schools have set up tree nurseries and soil conservation trials on their own farms.

The other main activities of the KMFP are:

- forest conservation – the forest boundary has been marked out clearly in collaboration with local people.
- controlled burning – fire is used for clearing forest, managing grassland, harvesting wild honey and disposing of farm waste, but can be very destructive. The KMFP has issued tools for fire-fighting to village representatives.
- controlling grazing – most households in Kilum keep chickens, plus a few goats or sheep. Goats and sheep are tethered throughout the rainy season but in the dry season they roam free for food, preventing natural regeneration. Trials have begun to rear goats and sheep in fenced areas, though fencing is expensive. Several species of tree and shrub are used as hedging, Guatemala grass has been introduced for dry season fodder, and the project is experimenting with making silage.
- sustainable harvesting – commercial exploitation of Pygeum bark started on Kilum in 1976, but over-exploitation has killed 80 per cent of mature Pygeum trees in the area. Illegal harvesting is still a problem. The KMFP is trying to encourage sustainable harvesting, which involves cutting bark every seven years to allow trees to regenerate.
- soil conservation – measures have been discussed with farmers since the beginning of the project. There are now 40 demonstration farms. The most effective measure is the use of

Figure 7.6 Tree planting in a nursery in Kilum.

contour hedges to prevent soil wash and increase soil fertility by fixing nitrogen and raising nutrient content to a level not normally available for farm crops.

- establishing tree nurseries – nurseries play a crucial role by supplying planting materials for soil conservation, agroforestry and fuel wood plantations. They can also be used for fencing, windbreaks, animal fodder, demarcation of the forest boundary and planting in degraded areas. An experimental nursery was set up in 1988 with a capacity of about 20 000 seedlings per annum. Farmers, women's groups and schools have been encouraged to establish their own.

The economy of Kilum once depended heavily on the forest. Hunting, woodcarving, traditional medicine and bee keeping still bring in income and their development is being supported. The income-generating capacity of the forest is a powerful argument for its conservation, and many argue that conservation will be successful if local people are involved in project management.

Trees and forests provide us with many things: firewood, oxygen, building and carving materials, medicines, food, and paper. Forests hold the rainwater which is so important for our water supply. Trees help to prevent soil erosion.

As our population grows, we cut down many trees for our own use. We cut down forests to make room for our farms and homes. Our natural forest is disappearing. Who is planting trees for tomorrow?

As we know, water is a limited resource. Rain that falls during the rainy season has to provide us with water during the dry season. Good, clean water is needed by everyone for cooking, bathing, drinking, and for growing our crops.

We are losing much of our water because of deforestation. Often our water is too dirty and polluted to drink, and it brings disease. Sometimes our streams dry up and there is not enough water for our growing population.

Land is one of our most important resources. We farm the land and get our food and energy from it. We build our houses and live on the land.

As our population grows, our need for land becomes greater. Will we have enough land for everyone? We must care for our land and use it wisely.

Figure 7.7 The project's view of unsustainable lifestyles.
These cartoons are from FEN, the KMFP magazine, highlighting the difficulties faced by the project and Kilum communities.

1 For each difficulty identified in Figure 7.7, explain:
   a) the effects on the ecosystem
   b) steps needed in ecosystem management to tackle the problem.

2 The KMFP team directors change every three years. You have to advise the next KMFP team in London on the best ways to manage an ecosystem under threat before they depart for Cameroon. Using all the material in this study, prepare a report of not more than 1000 words summarising the work of the current KMFP team. Identify for them what you feel still needs to be done.

Managing forests sustainably

The potential of agroforestry

This traditional form of sustainable development allows people to cultivate cash crops and rear livestock without damaging the forest ecosystem. The Chagga people practise a form of agroforestry on the southern slopes of Kilimanjaro in Tanzania. This imitates the stratification of the rainforest by using several layers of trees, bushes and vegetables (Figure 7.8). Each cultivated species is chosen according to available light conditions. At the highest level they grow banana, papaya and guava trees. Then come coffee bushes and finally, close to ground level, vegetables. Fish swim in the irrigation channels. Pigs, goats, cows and chickens provide protein and dung as an essential fertiliser. The crowns of some original rainforest trees protect the soil, ground surface and low growing plants from tropical storms, while their roots hold the soil in place. This system is successful and supports the highest rural population per square kilometre in Tanzania.

1 Using an atlas, draw an annotated sketch map of north-east Tanzania. On your map mark the location of Kilimanjaro and the natural vegetation found in this part of Africa.

2 Why do you think the slopes of Kilimanjaro support montane rainforest, while the surrounding lowlands are not forested?

3 List the advantages and disadvantages of agroforestry as a way of managing rainforest for the people and for the environment.

Sustainable timber production

International trade in timber is one of the major reasons for large-scale deforestation of rainforests. Timber industries in Brazil, Malaysia, Indonesia and India provide essential foreign earnings. Timber is mainly exported to MEDCs, particularly the USA, Japan and the countries of Western Europe. Demand for tropical hardwoods (for example mahogany, ebony teak and rosewood) is large and growing. One way to tackle the problem is for international trade organisations (the EU or the WTO – see Chapter 19) to encourage sustainable timber production. At the moment, those who adopt sustainable methods lose out because they produce less timber, so trade systems need to be altered in favour of sustainably-produced wood. The International Tropical Timber Organisation (ITTO) and the Forest Stewardship Council (FSC) are both working towards achieving this (see theory box on page 104).

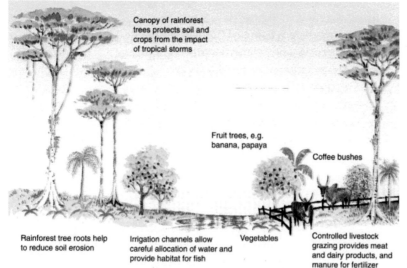

Canopy of rainforest trees protects soil and crops from the impact of tropical storms

Fruit trees, e.g. banana, papaya

Coffee bushes

Rainforest tree roots help to reduce soil erosion

Irrigation channels allow careful allocation of water and provide habitat for fish

Vegetables

Controlled livestock grazing provides meat and dairy products, and manure for fertilizer

Figure 7.8 Systems of agroforestry practised by the Chagga people.

Managing rainforests sustainably
The International Tropical Timber Organisation (ITTO)

The ITTO was set up in 1983 to work together with timber exporters and conservationists. One of its main objectives has been the 'Year 2000 Objective' – that by 2000, all tropical timber products traded internationally by member states would originate from sustainably managed forests. In 1983 only about 1 million hectares of productive tropical trees were being harvested sustainably, out of a total of over 800 million hectares. By May 2000, the ITTO found that a great deal had been achieved – perhaps more than most expected.

- Most countries have established forest estates and increased forest conservation.
- There are new initiatives involving local people in forest management.
- Local communities are helping to support sustainable forest management.
- Many countries are producing more value-added exports, for example wood is being processed into planks or furniture before being exported, earning more money as well as creating jobs.

But there are also problems such as illegal logging and poaching and inadequate forest management in some countries. Six countries (Cameroon, Ghana, Guyana, Malaysia, Myanmar and Indonesia) have been particularly successful though all still have some problems.

The Forest Stewardship Council (FSC)

The FSC is an international organisation founded in 1993 to support sustainable management of the world's forests. Its members include representatives from environmental groups, the timber trade, the forestry profession, indigenous peoples' organisations and community forestry groups from around the world.

The FSC is the only organisation offering credible world-wide timber certification for all forest types and plantations, and has received approval from NGOs such as WWF, Friends of the Earth and Greenpeace. By December 2000 the total area of certified forest was over 20 million hectares. The FSC has the support of several companies, who are committed to selling only certified timber and timber products. FSC labelling is preferred in the UK, Netherlands, Belgium, Austria, Switzerland, Germany, Brazil, the USA and Japan. This alliance means that the impact of the FSC trademark could be enormous. Buyers will have a way of identifying products originating from forest or woodland which is managed sustainably. A MORI poll conducted in 1990 showed that 80 per cent of consumers in these countries would buy 'green' products given the choice.

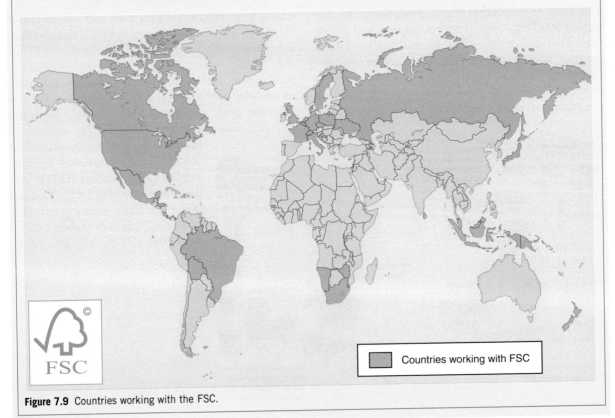

Countries working with FSC

Figure 7.9 Countries working with the FSC.

Harvesting timber sustainably can be profitable. A study in Peru showed that a hectare of forest could be worth about US $7000 if harvested sustainably, but if all the timber was cut at once the hectare would bring in only US $1000. Sustainable forestry is carried out on a small scale in the Peruvian Amazon. A local cooperative produces and sells wood in ways that do not damage the forest. The forest has been divided into 20m strips, which are felled using simple technology; no machines or vehicles are brought in. Felled trees are cut up before being removed on carts pulled by oxen. The felled area is narrow enough for natural regeneration, so no replanting is necessary. Wood is sawn into planks and exported, thus earning income for the community.

There is scope for reducing consumption of wood products in MEDCs which would place less pressure on tropical forests. Consumers also have the choice of buying products made of temperate hardwoods such as oak or ash from managed forests in Europe, rather than tropical woods such as mahogany, which is now a threatened species.

Far more paper is used than is needed, and a greater proportion could be recycled. Non-timber sources of paper such as hemp and agricultural waste are viable. Plantations on already degraded land could also be encouraged. If consumer demand fell to a level where trade in tropical timber ceased to be viable, one of the main causes of tropical deforestation and degradation would be gone.

1 What do you understand by the term 'sustainable use of tropical rain forest'?

2 Compare the objectives of the ITTO with those of the FSC. What difficulties does each face?

3 Which of the schemes do you think is likely to be most successful in preventing further deforestation? Justify your choice.

4 Debt for Nature is another scheme which aims to protect rainforest. Use the Internet to find out about this scheme and in which parts of the world it operates.

Summary

You have learned that:

- Many forests can be regarded as wildernesses but they may face issues of deforestation and degradation.
- Solutions lie in several strategies, all of which are based upon conservation, sustainable management and reforestation.
- There is often conflict between development and conservation. Conservation of environments involves achieving a balance between the two.
- Different groups and organisations play a part in ensuring forests are managed sustainably. These include private companies, NGOs and national governments.
- Strategic thinking is needed to protect and manage global ecosystems in a sustainable way, and for local developments to play an important role.

References and further reading

Parks or people? 39-minute video published by Educational Media Film and Video Ltd, Harrow Middlesex

RSPB, *Ecosystems and Human Activity*, Collins Educational (1994)

Web sites

Worldwide Fund for Nature: www.panda.org
Friends of the Earth: www.foe.co.uk
Greenpeace: www.greenpeace.org
ITTO: www.itto.or.jp
FSC: www.fscoax.org

Pressures on marine ecosystems

No one should underestimate the importance of marine ecosystems. Without them life on Earth would not be possible. Oceans account for over 70 per cent of the Earth's surface and provide habitats for 90 per cent of its life. Furthermore, marine ecosystems help to regulate the atmosphere and the world's climate, and are a major source of food. Like the world's rainforests, oceans are important to economic activities including many industries, for example as a source of medicines for the pharmaceutical industry.

This chapter will explore the social, economic, environmental and political significance of marine ecosystems. It looks at marine ecosystems and resources, their use, misuse, exploitation and management. It shows how human activity impacts their functioning and survival, referring to examples and incidents from around the world in both MEDCs and LEDCs.

Figure 8.1 Images of oceans and the role they play in everyday life on Earth.

Form groups of two or three.

1 Study the photographs in Figure 8.1.
   a) Identify a possible range of locations where each photograph might have been taken.
   b) On a large sheet of paper, write the letters A–F, well spaced over the whole sheet. Using the photographs A to F, identify as many possible links as you can. Draw lines on your sheet to show where you can see connections between the photographs, and annotate each line with a possible link.
   c) Identify a list of questions or issues raised by the photographs about the importance of oceans.

2 Each group should research one question or issue about the importance of oceans identified in 1c) and present findings to the rest of the class.

3 Classify the issues raised into social, economic, environmental and political. Decide which seem most significant and why.

What and where are coastal marine ecosystems?

Marine ecosystems are varied and have their own unique characteristics. Their significance is shown in Figure 8.2, where they are compared with some important terrestrial ecosystems. Some marine ecosystems are clearly of global importance. This part of the chapter explores two major marine ecosystems: coral reefs and mangroves.

Ecosystem	Mean primary productivity per area (tonnes per km²)	Area (millions of km²)	Mean global primary productivity (billions of tonnes)
Terrestrial			
Tropical rainforest	2200	17	37.4
Temperate deciduous forest	1200	7	8.4
Taiga	800	12	9.6
Temperate grassland	600	9	5.4
Desert	90	18	1.6
Cultivated land	650	14	9.1
Aquatic			
Open ocean	125	332	41.5
Coral reefs and algal beds	2500	0.6	1.6
Swamp and marsh	2000	2	4

Figure 8.2 Productivity of different global ecosystems, both terrestrial and aquatic.

1 Use Figure 8.3.
   a) Describe the distribution of coral reef ecosystems and mangroves.
   b) Suggest reasons for the distribution of coral reef ecosystems and mangroves.

2 Study Figure 8.2.
   a) How do aquatic ecosystems compare in terms of productivity with terrestrial?
   b) How significant are areas of open ocean in terms of area and mean primary productivity? Why should there be such a difference in the two values?

3 Use Figures 8.2 and 8.4.
   a) What is the difference between mean primary productivity per area and mean global primary productivity? Why should the two be so different in values for different ecosystems?
   b) Briefly describe how the mean primary productivity of coral reefs compares with other major ecosystems.
   c) Explain why coral reefs are almost equal in productivity to tropical rainforests but their mean global primary productivity is some 20 times less.

4 Suggest as many reasons as you can which would explain why some coral reefs are more productive than others.

5 Summarise the significance of marine ecosystems.

Coral reef ecosystems

Coral reefs are often referred to as the 'Amazon of the Oceans'. Like their land-based rainforest counterpart, coral reef ecosystems are some of the most productive ecosystems on Earth. They share other characteristics too, in terms of nutrient cycling, energy flows and their ecological value. Unfortunately, the similarity continues in terms of fragility and their susceptibility to human activity.

The global distribution of coral reefs is shown in Figure 8.3. Coral reefs are found between latitudes 30° north and 30° south at specific locations that fulfil their requirements. To survive, polyps need warm water year-round; they cannot survive in water colder than 18°C. They also require clear shallow water, less than 30m deep, for sunlight. Hence, most are located along the narrow edges of continental shelves, before water depth increases. The largest by far is the Great Barrier Reef, which runs in a 2000km stretch parallel to the eastern coast of Australia.

Figure 8.4 shows a typical underwater view of coral. Coral reefs consist of billions of coral polyps, which live together in reefs, or colonies. Each coral polyp is an animal 2–3cm in length that belongs to the same group as jellyfish and sea anemones. It feeds on minute organisms in the sea. Colonies of polyps establish themselves upon suitable surfaces, which fulfil their requirements for survival. Obtaining minerals from their food supply (minute organisms such as larvae and algae, or plankton)

enables each polyp to secrete calcium carbonate continuously around the lower half of its body, forming a protective chamber like a shell. This occurs at a slow rate – about 1cm per year.

Three-quarters of all living tissue within a coral reef is vegetable. Within each polyp are several yellow-brown granules, consisting of algae. These algae, which are primary producers, have the ability to convert solar energy into fuel through photosynthesis for the consumption of the next trophic level, the consumers. The vast array of colours in coral reefs is due to the presence of different algae reflecting different colours in the sunlight. They exist by absorbing waste from the polyp. They convert its phosphates and nitrates into proteins, and, with sunlight, use carbon dioxide to produce carbohydrates through photosynthesis. In this process they release oxygen, which is what the polyp needs to survive. The relationship is therefore a symbiotic one – the arrangement suits both the polyp and the algae, and each needs the other for survival.

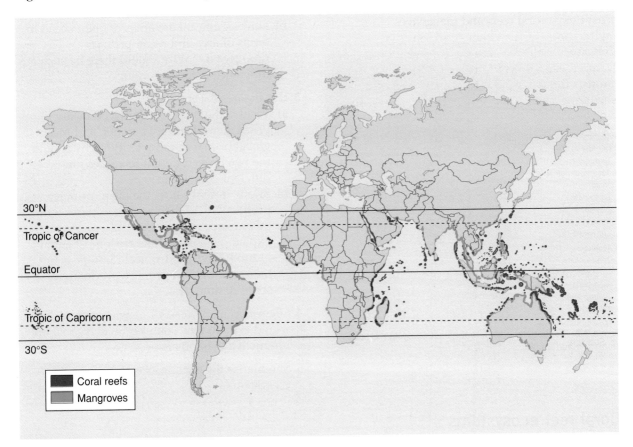

Figure 8.3 The distribution of coral reef ecosystems and mangroves.

Polyps reproduce by sexual (by means of fertilised eggs) and asexual means (by budding). When eggs hatch, new polyps swim and settle elsewhere, thus continuing the process of coral formation. Where budding occurs, filaments grow from the polyp to form buds, which secrete calcium carbonate on top of their parent. Thus buried, the parent polyp dies. The colony therefore consists of layer upon layer of limestone chambers, which accumulate as reefs or atolls. The process of coral building is slow, and a reef ecosystem may never recover if interfered with, either naturally or through human interference.

Reefs are self-sustaining communities. Corals are not only important for the mass of polyps that they support, but also for diverse marine life which is dependent upon the reef for food or security. Reefs contain thousands of species of fish. Some, like parrot fish, feed directly upon polyps, tearing coral to extract them. Starfish produce digestive juices which they squirt into the polyp casings. They then suck out the polyp as a soup. Other species use the protective network of coral on which to base or defend themselves. Clams settle on the coral bed and filter plankton from seawater. Eels live within the coral, pouncing on small fish. Damsel fish live within reach of branching 'antler' corals, filtering plankton from the sea while sheltering within the coral 'forest'. Small hermit crabs, carnivorous fish, sponges and sea horses all contribute to a hugely varied community.

Figure 8.4 Coral reef in the Red Sea.

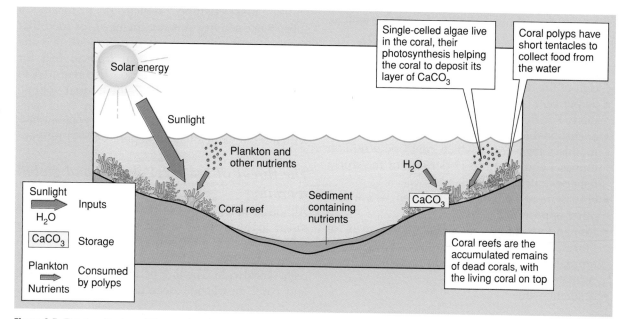

Figure 8.5 The functioning of the coral reef ecosystem.

Coral ecosystems

1 Describe the flow of nutrients within the cycle shown in Figure 8.5.

2 How is the cycle **a)** similar to and **b)** different from that of the forest ecosystem shown in Figure 6.21 on page 95?

3 Why is the kind of diagram used to show nutrient cycling within a forest ecosystem (Figure 6.21) inappropriate for a coral reef ecosystem?

The value of coral reefs

Some scientists liken coral reefs to oases within marine nutrient deserts. Open oceans are nutrient deficient when compared to coral reefs, which act as huge stores of nutrients. Their demise would therefore have a serious impact on the oceans and upon the people who live close to them. The value of coral reef ecosystems can be summarised as follows. They provide:

- as one of the most biologically productive and diverse ecosystems in the world, a source of food for millions of people, and a living for people in many atoll nations, the Indian Ocean and Caribbean islands
- sheltered lagoons and protection from coastal erosion
- protection from wave damage for mangrove ecosystems
- spawning and nursery areas for reef as well as offshore fish
- 10–12 per cent of the harvest of finfish and shellfish in tropical countries and about 25 per cent of the fish catch in LEDCs
- 90 per cent of the animal protein consumed on many Pacific islands
- a sustainable yield of fish, crustaceans and molluscs from reefs, which could be 9 million tonnes – equivalent to 12 per cent of the world fisheries catch
- employment and income in areas where few other opportunities exist
- tremendous tourist potential; coral reefs of Florida alone have generated an estimated annual income of US $1.6 billion from recreational uses
- aesthetic value.

Threats to coral reef ecosystems

Coral reefs around the world are under threat from both human and natural phenomena. This section identifies and explores some of these threats, in both LEDCs and MEDCs. Coral reefs cover only 600 000km^2 of the Earth's surface, tiny in comparison to other biomes (Figure 8.2). Already, 10 per cent have been degraded beyond recovery and another 30 per cent are likely to decline significantly by 2020. There are broadly two types of threat to coral ecosystems: those resulting from short-term human activity, and those arising from longer-term activity that causes global warming, sea-level change and the effects of El Niño.

Harmful fishing practices

Destructive fishing practices, such as blast and cyanide fishing, are becoming increasingly common. This is a clear result of competition for seafood for an ever-growing population in these increasingly popular coastal areas. NOAA (National Oceanic and Atmospheric Administration) report that more than 40 countries are known to have problems with blast fishing on coral reefs, and more than fifteen have reported cyanide fishing.

Fish trade for aquariums

Cyanide is used to stun and capture live coral reef fish for export. However, the consequence of this method of fishing is the death and destruction of corals and hundreds of associated organisms. Unlike blast fishing, which is primarily a subsistence activity, it is not the need for food that encourages this type of practice. Instead, it is the lucrative international trade in tropical fish for aquariums, and the live reef food fish required to support that industry. In 1995, the annual volume of the live reef food fish trade in Asia was estimated to be between 20 000 and 25 000 tonnes, with a retail value of approximately US $1 billion.

The threat of sea-level change and global warming

Although natural causes play a minor role in the threat to coral reefs, they compound the damage inflicted by human activity. The result has been to accelerate the destruction and deterioration of coral reefs worldwide. The link between global warming and coral destruction does not bode well for the future of these ecosystems. The effects of global warming are a threat to the survival of coral reefs. Inadequate levels of sunlight are a concern as sea-levels around the world are set to rise. Inhabitants of the many coral reef archipelagos, such as the Maldives, are Vulnerable becausethey are very low lying.

Greenpeace state that the sea-level rose by 10–25cm over the twentieth century, and will rise 15–95cm over the twenty-first century. If this continues, coral ecosystems may start to experience reduced light conditions that threaten growth. Some species grow quickly, as fast as 20cm per year, and would have no trouble keeping pace with sea-level rises. However, if species diversity is to be maintained conditions need to be optimal for all coral species, including slow-growing varieties.

Coral bleaching

A phenomenon known as coral bleaching has been causing damage to coral reefs on a global scale. Higher than normal sea temperatures are thought to cause this problem, which leads to the exclusion of symbiotic algae. Greenpeace reports that reef-building corals are currently living close to their thermal limit. Sea temperatures are said to be increasing at a rate of approximately 1–2 °C per century. At worst, this can lead to the death of corals, at best to their deterioration. There was catastrophic coral bleaching and coral die-off in 1998 (Figure 8.6), thought to be the most extensive in recent times. Tropical sea temperatures, at a 50-year high at that high at that time, were probably the cause.

Study Figure 8.6.

1 Describe the distribution of coral bleaching events in 1998.

2 Attempt to explain the distribution of the 1998 bleaching events.

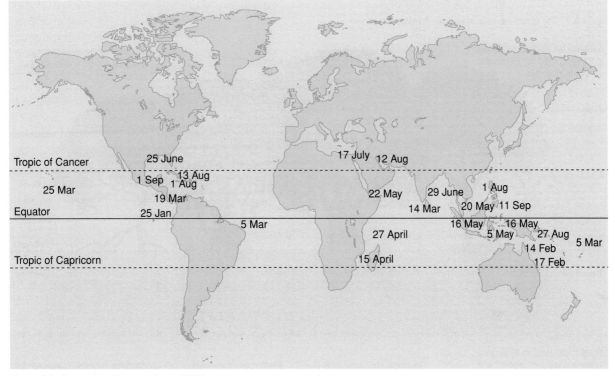

Figure 8.6 Coral bleaching events in 1998.

The effects of El Niño

Changes in weather patterns and phenomena like El Niño are also causing problems for reef ecosystems. The frequency and intensity of hurricanes has increased since 1990, which may be partly due to El Niño. Such storms have devastating effects on coral reefs, and the increase in wave energy during storms can have serious consequences. Sediment generated during storms can bury corals or whole coral communities. The El Niño effect has been strengthening since 1990, with more rapid cycles (see Chapter 3). Before 1980 El Niño disturbances did not exceed thermal tolerances of corals, probably because cycles were lengthy and temperatures had time to cool. It is only since 1980 that coral bleaching events have started to become more common and destructive.

Mangrove forest ecosystems

Figure 8.3 shows that mangrove ecosystems are as productive as their 'partner ecosystem', coral reefs. Mangroves grow in the swampy, muddy waters along coastlines, in what is described as the tidal zone. They are salt-tolerant plants that live on the margins between sea and land (and are therefore known as halophytic); the term 'mangrove' is not the name of a species but the name of a community of unrelated plants living in tropical and semi-tropical areas that are subjected to inundation by tides. They

have been found to exist best where seawater is diluted with about 50 per cent fresh water – hence the preference for low-lying coastal flats.

Few plants have evolved in ways that allow them to tolerate salt, and thus most mangroves are not subject to competition from other species. Mangroves tolerate salt in any of three ways, depending upon the plant:

- by preventing salt entering via root systems
- by excreting salt via glands in the plant – thus leaves may be coated with salt excreted via leaf pores
- by concentrating salt within bark or older leaves which return it to the mud or water when they fall.

Many also conserve water through thick 'waxy' cuticles (or 'skins') on the leaf which reduce the loss of water through transpiration. They have a clear structure (Figure 8.7).

Mangroves have unusual shapes, as low water reveals. Because much of their environment consists of silts and muds, which are mobile or unstable, they have developed root systems that enable them to remain standing (Figure 8.9). The biomass of the majority of mangroves is above ground level; most roots grow within the top 2m of soil or mud. Other species have stilt or spider roots (Figure 8.8), especially those found on the seaward side of a man-

Figure 8.7 The structure of a mangrove forest ecosystem.

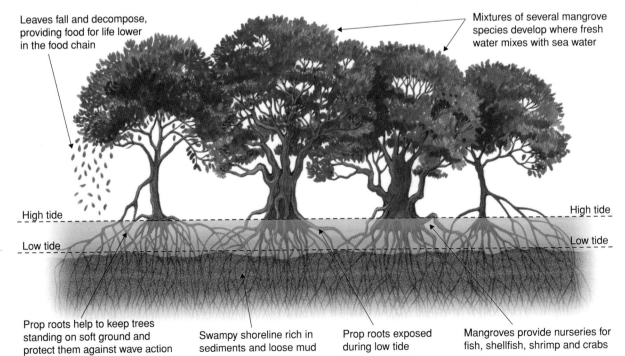

Leaves fall and decompose, providing food for life lower in the food chain

Mixtures of several mangrove species develop where fresh water mixes with sea water

High tide

High tide

Low tide

Low tide

Prop roots help to keep trees standing on soft ground and protect them against wave action

Swampy shoreline rich in sediments and loose mud

Prop roots exposed during low tide

Mangroves provide nurseries for fish, shellfish, shrimp and crabs

Figure 8.8
Root systems in mangroves exposed at low tide on a mud-flat. At high tide these help to trap the sediment shown at their base.

grove, which are oxygen-absorbing. Little oxygen is available in fine mud, and thus the roots are covered in breathing cells, known as lenticels, which draw in air. Oil spills can be fatal to these plants.

The value of mangroves

Some regard mangroves as muddy, mosquito- and crocodile-infested swamps. In fact, 75 per cent of commercially caught fish either spend some part of their life cycle in mangroves, or are dependent upon food chains that can be traced back to them. They also protect the coast by absorbing energy from storm waves and wind, and the sea by trapping sediment in their root systems (Figure 8.8). In this way, sediment clouds are prevented from reaching further out to sea where they could cause the death of whole coral communities.

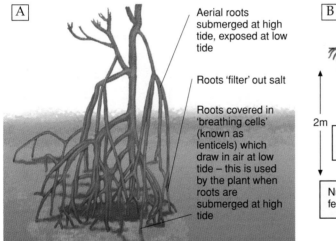

A
Aerial roots submerged at high tide, exposed at low tide

Roots 'filter' out salt

Roots covered in 'breathing cells' (known as lenticels) which draw in air at low tide – this is used by the plant when roots are submerged at high tide

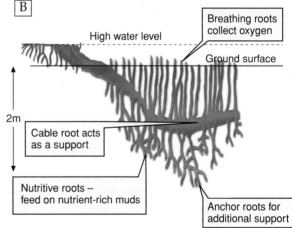

B
Breathing roots collect oxygen
High water level
Ground surface
2m
Cable root acts as a support
Nutritive roots – feed on nutrient-rich muds
Anchor roots for additional support

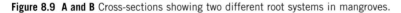

Figure 8.9 A and B Cross-sections showing two different root systems in mangroves.

Numerous medicines are derived from mangroves. Skin disorders and sores, including leprosy, can be treated with infusions or ashes from mangroves. Several conditions can also be treated from mangrove plants including headaches, diarrhoea, rheumatism and snake bites. They have other remarkable qualities. In draining the site of the Olympics village in Sydney before the 2000 Olympic Games, many pollutants would have run into Sydney harbour were it not for the mangroves fringing the edges of Homebush Bay. Many major pollutants, including heavy metals and dioxins, are reduced to harmless compounds after 'cycling' within mangrove communities.

1 To what extent is 'partner ecosystem' a suitable phrase to describe the relationship between mangrove and coral reef ecosystems? Explain your response using the following bullets as a focus for the role of mangroves in:
   • coastal erosion processes
   • ocean waves and currents
   • the marine nutrient cycle
   • sediment deposition
   • maintaining marine life.

2 Refer back to Figure 8.3 and an atlas. Describe and explain the distribution of mangrove ecosystems.

The pollution of marine environments

Look at the collage of photographs and newspaper headings in Figure 8.10. They refer to different incidents from around the world, where pollution of the marine environment is taking place.

Figure 8.10 Major marine pollution incidents.

Japan Battles Huge Oil Spill Off Tokyo with 130 Ships

From the *New York Times*, 3 July 1997.

Cypriot oiltanker burning in the Gulf of Genoa, Italy.

£4 Million Fine For Tanker Spill Is Reduced To £750 000

From the *Independent*, 17 March 2000.

Saundersfoot Beach after *Sea Empress* spill, Pembrokeshire.

Sea pollution puts killer whales under threat – Nature Watch

From the *Sunday Telegraph*, 20 February 2000.

Science: The Underwater Killing Fields

Polluted, Poisoned, Starved and Blown up – Coral Reefs Are Being Destroyed Faster Than Ever Before. But What Can We Do To Save the 'Rainforests of the Sea'?

From the *Independent*, 27 October 2000.

Team attend to Jackass penguin after oil spill on Cape Coast, South Africa.

1 Using the images and information in Figure 8.10, complete the table below by listing as many impacts the incidents would have had under the headings given. As you make the lists, try to categorise them into short-, medium- and long-term impacts.

2 Which incident would you say had the most serious short-term impacts? Which had the most serious long-term impacts?

	Short-term	Medium-term	Long-term
The physical environment			
Possible causes of the incident			
The economy of the area affected and beyond			
The social environment			
The political fallout			

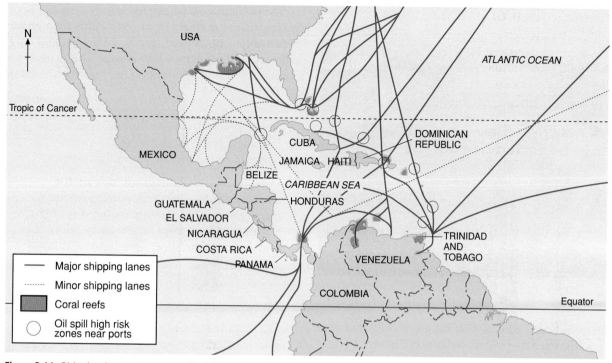

Figure 8.11 Shipping lanes and the threat of oil spills in the Caribbean.

Half of the world's population live within 60km of the coast, which is partly the result of the incredible productivity of coastal ecosystems. It is therefore no surprise that marine ecosystems are under threat from land-based pollution. As the world's population continues to increase and development along coastlines proliferates, threats from pollution will only become worse.

Approximately 80 per cent of marine pollution comes from land-based activities in the form of mangrove clearance, draining of marshland for agriculture, and the development of vacant land for settlements and tourism. The situation is exacerbated in LEDCs where population growth is outstripping the capacity to improve the infrastructure in order to deal with industrial, commercial and domestic waste, and where legal frameworks may be more tolerant of pollution incidents.

The Caribbean is especially under threat with 15 per cent of the world's coral reefs, through which pass almost 25 per cent of the oil transported worldwide by sea (Figure 8.11). Oil tanker spills are a common feature on news programmes today and can have devastating effects on marine ecosystems many kilometres from the site of the accident. In Trinidad, oil companies are increasingly present and are valuable assets to LEDCs. However,

tourism is an equally if not more valuable asset to a country like Trinidad. Obvious conflicts occur between the two, with coral reefs and other ecosystems suffering the consequences.

Feeding the world's people – the potential of aquaculture?

The demand for fish is increasing rapidly throughout the world. Ocean stocks are unable to provide the entire supply, and are in some cases dangerously low. Already Greenpeace and other environmental organisations are calling for a halt to fishing for deep-sea cod in the Atlantic Ocean, fearing the extinction of the species. Aquaculture is considered by many to be the solution. Aquaculture is better known as commercial fish farming (Figure 8.12) and may help to relieve the burden on oceans to provide food for the Earth's rapidly increasing population. However, a counter argument is that it has actually increased demand for some marine fish.

The fish farming industry is growing at such a rapid rate that more fish will come from farms than from the wild by 2020. Already, aquaculture provides 25 per cent of the world's seafood supply. The industry has become part of the globalisation process. A CNN report discovered that the seaside restaurants on the small island of Chios in Greece

Figure 8.12 A fish farm in Thailand.

were not only serving fish caught locally, but also fish from as far afield as India and China.

What methods are used in fish farming?

Aquaculture is already gaining its critics. Some of the destructive methods used today in the fishing industry are mentioned in Figure 8.14 on page 117. However, one less controversial method is Ice Shock. One of the biggest problems for the industry is the need to transport fish quickly to ensure quality and freshness. The Ice Shock method of fish farming overcomes this difficulty. Once ready to be harvested, fish are transferred from pens into a vat containing near freezing water. The fish die within seconds and remain fresh for up to twelve days, ensuring they arrive fresh and ready to serve anywhere in the world. This method of fish farming is considered by industry officials to be more humane than other methods of harvesting.

Managing other inputs for fish farming

Production methods used in aquaculture are coming under increasing scrutiny by national governments, environmental groups and consumers. The growth of young fish is accelerated by over-feeding and the use of antibiotics to ward off infection. Pesticides are used to kill marine or freshwater fauna. Conditions are often cramped, and faecal build-up in fish pens causes de-oxygenation of water. In Thailand, intensive shrimp farms appearing in large numbers in rice fields on the west coast pose a threat to mangrove forests from the use of pesticides, antibiotics and excess feed.

The public has so far proved less discerning about buying fish at markets or in restaurants than about genetically engineered food. Many mistakenly believe that the fish they buy is wild. This is likely to change as more information is publicised about methods adopted.

1 In pairs, identify the components of a fish-farming system by drawing a systems diagram of the inputs, stores and outputs.

2 Using the systems diagram, discuss the social, environmental, economic and health implications of the inputs required for fish farming. Make a copy of the table below and consider the short-, medium- and long-term effects.

Effects	Short-term	Medium-term	Long-term
Social Economic Environmental Health			

Developing sustainable aquaculture in Thailand

This case study looks at the threat to a coastal ecosystem in a LEDC, and how a local project has helped to develop a more sustainable future. It shows how attempts have been made to control over-exploitation of a marine ecosystem. The economic downturn in the Asian economy in the late 1990s following the devaluation of several Asian currencies such as the Thai Baht has created problems. Large trawler companies want the exclusion zone around Thailand to be reduced from 3km to 1km in an attempt to increase their catch. During times of recession, conservation laws and efforts come under pressure as politicians face tough questions on the economy.

Since 1993, Thailand has been the world's largest exporter of fish produced on commercial fish farms. As in many LEDCs, fish provides a major source of protein for Thai people. Of the top 40 countries where fish is the principal source of animal protein, 39 are LEDCs. The fishing industry – or aquaculture – is becoming increasingly important to their economies. Growth is fuelled by demands made by wealthier nations, searching for increasing volumes as well as varieties to satisfy ever more sophisticated or fashionable palates. The opportunity to earn much-needed overseas currency is one factor that is increasing pressure on marine resources. The result is an ecosystem damaged by over-use, and LEDC

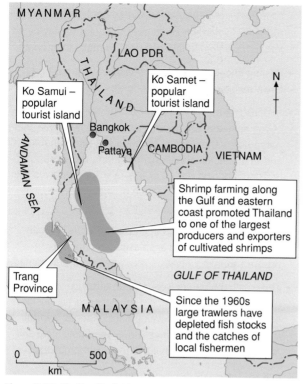

Figure 8.13 Thailand's fishing industry and the location of Trang Province.

Map labels:
MYANMAR
LAO PDR
THAILAND
Ko Samet – popular tourist island
Ko Samui – popular tourist island
Bangkok
Pattaya
CAMBODIA
VIETNAM
ANDAMAN SEA
Shrimp farming along the Gulf and eastern coast promoted Thailand to one of the largest producers and exporters of cultivated shrimps
Trang Province
GULF OF THAILAND
Since the 1960s large trawlers have depleted fish stocks and the catches of local fishermen
MALAYSIA
N
0   500 km

Yadfon work to conserve marine ecosystems on the west coast of Thailand

Yadfon means 'teardrop' and is the name given to the NGO working in Thailand to help poorer fishing families. As well as helping the poor, it also aims to conserve the local marine ecosystem, which provides their livelihood. Formed in 1985, it was the first Thai NGO devoted to coastal conservation.

The success of the organisation lies in involving the very people it is trying to help. Many different people at different levels have something to offer Yadfon as well as something to gain from its success. These people are referred to as 'stakeholders'; for fishing families, the stake is their livelihood and quality of life. Yadfon realised that to help the poor it would be necessary for them to work together as a team, rather than as individuals. If they were to take on large corporations and government agencies in their fight to protect the marine ecosystem, then they would have to learn new skills, build self-confidence, and in short create social capital in the community. They would also have to form alliances with other groups if their effort was to succeed. They saw five groups as key players:

- local communities
- civil servants

populations having to go without their traditional source of protein as fish stocks are exported.

The valuable mangrove forest ecosystem in Trang Province (Figure 8.13) on the west coast of Thailand has been under threat from deforestation for a number of years. Large swaths of the forest have been cut down by businesses for the production of charcoal. Local people worked for these businesses, not totally aware of the effects a depleted mangrove ecosystem would have on seafood supplies. An organisation known as Yadfon has tried to manage some of the mangrove problems, summarised in Figure 8.14.

- Continued haphazard removal of mangroves led to erosion and the silting of waterways, choking 'partner' seagrass and coral ecosystems.

- Destructive fishing practices were used by local fishermen, using dynamite, cyanide and pushnets which drag along the sea floor, destroying coral and seagrass species.

- Larger trawlers knowingly fished illegally within three kilometres of the shore. The use of destructive dragnets in this exclusion zone wreaked havoc on all 'partner' ecosystems.

Figure 8.14 Misuse of the marine ecosystem in Trang Province

1 Formation of community organisations that could initiate and carry out their own projects (investment in 'social capital')
2 Revival of the degraded mangrove forests by:
- petitioning government officials to prohibit further tree cutting in the communal area
- marking the boundary between communal areas and loggers' land
- replanting the mangrove tree, Rhizophora
- involving the provincial governor, who was shocked by the poverty and signs of child malnutrition
- creating an inter-village network, with regular meetings to share information and ideas
- training workshops and taking the local population on study tours
- gaining Government recognition as 'a community-managed mangrove forest'
- twice yearly planting festivals involving people from government, fishery and forestry officers
- encouraging small fishing people to stop using destructive fishing practices
- setting exclusion zones for boats and destructive pushnets with trunks of coconut trees
- placing marker buoys and signs.

Figure 8.15 How Yadfon revived coastal ecosystems.

- academics
- the media
- small business people.

1 Refer to theYadfon case study.
   a) Explain what you understand by the term 'stakeholder' and 'social capital'. What relevance does each have to this issue?
   b) Identify other stakeholders in addition to the fishing families.

2 Evaluate the role played by each stakeholder in contributing to Yadfon. Use Figure 8.15.

3 What are the potential benefits of involving stakeholders in the project?

4 Yadfon saw the small business link as the weakest in the chain. Outline the reasons why this was so.

5 Summarise how the 'social capital' of communities with whom Yadfon worked had improved.

- Fish stocks gradually increased as sea life returned to the area. Fishermen could save time and money by no longer travelling so far out to sea to make their catch.

- Fishing once again became a viable living; cutting down mangrove trees was no longer the only option.

- In 1995, a bonus was achieved by the revitalisation of the seagrass ecosystem, when dugongs made their home here. The dugong is related to the manatee and is a species almost extinct along the west coast of Thailand. The arrival of any rare species gives the whole effort a greater chance of success, and support from governing bodies.

- By involving the five groups over the years through consensus rather than aggression, each group ensured that conservation measures were maintained.

- The local community were now an effective voice and could face up to government officials and big business on equal terms. The development of social capital within the community meant they were now more self-sufficient and able to manage their own problems.

Figure 8.16 The results achieved from conservation work by the local community with support of Yadfon.

Summary

You have learned that:
- The world's coastal marine ecosystems are ecologically highly productive.
- Coral reefs can be seen as having a structure and function, and an ecological value.
- Mangroves play a very significant part in maintaining marine ecosystems.
- Both natural and human activities are leading to coral reef deterioration.
- Pressures on coastal ecosystems such as pollution and fishing are leading to depletion of fish stocks.
- Fish farming is a viable way of meeting demand for fish; but there are environmental costs.
- Protection and conservation of corals is taking place in some areas of the world through sustainable management of fisheries and pollution control. This contrasts with exploitation elsewhere.

References and further reading

Web sites

The Coral Reef Alliance: http://www.coral.org
Reef Relief: http://www.reefrelief.org
NOAA: http://www.noaa.gov
World Resources Institute: http://www.wri.org
Center for Marine Conservation: http://www.cmc-ocean.org

For regular updates on environmental issues, visit CNN's web page http://www.cnn.com and register to get regular emails
A similar service is provided by the Environmental News Network at http://www.enn.com

9 Fight the good fight

There are many organisations working on countless projects to protect the world's ecosystems. This chapter focuses on just one: Greenpeace. Greenpeace's homepage (Figure 9.1) highlights the diverse nature of this organisation's interests, from genetic engineering to nuclear energy. This chapter looks at one of Greenpeace's most visible campaigns: its fight to ban whaling.

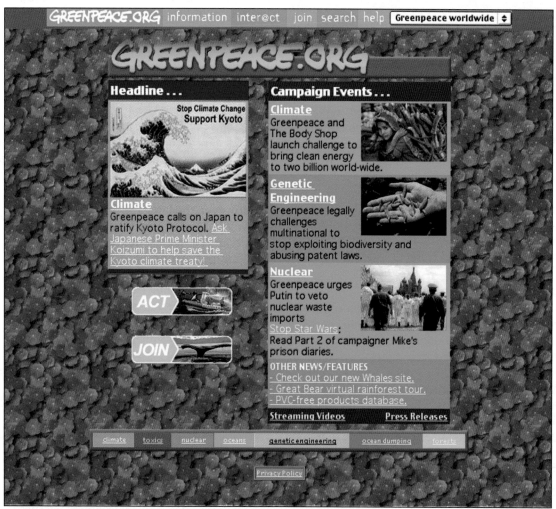

Figure 9.1 Greenpeace's home page, www.greenpeace.org

1 Using the home page for Greenpeace, summarise campaigns in which it is involved, and where these are taking place.

2 Produce a global 'hot spot' map showing key conservation issues in which Greenpeace and other organisations are involved.

The issue of whaling

Figure 9.2 Whales in the wild.

Whaling is an issue often associated with the Greenpeace organisation. You will read many articles calling for the worldwide ban on whaling, which quote conservation groups as well as governments from around the world such as the UK, New Zealand and the USA. However, there are countries that do not support this ban and are considered to be rogue nations. The country that receives most criticism is Japan; others include Norway, Greenland and Iceland.

The politics of whaling

The International Whaling Commission (IWC), based in the UK, was established in 1946. Accused of not being effective in its fight to protect whales, the commission banned commercial whaling in 1986. It currently has 200 members from 40 nations; its purpose is the conservation of whales and management of whaling. In 1972, it had fourteen members of whom eight were whaling nations. By 1982, this had changed to 39 nations, nine of whom conducted whaling.

New members of the IWC have caused controversy. Anti-whaling groups have accused Japan of encouraging LEDCs to become members of the IWC in return for foreign aid. Environmental groups argue that new members feel obliged to vote in favour of Japan when decisions are made to lift or impose bans on whaling. In order to make changes 75 per cent of the members have to vote in favour of the proposed change. The more allies Japan and other whaling nations have in the IWC, the harder it is for the anti-whaling movement.

Dominica, a tiny nation in the Caribbean, amazed delegates at an IWC meeting in Adelaide, Australia. The Dominican Environment Minister resigned over his country's vote against the motion for a protected whale sanctuary in the South Pacific. 'There is absolutely no reason for us to be held to ransom by Japan in return for promises of aid,' he announced.

Scientific research – is it needed?

Whaling nations such as Norway and Japan state that it is vital to learn more about whales and that they therefore need to catch whales for study. They are accused of using this as an excuse. Many conservation groups argue that research can be carried out without harming the animals. At present, most research carried out on the ecological role of whales, dolphins and porpoises does not involve killing the animal.

However, the Japanese answer that they need to know what is eaten by whales. In countries where the ocean is a main source of income and food, the growing population of whales is causing concern as their potential catches are consumed.

On the other hand, Greenpeace courts the world's media and has millions of supporters worldwide. Whaling is only one of their causes, but it really catches the public's imagination. The photograph in Figure 9.6 is used by anti-whaling groups such as Greenpeace to get their message across. Anyone faced with these sorts of images is led to one conclusion: whaling is barbaric, unnecessary and should be banned. However, there are two sides to every story, the issue of whaling included. The next section reviews how Iceland deals with the issue.

The view from Iceland, a whaling nation

This case study looks at whaling from a different perspective, a perspective not often aired by the world's press, and certainly not one shared by environmental groups such as Greenpeace.

Read the three articles in Figures 9.3, 9.4 and 9.5.

1 Identify the key players in the whaling debate according to these three articles.

2 In groups, categorise the key players as pro-whaling or anti-whaling.

3 Summarise the key arguments used by each group to support their point of view.

4 Is it important to know who is writing the article? Explain your answer.

40 per cent of Japanese indifferent to whaling issue, survey finds

While only one in ten Japanese say they support whaling against a slightly higher number who oppose it, nearly 40 per cent appear uncommitted, according to a survey. The survey, by the International Fund for Animal Welfare (IFAW) and Greenpeace International, covered 1185 adults across Japan. Only 10 per cent said they fear Japan's cultural identity would suffer if Japan were to stop whaling, while 35 per cent said it would not suffer very much or not at all. Only 18 per cent said they are prepared to face the consequences of continued whaling on the country's economy or international reputation.

On eating whale meat, 13 per cent said they have never eaten it and 48 per cent said they have not eaten it since childhood; only 1 per cent said they eat it once a month. Nobody ate whale meat more than once a month. Eleven per cent said they support Japanese whaling, 14 per cent said they oppose it, and 39 per cent said they neither support nor oppose it.

Kazuo Yamamura, director general of the Institute of Cetacean Research, said: 'Unlike rice, whale meat is not eaten so often by the Japanese people. However, the meat is a traditional cuisine. You cannot ignore local culture by calling it a minority.'

Figure 9.3 Adapted from the *Japan Times*, 21 September 2000.

Japan disregards Blair and Clinton and starts new whale hunt in North Pacific

Greenpeace today condemned Japan's decision to expand its 'scientific' whaling and to kill three protected whale species in the North Pacific, despite opposition from the International Whaling Commission (IWC) and appeals from President Clinton and Tony Blair.

'Japan has shown its determination to resume commercial whaling whatever the cost', said Richard Page of Greenpeace. 'The international community should intervene and stop Japan from riding roughshod over world opinion, scientific consensus and the will of the IWC.'

The Japanese fleet of catcher boats aims to kill 50 Bryde's and ten sperm whales this year in the seas off the coast of Japan, as well as 100 minke whales. Both Bryde's and sperm whales were heavily exploited in the past and their populations remain unknown. Japan kills over 500 whales annually via a loophole in the IWC's rules that allows whaling for scientific research. It claims that its hunt in the North Pacific is to research interactions between whales and their prey species. The meat will be sold as a delicacy in Japan.

Figure 9.4 Adapted from the Greenpeace web site.

Japan whales, the US wails

While President Bill Clinton is busy issuing threats against Japan, the Japanese are proceeding with their whale hunt. President Clinton announced that he will deny Japan fishing rights in US waters. Currently there is no foreign fishing in US waters, so this means nothing but maintaining the status quo. On a number of occasions the US has threatened to impose sanctions on countries such as Canada, Iceland, Japan, Norway and Russia because of their whaling activities. However, sanctions have never been implemented. There are several reasons for this:

- the Japanese catch complies with the UN Law of the Sea and the International Convention for the Regulation of Whaling
- US sanctions would violate World Trade Organisation (WTO) rules – Japan has indicated that if sanctions are imposed, it will complain to the WTO
- US groups are worried that imposing sanctions could damage sales to their most important agricultural export market, Japan.

US authorities also estimate that there are 2 million sperm whales worldwide. 'How can a catch of ten animals out of a total population of 2 million threaten the species?' asks Frovik.

Figure 9.5 Adapted from the High North Alliance web site.

Iceland is an isolated nation of 280 000 inhabitants bordering the Arctic Circle. Its economy is dominated by its reliance on resources from the ocean. Marine products account for nearly 75 per cent of Iceland's income as well as 50 per cent of all foreign currency earnings. Whaling is deeply rooted in Icelandic culture and references to whaling can be traced as far back as the thirteenth century.

The Marine Research Institute, Reykjavik, views the world's portrayal of the plight of whales as unrealistic. It takes the view that because of over-

Figure 9.6 A whale being flensed.

Figure 9.7 Minke whale harpooned by Japanese whaling ship in the Ross Sea.

Using the material in this chapter and further individual research, divide into two groups for a debate of the motion: 'The rights of people to whaling should be a matter for a country's population.' One half should take the role of Greenpeace and other anti-whaling bodies, the other the role of pro-whaling nations/bodies.

hunting of whales in the past, the whale has become a symbol of the crusade to conserve the environment. Instead of conserving and using whale stocks, environmental groups advocate a total ban. The Icelandic position on whaling has been that whales should be used sustainably.

In 1999 the Icelandic assembly voted to begin whaling in its own waters for the first time since 1989 in compliance with international law. It uses the following laws and protocols to support whaling in its own national waters:

- The United Nations Convention on the Law of the Sea (1982) clearly states that coastal nations can use the resources within their exclusive economic zone.
- The North Atlantic Marine Mammal Commission sees any total ban as conflicting with conservation and management of whale stocks.
- Any sanctions imposed in respect of whaling would violate international law for members of the World Trade Organisation.

So, who's right?

This issue will remain hot for many years. The questions remain:

- Should any country or group of countries impose cultural values on another?
- Should all whales be protected even when their numbers are considered to be sufficient by specialists in this field?
- Is the method of killing unacceptable?
- Should fisherman's livelihoods hang in the balance because of over-consumption of fish stocks by some whale species?

Summary

You have learned that:

- Different people play different decision-making roles depending upon their values and attitudes.
- Pressure groups exist to influence the ways in which decisions are made; some are extremely effective in gaining global media attention.
- People in government or specialists such as scientists may conflict with environmental pressure groups in the development of policies for conservation.
- Economic and environmental motives frequently conflict.

References and further reading

Web sites

Greenpeace:www.greenpeace.org
High North Alliance: www.highnorth.no
Japan Whaling Association:
www.jp-whaling-assn.com

International Whaling Commission:
http://ourworld.compuserve.com/homepages/
iwcoffice/

Heritage for the future

Managing special environments

Ecosystem management is becoming increasingly important at all levels – local, national and international. Examples of successful management are being sought around the world to see if they can be used with equal success in different settings. Many ecosystems have been designated as having global scientific value and are targeted for conservation. This results in conflict between development and conservation efforts, which is a common issue throughout the world.

How can development and conservation be balanced? Ecosystems of scientific value can also be of value in the development of a nation's economy. This chapter is about some of the conflicts between conservation and development. It shows how different strategies can be adopted,

through studies of World Heritage Areas with high biodiversity: the Galapagos Islands of Ecuador and the Daintree World Heritage Coast in northern Queensland, Australia. It also explores the effectiveness of global strategies for environmental improvement, in particular the 1992 Rio Summit.

The value of World Heritage listing – the Galapagos Islands, Ecuador

The Galapagos Islands lie on the Equator some 970km off the coast of Ecuador in the Pacific Ocean. There are six major islands two of which are uninhabited, twelve smaller ones and numerous islets. The population of 10 000 is growing at a rapid rate because of immigration. The catalyst for this is the development of tourism on the islands.

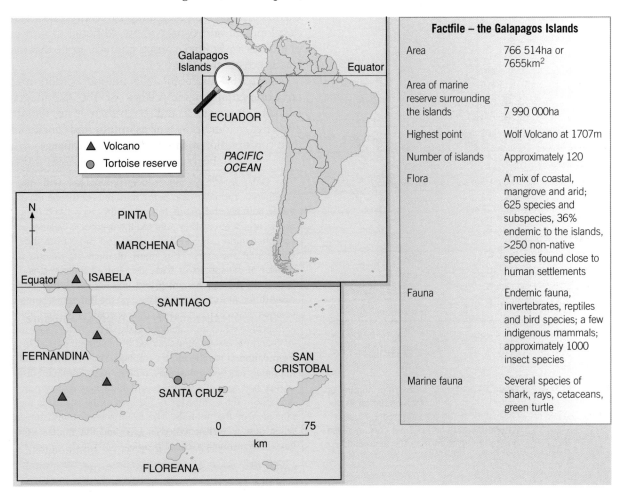

Factfile – the Galapagos Islands	
Area	766 514ha or 7655km^2
Area of marine reserve surrounding the islands	7 990 000ha
Highest point	Wolf Volcano at 1707m
Number of islands	Approximately 120
Flora	A mix of coastal, mangrove and arid; 625 species and subspecies, 36% endemic to the islands, >250 non-native species found close to human settlements
Fauna	Endemic fauna, invertebrates, reptiles and bird species; a few indigenous mammals; approximately 1000 insect species
Marine fauna	Several species of shark, rays, cetaceans, green turtle

Figure 10.1 The Galapagos Islands.

Tourist Mecca versus conservationist's dream

Figure 10.2 A threatened community? The Galapagos Islands (a) and its marine biodiversity (b).

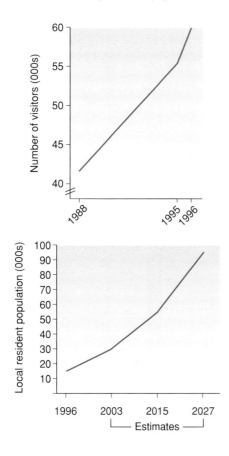

Figure 10.3 The increase in the number of visitors and local human population in the Galapagos. (Estimates assume 1.7 per cent natural increase and 6.1 per cent increase due to immigration from the mainland.)

Unique wildlife and gigantic volcanic peaks make for a destination for tourists seeking something different and special. Conversely it is an ideal site for the conservationist to protect and study, so the islands provide a classic example of conflict between development and conservation. Although numbers of tourists are limited, conservationists argue that the fragile ecosystem is under threat.

Figure 10.4 highlights the unique wildlife and environmental characteristics of the Galapagos Islands. However, if this ecosystem is to remain attractive to tourists as well as unique and functional then conservation management is imperative.

The Galapagos have never been connected with the continent. Gradually, over many hundreds of thousands of years, animals and plants from over the sea arrived there and as time went by they adapted themselves to Galapagos conditions and came to differ more and more from their continental ancestors. Thus many of them are unique: a quarter of the species of shore fish, half of the plants and almost all the reptiles are found nowhere else. In many cases different forms have evolved on the different islands. Charles Darwin recognized this speciation within the archipelago when he visited the Galapagos on the *Beagle* in 1835 and his observations played a substantial part in his formulation of the theory of evolution. Since no large land mammals reached the islands, reptiles were dominant just as they had been all over the world in the very distant past. Another of the extraordinary features of the islands is the tameness of the animals. The islands were uninhabited when they were discovered in 1535 and the animals still have little instinctive fear of people.

Figure 10.4 From the tourist guide, *South American Handbook*, by Ben Box.

Conservation management in the Galapagos

The Ecuadorian government designated the islands a national park in 1959 for their unique scientific interest; UNESCO, who placed them on the World Heritage list in 1978, calls them 'a natural laboratory of evolution'. But tourism as a means of economic development conflicts with conservation. UNESCO reports that the tourist industry is growing at an extraordinary pace. In the Asia-Pacific region alone, estimates indicate that tourist revenues, which were $805 billion in 1995, will grow at an annual rate of approximately 80 per cent by 2005. Figure 10.6 shows other barriers to effective conservation management.

1959	Designated a national park by Ecuadorian government.
1960	Ecuadorian government bans hunting of tortoises and seals, and plans to eliminate pests that have destroyed flora such as goats, control the pig population to conserve the tortoise population, and establish breeding programs for tortoise and land iguanas.
1974	First Management Plan approved. Revised again in 1984 and 1994.
1978	UNESCO placed the Islands on the World Heritage List.
1986	Galapagos Marine Resources Reserve (GMRR) created within 15 nautical miles.
1987	A draft Management Plan for the GMRR outlined four zones: • general use (for sustainable use of the reserve) • work and recreational fishing zones for residents • National Marine Park zones for human activities where natural resources are neither damaged nor removed • strict Nature Reserves where human access is not permitted. The plan was not approved until 1992.
1995	National Park Service given legal authority to patrol for illegal fishing.
1996	UNESCO decides it may put the islands on the World Heritage Danger List.
1997	President issues an emergency decree to draft a 'Special Law' for the islands, one objective of which is to control the population of the islands.

Figure 10.5 Towards a conservation management plan for the Galapagos Islands.

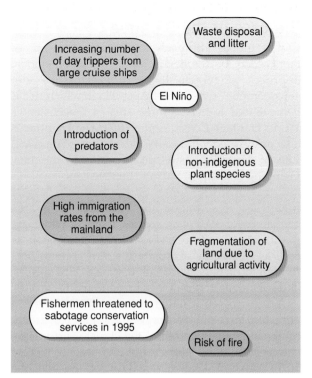

Figure 10.6 Barriers to effective conservation management.

You decide

1 Take each of the issues in Figure 10.6. Suggest:
   a) why each may be a risk
   b) what measures might be needed to prevent risks from occurring.

2 Form groups to represent the Ecuadorian government, UNESCO, the Galapagos National Park Service and a major tourist operator in the Islands. Using information in this section, each group should prepare a brief statement outlining how they would like to see the Galapagos Islands World Heritage Site developed and managed in the future.

3 After the presentations, consider the following:
   a) Is there common ground between the organisations?
   b) Who stands to lose most
      • if the Islands are not managed effectively
      • if they are managed too strictly?
   c) Should outsiders such as UNESCO or overseas nations have a say?
   d) Would the story be any different if the Islands were in an MEDC?
   e) Is it too late for the Galapagos Islands?

Local councils and conservation – the case of the Daintree

Can a global approach to the conservation of biodiversity be the best solution? Or is a regional approach preferable to take local issues into consideration? One area of Australia in which this is being tested is the Daintree area of Queensland's World Heritage Coast (Figure 10.7). The Daintree is also acknowledged as a World Heritage Site. One-fifth of Australia's bird species reside in the area, including cockatoos, parrots, honeyeaters, lorikeets and cassowaries; some of the world's largest butterflies live among the branches. The area contains over 3500 plant species, many of which are particular not only to Australia but to this region, as well as two-thirds of Australia's fern species, one-third of its orchids, half of all Australian bird species, and over a quarter of all fish, frog and reptile species.

Yet the region is under pressure. Tourism is fast attracting large numbers of people to the area, drawn by the attractive warmth of the climate and unique combination of coastline, forest and beaches (Figure 10.8). With Cairns International Airport less than one hour's drive away, numbers of tourists to this part of northern Queensland are rising fast. Many people see this area as an opportunity to move and adopt a new relaxed lifestyle while enjoying a quality of life that they feel cannot be had elsewhere. But the very numbers involved, and the building that is required to accommodate everyone, means that the character of the area is changing. Should it be protected from further development? If so, how?

Figure 10.8 The World Heritage Coast near Port Douglas.

	1991	1996–7	1999	% annual growth 1991–9
Day trippers	172 400	258 200	299 138	7.6
Overnight visitors	50 700	99 800	127 231	13.1
Total	**223 100**	**358 000**	**426 369**	**9**

Figure 10.9 Pressures on the World Heritage Coast – the growth in visitor numbers.

As a result of visitor pressure, population in the region is also threatening to rise as services and business opportunities increase. The local council has decided to put forward a plan to limit population growth in the area. It has revised downwards its previous estimates of the number of people who could be sustained within the area without environmental damage from 2400 people to 1200–1400. A limit of about 2400 has also been placed upon the number of overnight beds in the area. Most visitors for the foreseeable future are therefore likely to be day visitors.

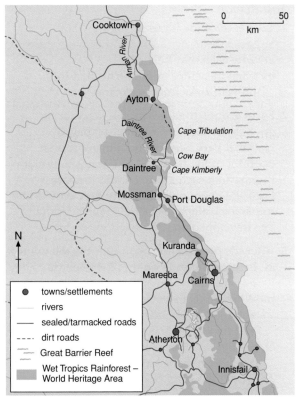

Figure 10.7 The Daintree World Heritage Coast in northern Queensland.

1 How far do you agree with the idea that a World Heritage area such as the Daintree should be limited in its population numbers?

2 Refer to Figure 10.9. Should a similar limit be placed upon visitor numbers? Why?

The Rio Summit

In 1992, the first Earth Summit was held in Rio de Janeiro in Brazil. Its purpose was to address problems of environmental protection and socio-economic development (Figure 10.10). The summit was ambitious in its aim that issues such as biodiversity should be addressed and that all countries should sign up to international agreements to protect and conserve species and the environment. Could worldwide co-operation and international legislation ever be effective in managing global ecosystems? The conference generated a good deal of enthusiasm, and a follow-up Global Earth Summit was scheduled for 2002. This section looks at attempts to manage ecosystems on a global scale through the adoption of global legislation.

Date: 3–14 June 1992

Cost: $123 million

In attendance: over 100 heads of state, 178 countries represented, 8749 media people

Objective: to address problems of environmental protection and socio-economic development

Agreements signed/endorsements:

- Convention on Climatic Change
- Convention on Biological Diversity
- Rio Declaration
- Forest Principles
- Adoption of Agenda 21 (a plan for achieving sustainable development in the twenty-first century)

Figure 10.10 The Rio Summit, 1992.

The achievements of Rio 1992

One of the most publicised achievements of the Rio Summit was Agenda 21 – the Rio Declaration on Environment and Development, and the Statement of Principles for the Sustainable Management of Forests. More than 178 governments adopted the

All Agenda 21 Issues	
Agriculture	Information
Atmosphere	Integrated decision-making
Biodiversity	International law
Biotechnology	Institutional arrangements
Capacity-building	Land management
Consumption and	Major groups
production patterns	Mountains
Demographics	Oceans and seas
Desertification and drought	Poverty
Education and awareness	Science
Energy	Small islands
Finance	Sustainable tourism
Forests	Technology
Freshwater	Toxic chemicals
Health	Trade and environment
Human settlements	Transport
Indicators	Waste (hazardous)
Industry	Waste (radioactive)
	Waste (solid)

Figure 10.11 Agenda 21 issues.

agenda and as a result, the Commission on Sustainable Development (CSD) was created to monitor and report on progress made on agreements signed in Rio. Figure 10.11 shows the ambitious nature and scope set by Agenda 21. In the UK, local councils have been required to adopt Agenda 21 policies for sustainable development in their localities.

The Rio Earth Summit has received much criticism. Many conclude that little has been achieved, with little sign of improvement. Even during the summit itself, rumours spread of 700 street children in Rio who were said to have been murdered before the summit in an effort to clean up the city before the world's media arrived.

However focused its aims, progress since the summit is far from good.

- The USA refused to sign the Biodiversity Treaty, fearing for their biotechnology industry. The Biodiversity Convention required those nations signing the treaty to produce national plans to recognise and locate the biodiversity within their borders and to create protected areas for their conservation.
- The USA complained further about requirements for biotechnology transfers to LEDCs from where raw materials for this type of research come. They wanted the freedom to research into genetic 'pools', many of which exist in LEDCs.

• The USA was accused by many of hindering negotiations at Rio. The US view was that measures to protect the environment might interfere with the workings of the free market or reduce the rate of economic growth. What solution or treaty would work without US support?

The role of transnational corporations

If global action is agreed to by governments, how can private companies be made to comply? According to the research organisation Worldwatch, the number of transnational corporations (TNCs) grew from 7000 in 1970 to an estimated 53 600 in 1998, with 450 000 foreign subsidiaries. Many critics of the achievements of the Rio Earth Summit blame TNCs for the lack of progress since 1992. TNCs are seen as primarily responsible for ozone depletion, global warming, toxic contamination, pesticide proliferation, international trade in hazardous substances and other practices that threaten human health and the environment. They are accused of generating economic growth and consumerism at the expense of people and the environment. Chapter 19 explores the issue of TNCs further.

1 Why would the support of the USA be essential to any negotiations or treaties about the environment?

2 How do you view the charges that TNCs are responsible for 'ozone depletion, global warming, toxic contamination, pesticide proliferation, international trade in hazardous substances and other practices that threaten human health and the environment'? Justify your views.

Global legislation and UNEP

Can global legislation conserve the world's marine ecosystems? A global framework has been established through the United Nations Environmental Programme (UNEP). UNEP has been successful in fostering agreement between governments on a regional scale through the Regional Seas Programme. Figure 10.12 shows the eighteen regional seas under UNEP.

Why regional and not one global convention? UNEP's view is that every regional sea has its own unique environmental problems and requirements. To try and apply a single approach to all areas would not only be difficult, but perhaps counter-productive as the needs of a particular region would not be met. Furthermore, interested parties, i.e. governments, are more likely to take part in a plan suited to their local needs, and as a result the conservation effort is more likely to succeed.

International agreements are in place to minimise impacts on marine ecosystems. UNEP describes the aim of these as an attempt to:
• regulate pollution from maritime activity
• control trade in endangered marine species
• curb the hunting of endangered whales
• protect coastal sites of universal value
• trace the effects of climate change on marine ecosystems
• deal with pollution from land-based activities.

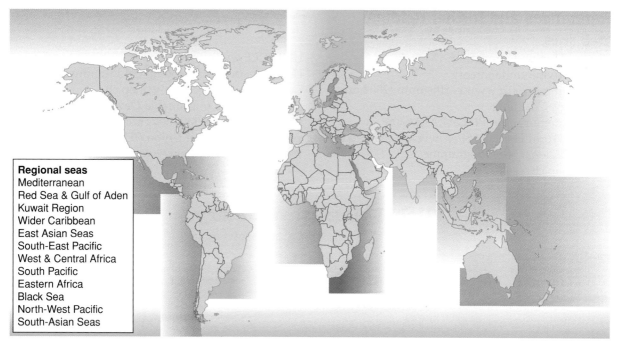

Figure 10.12 The UNEP regional seas.

Regional seas
Mediterranean
Red Sea & Gulf of Aden
Kuwait Region
Wider Caribbean
East Asian Seas
South-East Pacific
West & Central Africa
South Pacific
Eastern Africa
Black Sea
North-West Pacific
South-Asian Seas

1 What do you see as the strengths of the idea of international law? What are its weaknesses?

2 Make a copy of the table opposite. In pairs, identify what you see to be the strengths and weaknesses of the five management attempts to conserve areas of ecological interest.

3 Which actions, if any, seem most effective? Are others needed?

4 How effective do international agreements seem to be in controlling these issues? Should they be more effective? How could they be introduced and monitored?

Strategy	Strengths	Weaknesses
Actions taken by governments, e.g. the limitation on tourist numbers in the Galapagos Islands		
Actions taken by international organisations such as UNESCO to identify and conserve World Heritage Areas		
Local actions taken by councils, such as the attempts to limit population in the Daintree rainforest		
World Summits such as the Rio Summit in 1992		
Global legislation such as UNEP		

Summary

You have learned that:

- The conservation of environments conflicts with development.
- There are global strategies for the conservation of global ecosystems which are of scientific value. Some are considered to be of World Heritage value while others represent areas of high biodiversity.
- Strategic thinking is needed to protect and manage global ecosystems in a sustainable way, and for local developments to play an important role.
- World Summits bring attention to environmental issues and have some positive effects. However, they require the compliance of all countries, particularly those in the best position to help make them succeed.
- Worldwide legislation can be effective in maintaining marine ecosystems.
- Small-scale sustainable initiatives also bring success where they involve local communities in conservation measures.

References and further reading

Web sites

Charles Darwin Foundation:
www.darwinfoundation.org
Earth Summit 2002: www.earthsummit2002.org
Galapagos Coalition:
www.law.emory.edu/PI/GALAPAGOS
Natural World Heritage Sites: www.wcmc.org.uk
UNEP Regional Seas Programme:
www.unep.ch/seas

UNESCO: www.unesco.org
United Nations Environmental Programme –
Geneva Homepage: www.unep.ch
United Nations Sustainable Development Issues:
www.un.org/esa/sustdev/issues.html
World Conservation Union (IUCN): www.iucn.org
Worldwatch Institute: www.worldwatch.org

Global biomes: summary

Enquiry questions	Key ideas and concepts	Guidance and possible examples
Introducing Biomes What factors are responsible for the pattern of global biomes? What is the importance of global ecosystems? What are the threats to their survival?	• Concept of world biomes and their global distribution. Factors influencing distribution – role of climate. Variations in primary productivity. The increasing influence of human activities leading to very few truly natural ecosystems. • The importance of ecosystems environmentally (CO_2/O_2 regulatory mechanisms), hydrologically (micro-climate role) and economically (products, tourism, etc). • Threats from human activities and the loss of biodiversity.	• Chapter 5 How biomes function on the basis of primary productivity and physical conditions such as climate. The increasing pressure caused by human activities. The environmental and economic role played by biomes. Threats to biomes posed by human activities. The loss of biodiversity. The diversity of threats to ecosystems, e.g. exploitation, population, pollution, global warming – case studies in RTZ (Madagascar), Zanzibar.
Global ecological causes and management of threats **Either** Why has the degradation of the world's forests become such a global issue? Why are forest biomes difficult to conserve?	Choose one from forests or marine ecosystems to illustrate causes of ecological threats and their management: • Distribution of the world's major forest types. Comparison of structure/functioning and ecological value. • Issues of forest degradation in a variety of forests, looking at comparative causes and rates of destruction, and regeneration. Issues of wilderness and future of indigenous peoples. • Possible solutions to forest degradation, via conservation, sustainable management, reforestation.	• Chapter 6 The importance of ecological value of coniferous, deciduous, rainforests. Nutrient cycling, trophic levels, energy flows in temperate rainforests, boreal, and broad-leaf woodlands to assess causes and rates of degradation. The role of climate in differentiating forest types – coniferous, deciduous, tropical. Comparing forests – structure, function, productivity and value. Degradation, and rates of destruction and regeneration: Padley Woods. • Chapter 7 Forest conservation schemes – Korup and Kilum. Agroforestry. Debt for nature. Assessment of progress worldwide. Timber trade between LEDCs and MEDCs.
Or Why is it important to safeguard the world's marine ecosystems? What are the pressures on coastal ecosystems?	• Distribution of world's coastal marine ecosystems • Comparison of structure/functioning and ecological value. • An assessment of the natural and human causes of coral reef deterioration. • Pressures on coastal ecosystems – pollution, exploitation (fishing). • Protection and conservation of corals. • Development of sustainable use of fisheries.	• Chapter 8 The world distribution of coastal marine ecosystems. Nutrient cycling, trophic levels, energy flows, ecological value of coral reefs and mangroves. Pressures, e.g. bleaching, fishing and tourism, in coral reefs in contrasting areas. Fish farming and marine pollution. Sustainable fish management in Thailand, pollution control strategies contrasting with exploitation.
Global eco-futures How are individuals and organisations playing an increasing part in ecosystem management? What is the future for global ecosystems?	• Consideration of the roles people play as decision makers as individuals, group members, or in private companies or public organisations as scientists, managers etc. • Conservation of environments; the essential conflict between development and conservation in global ecosystems of agreed scientific value. • The need for strategic thinking to protect and manage global ecosystems in a sustainable way, and for local developments to play an important role. (Community forestry or local coral reef conservation.)	• Chapter 9 The role of decision makers in developing conservation areas; evaluating Greenpeace and the whaling issue in Iceland and Japan. • Chapter 8 Areas of world heritage value and high biodiversity – Galapagos and the Daintree. • Chapter 10 Global overview (e.g. Rio Summit). Global legislation (e.g. on marine ecosystems). Small-scale sustainable development – the Daintree; evaluating its success.

Global population

Introducing the global population challenge

People and the global economy

Figure 1 Demonstration in Prague, 2000.

Figure 2 TNCs dominate advertising in Oaxaca, Mexico.

In an otherwise peaceful country, riots stand out. They grab the attention of the media and lead to fears of lawlessness and violence. When riots occurred on the streets of two otherwise peaceful cities – Seattle in November 1999 and Prague in September 2000 – they were publicised across the world. What made them so newsworthy?

In each city at the time, the leaders of the world's richest industrial countries – the MEDCs – were meeting to discuss the global economy. Those who demonstrated were a loose association of anti-capitalists, anarchists or supporters of Jubilee 2000 – a campaign aimed at wiping out Third World debt.

What did the protesters hope to achieve? LEDCs spend millions of dollars every year repaying loans, as well as the interest on loans, provided by the industrialised nations. The Jubilee 2000 campaign believed that this debt should be written off. Governments of LEDCs would then be able to spend more money on economic development and welfare services such as health and education. Bono, lead singer with U2, met world leaders on behalf of the Jubilee 2000 campaign. He asserted that 19 000 children die every day as a direct consequence of Third World debt, i.e. money that could have been spent on health care instead of financing interest payments.

This was no idle claim. The United Nations Children's Fund (UNICEF) and most welfare organisations agree on the basis of global evidence that a direct consequence of cancelling Third World debt would include:

- education for all children of primary school age
- fewer deaths of a) women due to complications in child birth, and b) young children.

As an indirect consequence of these improvements to health and education, birth rates in LEDCs would begin to fall (see Chapter 13).

While the Jubilee 2000 campaigners talked to world leaders, rioters targeted high profile high street names such as the clothes retailer Gap. Anti-capitalists see TNCs such as Gap, Nike or MacDonald's as leading players in an increasingly global market-place. TNCs invest in numerous countries, connecting those countries by financial investment and with flows of goods. Thus it is possible to buy Gap or Nike products that have been made in India or Cambodia in high street shops. Changes in trade and transport have shrunk the world into one global village, or perhaps a global supermarket, a process known as globalisation. The anti-capitalists object to the way in which these global links exploit cheap labour in LEDCs, while consuming huge resources in transporting goods around the world.

Globalisation: linking child labour to the consumer society

The global nature of the economy means that children of school age who are working in Asia can be making clothes for high street shops in New York, Paris and London. Major TNCs such as Levi, Disney, Gap and Nike all have ethical policies which are designed to prevent child labour, and protect all labourers from discrimination and excessively long hours. However, protesters claim to have evidence that these codes are often broken. A reporter for the BBC uncovered factories in Cambodia making clothes for a number of retailers, including Gap and Nike. Women claimed to be working sixteen-hour shifts and the factories were employing girls as young as twelve (Figure 3).

collecting and recycling rubbish, or labouring in sweatshops, on building sites without safety regulation enforcement, or in the sex industry. Much of the work done by children is in the informal sector of the economy. As such, they have no entitlement to sick leave or holidays and no legal protection from excessive workloads or dangerous working conditions.

The next two sections of this book are closely linked. This section is about population, while the next focuses upon the global economy. What the protestors in Seattle and Prague were fighting for was as much an economic issue as one of population. This section explores the current issue of global population – its explosion in some parts of the world and stagnation in others. Youthful societies and issues of child labour are crucial in some parts of the world, while others are dealing with ageing societies and the costs of welfare in older age groups as more and more people survive longer. Who pays? Does the existence of a wealthy ageing world on (mostly) one side of the Equator (the North) therefore require a cheap reservoir of child labour to supply its consumer goods on the other (the South)? The issue is about the kind of world that people want to live in during the twenty-first century and beyond.

Figure 3 Child labour in India.

The International Labour Organisation estimates that 120 million children aged five to fourteen work full time, and a further 130 million work part time. The number of children working in Europe is increasing, but the vast majority of child labour occurs in poorer LEDCs. These countries are characterised by growing youthful populations. Nearly 50 per cent of the Kenyan population is under fifteen: imagine the challenge of providing adequate education for such a large proportion of a country. In India the proportion is lower, but the absolute number is huge: 386 million under-eighteen year olds in 2000. Of these it is estimated that at least 44 million are working and are therefore missing school. Most support their families in unpaid work around the home and farm, but many work in low-paid jobs such as

1 Parents and children in developing countries defend their right to use child labour. They see it as an important source of family income. However, some western pressure groups have attacked the use of child labour, because it deprives children of their education.

   a) Discuss the circumstances in which child labour is acceptable, and those where it would be unacceptable.

   b) What are the minimum rights we should expect for children under fifteen? Should education be compulsory? What about health and safety of child labourers?

2 Consider what could happen to the cost of high street clothes if Third World debts were cancelled. Is this acceptable?

Investigating world population growth

More than 6 billion people live on Earth today and the population is still rising. The most rapid rates of population growth are occurring in LEDCs, especially in sub-Saharan Africa and southern Asia. This chapter will investigate ways in which the population of the world is changing in time and space.

The growing world population

Human life probably first appeared on Earth around 3–4 million years ago, while the Earth was in the early stages of an ice age. When the ice age finally ended around 10 000 years ago, the world population had reached a total which was probably less than 5 million. It took until 1830 for the world population to reach 1000 million (or 1 billion). Since then, the world population has grown very quickly, doubling two and a half times between 1830 and 2000. By 1999 it had reached 6 billion and was rising by an extra three people every second.

Exponential growth

Figure 11.2 shows the usual way in which the changing world population is viewed. A long period of very slow population growth has been replaced in the last 200 years by an extremely steep curve, showing that the rate of growth is accelerating. This type of curve is described as exponential.

To understand this, imagine a small country with a population of just 100 000 people. Suppose that every year there are 5000 more births than deaths in this country. The population would rise to 105 000, then 110 000, then 115 000 and so on. The population would reach 150 000 after ten years. These figures show a regular progression known as arithmetic growth, i.e. growth by the same number each year.

But what if the population were to grow by 5 per cent of its total each year rather than by a fixed amount? After the first year the growth would be the same, i.e. 105 000. But in the following year it would grow by 5 per cent of 105 000 which is 5250, so the total

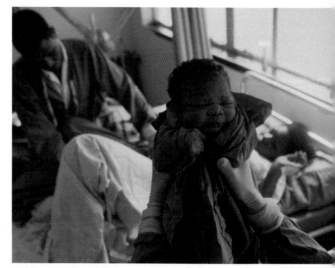

Figure 11.1 A maternity unit in South Africa.

population would be 110 250. The next year the population would rise to 115 763, then after ten years to 171 034. These figures, if plotted on a graph, give an ever-steepening curve and are known as exponential growth, i.e. the same percentage but an increasing number.

These numbers, of course, represent real people like the mothers with their babies in Figure 11.1. A country experiencing exponential growth has a youthful population. It faces a number of challenging

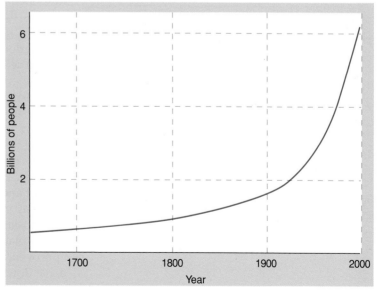

Figure 11.2 The exponential view of world population growth.

133

issues such as adequate provision of maternal health care and primary education. But it also has the potential advantage of a plentiful and vigorous workforce.

Rapid population growth since 1800 has been attributed to the industrial revolution. Industrial growth began in countries now known as the MEDCs of Europe in the nineteenth century. At the end of that century it spread to North America, before progressing to Australia and Japan. It was only in the second part of the twentieth century that industrialisation came to southern Asia and Africa. Population growth seems to have followed in a similar pattern: MEDCs experienced rapid growth in the nineteenth and early twentieth centuries, LEDCs later.

The logarithmic-logistic view of world population growth

The traditional view of population growth (Figure 11.2) contrasts slow growth prior to the industrial revolution with exponential growth as a result of industrialisation. But the shape of the growth curve changes significantly if plotted on logarithmic graph paper, where each axis progresses by a factor of ten in order to compress large ranges of data. This graph (Figure 11.3) indicates that global population growth

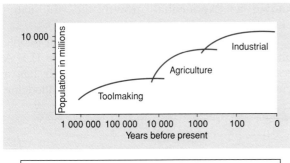

Environmental impacts of society			
	Toolmaking	Agriculture	Industrial
Scale of impact	Mainly local and short term	Local, regional and long-term impacts	Local, regional and global permanent impacts
Examples	Hunting affects local populations of animals	Forest clearance, soil erosion, extinctions of fauna due to hunting	Landscape change, air and water pollution common locally, acid rain, global warming

Figure 11.3 The logarithmic-logistic view of world population growth.

has occurred in three distinct phases. Each is attributed to a significant technological change, two of which occurred before the industrial revolution. This and the accompanying text suggest two important points.

- Population growth is spurred by technological change. The change from hunter gathering society to an agricultural society at the end of the ice age (10 000 years before present) encouraged population growth.
- Each phase of growth has been characterised by early growth followed by levelling out. This suggests that population finds its own natural level that is somehow determined (or limited) by technology.

Pessimistic or optimistic views on population growth?

The exponential view of population growth (Figure 11.2) creates an alarming and pessimistic view of the future for the Earth. Some believe that the Earth is already too crowded and that future population growth will create terrible problems as resources run out and the environment is degraded. These views are examined in Chapter 12.

Thomas Malthus, writing in the 1790s, was the first to identify exponential rates of population growth. He took a pessimistic view of its consequences, a view which became popular again after the publication of Paul Ehrlich's book *The Population Bomb* (1968). You can read more about Malthus in the theory box opposite.

Those who adopt Malthus' viewpoint now are described as neo-Malthusian. The neo-Malthusian view is that population growth is too rapid and must be slowed. It argues that rapid increase in population puts a strain on services and infrastructure, for example food, energy, housing, sewage systems and transport networks. Population growth therefore leads to poverty, and may result in famine or even civil war. These views tend to influence the press and general public leading to gloomy predictions about the fate of the world's mega-cities or of the world environment as a whole. Even the title The Population Bomb has violent and disastrous overtones.

Many governments who have adopted the neo-Malthusian view have encouraged methods of family planning, of which Malthus would not have approved. Governments who pursue policies to drive down the birth rate are described as having anti-natalist policies (see Chapter 13).

Malthus and exponential population growth

Thomas Malthus, writing in the 1790s, developed a predictive model of population growth which was based on his observation of population change in England at the time. Birth rates in late eighteenth-century Britain were high (38 per 1000 population) but death rates had been falling steadily since 1740, reaching 25 per 1000 by 1800. As the gap between birth rates and death rates widened, the population grew faster and faster. The population of industrial cities such as Birmingham and Manchester grew even more rapidly: natural increase was supplemented by migrants arriving from rural areas in search of work in factories.

The population growth of Manchester (Figure 11.4) was one of the most rapid of all British cities at the time. Plotted on a graph, these figures show a steep exponential curve whose gradient increases over time. Cities at that time relied more closely on food production in the neighbouring rural area than today, when food is imported from all parts of the world. Malthus predicted that rapid population growth would outstrip growth in local food supply. He believed that lack of food would result in malnutrition and famine. Overcrowding would lead to epidemics of disease, and the consequent collapse of society could result in civil war. He predicted that famine, disease and war would act as 'positive checks' on population growth, causing the population to fall to a level that could be maintained by the food supply. This pessimistic model is shown in Figure 11.5.

1773	36 250
1801	72 250
1851	303 500
1901	607 000

Figure 11.4 Exponential population growth in Manchester at the beginning of the nineteenth century.

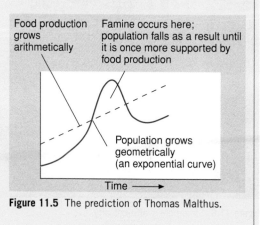

Figure 11.5 The prediction of Thomas Malthus.

Malthus suggested that his pessimistic prediction of overpopulation and its consequences could be avoided if people chose to limit population growth. He advocated delayed marriage and abstinence from sexual relations and described these decisions as 'negative checks' on population growth. Malthus himself did not believe that people should adopt any method of family planning since he thought this would lead to promiscuity.

The optimistic view of population growth

Other social scientists take an alternative, optimistic view of the consequences of rapid population growth. Such a view was put forward by Esther Boserup, a Danish economist, in 1963, and again by J Simon in a book *The Ultimate Resource* (1981). The Boserupian view is that people are intelligent animals who modify their environment and behaviour as necessary. Resource shortages force them to invent new processes and find new technologies: increasing food production, creating cheaper and more efficient energy and transport systems, overcoming resource and pollution problems. Exponential population growth creates more innovators and improved standards of living, not a slump towards famine and poverty predicted by neo-Malthusians. Environmental degradation need not be a consequence of population growth. The Boserupian view leads to the conclusion that people are innovators and a valuable resource. This idea has encouraged some governments (such as that of Singapore) to adopt pro-natalist policies, in which people are encouraged to have larger, not smaller, families.

Case study of Singapore: are people its greatest resource?

Singapore is a small city state at the tip of the peninsula of Malaya. Its aim is to become the wealthiest and most highly skilled country in Asia. It has the second largest container port in the world after Hong Kong, and is the world's leading manufacturer of computer disc drives. Its economy has grown over three times faster than the UK economy for every one of the last 30 years. Singapore has no natural resources. Its economic success is due to the technical skill of its manufacturing and service based industries which include electronics, medicines and petrochemicals.

Figure 11.6 Singapore – affluent city.

Singapore is only 42km by 23km in size and has very limited space. In the 1960s the Singaporean government was worried about overpopulation and introduced a family planning policy. Slogans such as 'Stop at two' encouraged people to have small families. Parents could have maternity benefits for the first two children only, and could be moved to the end of the housing waiting list if they had a third. The campaign was successful in that by the mid-1970s population growth had practically come to a halt.

However, in the 1980s the government realised that a young, highly skilled workforce was the key to the continued success of its industrial exports. The population policy was reversed, and in 1987 new slogans appeared, 'Have three, or more if you can afford it'. This new policy is carefully directed towards particular groups of women. The government would like well-educated young women to marry earlier and have more children. Women with better qualifications can claim up to Singapore $10 000 (£3750) for each of their first three children. At the same time, women who are poor or less well educated are offered cash incentives if they agree to be sterilised. Singapore still does not have enough people to fill all of its jobs, especially those that are low skilled and low paid, and 40 per cent of the workforce comes from overseas, mainly from Malaysia and the Philippines.

		Singapore	UK
Average annual incomes (GNP US$ per capita)	1991	12 890	16 750
	1996	30 550	19 600
% average annual growth rate in GNP (US$ per capita)	1965–80	8.3	2.0
	1990–6	6.6	1.5
Spending on education as a % of central government expenditure	1990–7	19	5

Figure 11.7 Singapore's economic success.

1 a) Choose suitable techniques to compare the economic indicators in Figure 11.7 for Singapore and the UK.
   b) Summarise the main differences between Singapore and the UK.

2 a) How much does Singapore's population policy owe to the thinking of Malthus and Boserup?
   b) Use Figure 11.8 to evaluate how successful each policy has been.
   c) Why should the government offer incentives for only some women to have larger families? Is this kind of discrimination acceptable?

3 How do you feel about Singapore's employers taking on so many foreign workers?

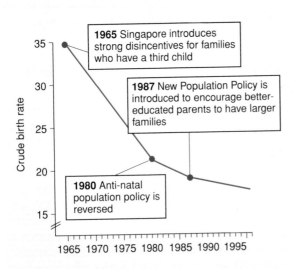

1965 Singapore introduces strong disincentives for families who have a third child

1987 New Population Policy is introduced to encourage better-educated parents to have larger families

1980 Anti-natal population policy is reversed

Figure 11.8 The fall of the crude birth rate in Singapore.

Investigating global patterns of population growth

Patterns of population growth over time are only one part of population study; the spatial dimension is also significant. How is population growing in different parts of the world? Where is it growing fastest? Figures 11.10 and 11.11 illustrate global patterns of population growth at the end of the twentieth century. These illustrate that birth rates are still high, and doubling times short, in poorer LEDCs. Populations are growing most rapidly in northern Africa, sub-Saharan Africa and southern Asia. Read the theory box on population change below to understand what is meant by different demographic terms.

Theory

Population change

The population of any region is a dynamic system. Inputs and outputs vary over time to create conditions of growth or decline in the overall population. The factors that influence growth or decline are also constantly changing. Figure 11.9 summarises the factors that affect population change.

Defining demographic terms

crude birth rate: the annual number of births per 1000 population.

crude death rate: the annual number of deaths per 1000 population.

doubling time: the number of years it takes for a nation's population to double in size. Short doubling times mean rapid growth. The shortest doubling times, for example in Gaza, are in the order of 20 years.

life expectancy at birth: the number of years a newborn baby could expect to live assuming he/she is subject to the normal

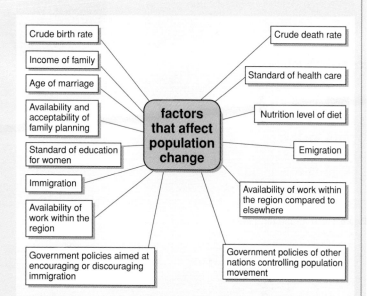

Figure 11.9 Population change: Inputs and outputs to the system.

risks of mortality (death) prevalent at the time of birth. The lowest life expectancy for any region is for sub-Saharan Africa where life expectancy is just 51 years.

maternal mortality rate: annual number of deaths of women from pregnancy related causes expressed as a number per 100 000 live births. This figure is as high as 1000 in some African countries, for example Eritrea, the Central African Republic and Mozambique.

natural increase or annual growth rate: the rate at which the population increases due to there being more births than deaths. Natural increase is measured as an annual percentage of the whole population. A growth rate of 3 per cent per annum, achieved in some African countries, would create rapid growth and short doubling times.

total fertility rate: the number of children that would be born per woman if she were to live to the end of her child-bearing years and follow normal patterns of fertility. Total fertility rate can be thought of as an average family size. Some European countries now have a total fertility rate that is below replacement level, i.e. where fertility is below two, the children will not replace the parent's generation.

under-five mortality rate: the probability of dying between birth and the age of five, expressed as a number out of every 1000 live births. The three highest under-five mortality rates are all in Africa: Niger 320; Sierra Leone 316; Angola 292. This means that almost one-third of children born alive in these countries die before the age of five.

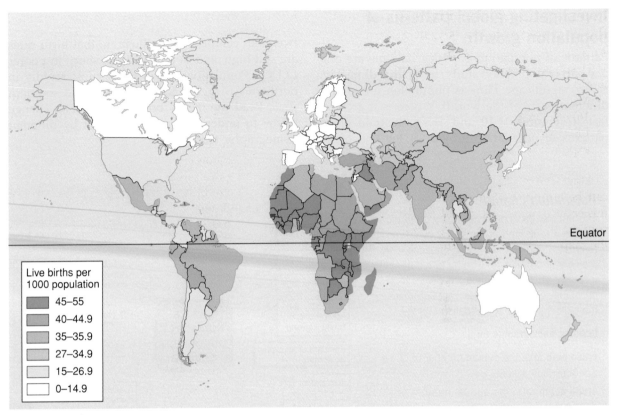

Figure 11.10 Crude birth rates.

Live births per
1000 population

45–55
40–44.9
35–35.9
27–34.9
15–26.9
0–14.9

Equator

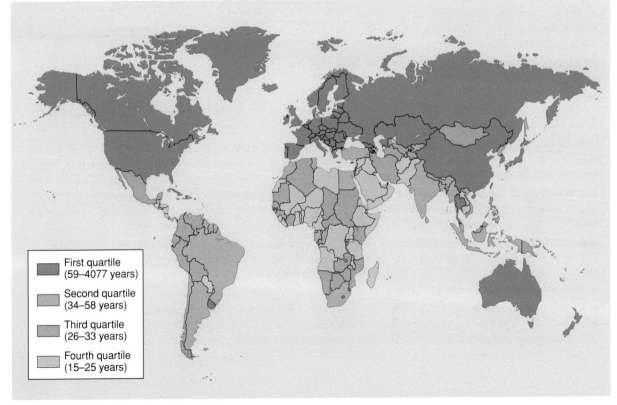

Figure 11.11 Doubling times of world population.

First quartile
(59–4077 years)

Second quartile
(34–58 years)

Third quartile
(26–33 years)

Fourth quartile
(15–25 years)

Population patterns in time and space: the demographic transition model

At a simple level, the maps in Figures 11.10 and 11.11 suggest a simple global pattern in which the world is divided into two parts:

- MEDCs north of the Brandt line (see Chapter 16) with slow growing or static populations
- LEDCs to the south, which have populations experiencing exponential growth.

However, to suggest that the world's economies can be simply divided into North and South is misleading. The real world is divided along a continuum from richest to poorest. Furthermore, the maps in Figures 11.10 and 11.11 are snap-shots in time. The reality is more complex; evolving economies suggest that populations follow a common pattern which can be divided into not two, but five stages of development. This model is known as the demographic transition. It is based on relative changes in the crude birth and death rate, and is shown in Figure 11.12. The demographic transition links a number of demographic changes to the evolution of the economy. Economic growth is shadowed by:

- declining death rates and birth rates
- declining fertility rates as people choose to have fewer children
- longer life expectancy as health care is improved.

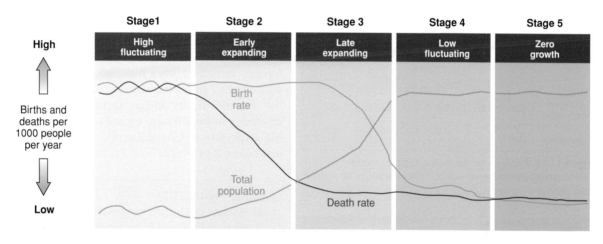

	Stage 1	Stage 2	Stage 3	Stage 4	Stage 5
Birth and death rate	Birth and death rates are high and fluctuate around 35 per 1000	Birth rate remains high but the death rate falls rapidly to around 20 per 1000	Birth rate begins to fall to around 20 per 1000 while death rate continues to fall to around 10 per 1000	Birth and death rates are low and fluctuate around 12 per 1000	Birth rates fall further and fertility falls below replacement level
Population characteristics	Population is small and will fluctuate but grows very slowly	Population begins its exponential growth, the proportion of under-15s expands	Population continues to grow, but the rate of growth is slowing	Population levels out, the proportion of under-15s and over-65s is similar	Elderly dependent population increases and population begins to decline
Timing of UK's transition	pre 1750	1750–1870	1870–1940	1940–2000	2000 onwards?
Current examples	Only isolated indigenous groups, e.g. rainforest tribes, currently in this stage	Poorer LEDCs of sub-Saharan Africa and southern Asia	Industrialising LEDCs such as those in South-East Asia or Latin America	Rich industrial MEDCs, e.g. USA and Japan	Some Western European nations, e.g. Italy

Figure 11.12 The demographic transition model.

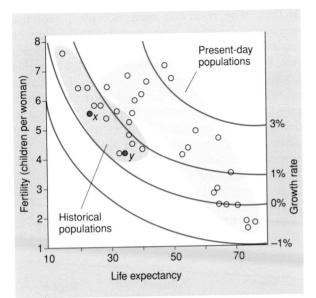

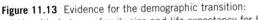

Examples

		Fertility	Life Expectancy	Growth rate
Historical population:	Spain (1797)	5.8	27	0.7
Present-day population:	Ethiopia (1997)	7.0	50	3.2

Figure 11.13 Evidence for the demographic transition: relationship between family size and life expectancy for historic and present-day populations.

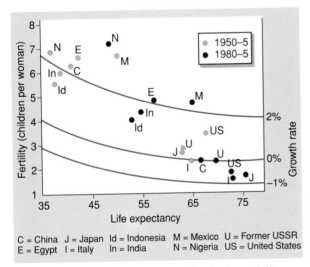

C = China J = Japan Id = Indonesia M = Mexico U = Former USSR
E = Egypt I = Italy In = India N = Nigeria US = United States

Figure 11.14 The relationship between family size and life expectancy for selected countries.

Figures 11.13 and 11.14 present further evidence of this demographic transition. They examine the relationship between fertility (family size), life expectancy and population growth rate. Figure 11.13 suggests that all historical populations are clustered in part of the graph where fertility is high but life expectancy is low. Consequently, growth rates were between 0 and 1 per cent. These historical populations conform to stage 1 of the demographic cycle. However, the present-day populations are spread over a much larger part of the graph. These points indicate that current populations fall into stages two to five.

Figure 11.14 examines the way in which selected populations shifted their position on the demographic transition between 1950 and 1985, a critical period of exponential growth in global terms. Some countries made more rapid progress than others. In Nigeria, for example, life expectancy was improved considerably. However, fertility remained very high, so growth continued well above 2 per cent, leaving Nigeria in stage 2 of the transition. In India, fertility did fall, but advances in health care meant a significant rise in life expectancy. Consequently, growth remained just below 2 per cent.

1 Study Figure 11.13.
   a) Match the following historical populations to points X and Y on the graph:

	Fertility	Life expectancy	Growth rate
Rural China (1930)	5.6	23	0.3
England (1650–1700)	4.1	34	0.2

   b) Copy the axes and sketch the cluster of present-day populations. Label those you consider to be in each stage of the demographic transition (stages 2–5).

2 Study Figure 11.14. Describe the changes made by each of the following countries. Try to predict from this graph the stage of the demographic transition.
   a) US
   b) China
   c) Italy

Case study: the demographic transition in Japan

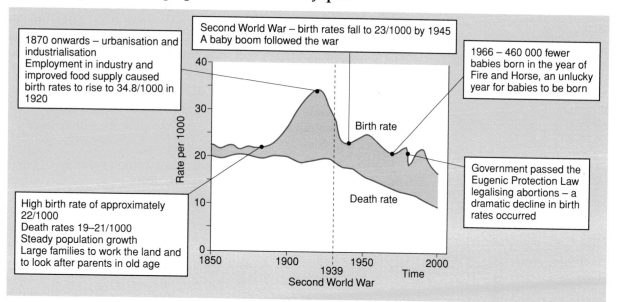

1870 onwards – urbanisation and industrialisation
Employment in industry and improved food supply caused birth rates to rise to 34.8/1000 in 1920

Second World War – birth rates fall to 23/1000 by 1945
A baby boom followed the war

1966 – 460 000 fewer babies born in the year of Fire and Horse, an unlucky year for babies to be born

High birth rate of approximately 22/1000
Death rates 19–21/1000
Steady population growth
Large families to work the land and to look after parents in old age

Government passed the Eugenic Protection Law legalising abortions – a dramatic decline in birth rates occurred

Figure 11.15 The demographic transition model for Japan.

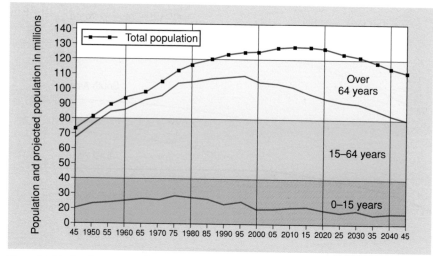

Figure 11.16 Predicted population structure, Japan.

Japan's population has moved through the stages of the demographic transition relatively quickly. Population growth was rapid in the early twentieth century. Japan's population doubled from 35 million in 1873 to 70 million in 1937, characteristic of the expansion of stage 2. After 1945, the Japanese government was worried that a rising population would result in money for economic growth being diverted into housing, education and welfare. Consequently, family planning and birth control were encouraged for the first time in the early 1950s, and abortion was legalised. The birth rate began to fall. As Japanese families became wealthier during the 1960s and 1970s, the birth rate dropped further. People were beginning to marry later and have smaller families, the result of living in a country where costs of living, especially housing, are very high.

Japan's current population clearly shows the characteristics of stage 4. Population growth has nearly ceased and the proportion of elderly dependants (aged over 64) is greater than at any other time in Japan's history. Forecasts and trends, shown in Figures 11.15 and 11.16, suggest that Japan will soon enter stage 5 of the demographic transition and population will begin to fall.

1 Use Figures 11.15, 11.16 and the text to identify when Japan moved through stages 2–5 of the demographic transition. Justify your decisions.

2 a) Use Figure 11.16 to estimate the proportion of elderly dependants in 1980, 2000, 2020 and 2040.
  b) Suggest what issues the ageing of Japanese society might raise for Japan.

3 Are there similar issues in store for the UK with its ageing population?

Predicting future population growth

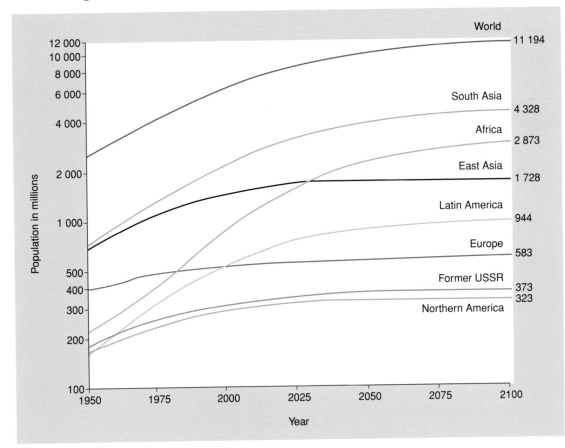

Figure 11.17 Predicted population change over the next 100 years.

The twentieth century was a unique period in the evolution of the Earth's human population. At no other time in history had rates of growth been so rapid, nor absolute totals of people so large. But population predictions shown in Figure 11.17 suggest something that Malthus, over 200 years ago, could never have foreseen: that the phase of expansion (exponential growth – stage 2 of the demographic transition) is followed by growth rates that slow and then level off. The rate of growth of the global population is already reducing. It will take another 100 years for growth to cease, and it is estimated that by then the population will have reached between 11 and 12 billion people.

These predictions leave a number of questions:
- Is 6 billion people already too many? Can the Earth cope with 12 billion? (Overpopulation is the focus of Chapter 12.)
- Figure 11.17 shows that the population of Africa and South Asia will continue to rise for some time. How can growth rates be reduced in the poorest LEDCs? The factors that influence fertility are studied in Chapter 13.
- How will ageing populations in stage 5 of the demographic transition affect a nation's economy? Chapter 15 examines issues facing countries with ageing populations.

Summary
You have learned that:
- The world population has grown exponentially, with the most rapid increase over the last 200 years. The population doubled two and a half times between 1830 and 2000.
- The most rapid rates of population growth are occurring in the LEDCs, especially in the countries of sub-Saharan Africa and in South Asia.
- Governments can influence population growth through policies that either encourage or discourage further growth.
- Trends in birth and death rates follow a pattern known as the demographic transition. The stage in this transition reached by different countries depends largely on the state of development of that country's economy.

References and further reading
Andrew Goudie & Heather Viles, *The Earth Transformed*, Blackwell Publishers (1997)
Philip Sarre & John Blunden, *An Overcrowded World?*, The Open University (1995)

Web sites
UNICEF, 'State of the World's Children 2000', to be found on UNICEF home page: www.unicef.org.sowc00/
United Nations Population Fund web site contains articles about issues such as reproductive health, reproductive rights and food security: www.unfpa.org/
United Nations statistical web site contains data on fertility: www.popin.org/

12 An overcrowded world?

By 1999 the Earth's population had reached 6 billion and was continuing to rise by 90 million every year. Some people take the view that the world is already overcrowded. They say that social and environmental problems such as poverty, lack of food and shelter, and increasing amounts of pollution are all evidence of overpopulation. Others say that continued growth inevitably leads to more problems as valuable resources such as oil, timber and even clean water run out. Is this inevitable?

Spaceship Earth

Figure 12.1 Spaceship Earth has limited resources.

Early exploration of the world gave people an incomplete view of the planet. Maps drawn by early European explorers show the known world (of Europe) in the centre. But the edges are hazy around unknown territory. Most European maps still show Europe in the centre – an example of Eurocentric perceptions of the world (i.e. Europe-centred). Some explorers embellished the edges of maps with sea monsters, suggesting fear of the unknown. To those whose sea expeditions took years to complete, the world must have seemed very large and its extent limitless, because they never saw the whole picture.

The first astronauts, orbiting Earth in the 1960s, were the first to see the world in its entirety, as in Figure 12.1. For the first time, it looked small and finite. Environmentalists working at this time used these images to illustrate that the world and its resources had limits. They were neo-Malthusians, with a pessimistic view of the way in which population growth was affecting the planet. They compared the Earth to a spaceship with limited supplies of food, water, energy, air and other essential life-supporting resources. They argued that the world was already overpopulated, that resources such as fossil fuels, minerals, clean water, and even clean air, had a finite limit and could eventually run out or be damaged beyond repair.

Ironically, many neo-Malthusian environmentalists live in MEDCs: the countries that consume the majority of the world's resources. The USA consumes 24 per cent of the world's energy with only 4 per cent of its population. But they are alarmed by population growth in LEDCs where resource use is currently low, but likely to increase in the future so that standards of living can improve.

Figure 12.2 When learning about other societies, we need to consider whether our point of view contains bias.

Over- or underpopulation?

A society with sufficient resources and appropriate technology to provide a satisfactory standard of living is said to have reached its optimum population. An optimum can exist at any density. Manhattan, in New York, has one of the highest population densities in the world, but many of its inhabitants have a very high standard of living. The urban environment has sufficient financial resources and sophisticated technologies (such as the subway system and high-rise housing) to enable many people to live comfortably in a confined space.

However, when too many people are added to a population it can create resource shortages and stretch existing levels of technology until they fail. This is described as overpopulation. People may have insufficient living space, fuel or sanitation; clean water and food may become scarce resources; traffic may become grid-locked; quality of life deteriorates. The ultimate consequence of such overpopulation might be famine or civil unrest as the fabric of society breaks down.

Underpopulation is said to occur where there are too few people to properly exploit available resources. As a result, there may be insufficient workers to provide food, adequate shelter, decent education or health care. Quality of life deteriorates. The consequence may be out-migration, as people leave to find a better quality of life elsewhere. Depopulation leads to the closure of services and, in extreme cases, houses and farmland may become derelict.

Overpopulation is closely related to the ecological concept of carrying capacity. Populations of, for example, laboratory mice grow until they run out of an essential resource such as water, light or clean air. At this point the population is said to have reached the carrying capacity of its environment, and the population crashes. This concept can be applied to human environments. New York can support more people than a similarly sized area of desert because a desert has fewer available resources, particularly water and shelter, and therefore it has a lower carrying capacity. However, human creations such as Las Vegas can extend or redefine carrying capacity.

1 Does the existence of homeless people in Manhattan provide proof that carrying capacity has been exceeded? What other evidence might you find to indicate that New York is overpopulated?

2 Study the photographs in Figure 12.4.
   a) In what sense could either, or both, scenes be described as overpopulated?
   b) Is overpopulation a negative term? To what extent is it a Eurocentric term?

Figure 12.3 Manhattan, New York – optimum population or overpopulation?

Figure 12.4 Images of overpopulation?

A Crowds enjoying the music at Glastonbury music festival.

B Large numbers of Rwandan Hutu refugees walk through Goma.

Does the Earth have a carrying capacity?

If the Earth has a finite carrying capacity for humans, it should be possible to identify resource shortages that will limit growth. Such an investigation was conducted in the early 1970s by ten industrial nations who were known as the Club of Rome. Scientists used computer modelling to try to predict what might happen in the future if resources continued to be used, and population grew, at the current rate. Their report, titled The Limits to Growth, was published in 1972. It made gloomy predictions about a world where continued industrial and population growth would consume both resources and food supplies. They forecast a world in which pollution would become a growing problem and where hunger and famine would become increasingly common during the twenty-first century. Their predictions are summarised in Figure 12.5. Environmental campaigners used the concepts of Spaceship Earth and Limits to Growth throughout the 1970s and early 1980s. They successfully pushed environmental issues up the political agenda. But their views on how best to tackle the world's population and resource issues were strongly challenged in the 1990s.

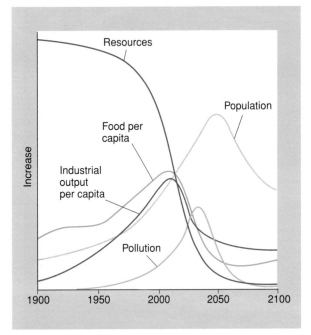

Figure 12.5 Computer modelling was used to predict these future trends.

1 Study Figure 12.5. Comment on the relationship between:
   a) resources and industrial output per capita
   b) industrial output per capita and pollution
   c) food per capita and population.

2 The five lines on Figure 12.5 represent five variables that are connected to each other. As one changes, it causes changes in one or more of the others. This is known as the independent variable. In your view, which is the most important independent variable in the graph? Justify your view.

Alternative strategies for balancing population and resource use

Limit population growth

A popular strategy advocated by many environmentalists and some governments, for example China and India, is to limit population growth. If effective methods of birth control can be enforced or encouraged, as in China's One Child Policy, then there should be an impact on the rate at which resources, including food, are consumed. This option is favoured by neo-Malthusians (see Chapter 11).

Technological change

A second strategy is to change the technologies of industrial production, waste disposal or food production to make the use of limited resources more effective. Technological change is not anticipated in the Limits to Growth model. However, there have been huge leaps in many aspects of technology since the early 1970s that have radically altered the way materials are used or food produced. Changes in computing, information communication, robotics and genetic engineering have altered not only technologies of production, but also ways in which ideas about production spread from one part of the world to another. Such changes were anticipated by Boserup (see Chapter 11) several years before the Limits to Growth model.

Reorganise society

A third strategy is to change the way society and production are organised so that everyone gets a fairer share of the limited resources that are available. Although only 25 per cent of the world's

Figure 12.6 'We must find a solution...'

Is the world overpopulated?

Neo-Malthusians say that the Earth is already over-populated. If that is so we should expect to see evidence in the form of:

- resource shortages that cause poverty
- food shortages that result in famine
- pollution and environ-mental degradation that damage human health or threaten human safety.

Hunger is a problem associated with the poorest LEDCs. Images of starving African children are used by the media, and sometimes by charities and relief organisations, to raise awareness in the West about poverty and famine in LEDCs. A popular perception is that famine is caused by overpopulation. Is this true?

Investigating famine in the twentieth century

'Food security, at the individual, household, national, regional and global levels ... is achieved when all people, at all times, have physical and economic access to sufficient, safe and nutritious food to meet their dietary needs and food preferences for an active and healthy life.' (World Food Summit, 1996)

Hunger may be divided into two types:

- acute hunger: short-term but intensive problems of food security which lead to famine. The worst famines in many people's memory may be those suffered in Ethiopia in the 1980s and again in the late 1990s. But, as we shall see, these were small scale compared to famines earlier in the century.
- chronic hunger: longer-term problems of food security, which cause long-term ill health, undernourishment and undernutrition. Chronic hunger leads to around 85 per cent of all deaths from hunger. Figure 12.7 shows the global pattern of undernourishment.

population live in MEDCs, they consume 75 per cent of the world's resources. The USA's population is about 4.3 per cent of the total world population, but it uses 29 per cent of the world's petrol and 33 per cent of the world's electricity. Efforts have been made in some parts of the world to redistribute wealth or land in a more even manner. Land reform in Kerala, India, has allowed even the poorest to own some land of their own. In the same state, improved education for women has allowed them to take more control in society and become wealthier and, indirectly, has reduced the birth rate. But changes such as these require political will, and may be more difficult to implement than either of the first two options.

---

1 Choose one of the alternative strategies for altering the outcome of the Limits to Growth model. Try to sketch a graph showing what might happen to each of the five variables. Annotate the peaks and trends on your graph to explain what is happening.

2 Study the cartoon in Figure 12.6.
   a) In what way do the figures represent cultural stereotypes?
   b) How is the imbalance in resources represented in the cartoon?
   c) Why is the figure on the right shown to be unable to make up his mind?

Deaths from famine, or acute hunger, are difficult to quantify accurately. Famines in the twentieth century often occurred at times of political instability or war. In confusion, authorities may have to estimate numbers of deaths. Underestimates may be made in order to diffuse political criticism. For example, there is no doubt that very many people died from hunger in North Korea during the 1990s, but this isolated government has kept details of this terrible famine from the rest of the world. So estimates of deaths from famine during the twentieth century vary widely; expert estimates

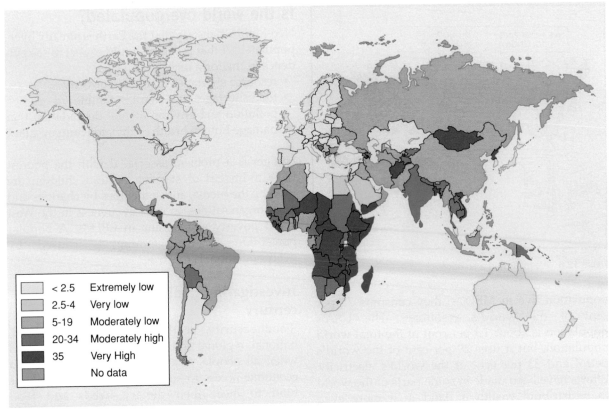

Figure 12.7 The global pattern of undernourishment.

range between 70.1 and 80.4 million. The number of deaths per decade is given in Figure 12.8. The data in Figures 12.7 to 12.10 suggests that:

- the last thirty years of the twentieth century saw a massive reduction in the number of deaths associated with famine, despite the rapidly rising world population
- the worst famines have occurred, not in Africa, but in Europe and Asia – three famines in the USSR claimed at least 18 million lives, and five famines in China claimed around 40 million
- the map of undernourishment indicates that the greatest number of hungry people in the world today live in China, India and the rest of South Asia. However, the greatest incidence of hunger (i.e. the largest proportion of the population who are undernourished) occurs in sub-Saharan Africa.

Decade	East Asia	Europe	South-East Asia	South Asia	Africa	Total
1900s					42 500	42 500
1910s					155 000	155 000
1920s	7 000 000	9 000 000				16 000 000
1930s		7 500 000				7 500 000
1940s	5 000 000	2 010 000		2 550 000	300 000	9 860 000
1950s	15 750 000				248 500	15 998 500
1960s	15 750 000				1 052 500	16 802 500
1970s			1 750 000	1 630 000	471 000	3 851 000
1980s					1 425 000	1 425 000
1990s			3 150 000		470 000	2 470 000
Total	43 500 000	18 510 000	4 900 000	4 180 000	4 164 500	75 254 500

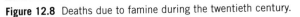

Figure 12.8 Deaths due to famine during the twentieth century.

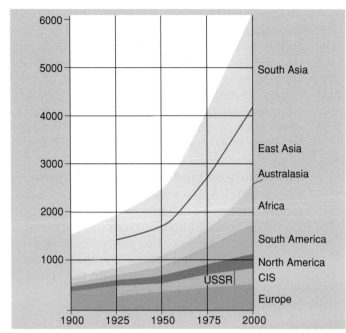

Figure 12.9 Population growth during the twentieth century by continent.

Region/country	Number of undernourished (millions)	% population who are undernourished
South Asia	283.9	23
India	204.4	22
Bangladesh	44	37
Sub-Saharan Africa	179.6	33
East Asia	176.8	14
China	164.4	13
South-East Asia	63.7	13
Latin America & Caribbean	53.4	11
Near East and North Africa	32.9	9

Figure 12.10 Number and proportion of undernourished, by region, 1999.

1 a) Use a suitable technique to graph the information in Figure 12.8. What spatial and temporal patterns are shown by the graph? Is the image of widespread famine in Africa in the 1980s, promoted by the media, accurate?

b) Compare Figure 12.8 to the rising population shown in Figure 12.9. Is it sensible to suggest that population increase is a possible cause of famine in the twentieth century?

2 Use Figure 12.10 to draw appropriate graphs showing the spatial distribution of hunger.

a) Use your graphs to describe the regions of the world that have:
- the largest absolute numbers of people suffering from hunger
- the largest proportions of people suffering from hunger.

b) Which, if any, of these regions has large or rapidly growing populations?

Why do problems of food security occur?

Policy in the 1970s was influenced by the thinking of neo-Malthusian scientists and the Limits to Growth report, which predicted that famine would be a consequence of overpopulation. It was thought that famine could be avoided in one of three ways:

- increasing food production – this was largely achieved by the introduction of higher yielding varieties of grain and the consequent use of green revolution technologies. More intensive use of herbicides, pesticides and fertilisers as well as improved irrigation and drainage allowed farmers to take marginal land into commercial production. Food production dramatically increased by improving yields per hectare and by taking more hectares of land into production.

- the stabilisation of prices – the payment of subsidies to farmers and the use of trade agreements between nations, for example between members of the EU, allowed farmers to produce food at guaranteed prices. Production increased as uncertainty was reduced.

- the introduction of strict family planning policies in some LEDCs – state control of population growth through family planning was seen as a key element of improving food security in countries such as India and China in the 1970s and 1980s. These anti-natalist policies are described in more detail in Chapter 13.

However, recent research has suggested that there is no simple link between population growth and famine. Indeed, food insecurity is not even necessarily about low levels of food production. Agricultural technologies have successfully increased food production so that never before has there been more food or more varieties of food available on the world market. So why are so many people still hungry?

It is now widely accepted that hunger occurs because of poor food distribution and the inability of some groups of people to obtain an adequate diet. Some people are rich enough or hold sufficient respect or political power to remain free from hunger even in the midst of famine. Professional people, shop owners, local government officers, policemen and soldiers are all examples of those who have good access to food during a crisis. Others have less secure access: those in rural areas who are far from shops or supplies of emergency aid held in urban areas, women, children and the elderly. During the 1984/5 famine in Ethiopia, while rural families, children and women starved to death, some of the aid intended to keep them alive was eaten by warlords and young male soldiers.

Case study of food security in Ethiopia

Famine in Ethiopia hit the public conscience when pictures of starving children saturated the media in the 1980s. Several hundred thousand people died in the 1984/5 famine. The public responded by donating millions in relief aid. But the public did not seriously examine the cause of the famine; it was assumed by many to be partly a result of overpopulation (Figure 12.11). In early 2000, images of starving African families were back on television, with a claim that up to 8 million people were at risk of a new famine. This time the media were more critical of the causes.

The World Food Programme (WFP), which is administered by the United Nations, blamed the crisis largely on natural causes. Although it acknowledged that other factors had contributed to the famine, it claimed that unreliable rainfall in the region of the Horn of Africa was the main reason for the food crisis. It claimed that the root cause of hunger in the region, which includes the countries of Ethiopia, Somalia, Eritrea and Kenya, was the failure of seasonal rains (Figure 12.12).

Ethiopia has two main growing seasons which correspond to two seasons of rainfall. Low rainfall during the main growing season in 1999 led to poor harvests at the end of the year. To make matters worse, the rains expected in February 2000, which allow a second yield of crops to be grown, arrived six weeks late. The WFP, anxious to avoid a catastrophe similar to the 1984/5

	Population in 000s
1950	19 573
1960	24 191
1970	30 623
1980	38 750
1990	49 240
1993	52 500 plus Eritrea 3 500
1997	60 148 plus Eritrea 3 409
Fertility rate	7 (fourth highest in the world)
Population growth rate	3.2% per annum

Figure 12.11 Demographic data for Ethiopia.

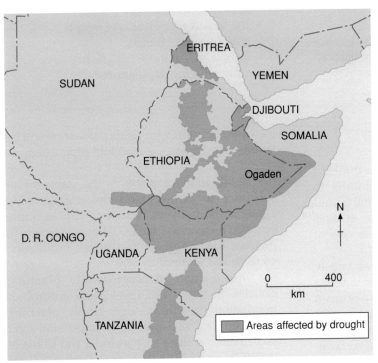

Figure 12.12 Greater Horn of Africa: drought affected areas.

famine, broke the news early to the western press.

While the media acknowledged that poor rainfall had played a contributing role, some commentators focused on political reasons for the crisis. The African editions of the Daily Mail and Guardian ran an article thus: 'Diplomatic sources in Addis Ababa describe the figures put out by the Ethiopian Authorities and by the United Nations – which claim that 8 million people are "threatened" with famine in Ethiopia – as "fanciful" and "exaggerated"'. Moreover, it suggested that the real cause of the crisis was not poor rainfall but the continued war between Ethiopia and Eritrea on its northern border.

The beginning of the article is reproduced in Figure 12.13 and comments from the article have been selected for comparison with the WFP point of view in Figure 12.14.

Ethiopian famine: Natural calamity or human disaster? Jean-Baptiste Naudet reports

Ethiopia has been fighting its neighbour, Eritrea, since May 1998. Two of the poorest countries in the world, they are now both calling on the international community to help them with a drought that could, they say, result in famine for millions. Is the disaster they face a natural one, or is it human?

Ethiopia accuses the West of waiting until there were pictures of starving children before responding to the crisis, and warns that another famine is on the horizon. Yet it has spent millions of dollars on arms that are being used in a conflict that has killed tens of thousands of people.

Figure 12.13 From the *Daily Mail* and *Guardian* (African edition), 1 May 2000.

Topic	Extracts from World Food Programme web site	Extracts from *Daily Mail* and *Guardian* (African edition)
Drought	Although its border war with Eritrea has displaced some 350,000 people and there are border clashes with Somali warlords, drought in the south and east of Ethiopia is having by far the greatest humanitarian impact.	Diplomats and aid workers in the region believe the two countries are suffering more from the war than from drought. They argue that the food crisis has less to do with lack of rainfall – which has not yet reached abnormal levels – than with the countries' insistence on fighting over 300km of rocky terrain.
War	Ethiopia's massive land offensive has also exacerbated food insecurity. There are reports of population movements in Tigray due to renewed fighting and the area requires food aid for internally displaced populations.	According to observers in Addis Ababa, the war is indirectly but 'largely' responsible for the food crisis in the south, since all the country's material, financial and human resources have been mobilised for the conflict with Eritrea.

Figure 12.14 Contrasting explanations for the 2000 famine in Ethiopia.

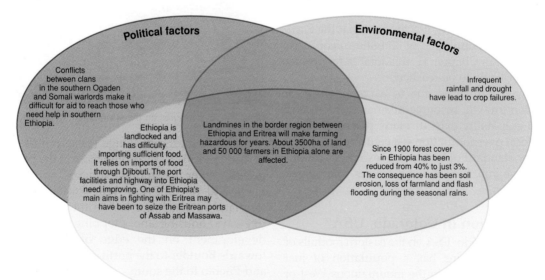

Figure 12.15 Factors which pose a threat to food security in Ethiopia.

1 Use Figure 12.11 and choose an appropriate technique to illustrate Ethiopia's growing population. Comment on the trend.

2 Use the news extracts and Figures 12.13 and 12.14 to describe ways in which the Ethiopian/Eritrean border war could:
   a) cause food insecurity in the war zone
   b) contribute significantly to food insecurity in the Ogaden region in the south-east of Ethiopia.

3 a) Draw a sketch map of the Horn of Africa. Add the labels from Figure 12.15 as annotations in suitable places on your map.
   b) Suggest strategies that could be adopted to remedy some of these problems.

4 Use this case study to illustrate why geographers must be critically aware of the limitations of the internet and news media as a source of data.

Is the concept of overpopulation redundant?

Famine is not an inevitable consequence of population growth. It may be triggered by disasters such as drought or floods, but it is usually caused by political failures such as war, food distribution problems, and the vulnerability of certain groups within society. Many now suggest that Spaceship Earth has the capacity to supply everyone with sufficient resources. However, a challenge remains to manage these resources effectively and equitably. If this could be achieved, it is thought that the Earth could sustain a population of 30 billion people. As we have seen in Chapter 11, this total is far greater than is ever likely to be reached.

However, hardships due to a combination of population growth, resource mismanagement and political culpability exist in many places. In these places, local overpopulation is a contributing factor to the low standard of living. Two examples follow. In each case you need to consider the role played by population.

Overpopulation in Colorado, USA?

The state of Colorado, USA, in the eastern foothills of the Rocky Mountains has a population of just 3.7 million. Like others in the mountainous West of the USA, it has a low population density of 12 people per km^2: only ten states have a lower density. As such, one would not expect the term 'overpopulation' to be appropriate. However, the combination of open space, economic growth and the beauty of the mountain landscape are attracting migrants from other parts of the USA and the population is rising rapidly. It grew by 149 per cent between 1970 and 1990; only seven states grew by a larger percentage. Between 1990 and 1996, 350 000 people moved into the state and an extra 1 million are forecast to move in by 2020. Most are well off and well educated: 27 per cent of Colorado's population over 25 have a degree.

Figure 12.16 Pressures on the environment in Denver, Colorado.

Cities in the Front Range (easternmost foothills of the Rockies) are absorbing most of the population growth. Ever expanding suburbs sprawl across greenfield sites. Every year 36 400 hectares of farmland or ranch are lost to the development of freeways, housing and shopping malls. Suburban development on the edge of Denver extends towards Boulder to the north and Colorado Springs and Pueblo to the south.

Suburbanisation is taking its toll. Commuter traffic emits particulates and gases that undergo photochemical reactions in the sunlight. The resulting brown cloud of smog that frequently hangs over Denver obscures the blue sky, limiting the clean air. But a greater limit to growth is the lack of water. The Front Range receives an annual total of just 355mm precipitation. The Midwest and mountain states receive the lowest precipitation totals in the USA. Moist Pacific air masses drop their precipitation over the western seaboard and are dry by the time they reach these central states. Moist Atlantic air similarly bypasses Colorado. Colorado's population relies mainly on the Denver basin aquifer for its water supply. This aquifer contains the same volume of water as Lake Erie, but it is a fossil aquifer: it was filled by rainfall long ago. Over-abstraction means that water is dropping faster than current rainfall is replacing it.

Families living to the west of Denver are already running out of water. Boreholes as much as 360m deep are running dry: rocks of the aquifer slope away to the east, and as water is pumped to supply new suburbs, the level drops. In some districts water levels have dropped by 240m. State law permits abstraction of 1 per cent of the aquifer each year, so the aquifer will run dry in 100 years. Denver has to find alternative supplies; it currently gets 50 per cent of its supply by transferring water from rivers flowing in the Front Range. But with rights to the use of surface water now all claimed, there will not be any additional water available for future growth. Population growth may not be sustainable unless methods of water conservation are introduced.

Overpopulated cities?

Half of the world's 6 billion people live in cities which are packed onto just 3 per cent of the Earth's land area. Many of the world's largest cities are in LEDCs, and 80 per cent of all urban residents will be in LEDCs by 2025. As these cities have experienced rapid growth, demand for land has brought into use land that is unsuitable for development: steep, unstable and deforested slopes that are vulnerable to landslides or mudslides; or riverbanks, floodplains or marshes that are vulnerable to flash floods.

Hazard mitigation in urban areas requires careful planning:
- land use zoning so that unsuitable sites, such as floodplains, are left undeveloped or are used for low risk land uses such as recreation
- application of strict building codes, for example using designs that are earthquake-proof.

But informal settlements are at risk because they are illegal and have been built without any planning control. Squatters build on any land that is available, including the sites that have been left vacant by the planners because they are unsuitable. Furthermore, informal settlements are built at high densities and are often poorly constructed, so the urban poor are most at risk from natural hazards such as earthquakes, mudslides, flooding, tropical storms or fire.

As vulnerable urban populations have grown, so have the number of casualties from natural hazards. In 1976 an earthquake killed 23 000 people in Guatemala. Guatemala City (population 1.3 million) was badly damaged. Some 1200 people died and 90 000 were made homeless. The majority of these casualties had been living in shanties, many of which had been built in gorges and ravines. Immediately after the earthquake most unsuitable sites were left undeveloped. High cost housing has been built on steep terrain to the east of the city, but it has been built to withstand shaking. However, since 1990 the city has grown rapidly in an unplanned fashion to over 2 million. The urban poor have either forgotten the earthquake, or consider it a remote risk – once again building is occurring on unsuitable sites. A recent survey identified 197 settlements, with a total population of 589 000, built on sites that are vulnerable to earthquakes, floods and landslides.

Figure 12.17 Demand for space leads to squatter settlements growing on land unsuitable for development.

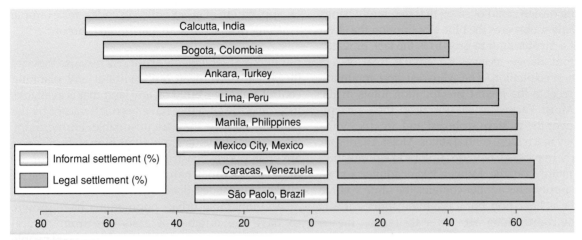

Figure 12.18 Percentage of informal and legal settlement for selected cities.

1 Use an atlas to locate each of the cities in Figure 12.18. Using the natural hazard map in your atlas, which of these cities is vulnerable to:
 a) earthquakes and landslides that result from shaking
 b) tropical storms and flooding or mudslides that result from extreme weather?

2 Explain why the number of people living at risk from natural hazards is likely to increase for the next 50 years.

3 Use the case studies of Colorado and Guatemala to explain:
 a) how lack of resources might limit the growth of local populations
 b) how technology can be used to overcome these limits to growth.

Summary
You have learned that:
- Crowded populations can create such demands on living space and other resources, for example clean air and water, that quality of life begins to deteriorate. This is known as overpopulation.
- Famine is seen by many as a symptom of global overpopulation. Overpopulation is also said to be the cause of environmental damage such as soil erosion, deforestation and pollution. Famine occurs as a result of unequal sharing of food resources: war, food distribution problems and the vulnerability of certain groups within society cause famine – not overpopulation.
- Global resources are not shared equally. The richer MEDCs consume around 75 per cent of the world's resources, despite having only 25 per cent of the world's population.
- Overpopulation may not exist at a global scale until population exceeds 30 billion. However, overpopulation may create stresses at a local scale. Rapid growth in some urban areas, for example, causes stresses on water supply and creates atmospheric pollution. City growth can be seen as unsustainable if limiting factors such as clean air and water are used up.
- Where population growth is uncontrolled, the urban poor make themselves vulnerable to natural disasters by building in unsuitable sites.

References and further reading
Jane Chrispin and Francis Jegede, *Population, Resources and Development*, Collins Educational (1996)
International Decade for Natural Disaster Reduction, *Cities At Risk: Making Cities Safer … Before Disaster Strikes*, Stop Disasters Publication (1996)
Philip Sarre and John Blunden, *An Overcrowded World?*, The Open University (1995)

Web sites
http://quake.wr.usgs.gov/
http://hoshi.cic.sfu.ca/hazard/idndr.html
http://www.fema.gov
http://www.unfpa.org/
http://www.popin.org

Issues facing youthful populations

This chapter investigates issues facing rapidly expanding populations in LEDCs. Why are populations there growing so quickly? What particular challenges are posed by such youthful populations?

Variations in total fertility rate: searching for explanations

It is a commonly held view in western societies that people in developing countries have too many children. There is a perception in the West that developing countries remain poor because they are caught in a poverty trap of their own making. Poverty results from populations that grow too quickly in countries that cannot afford care for its dependants. The idea is then translated from national to personal levels, i.e. families in LEDCs are poor because they have lots of children. This

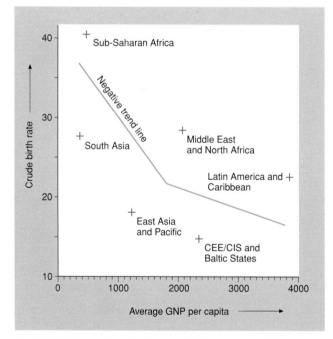

Figure 13.1 The relationship between GNP and crude birth rate.

view results from western perceptions about costs of raising a family. In Europe and the USA, feeding, clothing, health care and education of our children represent considerable costs. Pressures created by advertising in an affluent consumer society increase the need to spend money on the latest fashion, toys, computers, etc. for children.

That a link exists between wealth and the birth rate is demonstrated in Figure 13.1. It suggests a connection between the two sets of data. But is there a causal link between the two sets of data? And, if so, which set of data is dependent upon the other?

If it is true that developing countries are poor because people have lots of children, then the logical extension of the argument is that they will become richer if they improve, or enforce, methods of family planning. But what if people choose to have large families because they are poor? And what if the root cause of high fertility rates is another factor altogether? Obviously, governments that seek to reduce fertility rates effectively, and thereby slow population growth, need to consider these questions very carefully.

Why do total fertility rates vary?

Factors that stimulate change in total fertility rates are complex, and may be divided into economic, cultural and social. In many LEDCs, poor families regard children as an economic asset (Figure 13.3). Poor parents expect their children to help with chores, such as collecting water and firewood, and to look after younger siblings. Many are also expected to work on family smallholdings or to earn a wage. In countries without state pensions or other welfare payments, children are a guarantee of income when parents are too old to work. In countries where children are regarded as an economic asset, poverty leads to larger families, not the other way around.

Figure 13.2 Shoe shine boy working in Guatemala.

There is a negative side. Financial pressures to keep children away from school can result in both child labour and inadequate standards of education (Figure 13.4). UNICEF estimates that 130 million children of primary school age in LEDCs do not attend school (Figure 13.5). A further 150 million fail to complete primary education. They also estimate that 250 million children in LEDCs are trapped in child labour, and many receive no schooling at all. Some may see little relevance in attending school (Figure 13.6). Not only does this raise the human rights issue of exploitation, it also guarantees high birth rates in the next generation; education is a major factor in influencing birth rates.

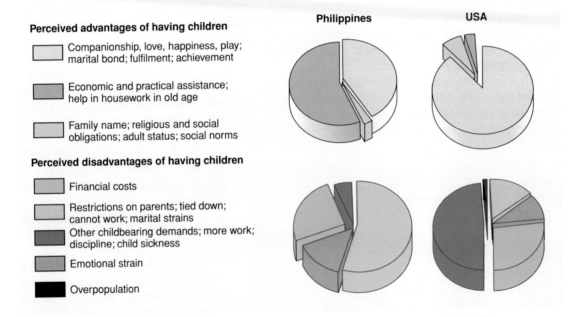

Perceived advantages of having children

- Companionship, love, happiness, play; marital bond; fulfilment; achievement
- Economic and practical assistance; help in housework in old age
- Family name; religious and social obligations; adult status; social norms

Perceived disadvantages of having children

- Financial costs
- Restrictions on parents; tied down; cannot work; marital strains
- Other childbearing demands; more work; discipline; child sickness
- Emotional strain
- Overpopulation

Figure 13.3 Perceived advantages and disadvantages of having children in the Philippines and the USA.

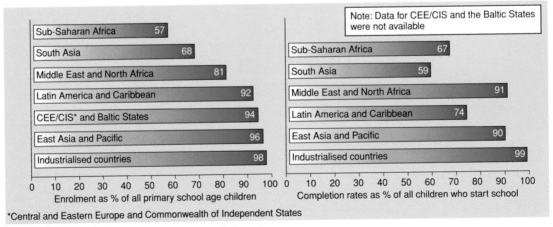

Note: Data for CEE/CIS and the Baltic States were not available

Enrolment as % of all primary school age children	
Sub-Saharan Africa	57
South Asia	68
Middle East and North Africa	81
Latin America and Caribbean	92
CEE/CIS* and Baltic States	94
East Asia and Pacific	96
Industrialised countries	98

Completion rates as % of all children who start school	
Sub-Saharan Africa	67
South Asia	59
Middle East and North Africa	91
Latin America and Caribbean	74
East Asia and Pacific	90
Industrialised countries	99

*Central and Eastern Europe and Commonwealth of Independent States

Figure 13.4 Primary school enrolment and completion rates.

When school is an income lost

The right to free education for children is enshrined in India's constitution. But in the poorest families, occupied with day-to-day survival, not all children can be spared for school. A child's time can be more valuably spent in the fields, or at home, than in the classroom. Education is a long-term investment that many families cannot afford; as well as the cost of books and a uniform, a child at school is a day's income sacrificed.

Thimmakka, from Basavapura village, expresses the sentiments of millions of parents in rural India: 'We have two pairs of bullocks and two fields. We need the help of our children to work on the land. So how can I send them all to school? This work has to be done so that we can all eat.'

Traditionally, education for girls has been seen as of secondary importance to that for boys. Often, girls are kept at home or are the first to be withdrawn from school when an extra pair of hands is required, such as when a younger sibling needs looking after. 'Why should my daughter be educated? After all she will soon get married and go to her husband's house', is a common cry.

Ponnuthi, a mother of four schoolgirls, disagrees: 'Whether they are boys or girls they should study. I have to be responsible for my children and they deserve a chance to become educated. They will have a better future. I have taken many loans and we are struggling but so what?'

Figure 13.5 Education and poverty.

The poor quality of education in schools is itself a depressant on the demand for education, even where access exists. Child labour experts have found that some children would rather work than be subject to a school regime that is irrelevant to their needs.

Assane, a 10-year-old shoeshine boy interviewed in the Senegalese city of Ziguinchor, made the case clearly:

'I don't need to go to school. What can I learn there? I know children who went to school. Their family paid for the fees and the uniforms and they are educated. But you see them sitting around. Now they are useless to their families. They don't know anything about farming or trading or making money … I know I need to learn to read and write [but] … if anyone tries to put me in school, I will run away.'

Figure 13.6 Why go to school …?

1 Study Figure 13.3. Discuss how perceptions of having children differ in the USA and Philippines. In particular, identify evidence to show that:
   a) poverty may influence decisions in the Philippines
   b) affluence may influence decisions in the USA.

2 Study Figure 13.4.
   a) In which region does primary education face the largest challenge? Justify your answer. What other information would be helpful in answering this more effectively?
   b) How do priorities for educators in South Asia differ from those in Latin America?

3 How important is it for all children to receive a basic primary education (Figures 13.5 and 13.6)? What are the gender issues? Why is quality of education an issue?

How do cultural and social factors influence fertility?

Economic needs among poor families may influence decisions to have children, but cultural and social factors are also important. Figure 13.7 summarises some of these factors. Perhaps the most crucial of these is the degree of autonomy enjoyed by women in society, i.e. their ability to act and make decisions independently. Full autonomy for a woman in society would mean:

- fertility rights: the ability to control her own fertility by use of contraceptives, to choose her sexual partner and the age at which she should marry
- ownership rights: the same rights as men to inherit, own and dispose of property
- educational rights: equal access to information, for example equal rights to education both at school and university; she would also have equal rights to express herself and her opinions, for example equal voting rights
- decision making rights: the same input as her partner to decision making within the household.

But many women do not experience full autonomy and each of these rights has some bearing on fertility rates. Many women do not have full fertility rights. Arranged marriages and even child marriage – although illegal – are common in India and other southern Asian cultures. Where this occurs, birth rates are higher. Another common example can be seen in women's lack of ownership rights. In most African cultures women do the bulk of farm work, but men own the land. Women are usually unable to inherit land when their husbands die. In such circumstances, women are more likely to be poor and feel they have no long-term security. A large family, especially several sons, could be an insurance policy against poverty in these circumstances.

Fertility is certainly influenced by beliefs, traditions and customs of society. Attitudes towards methods of family planning may be influenced by religious beliefs, and how widely those beliefs are acted upon. The Roman Catholic Church, for example, does not advocate the use of modern methods of contraception. However, many Catholics choose to ignore its teaching on this issue and many Catholic countries have low fertility rates; Italy has such a low fertility rate that, at 1.2, it is well below replacement level. So in relatively wealthy countries, where children are an expense rather than an asset, economic factors influence fertility more strongly than cultural.

Common cultural/social attitudes		
Value of women in society (female autonomy)	high	low
Average age of marriage	late	early
Cultural attitudes about gender of children	no gender preference	males preferred
Parental and government commitment to female education	high	low
Spending on welfare for women, e.g. ante-natal care	high	low
Availability of contraceptives and sexual health education/care	high	low
	↓	↓
	fertility decreases	fertility increases

Figure 13.7 Social and cultural pressures on the fertility rate.

The role of the state in controlling fertility

About 55 per cent of couples in LEDCs use some method of family planning. The use of family planning in LEDCs has increased fivefold since the 1960s and has contributed to significant reductions

Figure 13.8 Campaigning for small families in Mexico.

in average fertility over forty years; in 2000 average fertility was three to four, whereas in the 1960s it was six to seven. However, at least 350 million couples worldwide, many of whom say they want to space or prevent pregnancies, do not have access to the full range of modern family planning methods. A further 120 million women would like to use modern methods of contraception but cannot. They are prevented by one of the following:

- they need more accurate information
- contraceptive services are either unaffordable or unavailable
- partners, extended families or their community are unsupportive or hostile.

These estimates do not include growing numbers of sexually active, unmarried individuals who want access to modern family planning services.

Many states have taken direct action to try to control population growth. In most cases, the government has concentrated on promoting wider use of family planning. In Mexico, Catholic teaching on contraception had kept contraceptive use below 12 per cent. In 1973, anxious about future conse-quences of the population boom, the government reversed its family planning policy, making access to family planning a legal right, and legalised advertising and selling of contraceptives. Contraceptive use is now 53 per cent.

Other governments have gone further, attempting to enforce family planning in order to reduce population growth. In 1975 emergency laws were passed in India to enforce the sterilisation of large numbers of men. This led to massive public disorder and the government backed down. Nowadays, the government tries to persuade women to agree to sterilisation. In 1993, 4.1 million women were sterilised, but the campaign has little impact on fertility because those who volunteer are mainly older women who have already had several children.

Such attempts to enforce methods of family planning have been criticised by human rights campaigners. Strict family planning policies, like those introduced in China in 1979, have been blamed for the rise in female infanticide, i.e. the neglect and consequent premature death of young girls.

The 1994 population conference, Cairo

The UN has held international conferences on the topic of world population in 1974 (Bucharest), 1984 (Mexico) and 1994 (Cairo). These were attended by government representatives from LEDCs and MEDCs. They were important because they placed the debate on population growth within the wider context of the environment, the role of women and of sustainable economic development.

The conferences have consistently stated that it is not people (or population growth) that is the problem, but their poverty. Population growth is a symptom of that poverty. Economic development, which leads to higher living standards for the poorer members of the

global community, will lead to a reduction in fertility. The Cairo conference confirmed the importance of making modern methods of family planning available to all, but it condemned governments that tried to enforce family planning (Figure 13.8). It concluded that fertility rates should be reduced by a package of measures, to include:

- greater access to education, and equality for girls in the education system
- greater autonomy for women, and their involvement in development strategies
- improved health care and nutrition, especially to reduce infant and maternal mortality.

Figure 13.9 Girls catching up on their schooling in India.

7.12 The aim of family-planning programmes must be to enable couples and individuals to decide freely and responsibly the number and spacing of their children and to have the information and means to do so and to ensure informed choices and make available a full range of safe and effective methods … Any form of coercion has no part to play … Over the past century, many Governments have experimented with such schemes, including specific incentives and disincentives, in order to lower or raise fertility. Most such schemes have had only marginal impact on fertility and in some cases have been counterproductive.

11.2 Education is a key factor in sustainable development: … The reduction of fertility, morbidity and mortality rates, the empowerment of women, the improvement in the quality of the working population and the promotion of genuine democracy are largely assisted by progress in education. The integration of migrants is also facilitated by universal access to education, which respects the religious and cultural backgrounds of migrants.

11.3 The relationship between education and demographic and social changes is one of interdependence. There is a close and complex relationship among education, marriage age, fertility, mortality, mobility and activity. The increase in the education of women and girls contributes to greater empowerment of women, to a postponement of the age of marriage and to a reduction in the size of families. When mothers are better educated, their children's survival rate tends to increase. Broader access to education is also a factor in internal migration and the make-up of the working population.

Figure 13.10 Extract from the concluding document produced at the 1994 Cairo conference.

While global access to education has improved, there is still a gender gap: 75 per cent of illiterate persons in the world are women. Both the Cairo conference, and UNICEF see the need for children, especially girls, to have better access to educational services. The benefits of education are described in Figures 13.10 and 13.11.

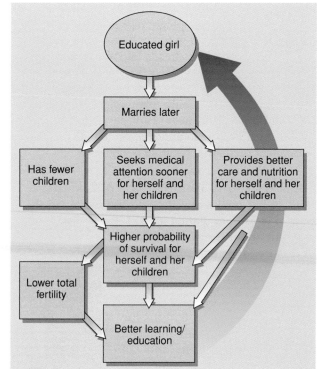

Figure 13.11 The benefits of investing in girls' education.

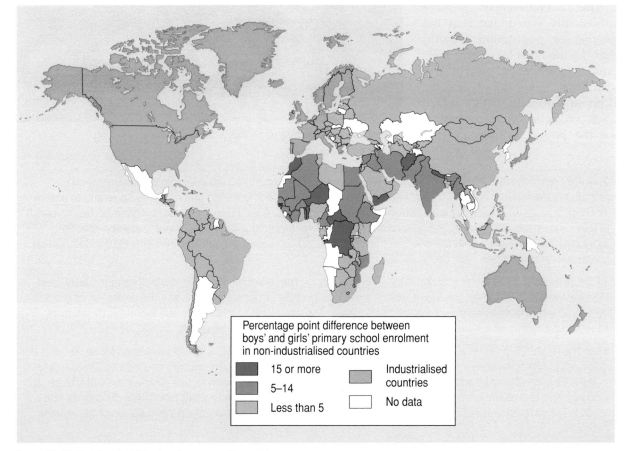

Figure 13.12 Boys' and girls' education across the world.

'Education For All' is a campaign by UNICEF and its partners to increase government spending on education so that all children receive primary education by 2010. They estimate it would cost an additional US $7 billion: less than is spent each year in the USA on cosmetics or in Europe on ice cream.

Education For All would be funded by the 20/20 Initiative, which would require LEDC governments to increase spending on basic social programmes from 13 to 20 per cent of government expenditure. Aid-giving MEDCs are encouraged to increase their official development assistance by 10–20 per cent.

	Current annual expenditure		Required additional average annual expenditure, US$ (billions)
	US$ (billions)	% of GNP	
Sub-Saharan Africa	7.0	1.9	1.9
South Asia	9.0	1.9	1.6
Middle East/North Africa	14.0	2.2	1.6
East Asia/Pacific	20.0	1.2	0.7
Latin America/Caribbean	30.0	1.8	1.1

Figure 13.13 Spending required to ensure primary education for all children by 2010.

1 Read Figure 13.10 and study Figure 13.11.
   a) 'The relationship between education and demographic and social changes is one of interdependence.' Summarise the ways in which education indirectly reduces fertility.
   b) Figure 13.11 demonstrates positive feedback. Explain what this means.

2 Use Figures 13.12 and 13.13 to compile a report on global access to education. Include in your report:
   a) detailed descriptions of regions where boys' enrolment in school greatly exceeds that of girls
   b) spatial similarities between patterns of gender inequality in school and patterns of fertility
   c) the spatial distribution of additional expenditure needed to ensure Education for All.

3 State what could happen without such spending.

Conflicts over fertility

The debate over fertility, and its control, has caused enormous disagreement. Opposing viewpoints, determined by cultural and religious background, lead to conflict. Roman Catholic representatives at Cairo were unhappy that they could not agree to the right of every couple to be able to choose methods of contraception. But they were, and still are, opposed by many women who want greater sexual autonomy. A third group is composed of conservative thinkers in MEDCs (for example the right wing/Christian coalition in the USA), who oppose what they see as society's liberalisation. They dislike ways in which western societies have changed since the 1960s. These changes include:

- co-habitation as an alternative to marriage
- widespread use of contraceptives
- liberalisation of divorce and abortion laws.

Figure 13.14 Women in Baghdad, Iraq.

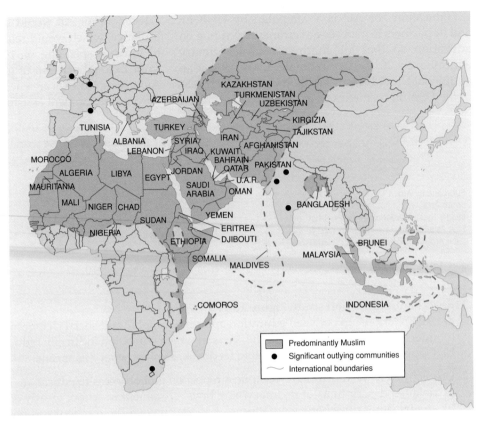

Figure 13.15 The realm of Islam.

In the 1980s, alarm caused by the spread of HIV and AIDS changed many attitudes about sexual relationships and triggered a call for a return to 'family values' by more traditional elements in society. This point of view is shared by many Islamic fundamentalists. The Islamic realm includes LEDCs in northern Africa and Asia: the very part of the globe that has the highest fertility rates (Figures 3.15 and 3.16).

The Islamic faith does not prevent the use of modern contraceptives. However, it attaches great importance to traditional family values that are patriarchal, i.e. father centred. In some Islamic states, traditional beliefs are in conflict with more progressive western viewpoints that are increasingly visible on television, in films and in advertising. In Egypt, fundamental Islamic groups oppose government policies that they see as too progressive and accommodating to western cultural values. Another example of this kind of political and religious opposition to cultural change can be seen in Morocco. Here the young king, who is also the country's supreme religious authority, has upset conservative Islamists in his country because he wants to give women greater autonomy (Figure 13.17).

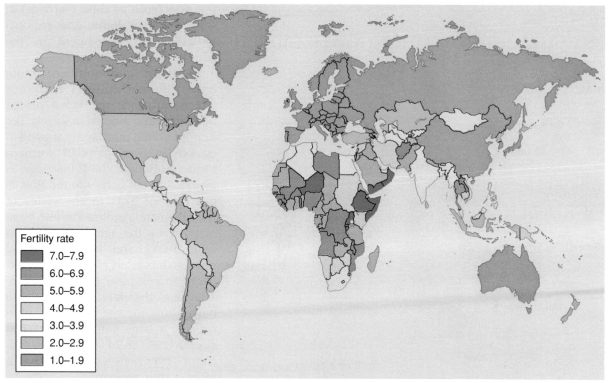

Figure 13.16 Global fertility.

Fury as 'King M-6' reforms status of Moroccan women

A rise in the legal age of marriage from 15 to 18; polygamy only with the permission of a man's first wife; an equal right to divorce, and a fair division of assets between the parties. What could sound more reasonable? In Morocco, these notions are enough to have wise men warning of civil war.

January 2000 will go down as when the new Moroccan revolution woke up to reality. It was when Islamic activists shouted down ministers in the capital, Rabat, and when a government plan to haul the treatment of women from the Middle Ages to somewhere near the 21st century became the litmus test for King Mohammed VI's ambitions for his country.

This was the month one of the most stable Arab countries became a battleground between modernisers and the forces of conservative Islam.

Morocco's Islamists are a minority, but a determined one.

They have the backing of conservatives in Mr Youssufi's eight-party coalition, and a natural recruiting ground in the mosques and universities.

The ingredients that have stoked Islamic movements elsewhere are only too visible here: massive unemployment, $19 billion of foreign debt whose mere servicing consumes one-third of the annual budget, rampant corruption and vast disparities between a tiny, super-wealthy elite and masses who live in grinding poverty.

The illiteracy rate is 50 per cent; as many live on £1 a day or less. Among women in the countryside, deprived of schooling, jobs and basic legal rights, those figures rise to 80 per cent or more.

The Islamists claim emancipation of women would lead to the collapse of the family, destruction of Islamic values and debauchery of every sort.

Figure 13.17 From the *Independent*, 3 February 2000.

1 a) Comment on the apparent link between the spatial extent of the Islamic realm (Figure 13.15) and global patterns of fertility (Figure 13.16).
  b) What other factors (economic, cultural, social) may account for high fertility in the Islamic realm?

2 Read the article in Figure 13.17.
  a) List ways in which the status of women will change if reforms are carried out.
  b) Suggest how each of these might influence reproductive patterns and birth rates in Morocco.

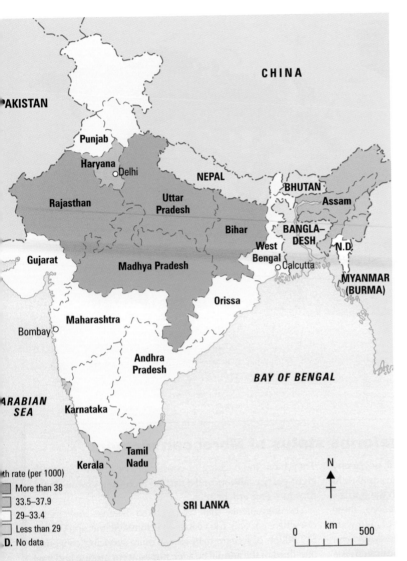

Figure 13.18 Regional variations in India's birth rate.

Map legend:

th rate (per 1000)
- More than 38
- 33.5–37.9
- 29–33.4
- Less than 29
- N.D. No data

practices (such as child marriage) in some parts of India, and regional variations in investment in the education system.

Northern and southern India have different cultural traditions which influence the value placed upon girls and women in society. For example, child marriage is an ancient custom in rural parts of northern India. Although child marriage is illegal, a recent survey found that 90 per cent of girls in the states of Rajasthan and Andhra Pradesh were married by the age of 15. Women who marry and begin a sexual relationship at an early age are less likely to complete their education. They are, therefore, more likely to have a low income and be more in need of a large family for financial support. A child bride has less control over her own fertility than a more mature woman.

By contrast, some southern Indian states depend less on traditional values and have adopted more progressive attitudes towards women. In Kerala, the socialist state has invested heavily in education and health care. As many women go

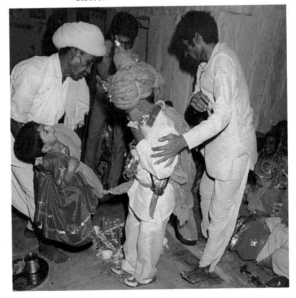

Figure 13.19 Child marriage, although illegal, is still common in some northern Indian states.

Fertility and the role of women: a case study of India

India, with a population of over 1 billion, is the second most populous country in the world. With an average fertility rate of 3.4, its population continues to rise rapidly at a rate of 1.9 per cent per annum. But its fertility rate hides significant regional and cultural variations. Figure 13.18 shows a large tract of northern India where birth rates are significantly above the national average. Contrast it with southern states, where birth rates are below the national average, and eastern states, a region in which there is huge variation in the birth rate.

The explanation for this striking pattern is complex. It includes regional variations in autonomy of women, the value placed on traditional

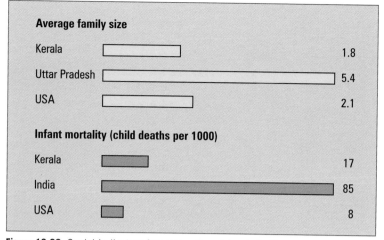

Figure 13.20 Social indicators for contrasting states in India, compared to the USA.

to school and university as men. Women have greater educational autonomy, and choose to delay marriage and pursue careers. Improvements in health care have reduced infant mortality, so women are confident that their children will survive and do not feel the need to have more in case of death in infancy. Twin improvements in health and education for women have dramatically reduced birth rates.

Gender inequality in India: investigating the sex ratio

Further evidence of India's regional and cultural inequality is given in Figure 13.21. It reveals variations in India's sex ratio: the number of girls and women to every 1000 boys and men. India averages 936 girls and women to every 1000 boys and men (a sex ratio of 936:1000). There is strong evidence to suggest that, if men and women are given access to a similar education, diet and medical care, women live longer then men. By contrast, therefore, the sex ratio in the UK (1036:1000) is weighted towards women. But India's male-dominated sex ratio indicates that life expectancy for girls in many parts of Indian society is lower than that for boys. Poor diet, inadequate education and health care are killing millions of girls unnecessarily. Indeed, for India to improve its sex ratio to that of the world average (a ratio of 1002:1000) it would require the survival of an additional 32.9 million women.

Figure 13.21 shows regional variations in the sex ratio; sex ratios are most unequal in northern states and become more favourable to women in the South. The explanation for this is that life expectancy for girls falls dramatically in a steep gradient from south to north. But what are the cultural explanations? The pattern and its explanations are similar to those relating to birth rates. Unequal sex ratios are due to the low perceived value of women in society. Poor parents who regard children as an economic asset favour boys, who are thought to work harder, will inherit the family land and will not marry out of the family. By contrast, girls leave the family to join their husband, often while in their mid-teens – not only is this a loss of labour, it also requires payment of a dowry to the husband's family. Dowry payment, like child marriage, is now illegal, but common in traditional northern states. Young girls, therefore, are sometimes neglected. They may be breastfed for a shorter period than boys. Poor parents who cannot afford full education and medical care for their children may choose to favour sons rather than daughters.

By contrast, women in southern states such as Kerala have greater sexual and educational autonomy. They marry later in life and experience lower rates of infant mortality.

List all the economic, cultural and social factors that may be responsible for the spatial pattern of fertility rates in India. How far do these contrast with:
a) the city or area where you live
b) other places you have studied?

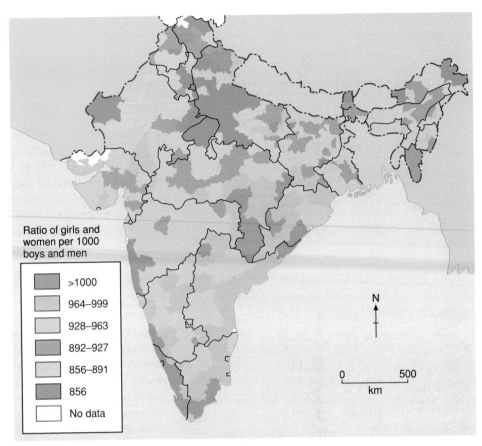

Ratio of girls and
women per 1000
boys and men

- >1000
- 964–999
- 928–963
- 892–927
- 856–891
- 856
- No data

N

0   500
km

Figure 13.21 Regional variations in India's sex ratio.

Summary

You have learned that:

- Doubling times are shortest and populations are growing most rapidly in the Sahel countries of Africa and in southern Asia.
- In LEDCs, poorer families choose to have large families for economic reasons. Social, cultural and religious factors also determine the birth rate.
- LEDCs are characterised by youthful populations, i.e. their populations have a large proportion of under-fifteens. It indicates that the population will continue to grow as these children reach sexual maturity – a situation regarded by some as a potential population explosion or time bomb.
- The fear of uncontrolled population explosion has lead some countries to adopt anti-natalist policies, where the state attempts to reduce birth rates. This raises concerns over the denial of the human right for individuals to be able to choose how many children they want.
- Apart from trying to lower the birth rate, youthful populations are facing other difficult issues. These include the use of child labour and the neglect of young girls in some societies.

References and further reading

Peter Atkins et al., 'India's missing millions', *Geography Review*, volume 13, number 1, Philip Allan updates (1999)

Carol Bellamy, *The state of the world's children 1999 – Education*, UNICEF (1999)

Philip Sarre and John Blunden, *An Overcrowded World?*, Open University (1995)

Web sites

Zero Population Growth, a US organisation that promotes policies designed to reduce population growth to zero: http://www.zpg.org.us

UNICEF in supporting education programmes at their web site: http://www.unicef.org.sowc00/

www.unfpa.org/

www.popin.org/

14 Migration and its consequences

Migration is a common phenomenon. Most people move at some point in their life because they change job, or because their family circumstances change and they need a bigger or smaller home. This chapter will investigate the reasons for migration, its consequences, and the way in which attitudes towards migrants may be changing.

Figure 14.1 Migration may be forced, as in photo A, or voluntary, as in B.

A Ecological refugees from the eruption of the Soufriere Hills Volcano.

B Economic migrant from Mexico crosses the border into the USA illegally.

Why do people migrate?

There are many reasons why people migrate. The photographs in Figure 14.1 illustrate the way migration can be divided into two main types: forced and voluntary migration.

Forced migration

Natural disasters such as floods, droughts, mudslides, volcanic eruptions and earthquakes leave people with no choice but to move for their own safety. Such migrants are ecological refugees. Figure 14.1A shows migrants forced to move by the eruption of the Soufrière Hills Volcano in Montserrat. The volcano began erupting in 1995 after being dormant for 400 years. A major eruption in June 1997 was successfully forecast and the southern half of the island was evacuated. The pyroclastic flows which followed the evacuation completely destroyed the island's capital, Plymouth. A population of around 11 000 before the eruption has been reduced to only 3000 today. Most of the refugees have moved to Britain, Antigua and other Caribbean islands, or the USA. Others moved to temporary shelters such as school and church halls in the north of the island before being rehoused. The south of the island is still an exclusion zone and uninhabitable.

Political instability may also force people to migrate. War or ethnic persecution may force groups of the population to flee from an area. These migrants are political refugees. Refugees from the former Yugoslavia, including the Kosovan refugees who fled the fighting with Serbia in the late 1990s, fall into this category.

A third factor is displacement that occurs when governments carry out major infrastructure projects, for example the building of dams, roads or tourist resorts. The World Bank estimates that at least 90 million people were displaced in the 1990s as a result of infrastructure projects. The massive development projects on the River Narmada in Maharashtra, India, are thought to have caused the displacement of 1.5 million people. In such circumstances, displaced people often receive scant compensation.

Voluntary migration

Many people migrate because they think they can find a better standard of living elsewhere. To escape low pay, unemployment and poor educational or health opportunities for their children, migrants choose to move in the belief they will be able to improve their standard of living as a result. These are known as economic migrants.

Figure 14.1B shows economic migrants trying to cross from Mexico into the USA. Around 900 000 farmers leave the arid and semi-arid lands of northern Mexico every year. Many are landless labourers who struggle with poverty because there is insufficient rural employment. They have two main choices:

- rural to urban migration – many rural families move to a city (Mexico City attracts thousands, but others move to towns such as Tijuana and Ciudad Juarez on the US border) in the hope of finding employment in manufacturing or service industries located there
- international migration to the USA – tens of thousands of Mexicans emigrate to the USA legally every year, and many others cross the border illegally; it is estimated that there are between 3 and 10 million illegal Mexican migrants living and working in the USA.

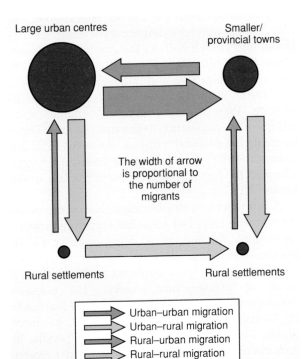

Figure 14.2 The types of migration flow common in MEDCs such as the UK.

Investigating patterns of migration

Patterns of migration are of great interest to geographers. What kinds of places commonly lose or attract migrants and what routes do migrations follow? Migration patterns are classified according to the type of places that lose and gain migrants. There are four main types of pattern (Figure 14.2):

- urban to urban
- urban to rural
- rural to urban
- rural to rural.

These movements can take place between countries but are more common within national boundaries – this is known as internal migration.

As a general rule internal movements within LEDCs are from rural to urban areas, while migration patterns in MEDCs are dominated by urban to rural movements. But this general pattern hides a more complex series of flows. For example, migration in rural areas of the UK involves at least two directions of movement:

- young local people are leaving the rural area in order to attend university or find work in cities
- older people are moving in to the rural area to enjoy early retirement or to commute to work.

Type of migration flow	1981	1986	1991
Urban-urban	13.9	11.3	38.0
Urban-rural	17.1	13.9	20.9
Rural-urban	18.4	15.4	19.9
Rural-rural	50.6	47.8	21.2

Figure 14.3 Types of migration in Malaysia, 1981–91.

1 Study Figures 14.2 and 14.3.
   a) Describe the way in which migration flows in Malaysia changed between 1981 and 1991. What might be the consequence for urban areas?
   b) Draw proportional arrows, like those in Figure 14.2, to illustrate migration flows in Malaysia in 1991.

South Shropshire: A case study of migration into a rural area

A level geographers at the Community College in Bishop's Castle, Shropshire, investigated some of the patterns common to migration within the UK. Local people who had moved from urban areas to live in South Shropshire were asked:

- where they had lived previously
- why they had moved
- whether the rural area met their expectations.

Sample size was very small. Only 18 people responded to the survey out of a total population of 1600 in Bishop's Castle. This represents a little over 1 per cent. Figure 14.4 shows the number of times that each migrant had moved. Four of the migrants had moved between several urban centres and had also lived abroad. The other fourteen had all lived in urban centres in England and Wales. The migration pattern of these fourteen is shown in Figure 14.5. Figure 14.6 shows the response to questions about whether the migrant perceived the rural area to offer a better quality of life than previous areas in which they had lived.

Number of moves	Frequency
1	1
2	0
3	9
4	4
5	1
6	2
7+	1

Figure 14.4 Mobility of the urban to rural migrants – number of homes since each migrant left the parental home.

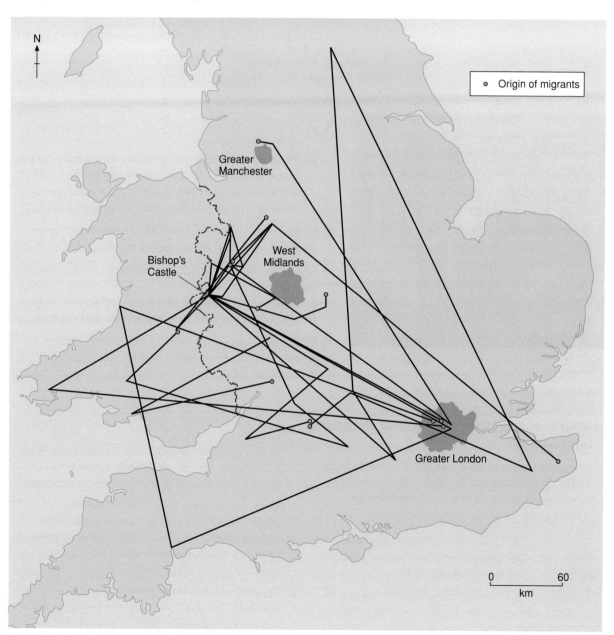

Figure 14.5 Movement of migrants to Bishop's Castle.

169

Figure 14.6 Migrants' perception of the rural area compared to previous homes. Migrants were asked to imagine that a ten-rung ladder represented quality of life. The top rung represented the best possible life, i.e. comfortable home, pleasant local environment and amenities, low levels of stress. The bottom rung represented the worst possible life, i.e. inadequate or insecure home, unpleasant local environment with unsatisfactory amenities, and high levels of stress. Migrants were asked to mark four points on the ladder, A, B, C and D.

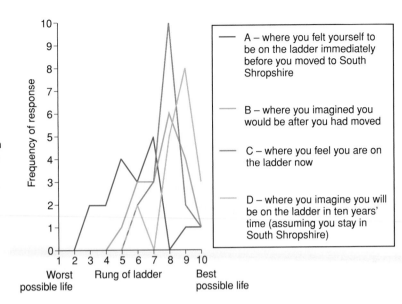

A – where you felt yourself to be on the ladder immediately before you moved to South Shropshire

B – where you imagined you would be after you had moved

C – where you feel you are on the ladder now

D – where you imagine you will be on the ladder in ten years' time (assuming you stay in South Shropshire)

Figure 14.7 Bishop's Castle in South Shropshire.

1 a) Suggest suitable techniques for plotting the data in Figure 14.4.
   b) What does the data tell us about the mobility of the respondents? What data would need to be collected to decide whether or not these people were more or less mobile than other people in the UK?

2 Describe the pattern of migration shown in Figure 14.5. Comment on the origin of the migrants.

3 Study Figure 14.6. What conclusion can you draw about:
   a) how people's quality of life has changed over time
   b) the difference between perception and reality?

4 What other questions might test whether or not people felt that their move had been a success?

Theory

Models of migration 1: patterns of movement

Ravenstein's laws

Ravenstein studied patterns of migration in the UK in the 1880s. From his research he developed a number of conclusions that are described as Ravenstein's laws. These laws were used as predictive statements to predict the usual pattern of migration. They need to be used critically today, as there have been many social and technological changes since they were written. Some of his laws are paraphrased below.

1 Most migrants move only relatively short distances. The number of migrants travelling further afield declines as distance increases. This inverse relationship between migrants and distance has become known as distance decay (Figure 14.8). The relationship occurs because of the friction of distance: movement is cheaper over short distances and it is easier to move to a known place nearby than to an unknown place some distance away.

2 People who do move long distances are largely unaware of the opportunities that are available (for example houses, jobs, etc.) at their destination. They therefore move to large, well-known urban centres rather than smaller settlements.

3 Migration occurs in stages. Ravenstein observed that as migrants left one place, they were replaced by new migrants moving in. This gives migration patterns a wave-like quality.

4 People in rural areas are much more likely to migrate than those in urban centres. Ravenstein was researching at a time when British cities were undergoing a period of exponential growth (see page 133) as a result of the twin causes of natural increase and rural to urban migration.

5 Ravenstein came to conclusions about the typical migrant:
- women are more likely to migrate within their country than men
- men are more likely to emigrate (i.e. move internationally) than women
- most migrants are adult.

Step migration and circular migration

Ravenstein's laws provided a focus for more recent studies of migration. Studies of migration patterns in LEDCs suggest that most rural migrants do not move directly to large urban centres. Instead, they move in a series of short steps over a period of time. In this model, most migrants are prevented from moving long distances by the friction of distance, i.e. the cost and inconvenience of travel. So they move from their rural home to a small market town. However, they do not settle in medium-sized settlements for long. Drawn by the prospects of better job opportunities in the larger urban centres they move again, each move being a step on a longer journey (Figure 14.9).

Other research has shown that many migrants do not settle permanently in their new homes. Many single migrants leave rural homes at times of unemployment, returning periodically to their rural families with money they have earned in the city. This is known as circular migration and is common where farm work is seasonal, for example in the Sahel and savanna climate zones of

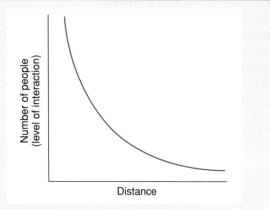

Distance

Figure 14.8 Distance decay effects.

Africa. Here farm workers are underemployed during the dry season so they migrate to urban centres and take up temporary employment, usually in the informal sector of the economy.

1 Consider each of Ravenstein's laws. What social and technological changes have occurred since Ravenstein that might alter predictions made in his laws?

2 Study the migration patterns in Figure 14.5. Did these migrants follow a) Ravenstein's laws, b) the distance decay model or c) a pattern of step migration? Explain your answer.

3 Study Figure 14.3 on page 168. How far does it support the theory that most rural to urban migration occurs in a series of short steps between urban centres of increasing size?

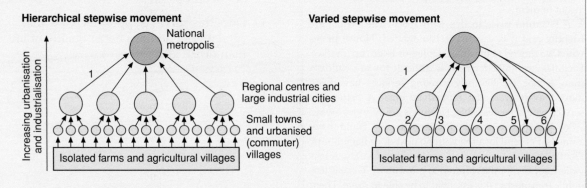

Types of stepped migratory movement originating from rural areas

1 Progressive movement from rural area to small town, to regional centre, to national metropolis
2 Progressive movement from rural area to regional centre and then national metropolis
3 Direct movement from rural area to national metropolis

4 Intention to move from rural area to national metropolis but eventually residing in regional centre
5 Intention to move from rural area to national metropolis but eventually residing in small town
6 Intention to move from rural area to national metropolis but eventually returning to rural area without residing elsewhere

Figure 14.9 Varieties of step migration.

Why do migrants move?

While some migrations are triggered by natural hazards, such as the eruption of the Soufrière Hills Volcano, others are forced by war or persecution. These migrants are forced to move for reasons of health and safety. But what reasons do voluntary migrants give for moving?

An understanding of the reasons for migration is important to planners. Rural councils in the UK need to understand migration patterns so they are able to forecast the demand for new housing in the countryside. In developing countries migration leads to massive demands on already crowded cities. Policy makers are keen to understand the forces that drive millions of people from their rural homes to live in cities that struggle to provide them with adequate housing, sanitation and clean water.

Why did people move to the study area in South Shropshire?

Respondents to the survey on South Shropshire provide an interesting source of personal attitudes towards rural areas and help to explain why so many people perceive cities to be stressful and congested, and rural areas quiet and tranquil. Figure 14.10 gives three sample responses suggesting a combination of positive and negative factors that influenced decisions to move. These are summarised in Figure 14.11.

---

1 It is a much healthier environment than living in a large town. It is a much steadier way of life. The roads are a lot quieter. Living in the country you get to know many people, so when you go shopping you can stop and have a chat to them.

2 A beautiful place to live with space. The people are friendly and it is easy to feel integrated. House prices when we moved to the area enabled us to go 'up' market. Facilities are limited which is difficult for my children (now teenagers). Recently banking services have been moved away from the immediate area. A better bus service would be desirable. Hospitals are 30 miles away.

3 We bought a house with land so we could have animals. Peaceful location with no next-door neighbours. Plenty of space for the children to play in safety. A less violent society for the children to grow up in. There is less public transport so it is essential to be able to drive. There are few leisure facilities locally so it is necessary to travel long distances especially where the children's interests and hobbies are concerned.

Figure 14.10 People's experiences of living in rural Shropshire.

---

1 Advantages of the new rural home (85 comments in total)

Friendly / well integrated community 9
Low population density / more space 8
Good local health care and schools 12
Less traffic or less noise 16
Less pollution / clean air 10
Beautiful surroundings 16
Slower pace of life 3
Less crime and vandalism / safer environment 5
Low cost of housing / low cost of living 6

2 Disadvantages of the new rural home (61 comments in total)

Hospitals and emergency services (police/ambulance) too far away 5
Poor choice of local shops / local shops more expensive / shopping involves travel 10
Poor range of leisure facilities: library, sport, cinema, theatre 6
Essential to have a car / poor public transport / poor road conditions 21
Not enough facilities for teenagers 6
Too few people (isolation) 5
Few local work opportunities or lower wages 8

Figure 14.11 Factors identified as advantages and disadvantages of living in South Shropshire.

---

1 a) Use an appropriate technique to represent the data in Figure 14.11.

b) Use your graph, and the responses, to summarise the advantages and disadvantages perceived by incomers to South Shropshire.

c) Does this survey support the view that rural areas provide a better quality of life than urban areas?

Theory

Models of migration 2: reasons for movement

Several models try to explain why migrants move; most are concerned with the decision-making process of individual migrants. The models identify factors that push people away from their existing home and pull them towards a new home. This push–pull model has been used for over 40 years to explain the behaviour of all migrants, but especially rural to urban migrants in LEDCs. Some commonly quoted push–pull factors are listed below.

Push factors include:

- natural disaster
- unemployment, underemployment or seasonal employment
- political, ethnic or religious persecution
- isolation
- lack of housing
- poor health or education services
- high crime rates or war
- congestion or too much noise.

Pull factors include:

- better health or educational facilities
- more work opportunities, higher salaries
- freedom of speech, political or religious freedom
- attractive scenery, slower pace of life
- more opportunities for social life and entertainment, 'bright lights'
- clean air, less pollution.

Lee's migration model

Social, environmental and economic factors contribute to the push–pull decision-making process. For example, drought (environmental) may combine with poverty (economic factor) to push migrants away from the countryside. In Lee's model, these factors have to be balanced against reasons for staying in the existing home, such as

- social – family ties (for example supporting elderly parents or caring for a young family), lack of education or illiteracy
- economic – the need to help run a family business, the cost of travel and setting up a new home
- lack of information about the destination, for example where to stay when the migrant arrives.

Lee called these 'intervening obstacles' to migration, which prevent some from moving.

He also identified 'intervening places'. Migrants move to intervening places rather than their original planned destination because of obstacles, such as cost and family pressures. Distance may prevent a migrant moving to a distant capital, but may favour a nearer town or regional centre, which becomes the intervening place.

The Todaro model

Todaro's model suggests that economic factors are the most influential of the push–pull factors. Individual migrants weigh up the economic costs and benefits of moving, comparing rural incomes with those that might be earned in the urban sector. Migration is likely where urban incomes are considerably greater than rural ones. A logical conclusion of this model is that policy makers can slow the rural–urban migration stream by creating investment and new employment in rural areas. Figure 14.12 provides evidence of higher wages that are available in urban Malaysia. Malaysia experienced rapid urbanisation during the late twentieth century as a result of rural to urban and urban to urban (step) migration. Its urban population rose from 34 per cent in 1980 to 58.8 per cent in 2000.

	1990	1995
Urban	1617	2596
Rural	951	1300
Average	1167	2007

Figure 14.12 Urban–rural wage differentials in Malaysia, 1990 and 1995 (figures indicate average monthly salaries in Malaysian rupees).

Household migration models

The Todaro model can be criticised for being too simplistic. Most migrants do not act as individuals but as part of a larger family unit. More recent migration models suggest that migrants consider the greater good of the family when they make their decision to move.

Two possible consequences of this new model are that:

- some family members may be of more benefit to the family if they stay at home than if they move. Such family members are described as tied stayers. For example, in Latin America, a son will have more work opportunities in the rural environment than a daughter. He will become a tied stayer while his sister moves to the city. Other family members may become tied movers if, at some later date, they also migrate in order to join a migrant who has permanently settled.
- other members of the family may be of greater benefit to the family if they migrate and send money home on a regular basis. The sending home of a regular remittance is recognised as a principal aim of many migrants. It was estimated in 1997 that the combined remittance of legal and illegal Mexican migrants in the USA to their families in Mexico every year was around US $6 billion.

1 Discuss the list of push and pull factors.
   a) Categorise the factors into social, economic and environmental factors.
   b) Which of these factors might explain rural to urban migration in LEDCs?
   c) Which factors might explain counter-urbanisation in MEDCs?

2 Refer to Figure 14.12. Use a suitable technique to illustrate the income gap between rural and urban areas.

3 Study the responses of the migrants to the rural study area in Figure 14.11.
   a) Categorise the advantages into economic, social, aesthetic/environmental factors. Which factor seems to be strongest?
   b) Study the disadvantages. Which of these would become push factors forcing the following people to leave the rural area:
   • an older teenager leaving school
   • a commuter with a comfortable car
   • a retired person with no car.

The impact of migration

Migration can have serious consequences for both the area that is sending migrants and the receiving area. These consequences, which may be a combination of benefits and costs, are of great interest to policy makers, who may want to limit the problems by controlling migration. So what are the consequences, and who pays the costs?

Economic costs and benefits

It is commonly assumed that source areas suffer as a result of losing economic migrants. It is said that rural areas in LEDCs lose 'the best and the brightest' as a result of urban migration and that older members of the family who are left behind struggle to work the land. However, this point of view ignores two important pieces of evidence:

• Migrants remit part of their income to the rural family. This money can be invested in businesses, home improvements or pay for the education of younger brothers and sisters. The amount sent home is significant: in 1995 it was estimated that Filipinos working in the USA sent back US $2.9 billion every year to families who remain in the Philippines. All Filipinos employed abroad sent home an estimated US $8.6 billion in 1999.

• The population of rural areas continues to grow due to natural increase but the amount of employment available to the rural workforce tends to decrease as mechanisation is introduced. Migration therefore helps to reduce competition for limited jobs as well as for limited resources such as land, clean water and wood fuel.

Studies of circular migration (see page 171) in the Machakos district of Kenya have shown that this seasonal movement has enormous benefits for the rural area. Circular migrants reduce demand on village food and water stocks during the long dry season helping to prevent the potential problems of overpopulation discussed in Chapter 12. Migrants earn money that is sent to rural families and invested in farms, for example to improve terraces and for tree planting schemes. It has also been used to diversify farm products. The growing cities of Mombassa and Nairobi have created extra demands for agricultural products such as meat, fruit, vegetables, timber and charcoal, which has meant increased incomes for farmers in Machakos.

Health and social risks

Migrants, especially women, are vulnerable to infringements of their human rights. Many cases have been documented of female migrants who, although believing they are contracted for a legitimate job, are forced to work in the sex industry. Female, and some male, migration to participate in the sex industry is depressingly common in Asia. Source areas are the rural districts of northern India, Nepal or Bangladesh. Receiving areas are the bars and brothels of India's growing cities or Bangkok, Thailand, which has an estimated 200 000 prostitutes.

Young women and men migrate as a result of rural deprivation; job opportunities for women in rural Asia are limited and wages are low. Many enter the sex industry willingly, as dancers or to work in strip-joints or massage parlours, in order to support rural families. A girl working in a massage parlour can earn ten times the amount of a waitress or a labourer on a building site. Others are reluctant participants in the sex industry. Those concerned about infringement of civil liberties report many cases of children who are kidnapped and sold as slaves into the sex industry. Other parents, apparently, willingly sell their children into the sex industry. Perhaps as many as 10 per cent of girls working as prostitutes are enslaved.

Women and men working in the sex industry are extremely vulnerable to the spread of sexually transmitted diseases (STDs). The number of women testing HIV positive has risen dramatically in Thailand. A further concern is the age of the prostitutes. UNICEF estimates that there are 100 000 girls under the age of eighteen involved in prostitution in Thailand. Of all girls aged eleven to seventeen, 20 per cent may be involved in the sex industry. One-third of child prostitutes test HIV positive.

Figure 14.13 The sex tourist industry in Thailand – nightclubs in Pat Pong, Bangkok.

Case study of female migration from Bangladesh to Malaysia

Research into migration of Bangladeshi women to Malaysia reported on several negative impacts:

- the cost of migration was considerable – families had to find 23 800 Taka (US $480) to pay for documentation and travel costs for the migrant
- young migrants had their education disrupted and felt isolated, leaving friends and family behind
- the economic slump in Malaysia in the late 1990s meant that many women were unable to work overtime and could not send enough money home
- women gained some independence but were also at greater social risk; condoms were expensive and understanding of their use to prevent the spread of STDs and HIV/AIDs was poor
- women felt vulnerable – they did not dare protest about discrimination at work for fear of deportation.

How do governments respond to migration?

It is estimated that 40 per cent of the urban expansion seen in LEDCs is due to internal migration. Planners struggle to provide adequate housing, sanitation and clean water in these developing cities. How can policy makers prevent this population movement into already crowded cities? There are a number of possible official responses when migration is seen to be too great.

Investment in rural development projects

The Todaro model (page 173), which influenced policy makers through the late 1960s, 1970s and 1980s, explained migration in terms of rural–urban wage differentials. The model was used to justify expensive investment projects in rural parts of many LEDCs. These schemes included major irrigation and HEP projects such as the Tucurui dam in Brazil, or the Narmada project in India. These projects required massive loans from the World Bank and MEDC partners, exacerbating problems of debt repayment. Some of them actually displaced rural populations, and many have been criticised for bringing too few benefits for rural people.

Land redistribution and the introduction of co-operatives

Socialist local governments in Kerala, India, were successful in redistributing land so that even the poorest families are not landless. But socialist schemes such as these have had little impact in most LEDCs where most governments follow capitalist principles.

Prohibit migrants from becoming urban residents

This technique was used in South Africa as part of the apartheid system. The settlement of black migrant workers was controlled with an official pass system. This has been adopted since in other LEDCs, most notably in China, which is currently experiencing the largest-scale internal migration in history. Millions of migrant workers flock to the coastal cities in search of work. As Figure 14.14 explains, the authorities avoid dealing with consequent welfare problems (such as provision of housing and education) by denying the migrants legal residence permits.

Tens of millions of peasants are setting off on China's new long march to find hope and work in the city

Ji Jianguo works long hours selling fruit at a Beijing stall. He sends money home to his parents and is saving a little so he can start a business. Floods recently drove him off his family's land in Anhui. He is one of 10 million peasants expected to leave their farms this year, adding to the 80 million who already live in shantytowns on the edge of China's big cities and along the coast.

The migration is changing China from a country where, only 15 years ago, 92% of the population were farmers to one where, although 72% live in rural areas, only 40% actually farm. Many leaders see the migrants as a threat to stability, and blame them for increased crime and overcrowded cities. The migrants are not allowed to become legal residents of the cities where they work, and so their children cannot attend school and health care is denied them. But the authorities know that China's economic boom is partly built on the migrant's remarkably cheap labour. Low-paid migrants have taken virtually all jobs in construction, sanitation and street vending.

Figure 14.14 Migration in China. From the *Guardian*, 3 November 1994.

Redirect migration to other reception areas

The governments of Brazil, Indonesia, Sri Lanka and Tanzania, among others, have used a policy of redirecting migrants to areas with low population densities – a policy known as transmigration. It is claimed to have two benefits:

- further urban overcrowding is avoided
- resource frontiers can be opened up by the migrants, i.e. the reception areas can be developed.

This policy has been used in Brazil, where poor migrants in the south-east region have been given incentives to migrate into Amazonia rather than to one of the cities in the south-east such as Rio or São Paulo. Transmigration has also been used in Indonesia (see case study below).

Encourage emigration instead of internal migration

Governments who are particularly concerned about overpopulation may encourage emigration in order to relieve population pressures. This policy was pursued in the nineteenth and early twentieth centuries by European powers who encouraged migration to the colonies. Now it is the LEDCs who pursue similar policies. The Bangladeshi government, for example, plays an active role in promoting emigration. Bangladesh is one of the most densely crowded countries in the world and 80 per cent of its population lives below the poverty line. Overseas migration, mainly to other Asian countries, is a major policy goal.

Case study of transmigration in Indonesia

Indonesia is a vast archipelago of 13 000 islands stretching over 5000km from west to east. With a population of over 205 million it is the fourth most populous country in the world. The population is very unevenly distributed. As shown in Figure 14.15, Java is very densely populated (with over 60 per cent of the nation's population occupying 7 per cent of the national area) whereas the Outer Islands have small populations and low densities.

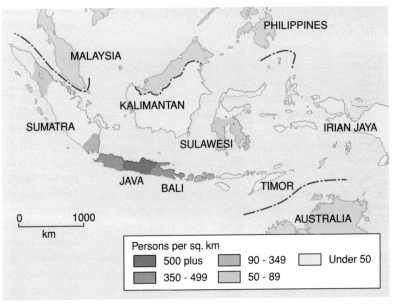

Figure 14.15 Population density in Indonesia.

The policy of redistributing this uneven population is known as transmigration. The first forced migrations were made by the Dutch colonists in order to provide cheap labour in the plantations of Sumatra. By 1950 around 200 000 people had been moved. Between 1950 and 1975 another 1 million migrants were moved, mainly to Sumatra and Sulewesi. During the late 1970s and 1980s the military government of Indonesia stepped up the pace of transmigration, moving another 2.5 million people, some of them to Irian Jaya (West Papua). The scheme was seen as a successful development project. The World Bank supported the policy and lent money for its implementation.

However, the numbers moved by the transmigration policy have made no real impact on the density of population in Java. Natural increase and the return of disgruntled settlers have contributed to increased growth of 18 per cent despite the policy. Furthermore, the World Bank and Indonesian government were put under pressure by human rights groups, such as Tribal International, to stop the scheme. They claimed that farming projects provided for the settlers were inappropriate and of little economic benefit. Other projects, including mining, logging, HEP schemes and the planting of oil-palm plantations, contributed significantly to deforestation and soil erosion and were damaging water systems. The projects also caused conflict between the transmigrants and indigenous peoples living in resettlement areas. For example, conflicts between the Indonesian army and the indigenous peoples of West Papua resulted in human rights abuses and hundreds of deaths.

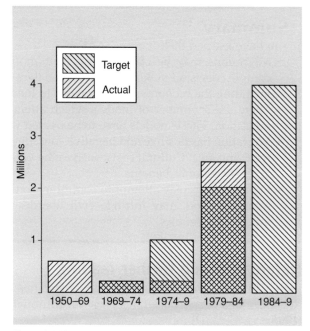

Figure 14.16 Transmigration totals in Indonesia.

The transmigration policy failed to meet targets, as can be seen in Figure 14.16 and the flow of official transmigrants slowed in the late 1980s and 1990s. The World Bank eventually withdrew support in the mid 1990s. But the policy has been successful in opening up new areas for development. In this respect it has a lot in common with the resettlement policies in Amazonia, Brazil. While official transmigration has slowed, the new opportunities in logging, construction and mining have triggered spontaneous migration. However, environmental damage and conflicts with local people continue.

Figure 14.17 Men from one of the hill tribes in Irian Jaya

Summary

You have learned that:

- Migrations may be classified by their motive (forced or voluntary). Migrants go through a complex decision-making process when they decide to move. A number of factors influence them, including the economic costs/benefits to the family.
- There are a number of models which attempt to explain patterns of migration, or reasons for migration. These models have to be treated with caution and weighed against evidence.
- Migration has positive and negative consequences for both the area sending the migrants, and the receiving area. Cultural costs, such as the vulnerability of single women, may have to be weighed against economic benefits.
- Policy makers may attempt to control migration flows within the country. These policies, such as transmigration, may infringe civil liberties such as freedom of movement and the rights of indigenous peoples.

References and further reading

Jane Chrispin and Francis Jegede, *Population, Resources and Development*, Collins Educational (1996)

Andy Owen, *Managing Rural Environments*, Heinemann (1999)

Web sites

http://www.SurvivalInternational.org

15 Issues facing the European population

This section has dealt so far with the global pattern of population change and resource issues; it has mostly explored changes affecting the majority of the world's population in LEDCs. The world is generally younger now than before, but people also live longer than at any time before. This chapter explores population issues in Europe, one of Earth's wealthiest continents.

Coping with population change in Europe

Towards the end of the twentieth century, fertility rates dropped to below replacement level in most European countries (Figure 15.1).

At present, there are several issues facing European populations.

- An ageing population poses significant problems of care – especially cost – for elderly people
- There is a shortage of skilled workers in countries such as Germany and the UK.
- It is already difficult to maintain viable communities in some of Europe's more isolated rural areas, for example northern Scandinavia.
- Economic migrants from northern Africa are entering Mediterranean countries such as Spain illegally.
- In the Balkans, ethnic conflict in the former Yugoslavia has created a refugee crisis. Meanwhile, economic failure in Albania has triggered illegal immigration into Italy.
- Conflict in the Caucasus (Chechnya and Azerbaijan) has created more refugees who may wish to enter Western Europe.
- Poverty and failing welfare systems in the former USSR are creating a crisis, especially for elderly populations.
- Illegal trafficking of economic migrants across Europe is causing misery, especially to women from Eastern Europe caught up in the sex industry.

Figure 15.1 Fertility rates in Europe.

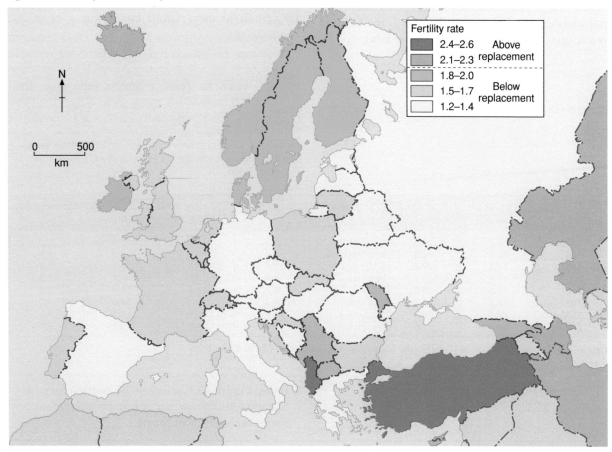

Fertility rate

2.4–2.6	Above
2.1–2.3	replacement
1.8–2.0	
1.5–1.7	Below
1.2–1.4	replacement

Population doubling times in Europe are the longest in the world. The number of people of working age compared to the number who are retired is falling. Currently the ratio is 4:1, but by 2050 it will have fallen to 2:1. Who will care for the retired and elderly? What will the declining fertility rate mean in terms of maintaining a bank of skilled workers? If shortages occur, where will the next generation of skilled workers come from? Should the UK encourage replacement migration in order to replace its own loss?

Ageing Western European population

In common with other affluent societies in Western Europe, the demographic structure of the UK is showing two significant changes:

- a fall in fertility as women choose to have fewer children
- an increasing proportion of elderly people as people live longer (Figure 15.2).

These two changes combine to form a population that is stable in size, but ageing. Figure 15.1 shows fertility rates in most European countries. Now below 2.1 in most countries, the population is below the replacement level needed to maintain population size. One in five women in the UK will never give birth to a child. Those who do are tending to leave the birth of their first child until later and later. The birth rate for women in their twenties is falling, while the birth rate for women in their thirties is rising. There may be many reasons for this trend:

- the failure rate of first marriages or partnerships may explain why some women do not start a family in their twenties
- many women, and also men, choose to delay the start of a family while they pursue a career.

But women who start a family later in life face the consequence of lower fertility. The chances of conception decrease rapidly at age 35 or above, making it likely that family size for older mothers is small. At the same time, in Western Europe improved standards in health care, greater affluence and greater knowledge about diet and fitness have lead to longer life expectancy. In 1995 there were just over 9 million people aged over 65 in the UK. It seems likely that by 2030 there will be over 14 million. Not only are more people living into retirement, many more people are living into old age, defined as 80 or over (Figure 15.3). Centenarians are increasing in number too. In 1951 about 300 people were aged over 100 years in the UK; by 2030 there could be as many as 36 000 centenarians.

	1901	1931	1961	1991	2021 (est.)
Males	45.5	57.7	67.8	73.2	77.6
Females	49.0	61.6	73.6	78.7	82.6

Figure 15.2 Life expectancy in the UK since 1901 (in years). The data show the average life expectancy for someone born in the years shown.

	Population in millions	% aged 0–16	% aged 65–79	% aged 80+	Total % age 65+	Millions of people aged 65 or over	Millions of people aged 80 or over
1971	55.9	25.5	10.9	2.3	13.2	7.4	1.3
1981	56.3	22.3	12.2	2.8	15.0	8.4	1.6
1991	57.8	20.3	12.0	3.7	15.8	9.1	2.1
2001	59.8	20.7	11.4	4.3	15.8	9.4	2.6
2011	61.2	19.2	11.9	4.7	16.6	10.2	2.9
2021	62.1	18.3	14.3	5.1	19.4	12.0	3.2
2031	62.2	18.3	16.3	6.6	22.9	14.2	4.1
2041	61.2	17.6	16.8	7.8	24.6	15.1	4.8

Figure 15.3 Ageing population in the UK – the increasing number of over-65s and over-80s.

1 Describe the pattern of fertility shown in Figure 15.1.

2 Using Figure 15.1, annotate an outline map of Europe with labels that summarise the main issues facing the continent.

Why are people living longer?
Medical factors

Several factors explain why Western European populations are living longer.

- More mothers receive pre- and post-natal care, which reduces infant mortality rates. In this way, the average survival rate increases and so too does life expectancy.
- 'Killer' infections such as smallpox, diphtheria, whooping cough and polio have either been eradicated or have been dramatically reduced because of child vaccinations. Many vaccinations remain effective for many years, such as BCG vaccinations against tuberculosis.
- Drug treatments have been developed for the most common causes of death. These include:
  - drug treatments which actually cure the cause of infection, such as drugs used to treat malaria
  - drug treatments for conditions that cure or arrest further deterioration, such as many drugs used in the treatment of cancer – the use of Tamoxifen in treating breast cancer has led to startling improvements in survival rates.

- Access to health care is available to more people as a result of government policies such as the introduction of the National Health Service by the UK government in 1948.

Economic factors

Improved standards of living usually result in people choosing to have smaller families. Where this is the case, evidence shows that smaller families result in lower infant mortality, which improves survival rates in the population as a whole.

Environmental factors

In the UK, smog caused by atmospheric conditions and emissions from coal-burning factories was the cause of bronchitis and lung conditions that killed many people in the early twentieth century. The Clean Air Acts of Parliament in the UK in 1956 reduced these emissions and people's health improved. Now an increase in the number of asthma cases is being attributed to car exhaust emissions; some feel that the UK government will have to take similar action again.

What impact do increasing numbers of elderly people have?

The increasing profile of those over 65 means that the geography of the population of the UK is changing. Figure 15.4 shows the proportion of elderly people living in different counties of the UK. For counties such as Cornwall or Dorset, increased proportions of elderly people put greater strain on health care resources. By contrast, fewer resources are needed for education.

---

1 Identify regions of the UK with the highest proportions of elderly people in Figure 15.4. Why should these counties or areas have the greatest numbers of elderly people?

2 What are the benefits and problems caused by high proportions of elderly people in a county or health authority region?

Figure 15.4 Where do elderly people live in the UK?
This map shows the distribution by county of people aged 75 and over in 1991.

The elderly
England and Wales = 7.1% of the population
East Sussex = 11.9% of the population
Cleveland = 5.4% of the population

% of population

- 10.4 and over
- 9.2–10.3
- 8.0–9.1
- 6.8–7.9
- 5.6–6.7
- 5 and under

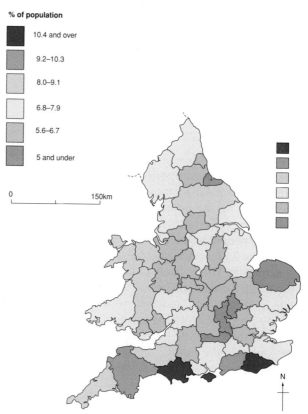

0   150km

Issues facing retired and elderly people

	Median age (years)		
	1950	1998	2050
World total	23.5	26.1	37.8
More developed regions	28.6	36.8	45.6
Less developed regions	21.3	23.9	36.7
Africa	18.7	18.3	30.7
Asia	21.9	25.6	39.3
Europe	29.2	37.1	47.4
Latin America and the Caribbean	20.1	23.9	37.8
Northern America	29.8	35.2	42.1
Oceania	27.9	30.7	39.3

Figure 15.5 Median age by continent, 1950, 1998 and 2050.

The ageing of the Western European population (Figure 15.5) has combined with a shortening of many people's working lives. Mechanisation and the globalisation of the economy have resulted in redundancies in expensive labour forces of European MEDCs. Many benefit from taking early retirement. A large population of wealthy retired people has opened up markets for the so-called grey pound. Companies selling leisure products, including DIY, gardening and travel, have benefited. However, many elderly people do not have surplus cash for new leisure opportunities. Poverty is a major issue, especially when the provision of special needs for elderly people can be very expensive.

> **1 a)** Use a suitable technique to analyse the data in Figure 15.5.
>
> **b)** Comment on the trend of the European population compared to other regions.

A pension crisis?

State pensions are supported by national insurance contributions made by those in work. The combined effect of an ageing population and the problems of maintaining full employment means that the ratio of working people to those over 65 is falling. In 2000 there were 3.71 working people to every person over 65 in the UK. This is likely to fall to 2.1 to 1 by 2040. As a result there would be less tax revenue to pay for state pensions and reduced welfare services for elderly people. Europeans are being encouraged to take out more private pension schemes while they are young. In the future, only the least well off will be able to rely on a state pension when they retire.

Providing adequate levels of health and social care

The World Health Organisation (WHO) warns that ageing European populations will lead to a big rise in cancers, heart disease and diabetes. Elderly people are also likely to suffer problems of dementia or reduced mobility due to arthritis. Providing treatment for the diseases associated with ageing will become more and more expensive as the proportion of elderly people increases.

The burden of care may be shared between the private and public sectors. At the moment elderly people can expect a package of care which might include:

- care assistants coming into the home to help dress or wash the elderly person
- provision of day care at a local centre
- the fitting of mobility aids in the home, such as stair lifts, grab rails and bath aids.

These might be provided through a combination of public welfare (social services), private care (for example private cleaners) and the voluntary sector (for example the Alzheimers Association who provide support for carers).

> **1** If survival rates continue to increase, what do you imagine will have to happen to:
> **a)** tax rates
> **b)** insurance premiums for health care
> **c)** the age at which people retire?
>
> **2** As a class, discuss whether the benefits of allowing people to survive for longer periods are worth the cost.
>
> **3** Would you support recent legislation from the Dutch parliament which made euthanasia (justifiable early death or mercy killing) legal?

Investigating the European migration issue

Should people have the right to move across Europe in search of work? If persecuted in your own country, would you expect to be given shelter in the UK? As individuals we expect certain rights: the right to work, to free movement and to free expression. Yet as a nation the UK guards its territory jealously to protect scarce resources such as jobs, housing and social care. Consequently, governments implement immigration controls to restrict numbers of overseas migrants entering the UK.

How are these controls implemented? Will it become necessary to change our perception of migration? It is helpful to distinguish between two types of migration:

- economic migration within and across Europe
- political migration – refugees, internally displaced persons and asylum seekers.

These are considered in turn.

58 dead in port lorry

The bodies of 58 people have been found in the back of a lorry at the English port of Dover. The driver of the Dutch-registered lorry, which arrived from Zeebrugge, Belgium, just before midnight, has been arrested. The 54 men and four women are thought to have been illegal immigrants and reports suggest that they are of Chinese origin. Two survivors, both men, have been taken to hospital. Home Secretary Jack Straw said he was appalled by the loss of human life caused by what he called 'the evil trade in trafficking'. Amnesty International described the deaths as 'a tragedy waiting to happen', and said it highlighted the desperate lengths some people were willing to go to to enter the UK.

Figure 15.6 From BBC news online, 19 June 2000.

Economic migration within and across Europe

Migration between the fifteen member states of the EU is relatively easy. Around 15 million economic migrants exist in the EU and the majority have moved from one member state to another. This free movement has benefits. Workers benefit from being free to pick and choose where they work, matching their skills and expertise to skill shortages in different parts of Europe. Employers are able to fill vacancies with the best recruits.

But ease of movement around the EU has created an issue which alarms the public and can endanger human life. Economic migrants from outside the EU have fewer rights to work in Europe than EU citizens. However, they are attracted by higher wages and better standards of living. They are sometimes aided by criminals who profit from trafficking people across frontiers. One attempt to smuggle Chinese migrants into the UK resulted in tragic loss of life (Figure 15.6).

Figure 15.8 The face of racism – the reception given to asylum seekers in Europe.

Figure 15.7 P&O use meters to measure carbon dioxide levels. The meters provide evidence of illegal immigrants stowed away on lorries.

Do European governments need to adopt a policy of replacement migration?

As populations stabilise and age, it may become necessary for European countries to adopt more open migration policies in order to replace their own population. Some Western European countries are finding it is becoming increasingly difficult to fill vacant posts in certain key areas of employment, for example nursing, teaching and IT. Key workers could be recruited internationally using a green card system – a policy known as replacement migration.

Policy makers wishing to adopt replacement migration as a strategy for solving the problems of an ageing population may have difficulties convincing those with nationalist views. Attitudes to migrant workers depend on the state of the economy. When unemployment has risen, or wages have failed to meet expectations, as happened during the 1970s and again in the early 1990s, attitudes to migrant workers in Europe have hardened and immigration controls have been tightened. Immigration then becomes an emotive issue: the popular press may portray migrants as 'scroungers' who have come to take away 'our' jobs. In extreme cases, migrant workers have been harassed and victimised, for example racial tensions became heightened in Germany in the early 1990s when neo-Nazis targeted Turkish migrant workers (Figure 15.8).

Germany woos Indian IT

German Foreign Minister Joschka Fischer has begun a visit to India aimed at wooing local software professionals with promises of special work permits. Mr Fischer is in the high-tech city of Bangalore where he told Indian information technology experts that his country was keen on tapping their expertise.

Germany has an acute shortage of computer experts and has already announced plans to issue 20 000 work visas – similar to the US green card – later this year to fill the vacancies. The plan to attract software experts from abroad led to criticism from German trade unions who feared job losses. But the foreign minister said there was no domestic opposition to recruiting overseas workers. 'We are living in a global era and a global economy. Indian engineers are welcome in Germany,' said Mr Fischer.

Figure 15.9 One consequence of Europe's ageing population. From BBC online, 17 May 2000.

1 Employers in the UK are finding it difficult to recruit computer technicians, health workers and teachers. Discuss this issue. Why are there recruitment difficulties in some skill areas? Is it a good idea to recruit from abroad? Who might object? If Germany needs to recruit from abroad, why is there still unemployment?

2 If Germany or the UK recruits Indian IT specialists, what are the advantages and disadvantages for India? Who gains most?

Theory

International interfaces for migration

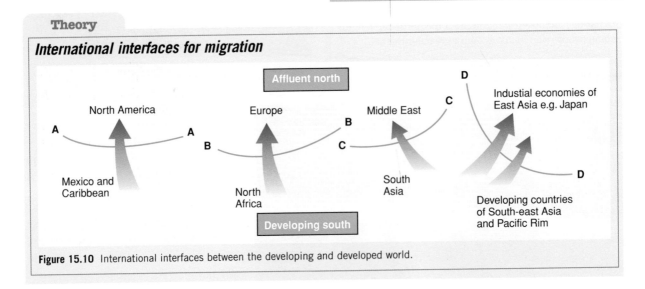

Figure 15.10 International interfaces between the developing and developed world.

Estimates of the total number of international migrants are very unreliable. Illegal migrants cross frontiers without proper documentation and are therefore missing from official records. So estimates are made over a large range: in the early 1990s it was estimated that the global population of international migrants was between 100 million and 120 million. The Todaro model (see page 173) predicts that economic migrants are motivated by wage differentials between sending and receiving countries. So we might conclude that most migration streams cross from poorer to richer nations.

One outcome may be south–north migration. Figure 15.10 illustrates the interfaces between rich MEDCs of the northern hemisphere and poorer LEDCs of the South over which these migration streams must cross. It indicates that there are four main pressure points:

- between Latin America, specifically Mexico, and the USA
- between the North African countries and the Mediterranean countries of Europe
- between the countries of South Asia and the Middle East
- between the countries of South–East Asia and East Asia.

This model of south–north migration is a particularly alarming one for policy makers in the MEDCs. The negative consequences of massive migration from LEDCs to MEDCs across these interfaces include:

- enormous pressure on limited resources, especially social housing and welfare, for example health care
- potential for political destabilisation: many western governments are concerned about the rise of fundamental Islam in Africa and South Asia (see pages 161–2) and would not want such views imported.

The interface model may itself be rather alarmist. In fact, most migrants move from one LEDC to another. The costs and social pressures of international migration are therefore largely met by other developing countries, not by MEDCs.

Political migrations – refugees, internally displaced persons and asylum seekers

Figure 15.11 The disputed Chechen territory.

The 1990s saw political change in Europe which meant population movement became possible or desirable for many more people. The collapse of communist control of central European countries such as Poland and of the USSR allowed border crossings that had not been possible for decades. As a result, nearly 1.7 million ethnic Germans returned to Germany between 1987 and 1993. At the break up of the USSR it was estimated that there were between 54 million and 65 million displaced people. Most of these had been forcibly transferred vast distances from west to east across the USSR by the Stalinist regime in the 1940s. In 1992 the member states of the CIS signed the Bishkek agreement, which allowed the majority of these people to return to their homelands.

Conflict in the former Yugoslavia and consequent persecution of ethnic minorities, a policy known as ethnic cleansing, gave rise to the largest number of refugees in Europe since 1945. In the early 1990s there were nearly 3 million refugees who had fled the conflict in Bosnia and Herzegovina. In 1999 a further 1 million refugees were forced to leave Kosovo. By the end of 1999, 660000 refugees had returned to Bosnia and the majority of the Kosovars had also returned. But 2 million people remained displaced. Of these, 1.2 million were internally displaced persons (IDPs), and 800000 were international refugees.

The movement of refugees produces enormous costs. Refugees incur financial losses as they leave behind their houses, possessions and jobs. Countries which receive the refugees may need outside assistance to provide shelter, food, water and health care. The United Nations High Commissioner for Refugees (UNHCR) is the international body that co-ordinates such operations. The atrocities committed in war and during episodes of ethnic cleansing leave lasting scars on refugees. Refugees may suffer from posttraumatic stress disorder and need counselling in order to overcome their experiences. The war in Chechnya, ongoing since 1996, displaced at least 300 000 Chechens. The drawings in Figure 15.12 were produced by children who were victims of the fighting as part of their therapy to overcome their trauma.

Those escaping war or persecution, but who have no legal right of entry to another European country because of immigration policies, may claim political asylum. It is estimated that there are 13 million people seeking political asylum in the world. In 1999, the UK gave refuge to 71 000 of them, or 0.05 per cent of the total, adding less than 0.12 per cent to the UK population.

Figure 15.12 Drawings by Chechen refugee children.

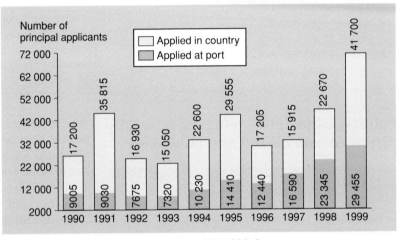

Figure 15.13 Applications for asylum to the UK, 1990–9.

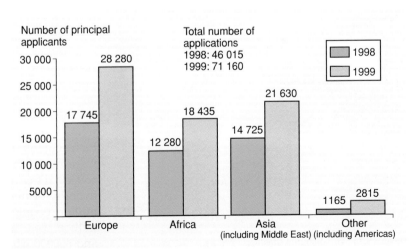

Figure 15.14 Asylum applications by area of origin, 1998 and 1999.

Assess the strengths of the following arguments, put forward during 2000, by different newspapers in the UK:

- 'The UK has a tradition of accepting refugees. Jews escaping from Hitler, refugees escaping from the terrors of Stalin, all have been accepted into Britain and gained hugely from it.'
- 'The UK neither has the resources nor the jobs available to take any more refugees, who should be sent back to their country of origin.'

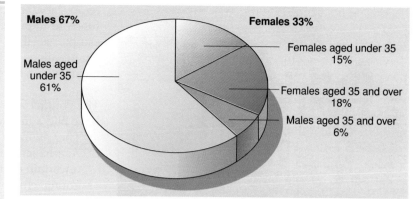

Figure 15.15 Applications for asylum to the UK by age and gender, 1999.

The refugee crisis in Azerbaijan

Azerbaijan came into conflict with neighbouring Armenia after the collapse of the Soviet Union in 1991. Azerbaijan is a nation of Turkic Muslims and Armenia is an Orthodox Christian country. The conflict is over the Nagorno-Karabakh region, an enclave populated largely by Armenians but located entirely within Azerbaijan. There has been a cease-fire since 1994, but the dispute is unresolved. Azerbaijan lost almost 20 per cent of its territory during the conflict.

The management of migration has become a huge challenge for policy

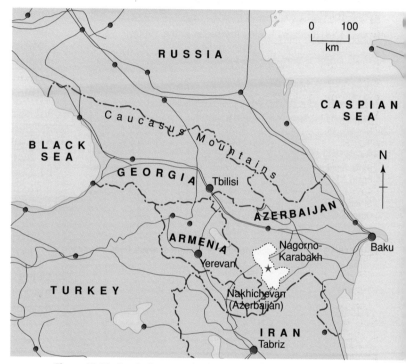

Figure 15.16 Azerbaijan showing the disputed territory of Nagorno-Karabakh.

Population structure

0–14 years: 30%
15–64 years: 63%
65 years and over: 7%
Birth rate: 18.08 births per 1000 population
Death rate: 9.47 deaths per 1000 population
Net migration rate: −5.92 migrant(s) per 1000 population
Life expectancy at birth: 58.51 years (males), 67.45 years (females)
Sex ratio (male:female)

- at birth: 1.05:1
- under 15 years: 1.04:1
- 15–64 years: 0.95:1
- 65 years and over: 0.65:1

Figure 15.17 Demographic factfile on Azerbaijan (2000).

makers in the Azerbaijan government and NGOs who are working with them. The former Soviet Union had restricted movement across borders. But the collapse of the USSR has opened up international frontiers. The poor state of the economy has encouraged economic migration. Most of all the government has to cope with refugees and IDPs from the conflict in Nagorno-Karabakh. The region worst affected by the conflict with Armenia has lost 40 per cent of its population to other countries.

There are nearly 800 000 refugees and IDPs who have been displaced by the fighting and who remain within Azerbaijan. Most of these have gained Azerbaijani citizenship, and become integrated into Azerbaijani communities. Over 50 per cent of IDPs have been found public housing, but a further 90 000 are still living in

Figure 15.18 Refugees leaving Azerbaijan in the 1990s.

Destination	Migrants	% of all asylum seekers from Azerbaijan
Germany	2816	45.3
Netherlands	449	39.4
Belgium	349	5.6
France	179	2.9
Switzerland	78	1.3
Spain	72	1.2
Austria	48	0.8
Sweden	46	0.7
Others	174	2.8
Total	**6211**	**100**

Figure 15.19 European destinations of asylum seekers from Azerbaijan, 1999.

temporary camps. There are insufficient public funds to improve the quality of life of those in the camps, so they require outside assistance from organisations like the UNHCR and International Organisation for Migration (IOM).

The conflict and refugee movement in the region have had a marked impact on the population.

- The average age at which girls marry in Azerbaijan has fallen from 23 to 17, due to the uncertain economic future.
- Young children are traumatised by events of war and separation from families.
- Lack of economic confidence and of credit from banks means that farmland is not properly cultivated.
- Governments are struggling to cope with the displacement of thousands of people.
- Individuals are seeking asylum in safer countries within Europe and elsewhere.

1 a) Comment on the main demographic features of Azerbaijan in Figure 15.17.
   b) Use the internet to compare these statistics to a Western European country of similar size, for example Austria or Finland. What significant differences do you find? How does the refugee crisis in Azerbaijan help to explain the differences?

2 Using a base map of Europe, produce a flow map of proportional arrows to illustrate the data in Figure 15.19.

Summary

You have learned that:

- MEDCs are characterised by increasing life expectancy and falling birth rates. As a result, the proportion of the elderly dependent population is increasing.
- A number of issues face such societies. These include the provision of health and social care for elderly dependants as well as an adequate pension to avoid poverty.
- International migration into and within Europe is a key issue for policy makers. The economic 'core' of the EU is a magnet to those from poorer countries outside.
- Ageing European populations may force governments to relax immigration control and adopt a policy of replacement migration.
- Political crises arising from change in the 1990s (for example Bosnia, Kosovo and the Caucasus region) have created problems for refugees and those who try to help them.
- The population of the member states of the EU can exercise a right to move across borders in order to find work. But strict immigration policies prevent other economic migrants from entering European countries easily.

References and further reading

John Cole and Francis Cole, *A Geography of the European Union*, Routledge (1997)

Jane Chrispin and Francis Jegede, *Population, Resources and Development*, Collins Educational (1996)

Philip Sarre and John Blunden, *An Overcrowded World?*, The Open University (1995)

New Internationalist, February 1995

OPCS, The 1991 Census

Geography Review, 'The Geography of age revealed by the 1991 census', January 1994

Web sites

UNHCR: www.unhcr.ch/

Refugee Council: www.refugeecouncil.org.uk

Global population: summary

Enquiry questions	Key ideas and concepts	Guidance and possible examples
The dynamics of population change What are the components of population change? How is population change measured and portrayed? How and why do rates of population change / vary spatially over time?	• The concept of population as a system with inputs, stores and outputs. Role of migration in system. • Natural change, migration balance and net change. • Census data and measures of change – birth, death, fertility, migration rates. Role of census in national and regional planning. • Portraying population density, distribution and change. • Global spatial variations in key measures of population change – causal factors. • The links between population change over time and development.	• Chapter 11 Population change – dynamics of natural change and migration components in contrasting countries. The global overview – birth rates, death rates, fertility. Assessment of key factors linked to economic development such as standards of health, welfare, education, role of women, etc. in the demographic transition. Demographic transition over time, examples from selected countries at different stages of development.
The implications of population change What are the global challenges posed by population change? What are the national challenges posed by population change? How do decision makers seek to manage population change?	• World population growth and future projections. • Population and resources – over-, under- and optimum (sustainable) population. Conflicting views of Malthus/Boserup. Limits to Growth model. • Coping with population growth (providing housing, work and services) and loss (maintaining viable communities). • Changing age and gender structures. Their implications for economic development and service provision. • Controlling numbers – contrasting attitudes, strategies and incentives. • Controlling movement within and across national boundaries – contrasting government policies.	• Chapter 12 Idea of exponential trend of global population increase. Assessing the balance equation of population and resources. Continental and national differentials. Role of technology in expanding resource base. Over - and underpopulation exemplified – global, Singapore, Japan. Are there global limits to growth? Assessment of issues in one rapidly expanding area and one area in decline – the notion of food scarcity in Ethiopia and 'overpopulation' in Colorado. Changing family structure (single parent/single person households). Economic impact of structure (e.g. dependency ratio). Gender imbalance (e.g. India). Implications of youthful (Chapter 13) and ageing population (Chapter 15 – Europe) for health and welfare services and employment. • Chapter 14 Assessment of impact of contrasting migration policies or plans, e.g. Indonesian transmigration. Classifications. Relation of migration in practice to theory. Urban–rural migration – South Shropshire. International female migration from Bangladesh to Malaysia.
The global challenge of migration What are the causes of international migration? What are the impacts of international migration? What are the key issues posed by international migration?	• Classification of migration by motive, duration. Analysis of decision-making factors – voluntary or forced. • Migration models – relevance of theories and models in understanding migration. • Pressure on the environment and resources. • Cultural and socio-economic benefits and costs. • Freedom of movement and civil liberties; refugees and ethnic cleansing. • The right to work; migrant workers and fluctuations in the global economy.	• Chapter 15 Major present-day patterns of international migration into and within Europe. Global refugee issues exemplified by displacement – Chechens, Azerbaijan. The key role of migrant workers and how it fluctuates (e.g. impacts of German reunification or Gulf War or SE Asia crisis).

The changing global economy
Introduction

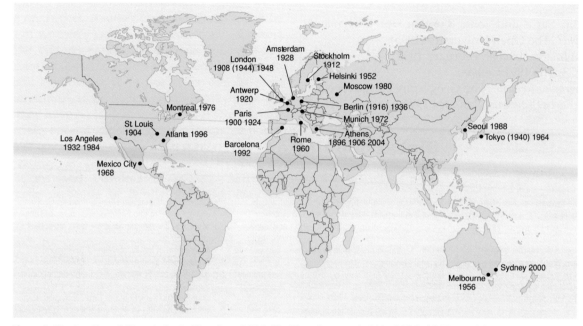

Figure 1 The location of Olympic host cities since 1896 (No Olympics were held in 1916, 1940 and 1944, although Olympic host cities were nominated for those years.).

The Olympics – dividing or uniting the world?

On 15 September 2000, the city of Sydney in Australia celebrated the opening ceremony of the 2000 Olympic Games, drawing together 11 000 athletes from 200 countries. Sport was held as a leveller of opportunity and of peoples with different outlooks and ways of life. In the Olympics, it was said, people could live as equals – apart from the stresses of racism, of poverty and of past mistakes.

Yet the Olympics show much about the world as it is, rather than the way we would like it to be. Figure 1 shows the location of those cities which have hosted the Olympics since the modern era began in 1896. Consider the location of these cities as a whole, and what they tell us.

The Olympics and economic development – the case of Eric Moussambani

Consider why the size of Olympic teams in Figure 2 might vary so much. A clear factor is the countries' level of economic development. At the 2000 Sydney Olympics, Eric Moussambani, a swimmer from Equatorial Guinea, won the hearts of the world with his swim in the 100m freestyle (Figure 3). The only swimmer who started legally in his heat, 'Eric the Eel' (as he became known) swam the slowest time on record; he had never competed in a pool of Olympic size because there were none in his country. In Equatorial Guinea:

- there are 0.4 million people
- infant mortality is high – 117 deaths per thousand live births
- Gross National Product (GNP) per capita was US $380 (about £260, or £5 per week) in 1995
- life expectancy in 1998 was 46 for men and 50 for women
- only 4 per cent of the population is aged over 60, reflecting the short life expectancy there.

In Australia, there are eighteen Olympic-size pools in Sydney alone, only one of which was used in the 2000 Olympics! In Australia:

- there are about 19 million people
- infant mortality is low – 5.8 deaths per thousand live births
- GNP per capita was US $18 720 (about £12 900, or £250 per week) in 1995
- life expectancy in 1998 was 75 for men and 81 for women

Other nations sending six or fewer competitors
Andorra
Haiti
American Samoa
Vanuatu
Tonga
Soloman Islands
Trinidad

■ Nations sending over 100 competitors

□ Nations sending six or fewer competitors

Figure 2 The number of competitors in the ten nations with most and least competitors at the 1988 Seoul Olympics.

Figure 3 Eric Moussambani at the 2000 Sydney Olympics.

Figure 4 Stadium Australia in Sydney – site of the 2000 Olympics.

- 12 per cent of the population is aged over 60, reflecting longer life expectancy.

Added to this, the sheer cost of staging the Olympics in 2000 (Figure 4), estimated at AU $1.8 billion (about £800 million), was beyond the reach of most countries in the world.

The Olympics and economic development – it's not so simple!

There seems to be a link, therefore, between a country's economic and social development. Yet it is not a clear link and, as this section shows, economic development is complex and changing. Figure 5a shows the top fifteen medal winners at the Sydney Olympics. Consider the extent of

Country	Number of medals won			
	Gold	Silver	Bronze	Total
United States	39	25	33	97
Russia	32	28	28	88
China	28	16	15	59
Australia	16	25	17	58
Germany	14	17	26	57
France	13	14	11	38
Italy	13	8	13	34
Netherlands	12	9	4	25
Cuba	11	11	7	29
Great Britain	11	10	7	28
Romania	11	6	9	26
South Korea	8	9	11	28
Hungary	8	5	3	16
Poland	6	5	3	14
Japan	5	8	5	18

Figure 5a The top fifteen medal winners at the 2000 Olympics.

Country	GNP in US$ (1995)	Literacy % (men/women)	Population in millions	Infant mortality rate per 1000 live births
1 United States	26 980	98/98	267.7	7.3
2 Russia	2 240	99/99	147.3	18
3 China	620	90/73	1236.7	31
4 Australia	18 720	99/99	18.7	5.8
5 Germany	27 510	99/99	82	5.1
6 France	24 990	99/99	58.6	5
7 Italy	19 020	99/99	57.4	5.8
8 Netherlands	24 000	99/99	15.6	5.5
9 Cuba	n/a	96/95	11.1	9.4
10 Great Britain	18 700	99/99	59	6.2
11 Romania	1 480	98/98	22.5	21.2
12 South Korea	9 700	99/97	45.9	11
13 Hungary	4 120	99/99	10.2	10.6
14 Poland	2 790	99/99	38.6	12.4
15 Japan	39 640	99/99	126.1	4

Note: Gross National Product (GNP) includes the value of all domestic and foreign output from a country, expressed in US$. It is divided by the population to produce GNP per capita.

Figure 5b Socio-economic data for the top fifteen medal winners at the 2000 Olympics.

Country	GNP in US$ (1995)	Number of medals won
Uganda	240	0
Vietnam	240	1
Burkina Faso	230	0
Madagascar	230	0
Niger	220	0
Nepal	200	0
Chad	180	0
Rwanda	180	0
Sierra Leone	180	0
Malawi	170	0
Burundi	160	0
Tanzania	120	0
Zaire	120	0
Ethiopia	100	8
Mozambique	80	1

Figure 6 Medals won by the fifteen poorest countries in the world at the 2000 Olympics.

economic development in these countries. Do the wealthiest countries win most medals? Compare Figures 5a and 5b.

An interesting question is 'Do the poorest countries win the least medals, or indeed any?' Of the 200 countries participating, 79 won medals at Sydney, which means that 121 countries did not win a single medal. The list in Figure 6 shows the fifteen poorest countries in the world, and the number of medals won in Sydney in 2000.

So there seems to be a link between sporting achievement and wealth. However, China's position of third in the medals table (Figure 5a) shows how the global economy is changing, and why. China was eleventh in the 1988 medals table. Chapter 21 shows how its economy is growing rapidly. In the past 20 years, a group of newly industrialising countries (NICs) have emerged in South-East Asia.

This section explores the reasons why there is a cluster of wealthy countries, why they are located in different parts of the world, and how a much larger, poorer group of countries has emerged. It shows how different countries and organisations, such as transnational corporations (TNCs), exert huge control over the way people live. It concludes with an assessment of different attempts that are being made to alter the balance of wealth, and the issues that stand in the way of a more equal world. Until the issues are resolved, the global order, as shown in the Olympics in Sydney, is unlikely to alter very much.

1 Either construct a scatter graph to show the relationship between medals won and GNP from Figures 5a and 5b, or key the data into a spreadsheet and carry out a correlation between the data. What do you notice?

2 What does this show about the relationship between the data? Why is this?

3 Now identify similar relationships between medals won and literacy, population and infant mortality. Give reasons for any relationships you identify.

References and further reading
You will find the following useful throughout this section:

Population Concern, Population and Development Database – a CD-ROM issued to all schools and colleges in 1998 with data for every country in the world

United Nations Development Programme, *Human Development Report*, published annually; those for 1998, 1999 and 2000 are especially useful for this section

World Bank, *World Bank Atlas 2000*

The state of the world

Identifying the development gap

In 1981, the Brandt Commission reported on world development. Its message was that the world consisted of two parts: a wealthy 'North' in which was concentrated a large proportion of the world's wealth, and a poorer 'South' (Figure 16.1). Its concern was the extent of poverty which affected two-thirds of the world's population, while the remaining one-third enjoyed much of the world's wealth, had better health care and longer life expectancy, and a better quality of life. This has since become known as the 'development gap', or disparity between the world's nations.

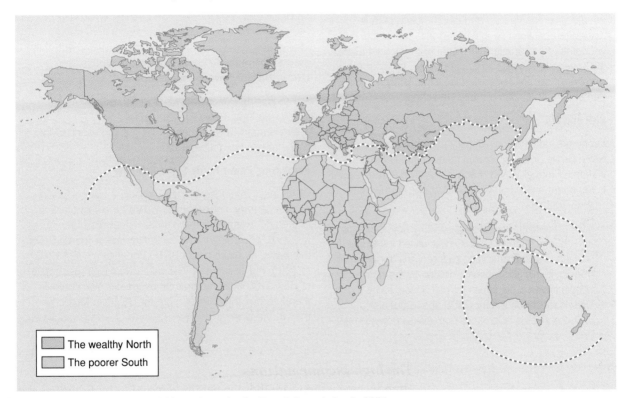

The wealthy North
The poorer South

Figure 16.1 The North-South divide as shown by the Brandt Commission in 1981.

This chapter will explore the geographical distribution of the world's wealth, identifying where it is greatest and least, and why. Many people now believe that the pattern is more complex than Brandt's division of the world as a result of economic development since 1981. Many countries that were in the South in 1981 have characteristics now that make them seem like highly developed areas of the North.

It all depends upon how development is measured, as the theory box on page 194 shows.

What is the global distribution of economic development now?

Many different words and terms are used to describe states of economic development, some of which overlap. At the time of the Brandt Report (Figure 16.1), people generally accepted two divisions – a rich and a poor world. Now, the United Nations uses the terms 'high income', 'middle income' and 'low income' countries to classify the world's 206 nations on the basis of characteristics that these countries share.

Defining and measuring 'development'

'Development' is difficult to define. To 'develop' means to 'change'; it also implies that things will alter for the better. 'Development' has come to mean the ways in which countries seek to develop economically and to improve their economic status. All countries try to promote economic growth as this will usually improve the standard of living for its inhabitants.

How is development measured?

Measuring development is difficult. Most measurements rely on data based on figures for income in the formal economy, and ignore informal and unpaid work. They are also average figures, and ignore how wealth is distributed between people or regions. Some data are economic, for example GNP, number of telephones per 1000 people, whereas others are social, for example number of people per doctor, life expectancy, percentage of children enrolled in school.

GNP and GDP

Economic indicators are usually presented in one of two ways: Gross Domestic Product (GDP) and Gross National Product (GNP). Each is slightly different, and it is important not to compare GNP in one country with GDP in another.

- GDP is the total value of goods and services produced in a country during a year. It is calculated by adding the value of all goods produced plus services (for example from tourism), and is usually divided by the number of people to give a per capita (or per person) value.
- GNP is much the same as GDP above, but also includes income that comes from overseas investment by organisations and residents. It therefore includes income from shares, or company profits from manufacturing or investment overseas (for example income returning to the USA from Coca-Cola or McDonald's franchises across the world). In this way, it is probably a better way of measuring income than GDP. Like GDP, it is usually divided by the number of people to give a per capita value.

Problems with economic indicators

In order to compare countries, money has to be converted into a common currency, usually US dollars. However, these figures do not say how much different currencies will buy in their own country. While GNP (average income) and GDP (total production) give an idea of average wealth and economic development, they are very blunt instruments. To improve on this, the United Nations have introduced:

- Purchasing Power Parity $ (PPP$), sometimes referred to as Real GDP per capita
- the Human Development Index (HDI), described in the theory box on page 201.

Purchasing Power Parity $ and Real GNP

PPP$ takes into account how valuable a currency is in its own country. For example, in 1998 the cost of living in the USA was about three times higher than in Morocco, according to the exchange rate of the US$. On this basis, Morocco had a GNP per capita of US $1240 in 1995, but based on PPP$ had a Real GNP per capita of US $3188 – nearly three times greater. You could therefore buy three times more for US $1 in Morocco than in the USA.

The high income nations

High income nations are those generally referred to by Brandt as the First World. They coincide with the 'high' category in Figure 16.3. These are the world's wealthy nations, or the North, so-called because most of these lie north of the Equator. In recent years, the term 'More Economically Developed Countries' (MEDCs) has come into use, and is used most often in this book. The term refers to the group of nations in Figure 16.4 whose GNP per capita is shown as high; it includes the USA, Canada, most of Western Europe, Japan and Australasia. This chapter shows how these countries have a disproportionate share of the world's wealth, trade, investment, use of resources and access to information.

How did there come to be a Third World?

It is tempting to think of LEDCs as poor, and always having been poor. This is far from the case. Historians tell of the wealth and sophistication of the Aztec and Inca empires in Central and South America. West Africa was home to many wealthy tribal groups with advanced medical knowledge. Australian aboriginal groups knew far more about living within and managing the Australian environment without damaging it than subsequent European settlers.

Much of the existence of the LEDCs can be explained by what has happened during the past 500 years. Between the fifteenth and nineteenth centuries, European countries sought land overseas as part of the extension of their political control. In doing so, they explored, invaded and took control of vast areas of the world. The extent of European rule in Africa is shown in Figure 16.2. The annexation of parts of the world by European countries is known as 'colonialism', and goes a long way to explain how and why the development gap has emerged.

Figure 16.2 European colonial rule in Africa by 1914.

- Spain conquered Central America together with the British, Dutch, Portuguese and French. Within 70 years of the arrival of Columbus, Spain had overthrown the Indian and Aztec empires and gained land and precious metals, especially gold and silver. Local labour was forced into the mines, or on to large plantations.
- In the Caribbean, sugar plantations replaced food crops grown for local people. The British and French became rulers, with slaves from West Africa at the bottom of the social pyramid.
- In Latin America, an estimated 7–8 million slaves were brought to Brazil alone between 1550 and 1850. The impact on Africa of removing millions of young men and women was to impoverish former wealthy and powerful African empires.

A few effects of colonialism have proved valuable, such as India's rail system. But for most, trade ties and economic links lasted well beyond independence. Most African states are still dependent upon European countries for trade and finance; many plantation owners and companies have stayed, and maintain control of land and resources. In South Africa, apartheid lived on until 1994, and the white population is still wealthiest. In Zimbabwe, land reform has led to conflict and loss of life as the President, Robert Mugabe, takes land back from white Zimbabwean landowners. The legacy of colonialism lives on.

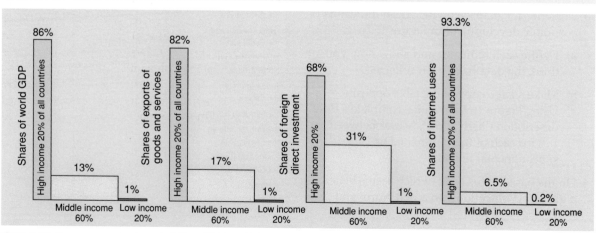

Figure 16.3 Some economic characteristics of high, middle and low income nations, 1997.

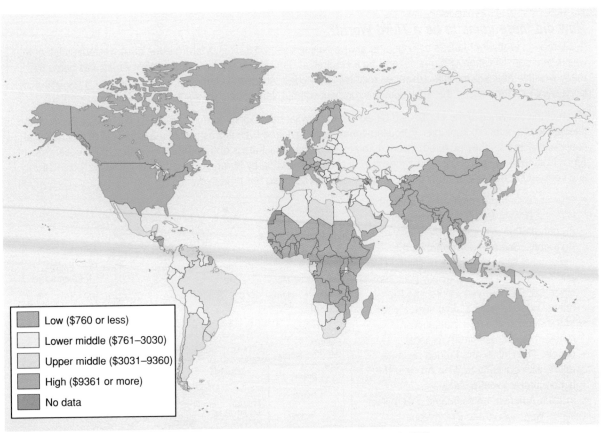

Figure 16.4 Global distribution of GNP per capita, based on 1998 data. All figures are in US$.

Legend:
- Low ($760 or less)
- Lower middle ($761–3030)
- Upper middle ($3031–9360)
- High ($9361 or more)
- No data

1 Using Figure 16.3, summarise the economic characteristics of high compared to low income countries.

2 Consider the economic indicators used to show key differences between high, middle and low income countries in Figure 16.3. Which other indicators would you suggest would also highlight differences between the North and South? Justify your choice.

3 Consider the maps showing social indicators of economic development in Figure 16.5a–c.

a) Define each indicator and show how you think the data have been collected.

b) Make a large copy of the table opposite. Using Figure 16.5a, b and c, complete a brief description ('high', 'low', 'varies between …') for each of the continental or subcontinental regions.

4 On the basis of this table, which seems better – a global classification into a rich North and poor South as used by Brandt (Figure 16.1), or the four divisions used by the World Bank (Figure 16.4)? Or are you able to reclassify using your own criteria? Explain your answer.

Region	Life Expectancy	Infant mortality	Child malnutrition
North America			
Western Europe			
Eurasia (Eastern Europe and CIS)			
Latin America and the Caribbean			
Middle East and North Africa			
Africa south of the Sahara			
Eastern Asia (China)			
South-East Asia and the Pacific Rim			
South Asia (Indian subcontinent)			
Australasia			

Figure 16.5 Three social indicators of development.

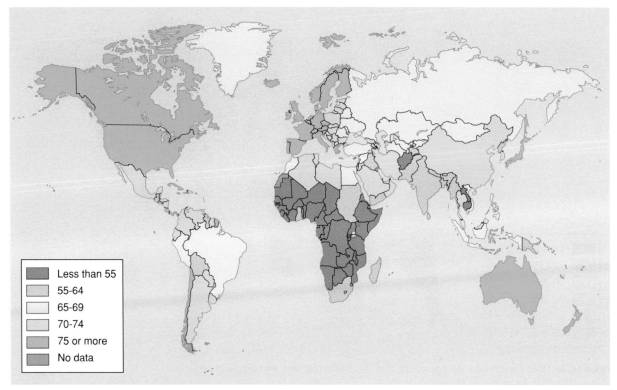

Figure 16.5a Life expectancy. All figures are in years.

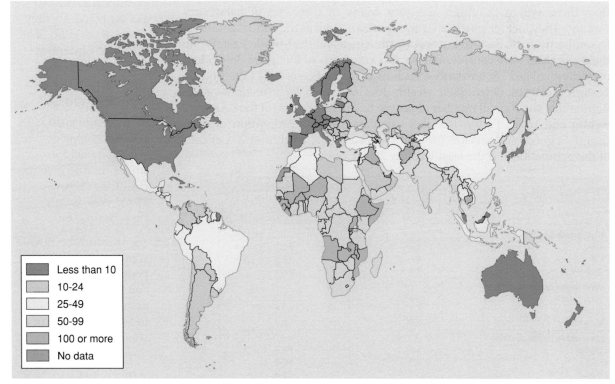

Figure 16.5b Infant mortality, i.e. deaths of children within their first year of life. All figures are per 1000 births.

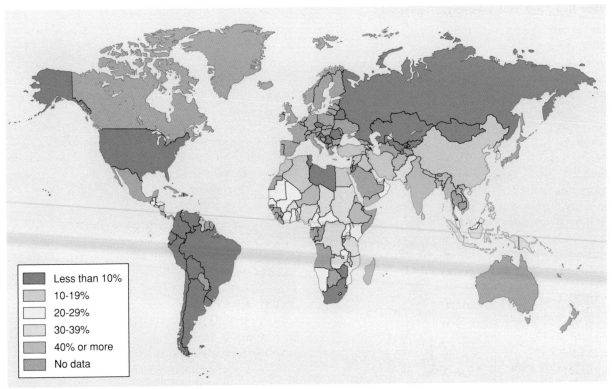

Figure 16.5c Child malnutrition. All figures are % of 0–15 year olds who are malnourished.

The upper middle income nations

Upper middle income nations are far more dispersed and individualised than those within the 'high' category. Many of these are in parts very wealthy. They include much of Latin America as well as individual countries in southern Africa, Eastern Europe, North Africa and the Middle East. While these countries have considerable wealth, standards of living are dependent on individualised circumstances, such as the presence of oil in the Middle Eastern countries. Often, their wealth does not reach large sections of the population, and a small number of people have a large share of the country's wealth and trade. Figure 16.6 is a calculation of the proportion of each country's goods and services (or GDP) owned by the wealthiest 20 per cent of the population and the least wealthy 20 per cent.

Country	% of GDP owned by the least wealthy 20% of the population	% of GDP owned by the wealthiest 20% of the population
High income countries		
USA	4.7	41.9
UK	4.6	44.3
Australia	4.4	42.2
Upper middle income countries		
South Africa	3.3	63.3
Brazil	2.1	67.5
Malaysia	4.6	53.7
Lower middle income countries		
Thailand	5.6	52.7
Peru	4.9	50.4
Russia	3.7	53.8

Figure 16.6 Distribution of wealth among upper middle and lower middle income countries, compared to high income countries.

1 Suggest why, in most countries, at least 40 per cent (and possibly up to 70 per cent) of all wealth is concentrated in the hands of the wealthiest 20 per cent of the population.

2 Why should such high concentrations of wealth be held in upper middle income countries (Figure 16.6)? Who would these people be?

3 As countries become wealthier, which people among a country's population gain most according to Figure 16.6? Why should this be?

The lower middle income nations

Lower middle income nations are more clustered than those within the upper middle category. They include countries within Latin America, individual countries in southern and North Africa, a large proportion of countries within Eastern Europe and the CIS, and the Middle East. Many of these are countries from the former Second World, a term for countries which formed the Soviet Union (USSR) before its break-up in 1991, together with the bloc of Eastern European communist countries whose governments fell after the collapse of the Berlin wall in 1989. These were centrally planned economies that were opened up to the global market during the 1990s and have since struggled. Many have serious currency weaknesses which has hampered investment and economic development.

The low income countries

Low income countries have become generally known as the 'Third World', and are also known as the world's poor nations, or the 'South', because most of them lie south of the Equator. They are sometimes referred to as the 'Two-Thirds World' because of the proportion of the world's population which lives there. In recent years, the term 'Less Economically Developed Countries', or LEDCs, has come into use, and is used most often in this book. The term refers to the group of nations in Figure 16.4 whose GNP per capita is shown as low; it includes the majority of African countries south of the Sahara, much of central and south Asia, and isolated countries within Central America.

Development as a continuum

However, the world cannot be divided even as simply as in the four-category division in Figure 16.3. There are huge differences in wealth within each of the four divisions. True, some MEDCs do have a very high GNP per capita, but others are much lower. Compare Luxembourg, which has the highest GNP in the world (US $45 100 per capita in 1998), with Slovenia (US $9780). Yet both are high income countries as shown in Figure 16.3. At the same time, low income countries range from China (US $750), where the economic growth rate was 9.6 per cent in 1998, to Ethiopia (US $100). However divisions are made, they are bound to mask differences within categories.

It is now more common to think in terms of economic development as a continuum. This recognises that even more complex categories than 'rich' and 'poor' exist, and that there are variations within categories.

Development and change – the NICs

In the last two decades of the twentieth century, the economies of several previously low income countries developed rapidly and to such an extent that they were very different from the struggling countries of Africa. Many of these now have GNP figures above many of the MEDCs. To walk through the streets of Singapore or Hong Kong today would be little different to walking around Paris or Los Angeles. Two groups of countries emerged in particular:

- those in Central and South America, such as Brazil and Venezuela, whose economies developed a strong manufacturing industrial base in the 1970s
- those in South-East Asia, such as Thailand, whose economies grew at a very rapid rate in the 1980s. Their development was based upon manufacturing and trade. Figure 16.7 illustrates just how rapidly their economies have developed – the name 'Asian tigers' is used to describe their aggressive push for economic growth. In Figure 16.7, 'real economic growth' refers to growth after annual inflation has been taken into account. By comparison, the UK was enjoying sound economic growth of 2 per cent in 1998! It is almost certain that China will follow this lead in the first decade of the twenty-first century.

These countries are generally referred to as 'Newly Industrialising Countries', or NICs. Chapter 18 on Taiwan shows how economic growth has occurred in one of these countries.

Country	Per capita GNP in US$		% annual real economic growth 1994	% average annual real economic growth 1990–8 (even including the 1997 recession)	% average annual growth in exports in the 1980s
	1973	1998			
Thailand	240	2 160	8.3	4.4	14.7
Malaysia	550	3 670	8.4	4.8	11.3
Singapore	1 580	30 170	8.8	6.7	4.2
South Korea	460	8 600	6.3	4.9	11.9

Figure 16.7 Changing levels of development – the case of four South-East Asian countries.
The countries shown underwent rapid economic development in the last quarter of the twentieth century.

Figure 16.8 Bangkok, the capital of Thailand, has many similarities with western urban areas.

Figure 16.9 Hong Kong – now one of the world's prime financial centres with much in common with western lifestyles.

The development gap

Even though development is shown as a continuum between MEDCs and LEDCs, it does not alter the fact that the last decades of the twentieth century witnessed an explosion in debt and poverty. There still exists a huge gap between the rich North (MEDCs) and the poor South (the LEDCs), which is referred to as the 'development gap'. There is a long way to go before the gap between MEDCs and LEDCs begins to narrow. The ways in which many LEDCs have tried to develop their economies have left them paralysed by debt. Malawi is among the world's poorest countries, with a GNP per capita of only US $210 in 1998. One quarter of this comes from overseas aid. It owed US $2.4 billion in debts in 1998, but earned only a quarter of this (US $549 million) in exports. One quarter of its export earnings is soaked up by debt repayment each year, and it has little chance at present of ever repaying its debts. This is no simple list of data; it translates into real life as Figure 16.10 shows.

A baby girl born in one of the least developed countries can expect to live barely 44 years – 2 years more than a baby boy. Her problems begin before birth since her mother is likely to be in poor health. If she is born in southern Asia, she has a 1 in 3 chance of being under-weight, a greater chance of dying in infancy and a high probability of being malnourished throughout childhood. She has a 1 in 10 chance of dying before her first birthday and a 1 in 5 chance of dying before her fifth. In some African countries her chance of being vaccinated is less than 1 in 2. She will be brought up in inadequate housing under insanitary conditions contributing to diarrhoeal disease, cholera and tuberculosis. She will have a 1 in 3 chance of ever getting enough schooling to learn how to read and write. She may be circumcised at puberty with consequent effects on her life as a woman and a mother. She will marry in her teens and may have 7 or more children close together unless she dies in childbirth before that. Ancient traditions will prevent her from eating certain nutritious foods during her pregnancies, when she most needs building up, and dangerous practices such as using an unsterile knife to cut the umbilical cord and placing cow-dung on the stump may kill some of her babies with tetanus.

She will be in constant danger from infectious disease from contaminated water at the place where she bathes, washes clothes and collects her drinking water. She will be chronically anaemic from poor nutrition, malaria and intestinal parasites. As well as caring for her family she will work hard in the fields, suffering from repeated attacks of fever, fatigue and infected cuts. If she survives into old age she will be exposed to the same afflictions as women in the rich countries: cardiovascular disease and cancer. To these she will succumb quickly, having no access to proper medical care and rehabilitation. She will not be able to pay anything herself: her country currently has less than 9 cents a year to spend on her health.

Some 24 million babies, one-sixth of the world total, are born in the least developed countries and too many of them will grow up in miserable conditions of life and health. Equity demands that the situation of these deprived infants be improved without delay.

Figure 16.10 The most deprived one in six.

At the beginning of the twenty-first century, awareness of the importance of social, political, cultural and environmental effects of economic change has created a different view of development. Economics is now balanced by a view that assesses people's quality of life and well-being. Development can be seen not just in terms of economic wealth, but also of social well-being and environmental quality. Aims such as justice, equality for the oppressed, freedom from pollution and environmental hazard are central to development. To this end, the United Nations uses a Human Development Index (HDI) to measure factors other than economic wealth (see theory box below).

However, high income does not necessarily convert into high HDI scores. Figure 16.11 shows how countries with similar HDI scores do not necessarily have similar incomes, and vice versa. It is a matter of how effective a country and its government are in converting income into human development.

a Country	HDI value	Real GDP per capita (PPP$)
Spain	0.894	15 930
Singapore	0.888	28 460
Georgia	0.729	1 960
Turkey	0.728	6 350
Morocco	0.582	3 310
Lesotho	0.582	1 860

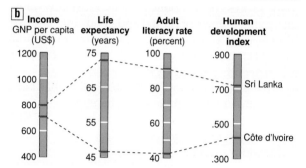

Figure 16.11 Contrasting HDI and Real GDP, 1997.
a Similar HDI, different income.
b Similar income, different HDI.

1 Study Figure 16.10. Which features of the girl's life are
   - within her control
   - outside her control?

2 How, if at all, should high income countries respond to situations such as this? Why?

3 Identify three courses of action which should be carried out in the poorest countries in order to attempt to improve this baby's prospects. Justify your suggestions.

Theory

The Human Development Index

The United Nations has introduced the Human Development Index (HDI) to measure not just the economic development of a country but also other factors which indicate development. The HDI uses three indicators of human well-being or deprivation:

- life expectancy
- education
- standard of living.

It averages these data for each country, and combines them into a single figure – the HDI – with a maximum possible value of 1. It is calculated as follows:

- The longest life expectancy in the world is 85 years and the shortest 25 years. In the HDI, values are converted to a number between 0 (worst) and 1 (best); 25 years count as '0' and 85 years as '1'. Any country whose life expectancy is 55 would therefore score 0.5, i.e. half-way between the lowest and the highest.

- Education is measured by averaging adult literacy rates to get one figure, and the number of years of schooling to get another. Lowest and highest values are expressed as a figure between 0 and 1; 75 per cent adult literacy would be 0.75 on the HDI. The same is done for schooling. If a pupil spends six years out of twelve in school, then this is expressed as 0.5 in calculating the index, i.e. 50 per cent of a twelve-year maximum.

- Standard of living is measured using a scale from the lowest PPP value (assessed by the United Nations in 1995 as US $200) to the highest (US $34 000). These are used as a scale from 0 to 1, as before, so that US $17 000 would be approximately 0.51.

The four indices – life expectancy, adult literacy rates, number of years schooling and standard of living – are added and averaged to give one figure, with 1 the maximum score. In 1998 Canada (with the highest score) had an HDI of 0.935, and Sierra Leone (with the lowest score) 0.252. The UK ranked tenth with 0.918.

The global economy in the twenty-first century

It is common now for people to speak of a 'global' economy and the process of 'globalisation'. What do these mean? Since 1980, the global economic balance has shifted. More and more countries recognise how important trade and investment are to the process of economic growth. Most now allow unregulated flows of capital and goods into and out of their countries in an attempt to attract investors from MEDCs. Like the colonialism of the fifteenth to nineteenth centuries, globalisation is being used to drive market expansion. 'Globalisation' has been used to describe the processes whereby:

- capital is moved across the world – over US $1.5 trillion is exchanged every day in the world's currency markets
- highly-skilled people, especially those with professional and IT skills, are moving around the globe to find employment where they are in demand
- instant communication takes place via the internet, email, cellular phones and global media networks
- new organisations are emerging and responding to change – global mergers of already huge transnational corporations (TNCs), expanding political organisations such as the EU, international trading groups such as the World Trade Organisation, and the United Nations increasingly trying to maintain global peace with its own forces
- global tourism takes more and more of the world's wealthy classes to new experiences overseas
- the world's media transmit news (for example the BBC, CNN) to virtually every country in the world via satellite networks.

However, this leaves power and influence in a very few hands, as Figure 16.12 shows.

Criteria	World's wealthiest fifth have	World's poorest fifth have
Global GDP	86%	1%
World export markets	82%	1%
Foreign investment	68%	1%
Telephone lines	74%	1.5%

Figure 16.12 Shares of the new global economy.

The communications revolution – who benefits?

The explosion in the global transport industry, together with a revolution in information and communication via the internet, has led to concepts of a 'shrinking' world. This further advantages the wealthier nations of the world and certain people within it (Figure 16.13).

Communication network	Issue
The internet	- Men constitute 83% of users in Japan, 93% in China. - Most users in the UK are under 30. - The Indian subcontinent has less than 1% of users. - 30% of those using the internet have a university degree.
Web sites and the new global language	- English is used as the global language on more than 80% of web sites.
Demand for skills	- In 1998, over 250 000 African professionals were working in the USA and Europe. In the EU, over half a million jobs are unfilled because of the lack of national skills.
Computers	- To buy a computer costs the average American one month's wages, the average Bangladeshi eight years' wages.

Figure 16.13 Issues in the communications revolution.

1 Using Figures 16.12 and 16.13, draw a 'futures wheel' like the one in Figure 16.14. On it, identify issues arising from these figures. Consider different scenarios, for example
- the internet – what happens if it remains a vehicle for a mainly young, male, well-qualified set of users?
- foreign investment – how and where will investment be made?
- demand for skills – who will the 'nouveau riche' be in the twenty-first century?
- web sites and the new global language – what happens to other languages?

2 Discuss as a class whether the 'new' economy and communications revolution has opportunities for all or just for a few.

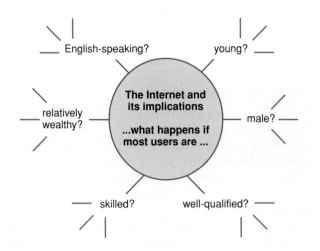

Figure 16.14 Futures wheel.

Summary

You have learned that:

- The world can be divided into groups of countries on the basis of common economic and social indicators, such as GNP or life expectancy. The most commonly used groupings are MEDCs and LEDCs, linked in turn to concepts of First and Third Worlds.
- The current pattern of global economic wealth shows a sharp contrast between a highly developed, wealthy North and a poorer South, separated by a widening development gap.
- Other groups of countries exist, such as:
  - the South-East Asian NICs, where rapid economic growth has enabled them to close the development gap with the North
  - the Second World countries of the former USSR, where change in government has led to rapid economic change.
- The concept of globalisation is used to describe attempts to reduce trade barriers between countries.
- The explosion in the global transport industry, together with a revolution in information and communication via the internet, has led to concepts of a 'shrinking' world. This further advantages the wealthier nations of the world.

References and further reading

Paul Harrison, *Inside the Third World*, Penguin Books (1993)
United Nations Development Programme, *Human Development Report*, published each year; 1999 and 2000 editions are especially useful
World Bank, *World Bank Atlas 2000*

Web sites

United Nations Development Program, web page http://www.undp.org

17 Going bananas?

The supermarket fruit display shown in Figure 17.1 provides a choice of different bananas. On the day that the photograph was taken, brands available were Del Monte, Chiquita, Windward Islands and the supermarket's own Organic label. How can customers know which ones they prefer? In fact, as this chapter will show, the label is everything and says far more than the name of the company from which it has come.

Bananas are, according to Fairtrade, 'the biggest fruit in the world'. Bananas:

- are the world's most popular fruit, worth more than £5 billion each year
- are the world's fourth most important crop after rice, wheat and maize in terms of value of production
- are the most popular fruit in the UK
- are the most valuable food product in supermarkets, outsold only by petrol and lottery tickets
- are worth annual UK sales of £750 million (2000)
- account for 28 per cent of all fruit sales in the UK
- have doubled in consumption in the UK since 1985; 95 per cent of households now purchase them.

Recently, the banana trade has become contentious and has involved some of the world's largest organisations, both private and public. This chapter investigates how there may be a price to pay for cheap bananas because of the conditions under which they are grown.

Figure 17.1 Supermarket banana counter.

Who controls what?

Over recent years the popularity of the banana has been on the increase. Consumption has more than doubled since the mid-1980s. In the same period the real banana price, taking inflation into account, has fallen by 35 per cent. Importers predict average annual growth of 5 per cent over the next five years. Over 75 per cent of banana sales are now through the major supermarkets. World exports of bananas virtually doubled to 12 million tonnes between 1988 and 1998.

Typical of most trade between LEDCs and MEDCs, bananas are imported into the USA and the EU – the two largest global markets for bananas. The largest exporting producers are:

- Ecuador (4 million tonnes)
- Costa Rica (2 million tonnes)
- Colombia (1.5 million tonnes)
- Philippines (1.1 million tonnes)
- Guatemala (0.6 million tonnes).

Of all world exports:

- Latin America accounts for over 83 per cent
- 11 per cent are from the Far East
- 3 per cent are from Africa
- less than 2 per cent come from the Caribbean.

The sources of imports into the UK are shown in Figure 17.2.

---

1 Identify the countries that supplied bananas to the UK in 1998, using Figure 17.2. Shade these in on a blank world map.

2 Draw flow lines to show volumes of bananas between banana producing countries and the two largest markets, the EU and the USA.

3 Using Figure 17.2, identify in a table:
   a) which countries have reduced imports to the UK
   b) which countries which have increased imports to the UK.

4 What are the implications for each group of countries?

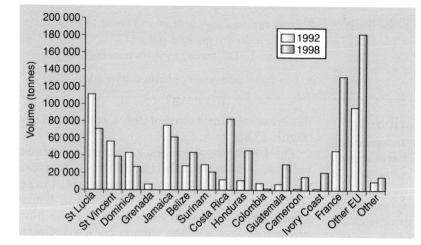

Figure 17.2 UK imports of bananas in 1992 and 1998. Note: France and the EU import from their own suppliers and re-export to the UK.

	Exports	Imports
Dominica		
Value	$60.8 million (1998)	$120.4 million (1998)
Commodities	Bananas 50%, soap, bay oil, vegetables, grapefruit, oranges	Manufactured goods, machinery and equipment, food, chemicals
Trading partners	Caribbean countries 47%, UK 36%, USA 7% (1996 est.) Netherlands, Canada (1996 est.)	USA 41%, Caribbean countries 25%, UK 13%,
St Lucia		
Value	$75 million (1998)	$290 million (1998)
Commodities	Bananas 41%, clothing, cocoa, vegetables, fruits, coconut oil	Food 23%, manufactured goods 21%, machinery and transportation equipment 19%, chemicals, fuels
Trading partners	UK 50%, USA 24%, Caribbean countries 16% (1995) Canada 4% (1995)	USA 36%, Caribbean countries 22%, UK 11%, Japan 5%,
Guatemala		
Value	$2.4 billion	$4.5 billion
Commodities	Coffee, sugar, bananas, fruits and vegetables, meat, apparel, petroleum, electricity	Fuels, machinery and transport equipment, construction materials, grain, fertilisers, electricity
Trading partners	USA 48%, El Salvador 10%, Honduras 6%, Germany 5%, Costa Rica 4% (1997)	USA 46%, Mexico 13%, El Salvador 5%, Venezuela 5%, Japan 4% (1997)

Figure 17.3a Trade flows between LEDCs and MEDCs.

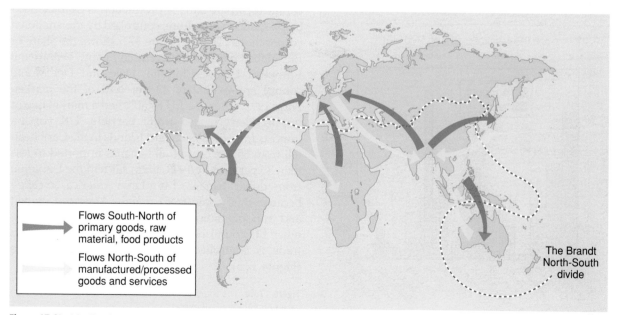

Flows South-North of primary goods, raw material, food products

Flows North-South of manufactured/processed goods and services

The Brandt North-South divide

Figure 17.3b Idealised map showing trade flows between South and North.

1 a) Describe the patterns of trade in the three countries shown in Figure 17.3a.
  b) How healthy do you consider this pattern to be? Give reasons.

2 How far do the countries in Figure 17.3a conform to the general pattern in MEDC–LEDC trade, as shown in Figure 17.3b?

3 Are these patterns confirmed by Figure 17.4?

The banana industry in the Caribbean

In the Caribbean, most producers are independent, small farmers. Caribbean growers have several disadvantages as far as banana cultivation is concerned. Growing areas are hilly or mountainous, with poor soil conditions and low yields. In addition, shipping, distribution and labour costs are all higher which contributes to a much greater production cost for Caribbean bananas. Caribbean producers are unable to compete directly on price. However, there are major obstacles to economic diversification away from bananas. Bananas are actually well suited to the climate, they recover well from hurricane damage, and a whole infrastructure has been built up to support the banana industry.

Although they only account for a small proportion of world trade, bananas are vital to the economies of many of the Caribbean states (Figure 17.4).

The UK is the sole market for most Caribbean bananas. Before 1992, the UK had been supplied mainly by the Windward Islands (St Lucia, St Vincent, Dominica, Grenada), Jamaica, Belize and Surinam. Under an exclusive export contract between Britain and the banana company Geest, Caribbean bananas were guaranteed a market outlet in Britain. Like many LEDC economies, Caribbean countries:

- depend on primary products, i.e. those that are produced from agriculture, mining, fishing or forestry
- are dependent upon a few markets to take most of their produce
- have little to fall back on in the event of a change of market (Figure 17.4).

The introduction of the Single European Market after 1992 was a major challenge to the relationship between the UK and the Caribbean. The Single European Market meant that special trade agreements that existed between individual members would have to be abandoned in favour of a joint policy for all EU countries. Most EU countries purchase their bananas from Latin American countries, where banana production is characterised by plantation agriculture, controlled by transnational corporations (TNCs). Figure 17.5 shows the share of the global banana trade by company. Within the European Union, Chiquita, Dole and Del Monte control approximately 43 per cent of the market. After 1992, when the EU established a market free of import charges and trade barriers, UK banana imports from the Windward Islands in the Caribbean fell from 65 per cent of all bananas imported to less than 35 per cent by 1998. Extra sales in the UK come from 'dollar' bananas from Latin America, so called because they come from mainly American owned and run plantations. Many are re-exported from other EU countries to the UK. The Latin American trade is controlled by a small number of TNCs (Figure 17.5).

Figure 17.4a The importance of bananas in the economy of producing countries.

Country	Value of banana exports (US $000s)	Value of all food exports (US $000s)	% food exports taken by bananas
St Lucia	32 497	38 706	84.0
Ecuador	1 058 729	1 564 825	67.7
Dominica	13 701	23 417	58.5
Saint Vincent/ Grenadines	20 546	42 182	48.7
Panama	138 748	293 888	47.2
Costa Rica	588 029	1 802 773	32.6

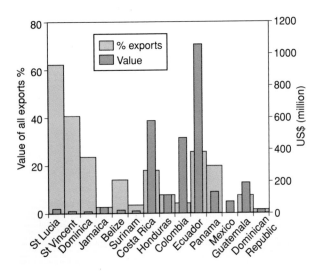

Figure 17.4b The importance of bananas in terms of value and as a percentage of all exports.

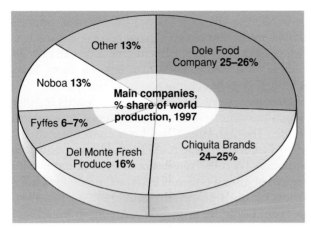

Figure 17.5 Ownership of the world's banana exports.

Giants step in – the effect of trade blocs on the banana trade

In recent decades, there has been a tendency for countries to group into large trading blocs. These consist of trading partners, which in some cases may go as far as seeking political, economic and even monetary union, for example the EU developed the Euro currency in 1999. The theory box below shows how these trading blocs have emerged.

The formation of the Single European Market in 1992 meant that members of the European Union had to work towards trading with the same group of countries. This affected arrangements for the import of bananas – Germany had previously had a tariff-

Theory

Trading blocs – what, and for whom?

An important feature of world trade has been the emergence of trading blocs, i.e. countries which choose to trade together as a group. The UK is part of the European Union (EU) which began as the Common Market in the late 1940s with a membership of six countries and has gradually expanded to include most countries in Western Europe. Other countries are likely to join in the first decade of the twenty-first century. The Association of South-East Asian Nations (ASEAN) joined together in 1967, and in 1992 the USA and Canada formed the North American Free Trade Association (NAFTA), with associated membership of Central and some South American countries. Blocs currently functioning are shown in Figure 17.6.

The advantages of a trading bloc are that countries may trade freely without paying duties, or tariffs, on goods produced within the same bloc. To countries outside the bloc there may be tariffs to pay on imported goods. The EU goes further and permits the free movement of people between European countries to work and settle. It has developed legal frameworks such as the European Court of Human Rights to which all its members are accountable, and in January 1999 launched a single currency.

The development of trade blocs accelerated in the 1980s and 1990s. More recently, West African countries look set to combine as a bloc. More significant is the role of the World Trade Organisation which represents 128 member countries (two-thirds of which are LEDCs). Formed in 1995, it represents a larger forum than any other organisation formed for the purpose of trade, but its role is to ensure that fair trade is established. However, there are those who suspect that its job is to create a global free trade area between countries, free of tariffs or duties. Consider the implications of this as you read through this chapter.

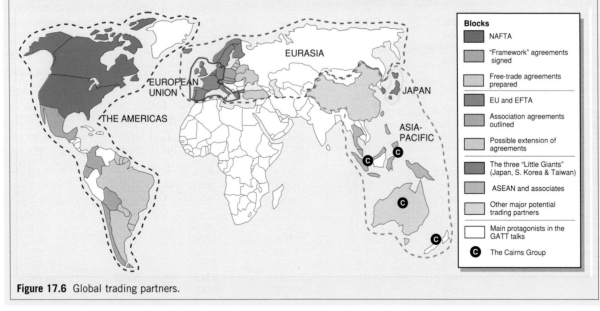

Figure 17.6 Global trading partners.

1 a) What would be the arguments for offering preferential conditions to countries in the banana trade such as those in the Caribbean?

   b) What would be the arguments against this?

2 Should the UK have maintained its preferential treatment for banana imports from the Caribbean, or was the WTO right to insist that it be removed?

free banana market, while the UK gave special treatment to imports from its former colonies in the Caribbean. A new banana regime was agreed in 1993 which used quotas and tariffs to give access to exports from African, Caribbean and Pacific countries. Imports from Latin America were thus limited both in volume and by higher prices.

However, this agreement went against moves towards greater globalisation and liberalisation of world trade, designed to establish ground rules for trade. The agreement has been challenged at the General Agreement on Tariffs and Trade (GATT), and its successor, the World Trade Organisation (WTO). Transnational banana companies think that the EU regime of giving preference to the Caribbean nations hinders their expansion. Chiquita pushed the USA to impose sanctions in 1999. Now 100 per cent tariffs are imposed on American imports of a long list of products which have nothing to do with bananas. For example, British packaging companies and French cheese and wine makers are subject to sanctions when exporting to the USA.

The effects of the WTO on the Caribbean producers

For the small farmers of the Windward Islands, the situation is becoming more and more desperate. As individual farmers on small plots of hilly land, they cannot compete with big companies. Dependent on the UK market for nearly 50 years, the farmers, and the economy of the islands as a whole, rely on the UK's willingness to buy their bananas.

Matters have been made much worse as result of the intervention of the WTO. Under pressure from the US government, backed by the interests of TNCs, the WTO is insisting that Europe ceases its preferential access for Windward Island bananas, even though they account for less than 2 per cent of world trade. Despite widespread concern about the social and environmental conditions in the Latin American TNC producers, Europe is not allowed to honour its commitments to discriminate in favour of Windward Island farmers. Farmers there cannot compete with the cost savings (for example low

Figure 17.7 Selected economic indicators for the Windward Islands. Note the changing economy caused by global changes to trade from the EU and WTO.

		Dominica	St Lucia	St Vincent	Grenada	Total
Number of active growers	1992	6 555	9 500	8 000	600	24 555
	1998	3 533	6 061	7 048	118	16 760
	% change	–46	–36	–12	–80	–32
Numbers in direct banana employment	1992	10 225	20 000	23 053	2 550	56 428
	1998	5 552	14 800	21 051	510	41 883
	% change	–44	–35	–12	–80	–26
Decline in active farmers and employees	1992–8	7 725	8 639	3 554	2 522	22 440
Population	1990/1	71 000	134 000	106 000	91 000	402 000
	1998	71 000	150 000	112 000	93 000	426 000
Banana exports (tonnes)	1990/1	56 617	133 777	79 561	7 486	277 441
	1998	28 135	53 727	38 890	94	120 846
As % all exports	1990/1	56.2	57.6	52.7	17.5	46.0
	1998	23.6	62.4	41.1	0.1	41.2
% workforce in bananas	1990/1	30.8	25.0	20.0	n.a.	25.3
	1998	33.0	35.0	34.0	0.1	34.0
% population dependent on bananas	1990/1	72.5	65.5	85.8	9.6	59.5
	1998	37.0	40.8	72.4	1.7	39.3
Pesticide imports ($000)	1990/1	2 105	5 336	1 946	738	10 125
	1998	20 000	3 978	2 500	900	27 378
Bananas yield (kg/ha)	1990/1	15 507	10 667	9 668	3 862	39 705
	1998	10 000	10 000	10 000	4 000	34 000

Figure 17.8 Caribbean and Latin American banana producers.

	Price paid for bananas to the company that supplies them			Price paid by these companies to growers in the Caribbean
	Oct 1998	Oct 1999	+/–	Oct 1999
Dominica	£6.38	£6.07	–5%	£3.27
St Lucia	£7.95	£5.62	–29%	£3.96
St Vincent	£6.54	£6.01	–8%	£3.96

Figure 17.9 Payments for bananas to companies and growers 1998–9 (equivalent £ per 18kg box).

wages and heavy use of chemicals) enjoyed by big plantation companies, and are losing their livelihoods. So for the Windward Islands and their farmers the future looks bleak. Prices are coming down and thousands of small farmers have already been driven off their land – or into farming marijuana – to make some kind of living.

Throughout the dispute, Caribbean banana exports to the EU have declined at a significant rate. Farmers have been leaving the industry, while banana importers, unable to get sufficient bananas, are turning to other Latin American countries for supplies. Many people have forecast the collapse of the Caribbean banana industry.

1 Explain ,using figure 17.7:
  a) the reduced production of bananas in the Windward Islands in the 1990s
  b) the decrease in the proportion of the population dependent on bananas.
  c) three other main changes shown in figure 17.7

2 a) How might those previously dependent on bananas now earn a living?
  b) Explain how the number of people forced to live in poverty has increased.

3 a) Using Figure 17.9, calculate the price per kg from a box of bananas paid to (i) growers in the Caribbean, (ii) companies that supply them for distribution within the UK.
  b) How does this compare with the price per kg in your local shop or supermarket?
  c) Explain the difference.
  d) Do you feel that the difference is justifiable?

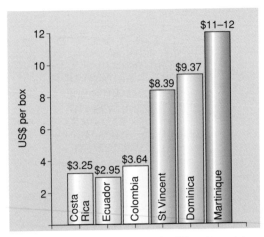

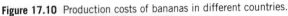

Figure 17.10 Production costs of bananas in different countries.

Figure 17.11 Large banana plantation in Colombia.

- Carlos works for the plantation workers' union, SITRAP, which campaigns to persuade banana companies to reduce aerial spraying. Carlos is one of the 20 per cent of Costa Rican banana workers left sterile after handling highly toxic chemicals.
- Juan handled the pesticide DBCP. His wife Maria gave birth to a baby whose head was four times bigger than his body.
- Although DBCP is now banned, five chemicals designated 'extremely hazardous' by the World Health Organisation are still used on plantations.

Figure 17.12 Health effects of working with plantation chemicals.

Latin American banana plantations

The banana trade is mainly in the hands of large TNCs which control huge tracts of land on which a monocultural (or single product) economy exists. Del Monte is now owned by a Chile based, Miami controlled and managed conglomerate, which is backed by money from the United Arab Emirates. Noboa is the largest company in Ecuador, owned by the richest man in Latin America.

Although Caribbean banana growers are losing market share to the banana plantations of Latin America, they still receive more for their work than plantation labourers. This is partly due to the control exercised by plantation owners to drive down prices. Figure 17.10 shows that, typically, a Latin American banana costs much less than half price of its Caribbean counterpart to produce. One factor which contributes to the lower production costs in Latin America is the economy of scale obtained due to the size of the plantations (Figure 17.11). Agrochemicals also contribute to a higher yield per hectare.

Environmental impacts of plantations

The EARTH College (Escuela de Agricultura de la Region Tropical Humeda) estimates that of the fungicide applied by aeroplanes some 40 times during each cultivation cycle, 15 per cent is lost to wind, 40 per cent ends up on soil rather than on plants and 35 per cent is washed off by rain. This results in a 90 per cent loss of the estimated 11 million litres of fungicide, water and oil emulsion applied each year to the banana production regions. Furthermore, for every tonne of bananas shipped, two tonnes of waste is left behind. Health effects are also serious (Figure 17.12).

The workers' living quarters are adjacent to the plantations. Although told to stay indoors with their families while spraying occurs, workers eat food plants from their private gardens, and wash with water that has been sprayed.

1 Make a copy of the table below and complete it, showing the advantages and disadvantages of plantation systems for growing bananas.

	Advantages	Disadvantages
Social Economic Environmental		

2 How far do the advantages and disadvantages balance each other?

3 Would you pay more for bananas that were produced by small farmers, or would you prefer cheaper bananas from TNCs? Explain why.

Living and employment conditions on Latin American banana plantations owned by TNCs

As well as being forced to endure appalling working conditions, plantation workers are also paid pittance wages. In Ecuador, plantation workers are paid just $1 per day. When workers try to organise into trade unions they are often met with violent suppression. Increasing production – and declining retail prices – means that producers are getting prices as low as $2 for a 40lb box (3 pence per pound) – which does not even cover the cost of production. Banana workers' wages have been falling. An eight-hour working day in Costa Rica in 1993 would earn a monthly wage of $250, while the same amount of work four years later was worth $187. Working conditions consist of working days of 12–14 hours for wages which are not sufficient to cover the basic needs of subsistence for a family, dismissals without any social security or redundancy payments, lack of medical attention, lack of educational opportunities and no rights to maternity leave.

In Guatemala, the wage rate of 40p per hour was due for review in August 1999. A strike in March 2000 resulted in a large-scale firing of workers. The Big Three (Chiquita, Dole, Del Monte) have begun recognising independent trade unions, but there is a long way to go.

Plantation companies often control all aspects of life, including schools, healthcare, water and electricity supplies, housing, and the supply of cooking equipment, transport, recreation facilities, books for the union library, football shirts, toys – everything apart from the Catholic Church (where they control the electricity supply).

Figure 17.13 From Fairtrade, August 2000.

Fairtrade – a way forward

A second impact of the WTO has been a ruling that countries should not discriminate between products on the grounds of the social or environmental conditions under which they were produced. This leaves few ways for European consumers to support disadvantaged producers, such as those in the Windward Islands. Now, a new voluntary labelling scheme has been introduced, known as 'Fairtrade'. A Fairtrade label is awarded to products which meet certain standards of production and trade, with better deals for producers. Fairtrade bananas have established a market share of between 5 per cent and 13 per cent in EU countries where they are available.

Fairtrade also establishes:
- direct trading links with producers in developing countries, cutting out local dealers
- guaranteed prices to producers
- a 'social premium' to producers, for investment in social and environmental improvements
- credit allowances or advance payments
- long-term trading relationships to enable planning.

Over a third of the EU population said they would be prepared to pay a premium above the price of normal bananas for Fairtrade bananas. Over 70 per cent of UK consumers say they care about the conditions endured by people who produce goods for consumption. The first Fairtrade bananas from Costa Rica entered the UK in January 2000, and were offered for sale in 1000 Co-op stores, followed by boxes of Windward Islands bananas in July 2000. The importing company, Geest, was shipping 144 000kg a week by autumn 2000 and increasing volumes as consumer demand dictated. If the market can reach 8 per cent of demand, the UK could import 50 000 tonnes of Fairtrade bananas, which represents 36 per cent of the Windward Islands' current production. The initial results have been encouraging with the Co-op selling its 8 millionth Fairtrade banana in July 2000 and Fairtrade accounting for 7 per cent of bananas sold in the Sainsbury's stores where they were stocked.

Costa Rica is now the major supplier of Fairtrade bananas to Europe. Since beginning to sell on Fairtrade terms, the cooperative that supplies most bananas has stopped using paraquat and other herbicides, reduced the use of chemical fertilisers, started recycling all plastic waste, cleared up a rubbish pit, and started planting trees along canals. Employed workers have enjoyed considerable wage rises recently, and the social premium has funded an agronomist and five environmental specialists, and also repairs to housing.

The Fairtrade social premium has been used to cut the use of harmful herbicides consequently providing more work in manual weeding, and to pay end of year bonuses and subsidies for union expenses. There are plans to expand into organic production, and a social and environmental action plan is also being implemented.

a Elia Ruth Zúñiga works in the packing plant for Coopetrabasur. She said that 'with Fairtrade our salary has increased quite high, so that we have a better life for our families. We have water, we have electricity and we have a house given to us by the company. Everything here was in a bad condition due to contamination. Rivers didn't have any fish. Due to chemicals we were losing everything. Water was really contaminated. Now it's different, we don't use chemicals. I would like the markets to get bigger in Europe – that would be great for us.'

b Caphias Duncan, 61, lives on his own in a dark room at the far end of a disused dance hall in St Vincent. He has three acres of bananas and has recently joined the farmer's group that is registered to supply Fairtrade bananas to the UK. He laments the current situation: 'The price we get is bad enough. Before it was much better than now. The cost of living has gone up, the cost of fertiliser has gone up, the price we are left with has gone down. It's much more difficult to grow bananas now and it's just not worth it. My sons have gone to the hills to grow marijuana. It's less work and more pay, but it's illegal.'

Figure 17.14 The effects of Fairtrade on people's lives.

1 Make a copy of the table below and complete it, showing the advantages and disadvantages of the Fairtrade system for supplying bananas.

	Advantages	Disadvantages
Social Economic Environmental		

2 How far do the advantages and disadvantages balance each other?

3 How does this balance compare with the plantation system?

4 Do you count yourself among those who would pay more for Fairtrade bananas, or would you prefer cheaper bananas from TNCs? Explain why.

Summary

You have learned that:

- Many food products come from LEDCs to supply the western economies of the EU and the USA.
- Several LEDCs depend on bananas, and on western countries to buy them.
- The development of trade blocs has protected the rights of richer nations at the expense of poorer nations. This has led to uneven distribution of wealth in the areas of flows of trade, technology, food resources, investment, aid and people.
- The development gap, described in Chapter 16, is enhanced by the flow of trade and goods between MEDCs and LEDCs. Countries of the South are dependent on the markets of the North. Similarly, countries of the North depend upon countries in the South for food and raw materials. This is known as 'global interdependence', and largely works in favour of countries in the North.
- Even though LEDCs supply food to MEDCs, the ownership of land, and the way it is managed, is often in the control of MEDCs.
- Small farmers compete with large plantation producers, often on disadvantageous price terms.
- Plantation farming has been criticised for its heavy use of environmentally damaging chemicals.
- There are alternative systems for the production of food, such as that run by Fairtrade, but these may be at greater economic cost.

References and further reading

Food & Agriculture Organisation (FAO) of the United Nations
Claire Godfrey, *A Future for Caribbean Bananas*, Oxfam (1998)
New Internationalist, October 1999

Web sites

Unpeeling the Banana Trade, Fairtrade Foundation, August 2000 – can be found on the Fairtrade web page:
http://www.fairtrade.org.uk/unpeeling.htm
The Caribbean Banana Exporters Association web site: http://www.cbea.org/

The global shift – Taiwan

Economic change due to the transition to a global economy creates stress in societies. Trade barriers are reduced in some places and erected in others, and investment capital moves around the world in search of the best returns. This chapter investigates Taiwan, where rapid economic change has been experienced. It looks at the cultural, social and environmental effects of this change.

Taiwan – a newly industrialising country

Since 1950 the Western Pacific Rim of Asia (Figure 18.1) has become a major global economic core area, and now ranks alongside North America and Western Europe. Since the mid-1980s, the centre of this core area has shifted south from Japan to include the Asian 'tigers' (Taiwan, Thailand, Malaysia, South Korea, Hong Kong and Singapore).

Chapter 17 has shown how these countries have grouped into ASEAN – an Asian economic trade bloc. Figures 18.3 and 18.4 show how the symbols of economic growth and consumption are already apparent. Parts of China are now developing even more quickly and look set to take over a core role in the twenty-first century.

Taiwan and the NICs

Taiwan has become an important part of the economic core area and is now a global economic force. It is grouped with the NICs, found mainly in South-East Asia.

Rapid industrialisation has resulted from investment by TNCs, which take advantage of low wage rates and tax incentives to produce manufactured goods for richer MEDCs. Special coastal zones have been designated to encourage

Figure 18.1 The Western Pacific Rim.

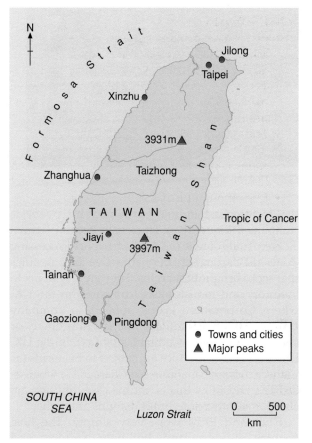

Figure 18.2 Key features of Taiwan.

In 1998, Taiwan could boast the following:
- Manufacturing accounted for 78 per cent of total industrial production and 26 per cent of the national workforce.
- The total production value of the IT industry was US $30 billion, up 21.4 per cent from 1996.
- Taiwan was the world's third largest computer hardware supplier after the USA and Japan.
- Some 900 computer hardware manufacturers provided jobs for approximately 100 000 employees, producing desktop PCs, scanners and CD-ROMs.
- 13 automobile manufacturers had contracted joint ventures with overseas makers, mostly from Japan.
- The China Motor Corporation maintained its traditional top position, producing over half of the 105 000 commercial vehicles sold.
- Taiwan was the third largest producer of artificial clothing fibre.
- Labour-intensive industries have gradually been replaced by capital- and technology-intensive industries, such as the production of chemicals, petrochemicals, information technology, electrical equipment and electronics.

Figure 18.3 Production in Taiwan in 1998.

Figure 18.4 An alleyway market in Taichung, Central Taiwan.

the location of industries owned by overseas companies (Figure 18.5). These have become known as Free Trade Zones (FTZs) and Export Processing Zones (EPZs), and are very attractive to companies that seek high profit margins. They are free of tax to investors and industrialists (compared to the UK, where Corporation Tax is applied to company profits, and where profits on the sale of property or shares are subject to Capital Gains Tax). In the UK, imports of some produce are subject to EU tariffs (as with Caribbean bananas – see Chapter 17) whereas in FTZs and EPZs this is not the case. Imports are cheaper and therefore profit margins are higher.

FTZs and EPZs work very simply. The host country provides land, buildings, services and

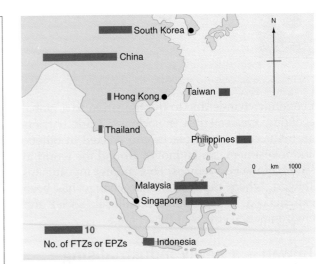

Figure 18.5 FTZs and EPZs in the West Pacific.

labour. The overseas company brings in raw materials, part-finished goods, management, technology and capital. The host country receives rent and payment for services, wages and experience. The overseas company exports goods and makes profits.

The attractions for industrialists are cheap labour, no unions to enforce wage rates or monitor working conditions, no customs import or export duties, no local taxes, long periods between tax payments (known as 'tax holidays'), subsidised services, cheap loans, and unlimited profits which can be taken out of the country without restriction. Workers can find the situation less attractive (Figure 18.6), but conditions improve when better paid work becomes available elsewhere in the country, as is now happening in Taiwan.

In Kaohsiung Export Processing Zone in southern Taiwan, as in most Asian FTZs, 85 per cent of the labour force are young women whose wages are lower than those of men doing similar work. Employers exploit the cultural training of the girls and say that they are 'obedient and pay attention to orders'. Beside causing 'less trouble' than boys, they say, their 'nimble fingers' are better for work in electronic assembly and textiles.

Low wages are backed by insecurity of job tenure and poor working conditions. Eye ailments are common in electronics assembly workshops. Near to the EPZ the women live in bare dormitories with very basic amenities. Sexual exploitation is common, but many girls are encouraged to continue work as their income is vital to the family. And this is in a country which has managed the distribution of wealth more equitably than most.

Figure 18.6 Working in a Free Trade Zone.

1 Form three separate groups. Select one of the following people:
 • a potential investor
 • a local person looking for work
 • a human rights activist.

 Discuss the description of FTZs and EPZs above and in Figure 18.6 from the point of view of the person you have selected.

2 Present your group's findings to the other groups and discuss different viewpoints that are expressed. Can the viewpoints and priorities be reconciled?

Taiwan's history

Taiwan's history has been complex but explains why economic development has occurred here. In 1945, after nearly 50 years of Japanese occupation, Taiwan once again became part of China. In 1950, communists under Mao Tse-tung drove Nationalist Chinese out of mainland China. Their leader Chiang Kai-shek and a million followers occupied Taiwan. Chiang Kai-shek kept the country under military law until July 1987.

Wages per month	US$	$ annual	£ 1997
Mining and quarrying	1414	17 000	11 300
Manufacturing	1229	14 750	9 800
Electricity, gas and water	2733	32 800	21 900
Construction	1290	15 500	10 300
Commerce	1234	14 800	9 900
Transport, storage and communications	1675	20 000	13 300
Finance, insurance and real estate	2079	24 950	16 600
Business services	1642	19 700	13 100
Social and personal services	1265	15 200	10 100

Annual leave entitlement

 • 7 days per year for 1–3 years employment

 • 10 days per year for 3–5 years employment

 • 14 days per year for 5–10 years employment

 • 14 days plus 1 additional day for every year over 10 years to a maximum of 30 days per year.

Figure 18.7 Wage levels and holiday entitlements in Taiwan in 1998. These are official government wage levels. As Figure 18.6 shows, other, illegal, workers do not have these same entitlements.

The USA poured arms and aid into Taiwan to prevent further expansion of communist China. The Chinese tradition of hard work and commitment to learning enabled the Taiwanese to develop industry and commerce and dramatically improve most people's standard of living. Since 1987 democracy has gained strength, and Taiwan now has free elections with greater attention to human rights. Taiwan has now passed through the phase of low wages and overseas exploitation, though this has often been replaced by similar conditions in home-grown companies. Taiwan is no longer a 'low wage cost' location compared to other regions of South-East Asia (Figure 18.7). In fact Taiwanese companies are themselves now investing overseas in textiles and electronics in countries like mainland China whose economies are less industrialised.

Economic issues: how will the rest of the world compete?

Taiwan has twelve TNCs each with market values of over US $2.5 billion as well as many smaller ones. These are now investing in factories in other areas of East Asia to provide low wage labour for its manufacturing. The financial and management success of Taiwanese firms is exemplified by Delta Electronics and its worldwide links. Taiwan, like Japan, is now investing in higher income areas such as the UK (for example Telford where Taiwan's Tatung factory is located), with grants and tax incentives from the host government.

Should the UK welcome Pacific Rim investment? What measures, if any, should be taken to control it?

Social and cultural issues: Where do you begin?

Value systems and cultural norms from the USA and Japan are making a tremendous impact on the younger people of Taiwan. Westernisation is an established fact – American comics in Taiwanese translations, fast foods competing with traditional Chinese dishes, clothes displayed on western dress models in shops, consumerism, computerisation and so on. Taipei (Figure 18.8) is indeed a 'global' city, where someone from the wealthy North would not feel out of place.

Traditional family structure is holding so far, but is under stress. At present older women are willing to mind their grandchildren while their daughters

Figure 18.8 Central Taipei. Taipei is a growing modern industrial and commercial city. It is now becoming congested with people and traffic (mainly taxis, buses and scooters), and an American-style Rapid Transit System is being constructed.

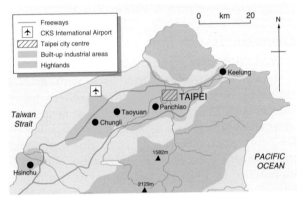

Figure 18.9 Taipei conurbation and northern Taiwan.

go out to work, enabling young Taiwanese women to succeed in business. But will *they* be willing to mind *their* grandchildren? The ambitions of the younger generation are different from the generation before. As well as cultural issues there are social issues, one of which is the fate of illegal migrant workers.

Illegal migrant workers in Taiwan

In the back streets and outer suburbs of Taipei (Figure 18.9) there are hundreds of small independently owned factories, many of which produce partly finished goods and components for bigger companies. These bigger companies supply products to Europe and North America. The economic boom has created a labour shortage – unemployment in Taiwan has been under 1 per cent for many years – and although some overseas labour is recruited legally, it has not been government policy to attract large numbers of immigrants. Agents recruit workers and arrange illegal entry into Taiwan, where they are virtually hidden in factories where they work. In small and medium-sized factories in Taipei and central Taiwan, there are about 10 000 legal immigrants but 50 000 illegal workers. Their status means they are outside the protection of the law, and Kanishka's story (Figure 18.10) shows what happens.

An interview with Kanishka, a Sri Lankan migrant worker

Q How much did you pay your Sri Lankan agent in order to come here?

A I gave 35 000 in my country's currency.

Q What is that in UK pounds?

A About £600. After I came to Taiwan they also deducted £700 from my salary.

Q How many foreigners were working at this company when you arrived?

A Maybe 23.

Q From what countries?

A Bangladeshis are the majority. At that time there were five Sri Lankans and four Thailand people.

Q Can you describe an incident you remember well?

A I remember one incident. There were four Indonesians in the factory. Three of them had come to the end of their one-year agreement. They went to the office to ask for their passports back. The boss was very angry. He gave them their passports and told them to leave the company immediately. Then there was only one Indonesian. The boss took revenge on him. He shouted at this guy and took him into the room. He used the electric gun on him, the Indonesian man told me he used it on him in the room. I heard him screaming in the room. We were very afraid. Then I saw him come out and near the elevator I saw the boss kick him. Then one Malaysian stopped the boss. On the day he mistreated the Indonesian guy I went to the office because the boss deducted £50 from our salaries per month. I don't like because my agent didn't tell me about that. The boss was very angry and he shout loudly. Anyway the boss was very angry and he called the Malaysian to come and translate, also he called a Filipino. I asked him why he deduct £50 from our salaries. The Malaysian guy told me the boss is very angry, that he takes this from all the salaries of foreigners and he will return it after 6 months. I said he cannot do that. The boss got very angry. He shout very loud at me: 'Any question? Any question?' He is a big man, maybe a six-footer.

Q Is there anything else you would like to say?

A I like Taiwan. But I don't like to work any more in that factory. Very hard. If people are kind OK. We can work hard. We can work very hard for them that's OK. But we must not always be afraid, we must have our human rights.

Figure 18.10 Kanishka's story. Kanishka, who is 28, is one of about 3000 Sri Lankans in Taiwan.

1 Work with a partner.
   a) List the issues arising from Kanishka's story in Figure 18.10.
   b) Who can do what about each issue?
   c) What are the possible remedies for human rights violations in such circumstances?

2 Consider Kanishka's story and other evidence in this section. In a group, discuss:
   a) how far people in the UK face similar cultural and social issues to those in Taiwan
   b) what, if anything, you feel can or should be done about these issues, and by whom.

Environmental issues: must growth cause pain?

Rapid industrialisation and urbanisation seems to be almost impossible without environmental cost, particularly pollution. In capitalist free-market economies, infrastructure and legal controls inevitably lag behind developments in agriculture and industry. Profit and immediate improvements in personal and family circumstances are priorities for people. Environmental issues are lower on their list. Most environmental problems are common in Taiwan – polluted rivers, air unfit to breathe in Taipei for an average of 62 days per year, and crops contaminated with pesticides and heavy metals. Taiwan is becoming an environmental nightmare. Figure 18.11 provides one way of looking at these problems.

Agricultural development has aggravated this situation. Farming is mechanised and intensive, and the 'green revolution' increased the use of pesticides, fertilisers, irrigation and intensive rearing methods (Figure 18.14). Demand from consumers in towns and cities means that water polluted by industrial waste and sewage is used for irrigation without treatment. The extent of Taiwan's polluted rivers is shown in Figure 18.12. Many soluble pollutants transfer easily into the food chain. In addition, farming methods themselves create problems (Figure 18.13). Even recently developed and highly productive aquaculture is in serious difficulty (Figure 18.14).

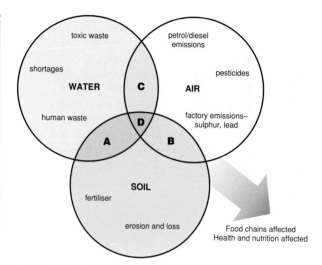

Figure 18.11 Venn diagram showing aspects of environmental pollution in Taiwan.

1 Make a copy of Figure 18.11. Identify some of the effects of pollution in the overlapping sections A, B, C and D.

2 Do the environmental problems illustrated in Figure 18.11 require different or similar solutions?

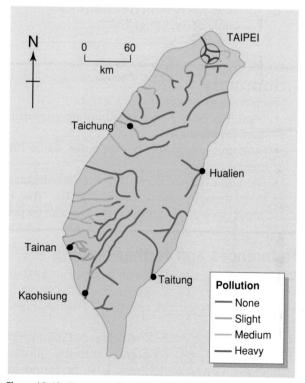

Figure 18.12 River pollution in Taiwan.

High crop yields in the lowlands of Taiwan have been obtained by liberal use of fertilisers and pesticides. Taiwan is among the top users of chemical fertilisers in the world. Heavy use contributes to soil acidification, zinc losses and reduced soil fertility. Nitrogen and phosphorous run-off stimulates the growth of algae in rivers and lakes, and contaminates groundwater. Pesticides contaminate freshwater sources. Farmers apply an average of 4kg per hectare per annum and now use almost 1 per cent of the world's pesticide. Pesticide abuse is encouraged by aggressive marketing of some 280 brands by private companies, with no effective government regulation of the trade.

Figure 18.13 Agriculture – a toxic growth?

Hailed as the success story which 'every country in the business is scrambling to emulate', Taiwanese aquaculture has achieved fantastic growth rates, with prawn production, for example, increasing 45 times in just 10 years. Like other industries in Taiwan, aquaculture is made up of thousands of small, specialised producers throughout the country, most of them in coastal areas. They are dependent on rivers and wells for clean fresh water, which is fast becoming a scarce commodity. Thus, mass deaths of shrimps and fish regularly occur as a result of toxic chemical waste from upstream industries. In one incident, millions of dollars, worth of cultivated oysters had to be destroyed after they turned green. Local newspapers traced the pollution upstream to scrap cable and wire processing factories that did not have wastewater treating equipment.

Figure 18.14 Aquaculture – the lethal loop.

Redressing the balance

1 a) Identify from Figures 18.12-18.14 the environmental problems facing agriculture in Taiwan.

  b) What do you feel is the cause of each problem?

2 a) What are your own reactions to the agricultural situation in Taiwan?

  b) Are your reactions or concerns social, economic or environmental?

3 What could be done to address environmental problems in farming in Taiwan by:
  • farmers
  • wholesalers and shopkeepers
  • consumers
  • exporters
  • local and national government
  • people outside Taiwan?

Summary

You have learned that:
  • There has been a shift of economic growth into East Asia, where political and cultural climates have promoted it.
  • Economic expansion has in some cases been at the expense of human rights and environmental costs.
  • Economic change may bring with it cultural change which can be irreversible.
  • Even though 'global forces' and the 'free market' are fundamental to economic change, the importance of government policies can be paramount.

References and further reading

Rapid economic development in the Far East is explored in:

W Bello and S Rosenfeld, *Dragons in Distress*, Food First (1990)

R Hodder, *The West Pacific Rim*, Belhaven Press (1992) 'Easy reading' on economic activity, global economics, Taiwan and Ghana is to be found in publications from the Development Education Centre, Birmingham:

Beyond the backyard (1993)
The global money machine (1994)
Can you be different? (1994)

Web sites

The CIA Factbook web page has data on every country in the world:
http://www.odci.gov/cia/publications/factbook/geos/tw.html

The global economy – transnational corporations

This chapter looks at globalisation of the economy and how transnational corporations (TNCs) operate. It explains why there has been a global shift in the location of production and how the global organisation of production affects employment in countries at different stages of development. The role of TNCs is explored, together with the benefits and problems that they may create in different parts of the world.

Global control – the emergence and growth of TNCs

Increasingly, huge wealth and giant TNCs are in the hands of a very few nations and institutions – and therefore a very few people. TNCs have not suddenly appeared, but have developed steadily with the market economy. The largest of these companies now match or exceed the size and scale of some nations in wealth, power and trading. Figure 19.1 shows sales of the world's largest companies in 1997 compared to annual GDP of selected countries. The TNCs are generally located in the richer North and in the NICs of South-East Asia (Figure 19.2).

Country or corporation	GDP or total sales
General Motors	164
Thailand	154
Norway	153
Ford Motor	147
Mitsui & Co.	145
Saudi Arabia	140
Mitsubishi	140
Poland	136
Itochu	136
South Africa	129
Royal Dutch/Shell Group	128
Marubeni	124
Greece	123
Sumitomo	119
Exxon	117
Toyota Motor	109
Wal Mart Stores	105
Malaysia	98
Israel	98
Colombia	96
Venezuela	87
Philippines	82

Figure 19.1 The world's most valuable corporations in 1997, based upon total sales compared to the total GDP of selected countries (in US$ billions).

Figure 19.2 The global distribution of TNCs.
This shows the number of TNCs with a market value of over $3 billion in the mid-1990s.

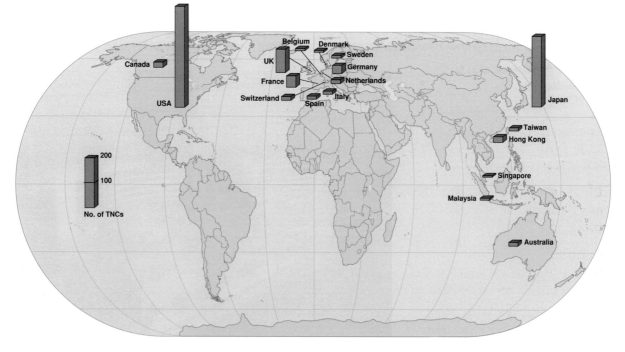

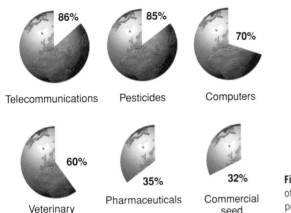

Bank	Since 1992, has taken over or merged with:
Lloyds	Cheltenham and Gloucester, TSB
Barclays	Woolwich
Bank of Scotland	NatWest
National Australia Bank	Yorkshire Bank, Clydesdale Bank
HSBC	Midland Bank
Royal Bank of Scotland	Abbey National

Figure 19.4 Consolidation in the UK banking industry, 1994–2000.

Telecommunications 86% Pesticides 85% Computers 70%

Veterinary medicine 60% Pharmaceuticals 35% Commercial seed 32%

Figure 19.3 Market share of TNCs in selected products in 1997.

Company data change from year to year, and in the last years of the twentieth century mergers created new corporate giants at the rate of about one every two weeks. Broadly, TNCs have grown in two ways:

1 By **natural growth**, generated by the effective creation of products which sell well, and which feed further investment by the company. For instance, the development of production lines in the Industrial Revolution replaced individual craft skills but made products cheaper. In turn, companies invested profit into research and development of new products.

2 By merger with and acquisition of other companies. These take place in two ways:
  • By **consolidation**, i.e. the acquisition and merger of companies which deal in similar businesses. In 2000, drug companies Glaxo and SmithKlein Beecham merged to form GlaxoSmithKlein (whose new headquarters in

west London is shown in Figure 19.5), and Barclays Bank took over the former Woolwich Bank. The aim of such mergers is to increase corporate share of the market. Figure 19.4 shows mergers in the banking industry in the UK. As changes in ownership occur frequently, these should be watched carefully.
  • By the **acquisition** of companies which deal in different product lines. These enlarged companies are known as 'conglomerates' and are often controlled by corporate investment houses or companies which see strength in diversifying their range of products. Often, the controlling company is an investment house whose name is unlikely to be recognised in the street and which has little expertise in the product. An example is Itochu (Figure 19.6), one of the large corporations shown in Figure 19.1. Profit levels are similarly astounding: for the

Figure 19.5 The new headquarters in west London of GlaxoSmithKlein.

1 How does Itochu describe itself?

Itochu describes itself as 'a global trader, financier and investor with consolidated revenues last year in excess of $130 billion'.

2 What are its product ranges?

Its products currently include goods in textile & apparel, finance & logistics, food & general merchandise, metals, machinery, aerospace & electronics, and chemicals & plastics.

3 What brand names would I have heard of?

Its more common trading names include:
- Compaq computers
- Fashion names – Dunhill, Emporio Armani, Vivienne Westwood, John Rocha.

4 What does it do in Europe?

Its European operations include:
- wholesale distribution of tyres, paper, building materials and foodstuffs from non-European sources, such as coffee, sugar, cocoa, sugar, nuts and seeds
- handling and supplying iron ore, coal and precious metals and the manufacture and processing of steel products, including pipes to the oil and gas industry
- manufacturing flat and long steel products, mobile phones, aero-engine spare parts and office automation equipment
- trading in aluminium, copper, zinc and other metals.

Figure 19.6 Have you ever heard of … Itochu?

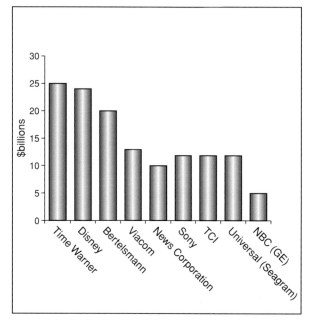

Figure 19.7 Media giants – total sales (US$ billion).

three-month period to November 2000 Shell returned profits of £2 billion! British Telecom shares collapsed when it was learned that profits for a three-month period in 2000 had fallen to £1 billion from £1.7 billion in the same period in 1999. It is easy to become engrossed in the figures; they are huge and almost meaningless. It is sometimes more relevant to see how mergers and acquisitions affected people's lifestyles – the music they listen to, the food they eat, the newspapers they read. Figure 19.7 shows how mergers in the media industry have affected what we see on television, hear in music, watch in films or read in newspapers. Television ownership doubled worldwide between 1980 and 1995 and at the same time programming was becoming concentrated in the hands of fewer people.

1 Select one of the following large TNCs. In many cases you may not have heard the names, but will certainly know some of the products:
   News International, Vivendi, Diageo, Seagram, Sony, Axa, General Electric, AT and T, Dupont, Exxon, Philip Morris, Unilever, General Motors, or another of your choosing.
   a) Using an internet search engine, find the company home page.
   b) In pairs, carry out an enquiry with questions similar to those for Itochu, i.e.
      - How does the company describe itself?
      - What are its product ranges?
      - What brand names would I have heard of?
      - What does it do in Europe?

2 What links does the company have with LEDCs? How clearly are these stated? How are these portrayed?

3 What are the implications of this company for you and/or your family and friends, and your lifestyle?

4 Study Figure 19.7.
   a) What are the issues involved in having fewer and larger companies in control of the media?
   b) Are these issues largely beneficial or detrimental for people?

Barbie goes global!

In 1945, two men operating out of a converted garage in California formed Mattel, a company producing children's toys. By 1960, the company had a sales turnover of almost US $100 million. By the process of growth and acquisition of other companies, Mattel underwent huge expansion during the last years of the twentieth century. Its products are known throughout the world, so that it is truly a global company. However, it also operates globally, seeking new locations for the manufacture of its products.

Mattel – the house that Barbie built

Mattel is the house that Barbie built. It is the world's number one manufacturer of toys, and its headquarters is based in El Segundo, California. In addition to the world's best-selling toy, the Barbie doll, Mattel produces Fisher-Price toys, Hot Wheels cars, and action figures and toys based on Disney characters and the Harry Potter children's books. It operates across the world, making products in some countries and selling them in over 150 countries worldwide. Toys"Я"Us and Wal-Mart account for about 33 per cent of sales, but the company hopes to reach customers in new and more direct ways, especially through catalogue and online sales.

The company concept of Barbie

The whole concept of Barbie is based upon the American dream. For children, her glamorous lifestyle and image, together with accessories such as The Barbie Dream House, have reflected the dream of suburban consumerism in the USA. The range of products is huge (Figure 19.8). Since the early days of a small company in 1945, its sales had leapt to US $4.67 billion worldwide by 2000 (Figure 19.9). It has carved out a niche market in children's toys, the largest part of its market being focused upon two main customers – girls, and infant and pre-school children (Figure 19.10).

Like many TNCs with global sales in so many countries, the largest of Mattel's markets is nonetheless the USA (Figure 19.11). Here, competition for leadership in the toy market is intense, but the financial reward for the company that can maintain its position is huge. Its chief competitor, Hasbro Inc., has sales only 20 per cent less, though its other competitors lie well behind these two. How does Mattel maintain its position as the leading company?

The theory box, 'The global thirst for consumerism' on page 223, shows how large the children's toy market is. It also shows how the global market is confined to those countries which lie in the economically developed North. What do companies like Mattel mean for LEDCs in the South?

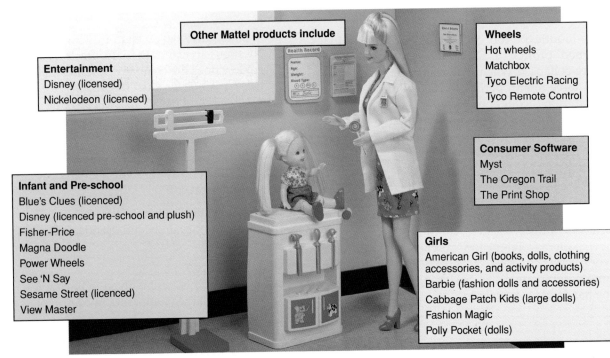

Entertainment
Disney (licensed)
Nickelodeon (licensed)

Other Mattel products include

Wheels
Hot wheels
Matchbox
Tyco Electric Racing
Tyco Remote Control

Consumer Software
Myst
The Oregon Trail
The Print Shop

Infant and Pre-school
Blue's Clues (licenced)
Disney (licenced pre-school and plush)
Fisher-Price
Magna Doodle
Power Wheels
See 'N Say
Sesame Street (licenced)
View Master

Girls
American Girl (books, dolls, clothing accessories, and activity products)
Barbie (fashion dolls and accessories)
Cabbage Patch Kids (large dolls)
Fashion Magic
Polly Pocket (dolls)

Figure 19.8 Barbie and selected brands from Mattel, Inc.

The global thirst for consumerism

The consumer economies of the USA and the EU have never been bigger. Up to 2000, the USA had enjoyed ten years of continuous economic growth, unparalleled in its history. Both in Western Europe and in the USA, incomes and share ownership increased several times. With annual global spending on goods and services approaching US $24 trillion, it has never been better to be a consumer – that is, if you belong to the minority of 'those who have'.

Among the biggest sectors of American consumerism is the economic boom in children's toys and electronic goods. The giant American corporations of Mattel, Disney, and Hasbro supply children's markets, while Japanese electronics companies such as Sega and Nintendo have established bases in the USA. Toy sales in 1998 in the USA amounted to US $27.2 billion, of which US $6.2 billion was spent on video games and US $21 billion on traditional toys. Most are imported: in 1998, imports totalled US $14.3 billion while exports were just over US $1 billion.

By 1999, Western Europeans and North Americans spent annually between them:

- US $12 billion on perfume – twice the amount needed to give everyone in the world basic education
- US $17 billion a year on pet food, while a quarter of the 4.5 billion inhabitants of developing countries lack adequate housing
- US $8 billion on cosmetics – the Broadway show *Cats* is said to have used more than 18 000 eyeliners in its first fifteen years.

Consumerism is said to feed global disparity and the development gap. Put into plain language:

- One-fifth of the world's richest people consume 85 per cent of all goods and services, whereas the one-fifth on the other side of the income spectrum consume 1 per cent
- One child in an industrial country consumes and pollutes the same amount as 30 children in LEDCs over a lifetime.

1994	1995	1996	1997	1998	1999
3.21	3.64	3.79	4.83	4.78	5.51

Figure 19.9 Recent sales at Mattel (figures in US$ billion).

	US$
• Girls	1,783,120
• Boys–entertainment	1,195,811
• Infant/pre-school	1,625,337
• Direct marketing	357,995
• Other	19,396
Adjustments	311,717*
Total	**4,669,942**

* Adjustments are usually costs that are one-offs borne by a company, for instance redundancy payments when it makes workers redundant.

Figure 19.10 How does Mattel make its money? Sales by category, 2000.

2000 sales	% of total
USA	71
Other countries	29

Figure 19.11 Geographical location of Mattel sales, 2000.

1 Using Figure 19.12, make a large copy of the following table and identify features that have helped Mattel to develop by growth in sales and products, and those that have led to growth by acquisition.

Date	Growth of the company through the development of products	Growth of the company through acquisitions of other companies

2 a) Identify and list from Figure 19.12 the problems that the company has faced.
   b) How would you explain these?
   c) In which decade have most of these occurred?

3 a) What patterns do you notice about Mattel's company acquisitions?
   b) How would you explain these?
   c) In which decade have most taken place? Why?

4 Which seems most beneficial for Mattel – growth by the development of new products or growth by acquisition of other companies? Why do you think this is?

5 a) Suggest reasons for and possible benefits which could result from selling children's clothing online and by catalogue.
   b) Why should so many companies seek to sell their goods in this way?
   c) What are the risks in selling in this way?
   d) How might selling online change the geography of how the company sells its goods?

The development of Mattel

Figure 19.12 shows how Mattel has grown since its origins in 1945. Its position as a global toy supplier is fairly recent but its role as a global player is not. Consider how the company has 'gone global' and why this is.

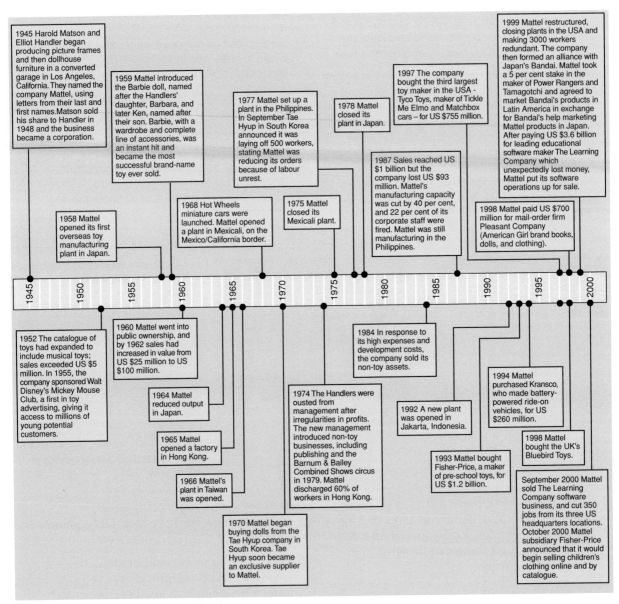

Figure 19.12 The history of Barbie and Mattel.

Barbie's global shift

In spite of global changes in the location of production, Mattel still retains a large number of subsidiaries and branches in the USA (Figure 19.13). Many of these are not manufacturing plants, but distribution depots and marketing and management functions. Typical of TNCs is the control structure with headquarters in one location and distribution and marketing in other, often cheaper, locations.

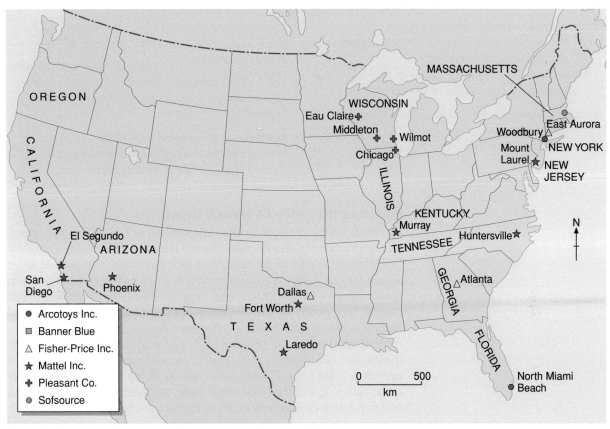

Figure 19.13 Location of Mattel subsidiaries and branches in the USA.

However, most manufacturing of Mattel products is now carried out outside the USA. In the 1950s, Mattel began to manufacture Barbie dolls in Japan. Mattel has factories in China, Indonesia, Italy, Malaysia, Mexico and Thailand. It also has suppliers in Germany. In 1996 Mattel opened a US $26 million model car toy factory in the Bangpoo Industrial Estate in Thailand's eastern seaboard which employs 1200 workers. A second phase will employ a further 2000 workers. The firm expected to generate export revenues of US $40 million from the new plant by the year 2000.

Location	GNP per capita in US$	% annual growth in GNP	% of children aged 10–14 who work	Comment
China	620	6.9	12	Known internationally for its disregard for human rights. Huge economic potential of 1.25 billion people and a rapidly developing economy.
Indonesia	980	4.7	10	Now politically unstable, losing a long-term president and involved in a civil war in the late 1990s.
Malaysia	3890	4.0	3	Slower economic growth after rapid growth of up to 10% in 1990s.
Mexico	3370	0.9	7	Joined NAFTA in the late 1990s, creating a tariff-free market with the USA.
Thailand	2740	5.2	9	The number of children working has dropped sharply in recent years – government laws are now phasing it out. Minimum wage is now approximately £80 per month.

Figure 19.14 Wage rates and economic characteristics of some countries in which Mattel manufactures its products, 1998.

1 On a world map, identify and label
  a) in one colour, countries in which Mattel manufactures its products
  b) in a second colour, locations of its subsidiary companies or branches.

2 Mattel describes itself as a 'global consumer products company'. How far would you agree with this statement?

3 Identify from Figure 19.14 why Mattel should want to manufacture its products in all the countries shown.

4 Why might the governments of these countries also be happy to welcome companies such as Mattel?

5 For the countries shown in Figure 19.14, what are the potential benefits of Mattel locating there. What are the potential problems?

Keeping the price of Barbie down

In recent years, changes in the company have led Mattel to rethink where production should take place. Like other TNCs, the company has undergone part of the process of globalisation – where companies search for the cheapest areas of production across the globe in order to maximise profits. The creation of large free trade areas within which people and goods can move easily without tariffs or penalties has helped to create giant trading areas (see Chapter 17, page 207).

NAFTA, formed in 1994, created a free trade area within which duties for qualifying goods would be eliminated by 2003 for its members – the USA, Canada and Mexico. It has had effects upon the USA, where goods have become more competitive. Companies can make quick decisions to relocate to countries where costs are cheaper.

Company	Year ended	Sales (US$ bn)	Sales growth 1999	Sales per employee in US$	Largest region of sales
Mattel	Dec 99	5.515	15.3%	177 902	USA (72.2%)
Hasbro Inc.	Dec 99	4.232	28.1%	445 501	USA (66.6%)
Sega Corp.	Mar 99	2.090	−22.3%	525 824	Japan (78.7%)
Alliance Gaming Corporation	June 99	0.458	9.8%	199 209	USA (76.5%)

Figure 19.15 Sales comparisons of Mattel and its chief competitors for the year ending 1999.

Figure 19.15 helps to explain the global search for the cheapest locations. Most of Mattel's sales are in the United States: in 1999, sales there were nearly US $4 billion, over 72 per cent of the total. The company currently employs 30 000 people. With sales of US $4.6 billion, this equates to sales of US $153 333 per employee. Compare this with sales per employee values for its competitors. The only way perceived by the company to cut its costs is to reduce its single biggest cost – labour.

US toy factories have cut a one-time American workforce of 56 000 in half and sent many of those jobs to LEDCs, often where wages are lower.

Independent Monitoring Council Completes Social and Human Rights Audit of Mattel's Mexican Plants

As part of a continuing commitment by Mattel to monitor its worldwide manufacturing facilities, the Mattel Independent Monitoring Council (MIMCO) today released results from its first audit of Mattel's two company-owned and operated manufacturing facilities in Mexico...

...In terms of working conditions, onsite medical facilities, worker training, wages, and overtime hours, the MIMCO audit results document that both Mexican facilities (Monterrey and Tijuana) are in overall compliance with both applicable county laws and Mattel's Global Manufacturing Principles (GMP), Mattel's self-imposed global manufacturing code of conduct. Overall, the two facilities provide a safe and pleasant working environment, and offer wages and benefits that exceed Mexican labor laws...

...Upcoming phases of the audits include Mattel owned or controlled facilities in China, India and France and key vendors around the world. In addition, MIMCO will be verifying that Mattel has complied with the issues addressed in the first report detailing facilities in Indonesia, China, Malaysia, and Thailand.

Mattel press release, 25 May 2000

Follow-up audit reports; Guan Yao, China

The MIMCO follow-up audit report for the Mattel facility in Guan Yao illustrates a considerable effort made by management to address the issues of concern expressed by MIMCO in its first audit report and take the necessary remedial actions to successfully meet MIMCO's recommendations. Guan Yao has substantially enhanced its payroll structure, maternity leave program, and maintenance of employee records. MIMCO found significant improvement in the employee living and working conditions with the building of new dormitories, canteen and on-site medical facility, as well as the installation of a new ventilation system.

Mattel press release, 7 May 2001

Figure 19.16 Press releases from Mattel's website, www.mattel.com.

Mattel Global Manufacturing Principles

Mattel now produce the bulk of their toys in China. The industry adopted a code of conduct which calls upon companies to monitor themselves. This places nothing upon companies other than a moral obligation. However, it is a move forward and compares very well with other companies whose image is occasionally tarnished.

While Mattel has an internal monitoring program, it was the first toy company to utilise external independent monitoring which publishes objective reports of Mattel facilities and sub-contractors on GMP progress.

Figure 19.17 Statement from Mattel's website regarding social and environmental responsibilities.

Mattel's Global Manufacturing Principles apply to all parties that manufacture, assemble or distribute any product or package bearing the Mattel logo. These cover:
- hiring, wages and working hours
- age requirements
- forced labor
- discrimination
- freedom of expression and association
- living conditions
- workplace safety
- health
- emergency planning
- environmental protection
- evaluation and monitoring

Mattel has initiated a three-stage auditing process - that is overseen by an independent monitoring council to thoroughly inspect facilities around the world.

No one under the age of 16 will be employed. If the local law requires a higher minimum age, will comply with the local law.

However, there are other responses by companies such as Mattel to pressure from organisations such as Greenpeace. The adoption by Mattel of certain principles, such as those shown in Figure 19.17, was announced in 1997.

GREENPEACE APPLAUDS MATTEL'S DECISION TO REPLACE PVC WITH PLANT-BASED PLASTICS IN TOYS

Greenpeace today applauded the decision by Mattel Inc. to remove PVC from its toys and switch to plant-based plastics. Mattel will start selling the new, environmentally friendly products as soon as 2001.

The move followed a year of discussions with Greenpeace. While petroleum-based alternatives to PVC materials in toys have been available for many years, Mattel has gone a step further by switching to non petroleum-based plastics. 'Children born today can now look forward to playing with PVC-free toys that are made of environmentally friendly, bio-based plastic,' said Axel Singhofen of Greenpeace.

Mattel's policy comes on the heels of the EU ban on six toxic softeners found in soft PVC toys marketed for teething. In the US, where Mattel is based, the federal Consumer Product Safety Commission has only asked for voluntary removal of phthalates in teething toys and rattles. The EU rejected a similar offer by Europe's toy industry and instead adopted a ban on these products. It has legally banned soft PVC teething toys but does not require outlets to withdraw these products from their shelves. Nor does its ban cover other toys that children could put in their mouths.

Vinyl is the only plastic connected to dioxin and the release of chemical softeners known as phthalates. Phthalates have been linked to damage to the kidneys, liver and testicles in animal experiments.

Mattel joins several other global companies that have decided to replace PVC in their products including LEGO, IKEA, Nike, The Body Shop, General Motors, Honda, and Baxter Healthcare.

Figure 19.18 From the Greenpeace web site, 8 December 1999.

1 Do you see Mattel's response to child labour concerns (Figure 19.17) or its decision to replace PVC in toys (Figure 19.18) as proactive (i.e. it introduced measures that it believed to be right), or reactive (i.e. it reacted to outside pressures)?

2 Which other cases do you know of where companies have responded similarly?

3 How far should companies be responsible for:
  a) moral concerns such as child labour
  b) environmental concerns such as the use of toxins?

4 Environmental and social concerns such as these are, it is often argued, burdens on companies such as Mattel, forcing them to increase prices.
  a) How would you persuade the board of Mattel that their decision is one that should not place a financial burden on the company?
  b) How would you convince other companies to follow suit?

Ironically, the US toy industry and other industries unrelated to bananas found themselves caught up in trade sanctions against Europe. Some American companies that import from the EU found that they had to pay duties on those products (Figure 19.19) in 1999 as part of the banana wars.

Since, in the end, toys were not included in the sanctions, Mattel never did pay duties on toys imported from the EU.

Banana sanctions bite again

US trade experts heard a number of concerns from US importers about plans to impose import duties on millions of dollars in goods from the European Union in a dispute over bananas. Experts from the US Office of Trade heard from importers of food, furs, luxury leather goods, toys and other items targeted for sanctions.

The President of Louis Vuitton told the panel that the proposed 100 per cent tariffs would hurt sales of their luxury handbags and other luxury goods and force layoffs at their 97 wholesale and retail outlets in the United States.

Mattel Inc. urged the panel to drop import tariffs on toys, saying two of their doll lines, Corolle and American Girl brands, are sourced almost exclusively from Europe. The proposed tariffs could result in the collapse of the entire line of American Girl dolls, a highly popular doll sold exclusively in the USA and five of the six dolls are made in Germany. 'For this line to bite the dust, it would have a very direct impact on those 850 US workers there,' Mattel's representative told the panel.

Chiquita told the panel that the USA and Latin American producers are losing US $2 billion in banana sales in Europe a year because of European import rules that favor Caribbean producers.

Figure 19.19 From Reuters, 9 December 1999.

Summary

You have learned that:

- The rise in the global economy is to a large degree the result of efforts by large TNCs.
- TNCs illustrate the global shift in the relocation of industry to cheaper wage economies.
- TNCs play a large role in our lives, from controlling food that is eaten to the news that we hear.
- TNCs play a major part in the global organisation of production and employment. In the main, they sell in MEDCs and produce in LEDCs.
- The impact of TNCs and the global economic shift has made itself felt in countries at different stages of development. In MEDCs, TNCs control much of what is consumed. In LEDCs, they control how people work and for what wages.
- The control exerted by trade organisations such as the WTO mirror the control managed by TNCs.

References and further reading

'Globalisation: peeling back the layers', *New Internationalist*, November 1997

'The big jeans stitch-up', *New Internationalist*, June 1998

'The Mousetrap: inside Disney's dream machine', *New Internationalist*, December 1998

United Nations Development Programme, *Human Development Report 2000*, Oxford University Press

20 The impact of changing employment patterns

This chapter looks at changes which are happening to employment in the West Midlands, one of the UK's eleven economic regions. The region has traditionally been part of the UK's major 'core' region of economic development, which spans the area from the North Midlands to the South-East of England.

In recent decades, Birmingham's economy has been affected by global changes, already described in this section. Employment in some sectors has fallen rapidly while in others it has increased. People's lives have been affected by changes, the causes of which are often a long way removed from where people live. People on the receiving end of changes in the global economy, such as those who become unemployed, often feel removed from the causes of change and unable to influence them. This chapter shows different ways in which changes can affect people for better and for worse.

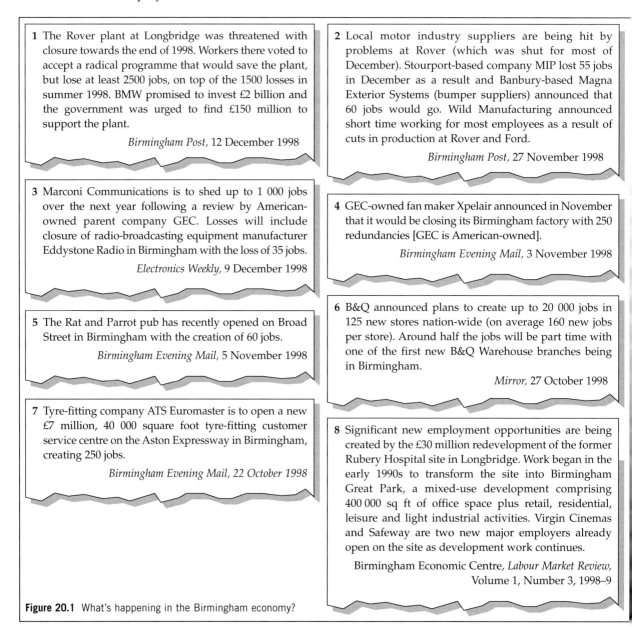

1 The Rover plant at Longbridge was threatened with closure towards the end of 1998. Workers there voted to accept a radical programme that would save the plant, but lose at least 2500 jobs, on top of the 1500 losses in summer 1998. BMW promised to invest £2 billion and the government was urged to find £150 million to support the plant.

Birmingham Post, 12 December 1998

2 Local motor industry suppliers are being hit by problems at Rover (which was shut for most of December). Stourport-based company MIP lost 55 jobs in December as a result and Banbury-based Magna Exterior Systems (bumper suppliers) announced that 60 jobs would go. Wild Manufacturing announced short time working for most employees as a result of cuts in production at Rover and Ford.

Birmingham Post, 27 November 1998

3 Marconi Communications is to shed up to 1 000 jobs over the next year following a review by American-owned parent company GEC. Losses will include closure of radio-broadcasting equipment manufacturer Eddystone Radio in Birmingham with the loss of 35 jobs.

Electronics Weekly, 9 December 1998

4 GEC-owned fan maker Xpelair announced in November that it would be closing its Birmingham factory with 250 redundancies [GEC is American-owned].

Birmingham Evening Mail, 3 November 1998

5 The Rat and Parrot pub has recently opened on Broad Street in Birmingham with the creation of 60 jobs.

Birmingham Evening Mail, 5 November 1998

6 B&Q announced plans to create up to 20 000 jobs in 125 new stores nation-wide (on average 160 new jobs per store). Around half the jobs will be part time with one of the first new B&Q Warehouse branches being in Birmingham.

Mirror, 27 October 1998

7 Tyre-fitting company ATS Euromaster is to open a new £7 million, 40 000 square foot tyre-fitting customer service centre on the Aston Expressway in Birmingham, creating 250 jobs.

Birmingham Evening Mail, 22 October 1998

8 Significant new employment opportunities are being created by the £30 million redevelopment of the former Rubery Hospital site in Longbridge. Work began in the early 1990s to transform the site into Birmingham Great Park, a mixed-use development comprising 400 000 sq ft of office space plus retail, residential, leisure and light industrial activities. Virgin Cinemas and Safeway are two new major employers already open on the site as development work continues.

Birmingham Economic Centre, *Labour Market Review*, Volume 1, Number 3, 1998–9

Figure 20.1 What's happening in the Birmingham economy?

Changing employment patterns

Consider the news items from newspapers and journals in 1998 (Figure 20.1). They show a changing economy in the West Midlands. This is part of a general structural change in economic activity that is taking place globally. In the traditional industrialised countries of Japan, Western Europe and North America (the world's MEDCs), several employment changes have taken place in recent years.

- There has been a decline in manufacturing and a rise in service employment. In these nations, fewer people are needed to produce all the goods that can be consumed or sold elsewhere. Goods can be also produced more cheaply in other countries. By 2000, 75 per cent of UK employment was in the service sector, and less than 18 per cent in manufacturing. Leisure industries are increasing while manufacturing is less significant. In contrast, other 'newer' industrial nations, like the 'tiger' economies of South-East Asia, are developing manufacturing industries. This has been described as a geographical model (see theory box below).
- More people are in employment now than before. The majority of households have more than one wage earner, and more people are working part-time. More women are in paid work now than at any time, excluding wartime.

Changing employment patterns in the West Midlands

In the UK, employment change has been more marked in some regions than others (Figure 20.3). Traditional manufacturing areas like the West Midlands (Figure 20.5) have experienced dramatic falls in employment and production (Figure 20.4). By 2000, 51 per cent of working men and 81 per cent of women in this region were employed in service industries. In some sectors growth has been rapid. In a sample of over 13 000 Birmingham companies in 2000, 'fast employment growth companies' accounted for 49 242 new jobs out of a total of 53 707. While they represented only 9 per cent of all companies, they created 92 per cent of all new jobs between 1995 and 1998.

---

1 What is meant by 'fast employment growth companies'? Give examples and say why this term is used. Why should such companies generate so much employment?

2 What are the benefits and problems generated by 'fast employment growth companies' compared to more traditional employers?

Theory

Employment change over time – the Clarke sector model

Economic change and development is followed by a change in employment structure. As one economic activity grows, profit and investment from that is directed to other successful and related activities. Hence it is possible to see a change from agricultural economies to industrial economies, and later the emergence of service economies. One economic sector tends to dominate investment and employment at different stages. The general change from one sector to another is shown in Figure 20.2.

Like most geographical models, it is helpful in simplifying reality. However, it is rather unsatisfactory because it runs a risk that people might think that all countries have to develop in this way. It should not be read as assuming that this *must* happen, only that it *has* happened in most western industrialised economies. It can be illustrated using employment data from the West Midlands (Figures 20.3 and 20.4).

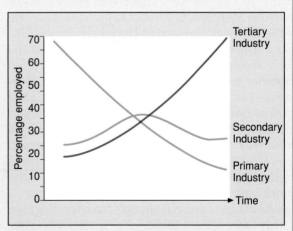

Figure 20.2 Clarke's sector model of employment over time.

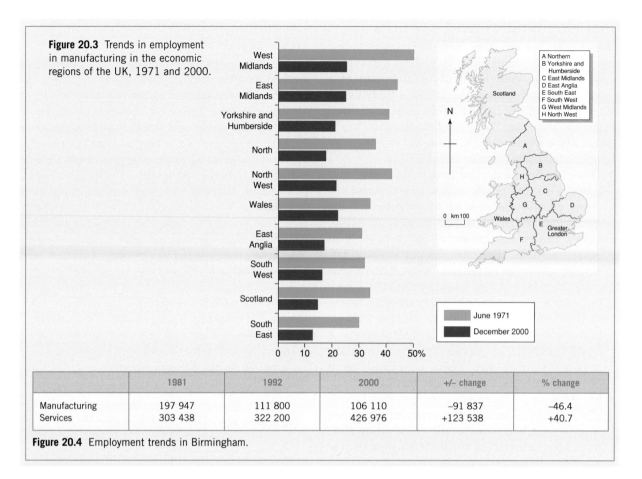

Figure 20.3 Trends in employment in manufacturing in the economic regions of the UK, 1971 and 2000.

	1981	1992	2000	+/– change	% change
Manufacturing	197 947	111 800	106 110	–91 837	–46.4
Services	303 438	322 200	426 976	+123 538	+40.7

Figure 20.4 Employment trends in Birmingham.

The geographical location of the West Midlands

Figure 20.3 shows the location and boundaries of the West Midlands Economic Region. At its centre is Birmingham, the second largest city in the UK, and a major economic unit. It has been one of the UK's major industrial regions for nearly three centuries first with coal and metal-working, then engineering. As one industry has developed, it has spawned others related to it and depending upon it. This is known as an 'agglomeration' or 'multiplier effect'. Part of the reason for its growth is its accessibility due to its location in the centre of England and Wales. Figure 20.5 shows how motorway and rail networks, as well as a significant international airport, make Birmingham a very accessible 'second city' in the UK after London. This has helped to make the West Midlands part of the UK's 'core' economic region. The idea of 'core' and 'periphery' regions is explained in the theory box on page 234.

Employment change still brings a large number of commuters into the city. Figure 20.6 shows the leisure industry emerging within the CBD of Birmingham. The total number of jobs within the city has risen from 466 000 in 1991 to over 530 000 in 2000. The regenerated CBD and 'global city' has provided jobs and opportunities for professional and financial services, as well as some in tourism. These jobs bring in people from across the West Midlands and beyond. The 1991 census showed how the proportion of jobs taken in Birmingham by people living outside the city boundary had increased to 35 per cent, doubling in 30 years.

The flight from urban centres

However, the concentration of economic activity within Birmingham is changing. Costs of labour, land, buildings, plant, borrowing, marketing and sales, and management are now high. Many industries now deal with very light materials or high value, low-weight consumer goods that need to be distributed quickly; their employees may be salespeople or IT consultants travelling to customer sites. 'Time' is now more significant, making sites accessible to motorway access more favoured. City centre locations may be close to people, but traffic congestion into the CBD reduces speed of travel.

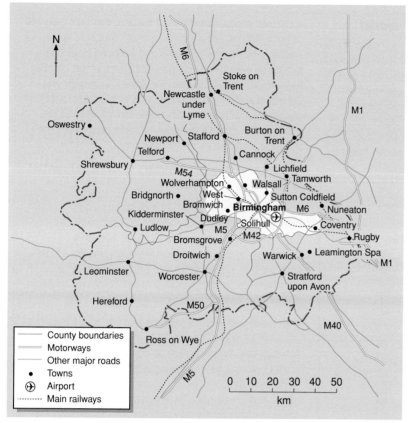

Figure 20.5 The West Midlands region and transport links.

As a result, the city of Birmingham itself has tended to lose more companies than it gains through company relocations. The infrastructure of Birmingham in the past has led to a concentration of transport and service links within the central urban zone of the West Midlands. But between 1988 and 1998, the city of Birmingham had the highest net outflow of relocating companies of all local authorities in the West Midlands. Overall, 37.5 per cent of Birmingham businesses that changed location between 1988 and 1998 chose to move away from (as opposed to within) the city. Relocation away from the city resulted in a net loss of 7.3 per cent of the total number of

Figure 20.6 Recent developments in service industries – development and leisure facilities to the west of Birmingham CBD.

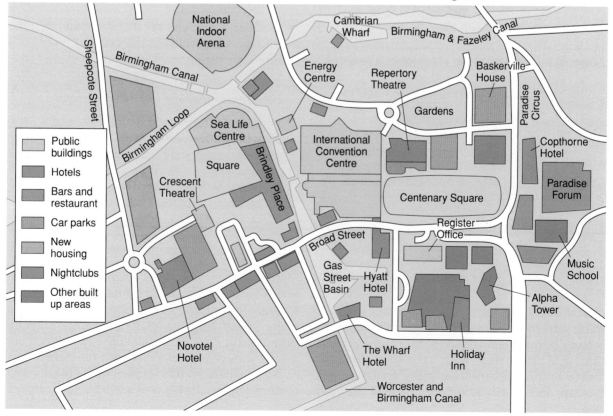

Friedmann's core and periphery model

Friedmann's concept of core and periphery (Figure 20.7) is useful in geography because it helps to show how some areas become more economically developed than others, and why some people and some regions are wealthier than others. Friedmann perceived economic growth as having a pre-industrial phase (Stage 1 in Figure 20.7), a transitional phase with limited investment (Stage 2), an industrial phase (Stage 3) in which sub-centres begin to develop, and a post-industrial phase (Stage 4).

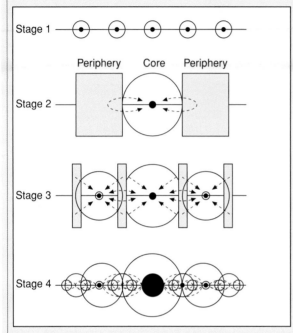

Figure 20.7 The concept of core and periphery in geography.

To understand the model, imagine a wealthy region – South-East England is usually taken as the 'core' region of the UK. Here, employment develops using high technology, offers higher pay than elsewhere and promotes high capital investment. The region's wealth attracts high densities of service industries designed to provide for the population, and demand means that house prices are higher there than elsewhere.

Now consider the opposite. Regions on the 'periphery' attract employment using lower technology, with lower pay

and lower capital investment. However, there are benefits, as such regions are often cheaper for people to live in. Traditionally, Northern Ireland and Scotland have been quoted as examples of peripheral regions of the UK. But this should not detract from the economic growth that does occur. Figure 20.7 shows how one set of processes cannot exist without the other. The formation of capital and wealth – core processes – is made possible by the labour and resources in the periphery.

Why are economic core/periphery concepts so important to geography?

These concepts present different patterns over space. It is usually easy to recognise core and peripheral regions using simple economic data. Economic processes tend to be separated geographically. Usually, core processes concentrate in affluent areas while peripheral processes produce areas which are relatively poorer with higher unemployment.

Within the world, different core and periphery patterns occur at all scales. Global core regions such as North America and Western Europe contain many smaller-scale core regions, for example southern California or Berkshire. Similarly, global cores may contain small peripheral areas, such as Western Ireland or Labrador. Again, global peripheral areas such as Latin America and Africa contain smaller core regions like São Paulo or Accra.

1 How far would you say that the West Midlands is part of the UK's core economic region?

2 Within the West Midlands, identify peripheral areas and justify your choice.

3 How could the West Midlands core and periphery alter over time if
   a) traffic congestion in the central urban area is not resolved
   b) new grants are offered to attract investors to places such as Tamworth or Telford?

businesses, 6.2 per cent of jobs, and 5.8 per cent of turnover.

Traffic congestion and high office rental costs are starting to affect the region. Although nineteenth-century Birmingham was at the hub of the English canal and rail system, both have since declined. Canals and canal banks are being revitalised for tourism, and the city is still the centre of the busy

Midlands rail network as well as an important Inter-City node. However, the rail network reflects nineteenth-century technology and requires a major overhaul, especially in track layout; Birmingham New Street station is renowned for delays, as several lines focus upon the station.

Again, although Birmingham in the twenty-first century (Figure 20.6) is well served by motorways, congestion has become rife. With its urban motorways – the M5, M6, and A38 (M) – Birmingham was dubbed 'motorway city' in the 1970s. Since then, orbital motorways have added to the network. These include the M42 (access to the South and East), the M6/M1 (to the North and London), the M40 (to the South-East and London) and the M5 (to the South-West). Construction has recently begun on a further northern link toll motorway to take traffic away from the congested M6. But the motorways largely reflect traffic levels in the mid-twentieth rather than the twenty-first century, and the M5-M6 junction passing through the centre of the conurbation is almost always congested at peak times for several kilometres (Figure 20.8a). For both office-based businesses and manufacturers, the city has become congested and expensive. The NEC (Figure 20.8b) is typical of the way in which economic activity has refocused upon the urban edge, where accessibility is improved.

Growth on the urban fringes

Other areas of the West Midlands have grown rapidly in recent years. Manufacturers are moving away from centres such as Birmingham and Wolverhampton, leaving behind a core of specialist retail, property, legal and financial functions. Manufacturing and distribution are more likely to be located on urban peripheries, together with retail parks, supermarkets and servicing companies. The main determinant of investment in warehousing is proximity to the motorway networks. Concentration of warehousing and distribution in areas close to the M6, the M42 and M69 has contributed to relatively high levels of investment in Staffordshire as well as Tamworth and Coventry. Equally, some development has been concentrated along the A38 in East Staffordshire, along the M40 in Warwickshire and the M5 corridor in Wychavon and Worcestershire.

New growth points such as Telford (Figure 20.9) and Tamworth have drawn companies away from the traditional industrial areas of Birmingham, Wolverhampton, Walsall and Wednesbury. This has been the result of 'inward investment' in the UK or from overseas. A system of benefits has been established to promote inward investment, especially from overseas companies. Companies have been drawn to Telford because of government grants available to them, such as tax-holidays and rent or building grants, but also because of the accessibility of the new town and quality of life that

Figure 20.8a Congestion at the intersection of the M5 and M6 motorways has led to the relocation of many companies away from the West Midlands conurbation.

Figure 20.8b Outer-city development – the NEC. On the south-eastern edge of the city, the centre attracts 4 million people each year, and supports 12 000 full-time jobs. Its accessibility next to the motorway and close to the International Airport has been a major factor in its success.

it offers. The A38 corridor towards Tamworth and Burton-on-Trent has developed with the opening of Toyota's car assembly plant at Burnaston.

Figure 20.9 New industrial sites in Telford.

Figure 20.10 The Rover–BMW Longbridge Works. This is still a major car producer in spite of plans to close the works in 2000.

1 On a map of the UK, mark the location of Birmingham and UK motorways. Using an atlas, show how far you could travel along motorways in one, two and three hours, assuming an average speed of 90km/h. This will produce a 'time–distance' map, and give some indication of what geographers call the 'centrality' of the West Midlands.

2 Which other regions or cities in the UK would have similar good access? Which would have poor access?

3 Make a sketch copy of Figure 20.5 showing transport links within the West Midlands. Annotate it with:
   a) reasons for economic relocation of companies in Birmingham
   b) growth points along the motorways of Staffordshire, Warwickshire and Worcestershire.

4 Why should Telford and Tamworth be such significant growth points in the West Midlands for inward investment?

The fate of the car industry

Much of Birmingham's engineering industry is related to the motor industry. Not only are car sales a barometer of affluence and thus strongly hit by recessions, but car manufacture is also one of the most 'globalised' economic activities. Japanese and American sales and investment in the UK are a clear indication of this globalisation. Birmingham's car industry has survived with the Longbridge Works (Figure 20.10) going through several ownership changes – first Austin, then a nationalised BMC, then British Leyland, Rover, BMW, and most recently a local buy-out. Overseas ownership has proved difficult and BMW, Longbridge's previous owners, planned to close the plant in early 2000. A local rescue plan was accepted, and although unemployment has risen as the plant has cut back its labour force, it is possible that it could survive in the medium term. Its partner Land Rover plant in Solihull was sold to American-owned Ford by BMW in 2000. Ford had already taken over the Jaguar plant in east Birmingham.

Why have such changes taken place? That Rover has survived at all is surprising in view of the current global trends towards larger and more diversified companies (Figure 20.12). Small units of production are largely unviable for companies now, including highly specialist companies with top brand names. Even Rolls Royce and Bentley are now linked with or owned by large TNCs which can support research and development on the one hand, or gain advantage of cost benefits on the other. Ford purchased Land Rover for its name and for a slice of the quality market in which there have been increasing sales.

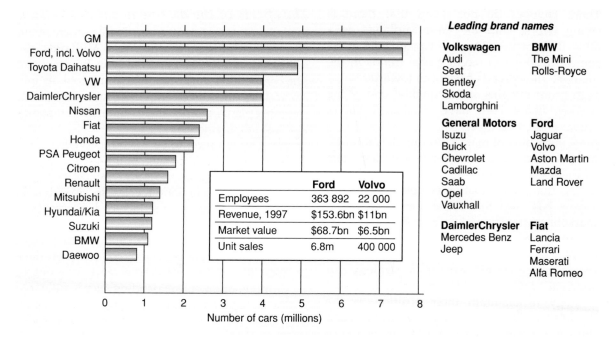

Leading brand names

Volkswagen	BMW
Audi	The Mini
Seat	Rolls-Royce
Bentley	
Skoda	
Lamborghini	

General Motors	Ford
Isuzu	Jaguar
Buick	Volvo
Chevrolet	Aston Martin
Cadillac	Mazda
Saab	Land Rover
Opel	
Vauxhall	

DaimlerChrysler	Fiat
Mercedes Benz	Lancia
Jeep	Ferrari
	Maserati
	Alfa Romeo

	Ford	Volvo
Employees	363 892	22 000
Revenue, 1997	$153.6bn	$11bn
Market value	$68.7bn	$6.5bn
Unit sales	6.8m	400 000

Figure 20.11 The world's top fifteen car manufacturers in 1998.
The graph and inset table show turnover and sales of the world's top car manufacturers. Rover is probably too small to be economic in the current global market unless it can produce specialist products.

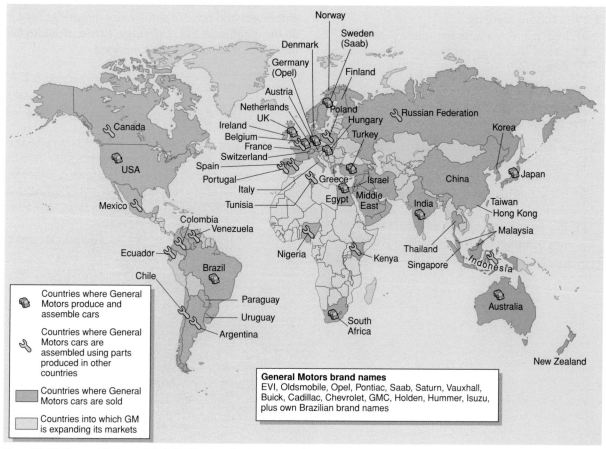

Figure 20.12 General Motors, global distribution of sales, production and assembly of vehicles.

These changes do not mean that there is anything wrong with the West Midlands as a location. It is a matter of how well companies in the region can respond to recent global trends in the car market. These trends have been towards:

- high profit margins at the 'quality' end of the market; hence Ford have purchased Volvo, Jaguar and Land Rover
- mass marketing of mainstream models through new, mechanised and more efficient plant such as Toyota's plant at Burniston
- a view that the car market is a global market – Toyota has used the UK as part of a global marketing strategy and as a foothold into the EU; their models are the same irrespective of the country they sell in
- enlarging company size as a strategy for survival – General Motors have a global strategy to maintain their position as the world's largest manufacturer (Figure 20.12) and the UK is simply a part of a larger picture in which sales, manufacturing and assembly are managed holistically from the USA.

1 Why should there be:
   a) high profit margins for 'quality' cars
   b) a view that large companies are more able to survive?

2 What are the benefits for consumers and producers of having global car models such as the Toyota Corolla? What are the problems?

3 Give examples of other industries in which:
   a) smaller companies are merged with or swallowed by larger ones
   b) mass production is seen as the way for survival
   c) the same products are available almost anywhere in the industrialised world.

The effects of the decline in car production

In spite of investment from Toyota, there were employment losses in the West Midlands car industry in the 1990s, particularly in Birmingham. The competition in car manufacturing took its toll. As well as the direct employment losses in car assembly plants, supply and component companies also lost employment.

- Fort Dunlop used to be a production centre for tyres; now its imposing building is used for cultural activities.
- BSA once made motorcycles in Sparkbrook; now the site of its large factory is a greenfield recreation area.
- Lucas, which for years manufactured car batteries and electrical car components, have been forced to 'restructure' and pull out of Birmingham, while expanding successfully into the aerospace industries.

As a result, unemployment is high in many traditional manufacturing areas, especially in Birmingham (Figure 20.13). Districts of Birmingham such as Longbridge have relatively few other employers and none of similar size (Figure 20.14). Of all the employers in Longbridge, Rover provides far more jobs than all the rest combined.

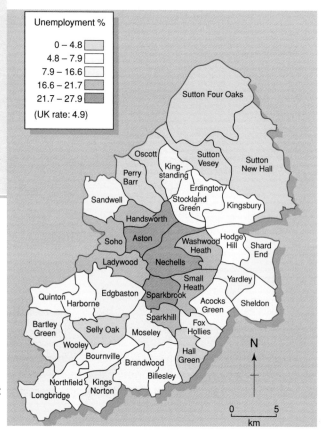

Figure 20.13 Unemployment in Birmingham in 2000.

	Male		Female		All
Industry	F/T	P/T	F/T	P/T	
Agriculture, fishing, energy & water	0	0	0	0	0
Manufacturing & construction	13 900	0	1 100	0	15 100
Distribution/hotels/restaurants & transport & communications	300	100	200	400	1 000
Banking, finance & insurance etc.	100	0	0	0	100
Public administration	300	100	800	800	1 900
Other services	300	100	300	300	1 000
Totals	**14 800**	**300**	**2 400**	**1 600**	**19 100**

Figure 20.14 Numbers of jobs in Longbridge in 2000(F/T – full time; P/T – part-time).

	Male		Female		Total	
	No.	%	No.	%	No.	%
Birmingham	27 203	11.8	7 833	4.5	35 047	8.7
West Midlands Region	81 700	5.7	24 900	2.2	106 600	4.1
UK	802 500	5.0	244 800	1.9	1 047 300	3.6

Figure 20.15 Seasonally adjusted unemployment in Birmingham, the West Midlands Region and the UK, October 2000.

1 Describe the pattern of unemployment in Birmingham (Figure 20.13). How is this a) similar to, or b) different from patterns of unemployment in other cities that you know of?

2 Describe the pattern of employment in Longbridge (Figure 20.14). How is this a) similar to, or b) different from patterns of employment in other cities that you know of?

3 How serious is the dependency in Longbridge (Figure 20.14) upon employment in one major industry? How could the geography of unemployment in Birmingham be altered if the Rover plant in Longbridge were to close?

4 Study Figure 20.15. Why should:
 a) more men than women be registered unemployed in the West Midlands
 b) a higher percentage of people be unemployed in Birmingham than in the West Midlands as a whole
 c) unemployment in the West Midlands be higher than in the UK as a whole?

What has caused employment change in Birmingham and the West Midlands?

- **Kondratiev waves:** Each successive major innovation leads to a surge in production and increase in global GDP – or a Kondratiev wave. Electricity brought a rapid increase in production, while microelectronics and robotics have brought the most recent wave. Each wave favours geographical areas that are early in exploiting it.
- **The growth of consumer and service markets:** This has followed the increase in GDP. As wealth increases, so demand for goods and services increases from retail to education, tourism and health care. These take over as companies produce consumer goods in countries where costs may be cheaper.
- **Spatial separation**, made possible by technological developments in production, distribution and communication: Manufacturing, marketing, research and management for a product can each take place in different locations. British Airways now has its accounting division in Delhi, where it pays workers 10 per cent of what it would pay workers in London. Agglomeration and the multiplier effect therefore apply far less now than they did.
- **Globalisation:** This is the process of concentrating ownership and power in the hands of a few nations and TNCs. Decisions are more likely to be made now by companies with few links to the West Midlands, and which pursue a global rather than local policy.
- **Waves of recession and recovery** that make sustained growth difficult to achieve: 'Slumps and booms' affect all market economies, though recessions hit different countries at different times.
- **Mechanisation and computerisation:** These have reduced the labour needed in manufacturing, and now in services as well, leading to 'increased productivity'.

- Girls outperform boys in both primary and secondary schools.
- On average, attainment of Pakistani and Bangladeshi is lower than that of Indian or white pupils. Of concern are African-Caribbean and Pakistani boys, who perform poorly in terms of higher-grade GCSE passes.
- People in work are better qualified than those who are unemployed.
- Some 24 per cent of people have no qualification equivalent to an NVQ at any level. Worryingly, 19 per cent of those in paid employment are unqualified.
- Training and learning opportunities favour the already well trained and qualified.
- In 1998, Birmingham was ranked fifth out of 366 local authority areas in England on an 'Index of Local Conditions', combining thirteen indicators of socio-economic deprivation. It has ten of the 30 most deprived wards in the country.
- Many ethnic minority groups in Birmingham experience deprivation as result of a combination of factors, including discrimination, low qualifications and skills, and low participation in training and education, which leads to high unemployment rates.
- Disabled people were three-and-a-half times more likely than non-disabled people, and non-white people three times more likely than white people, to consider discrimination as a barrier to employment.
- Against popular expectations, men were two-and-a-half times more likely than women to find discrimination as a barrier to getting a job.

Figure 20.16 Findings of the 1998 Household Survey on skill and employment in Birmingham.

What impact has employment change had on the West Midlands?

In Birmingham, as elsewhere, change in employment patterns is one of the most obvious results of change in economic activity. The loss of manufacturing employment has been continuous since the 1960s. Poverty is concentrated in the inner city (Figure 20.13), where reliance on welfare benefits is high and the urban and housing quality is poor. Urban regeneration projects are making improvements, but lack of employment opportunity is still the crux of the problem. The findings of the 1998 Household Survey on skill and employment in Birmingham found a concentration of problems in inner Birmingham, which did not match opportunities outside (Figure 20.16). What is emerging is an urban region of 'haves' and 'have-nots'.

1 Summarise the key issues in Figure 20.16. How serious are these issues to people **a)** locally in Birmingham, **b)** in the West Midlands, and **c)** elsewhere in the UK?

2 The UK government has recently introduced funding for 'Education Action Zones' (EAZ) designed to raise levels of educational attainment in inner city areas. How far should Birmingham qualify for this, in your view?

3 In groups of two or three, identify targets that you feel would help to solve the following problems in inner Birmingham. Present your targets to the group with a justification for each one.

- Boys attain lower GCSE grades than girls.
- Low attainment among African-Caribbean, Pakistani and Bangladeshi pupils in general and boys in particular.
- Unemployed people are less well qualified than those who are employed.
- One further problem in Figure 20.16 of your choice.

4 What do you see as the problems ahead if these issues are not addressed?

Summary

You have learned that:

- There has been a shift in economic activity within the West Midlands region, which reflects the general global shift from manufacturing to service employment.
- Although the West Midlands remains a successful manufacturing region, employment in service industries is outgrowing that in manufacturing, and there is a tendency to shift to outer city locations.
- The infrastructure of the West Midlands, especially its transport links, reflects earlier needs rather than those of the twenty-first century. As a result of urban congestion, many industries are seeking outer-region or greenfield sites.
- Many traditional industrial areas in the UK have been adversely affected by global changes that have seen mergers among companies, relocations to other parts of the world and changes in company ownership.
- The effect of change has been to provide benefits for a more affluent group while bringing poverty and poor life chances to others.

References and further reading

Graham Butt et al., *Birmingham: decisions on development*, Development Education Centre, Gillett Centre, 998 Bristol Road, Birmingham B29 6LE (1998)

For economic information on the West Midlands and other economic regions of the UK, try HMSO (published annually) *Regional Trends*, available from most libraries

Web sites

Useful web pages for up-to-date information on the West Midlands include

The Birmingham Economic Information Centre: www.birminghameconomy.org.uk

For information on car companies, visit the company web pages; General Motors has information on all its global activities on www.gm.com/company/corp_info

What will the global economy look like in future?

China – the next tiger?

China – with one-fifth of the world's people – has for years been sheltered from the western economy by a totalitarian government whose politics have encouraged a communist style of centralised development. Largely removed from western influence, using import controls upon goods, restricting the movement of people and with little attention to international currency markets, China has developed in ways that have been geared towards providing for its own people.

The Chinese government has now adopted a policy of greater contact with the West, of opening up to western companies and of trade agreements. The process of transfer to a more western-style economy is likely to be finalised in 2001 when China becomes a member of the WTO (see Chapter 17). This means that it will have to remove trade tariffs and barriers that have protected its economy for over 50 years. Its companies will be able to invest overseas, and western companies – particularly TNCs – will be keen to invest in China. China's fast economic growth rate of 8.2 per cent in the first nine months of 2000 and a population of 1.2 billion provides a market that few MEDC companies can resist.

Names familiar to westerners – Starbuck's coffee, McDonald's, Shell petrol – are found now in Chinese commercial life. Shanghai (Figure 21.1) has a more commercial appearance, with advertisements on the streets (Figure 21.2). Traffic-jammed streets sprawl around new buildings that spring up, covered in bamboo scaffolding. Shiny new glass-and-concrete office blocks and factories stand close to small, grimy workshops offering everything from car parts to paint. The city and its surrounding area have a population of 7 million, and a GDP growing at 12 per cent a year. How will China cope with change? What will the impact be on western companies? Who benefits? Some of the effects are described in Figure 21.3.

Figure 21.1 Shanghai – no longer the appearance of a Far Eastern city as new office blocks appear.

Figure 21.2 Street scene and common brand names in Shanghai.

Sector	Likely outcome	Comments and reasoning
Agriculture	Farming will be hard hit	WTO membership will reduce import tariffs, permit trade, and cut subsidies on farm products. China's farms average only 0.1ha of land per farm worker, compared to 1.4 in the USA and 0.5 in Europe. Prices are higher than those on international markets. China cannot compete with the USA, Canada and Australia in trade in food at present. Some 900 million people make their livelihood from the rural economy, but 100 million of these are seasonally unemployed and could lose their jobs. Food technology and genetically modified crops could boost the efficiency of domestic production.
Oil and petrochemicals	Rapid growth	PetroChina, China's largest oil company, has had substantial investment from BP. US $3 billion has been invested by foreign companies in the second and third largest Chinese oil companies. Royal Dutch/Shell are investing in a US $4 billion petrochemical complex in which Shell has a majority stake. Exxon Mobil is planning to open 500 service stations.
Textiles and labour intensive industries such as toy making, shoe manufacturing	Likely to gain	Government restrictions on China's textile exports will end in 2005, after which textile exports will increase by 20 per cent and clothing 200 per cent. Supplies of cheap labour from the countryside will be inexhaustible in future, and make Chinese goods cheap for many years. However, the area is known for product piracy. The Rongguang rubber shoemaker in Ruian is a classic sweatshop. Started by local farmers in 1987, it produces 50 million pairs of trainers and casual shoes a year. The factory is packed with women hunched over old sewing machines and men handling hot rubber extruders. Other factories produce shoes with slightly altered Nike logos. Recent Hollywood movies are available on DVD in cassette stores for US $1.20. Shanghai authorities are trying to reduce piracy and to encourage companies to focus on quality. Shoemaker Aokang has built up a quality leather shoe company in China and hopes to sell abroad. With Italian machinery and a team of 60 designers, it is planning to increase sales and exports.
Automobiles	Could be the worst hit industrial sector	Tariffs on imported cars and parts (designed to protect the car industry) will be cut. Many factories are considered small and inefficient. Only 40 of the 136 domestic manufacturers are likely to remain in business, and four or five large manufacturers will dominate the market. As many as 20 per cent of the workforce in state-owned industries could be made redundant. Shanghai's old state-owned car factory produced 100 000 cars annually, each consuming 16 litres of petrol per 100km! A new plant jointly owned by VW and General Motors has an annual capacity of 250 000 cars, produced by one-sixth the number of workers, and each vehicle consumes 6 litres of fuel every 100km. After 2001, overseas competition means that car-makers will have to reduce costs by 10–15 per cent every year. Car parts may have to be bought from cheaper countries such as Malaysia, Thailand and Brazil.
Telecoms and Internet	Huge potential as the market opens up to foreigners	Foreign companies will be allowed to own up to 49 per cent of telecoms companies, and hold a 51 per cent interest in internet providers. Vodafone has a 2 per cent stake in China Mobile (of US $2.5 billion!), Hutchison in China Unicom, and China Telecom could offer a stake to a foreign investor.
Retail	Likely to expand	China is lifting restrictions on retailers, raising the prospect of competition for local stores, many of which are unused to competition. WalMart, which opened its first store in China in 1996, now has eight and is planning to expand. Carrefour, the French retailer, boasts 26 stores in fourteen cities. Metro, the German retailer, has ambitious expansion plans, as have all five of Japan's top retailers. Urban incomes are tempting. In 1998, urban incomes in Shanghai were ten times higher than rural, and increased 8.4 per cent in the first nine months of 2000.
Service economy	Rapid growth	The service sector increased from 20 per cent of Shanghai's economy in 1980 to 50 per cent in 1999. The transition has come from manufacturing. There were 500 000 female textile workers in 1980. Now, there are 160 000. Most have moved into service industries – restaurants and hotels.
Financial services	Expanding	Foreign insurance companies will be allowed in to operate in China, together with foreign banks. Local insurance companies will be vulnerable to competition.

Figure 21.3 How different economic activities will cope with exposure to trade with western economies.

Figure 21.4 Rural China – in for a rude awakening to western economics?

1 Study Figure 21.3. Make a copy of the table opposite and assess the costs and benefits to China of the changes that are likely to result from WTO membership. Add at least two other changes that you feel are likely to happen within China as 'westernisation' spreads.

2 Using three different highlighters, identify costs and benefits that are social, economic and environmental. What patterns do you notice?

3 Do you see the changes as beneficial for China or not?

4 'We're all the same now – there'll be nothing left soon but western culture'. How do you view the westernisation of China?

Sector	Costs	Benefits
Agriculture		
Oil and petrochemicals		
Textiles and industries such as toy and shoe manufacture		
Automobiles		
Telecoms and internet		
Retail		
Service economy		
Financial services		

The changing geography of technology and work

New technologies have made possible a huge growth in global communication. The widespread growth in MEDCs of ownership of personal computers (Figure 21.5) and use of the internet has led to an increase in demand for telephones (Figure 21.6). The UK has undergone two major number changes since 1994 to cope with demand for telephone lines, as companies expand communication networks and more people purchase computers and fax machines for use at home.

Although these have huge implications for social and home life, they also have an impact upon the ways in which people are now able to work. Home offices – used by parents and their children – are increasingly commonplace. For some, the opportunity to work at home is now part of their employer's policy. The British Airport Authority allows its staff car park permits for only four days per week at its company headquarters at Heathrow airport in London in response to demand for parking space and in the hope that staff will work from home one day a week.

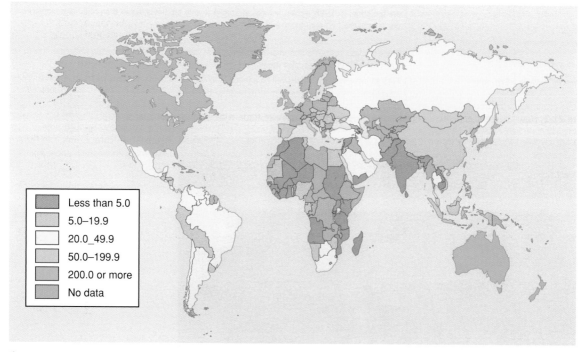

Less than 5.0
5.0–19.9
20.0_49.9
50.0–199.9
200.0 or more
No data

Figure 21.5 Global distribution of personal computer ownership, 1998.

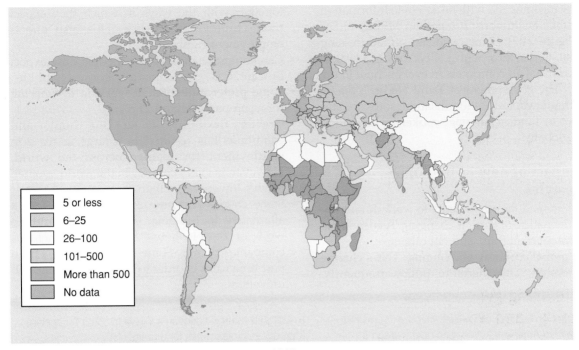

Figure 21.6 Global distribution of telephone main lines, 1998.

1 Describe the distribution of personal computers (Figure 21.5) and telephone lines (Figure 21.6). To what extent are the two related?

2 What are the advantages and disadvantages of working at home for **a)** employers, **b)** employees?

Changing technology – but for whom?

While communications technology has brought huge benefits for some, it has also exposed how many people are being left out of the revolution. The United Nations Development Programme in 1999 noted how there are increasing numbers of those who are marginalised – many living in rural areas, the elderly, women, people living in LEDCs

Figure 21.7 Internet users, 1998.

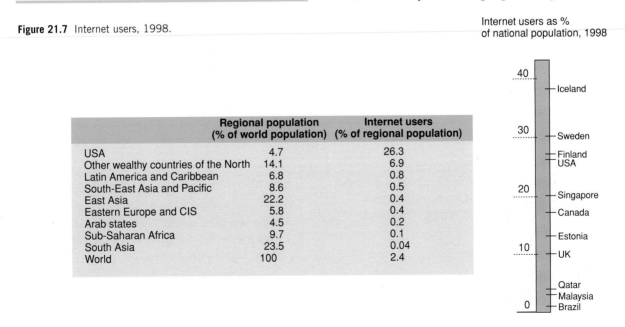

	Regional population (% of world population)	Internet users (% of regional population)
USA	4.7	26.3
Other wealthy countries of the North	14.1	6.9
Latin America and Caribbean	6.8	0.8
South-East Asia and Pacific	8.6	0.5
East Asia	22.2	0.4
Eastern Europe and CIS	5.8	0.4
Arab states	4.5	0.2
Sub-Saharan Africa	9.7	0.1
South Asia	23.5	0.04
World	100	2.4

with low incomes and with no access to information or to public institutions. It noted an MEDC–LEDC split (Figure 21.7). Some countries are addressing the issue. Costa Rica, with a GNP of US $2680 in 1997, has installed computers in every school in the country. The government of Tamil Nadu, India, is promoting keyboard standardisation, software and web sites in Tamil, a language spoken by 75 million people globally.

The impact of new technologies on lifestyles

Technology and the opportunity to work differently means the nature of work is changing. As usual, the arrangements suit some and not others.

- The global economy is changing. TNCs change ownership, and therefore policy, frequently, together with the ways in which they expect their employees to work. This also affects employment rights.
- Careers are changing. Few people now expect or want, and few companies offer, a 'job for life'.
- Some prefer independent working to working for a company (Figure 21.8).
- Greater flexibility in working hours and conditions has resulted in a large increase in employment for women across the world. However, in every country in the world, women receive lower wages than men.
- Some choose part-time or flexible work as an alternative to full-time. Others have part-time work or flexible hours forced upon them as companies change. Some – like students – fit in part-time work in order to pay their way through university.

a Mick set up as an IT consultant after leaving his last employer, an American software company based in London. He left because he was fed up with the corporate structure. The company used improvements in technology to set up teleconferences twice a week between London and the USA. To fit in with US times, these would occur at 4 p.m. on Monday and Friday, often lasting two to three hours. He got fed up with being late home, having to travel to the USA four or five times a year (sometimes for two or three days, arriving back in London at 6 a.m. and having to attend meetings at 9 a.m.). His US colleagues had ten days annual leave and resented the UK's signature to the EU Social Chapter that allowed four weeks leave as well as public holidays, paternity leave, etc. Now he works as a consultant, often for the same people that he used to work for! He is free to choose whom he works for and when, and can earn double the salary and holiday that he used to. Technology has allowed him to work independently; a laptop computer and mobile phone make him contactable and able to work anywhere in the world.

b ACP Television is based in a village in south Shropshire. It produces programmes for a range of TV companies, including the BBC (it produced 'Australia 2000' in 1999) and Channels 4 and 5, and also works for a number of companies who want, for example, marketing videos or promotion materials. Located 90 minutes' drive from Birmingham Airport or Birmingham International railway station, the director of the company, Sandra Keating, prefers to travel to London rather than live there. Technology has meant that she can work with a director or executive producer at a distance, thanks to fax and email. Regular meetings with clients usually take place in London or Birmingham.

Figure 21.8 Two examples of independent working.

1 How would the people in Figure 21.8 do their jobs differently without communications technology such as computers, email and mobile phones?

1 Study the data in Figures 21.9, 21.10 and 21.11

  a) Identify the issues shown in the data.

  b) Identify who benefits and who does not.

  c) France recently introduced a maximum 35-hour working week. What might be the arguments for a shorter working week? Are there arguments against it?

How long shall we work in future?

However, working practice often counters any benefits offered by changing laws and technologies. In the late 1990s:

- only 5 per cent of men in the EU took paternity leave on offer
- in Austria, women made up 98 per cent of part-time employees
- in Germany, a third of women worked less than 35 hours per week compared with only 2 per cent of men.

Working hours vary by country, but do not produce GNP in relation to effort. With a per capita GNP of US $34 890, Danish workers worked the hours shown in Figure 21.9. UK workers worked the hours shown in Figure 21.10, yet GNP was 40 per cent less at US $20 870. Neither does the length of the working day bear any relation to GNP in LEDCs; there, too, it does not favour those who work the longest hours. Figure 21.11 shows how the issue of working hours is gender-related.

	% of the working population in work		
	< 30 hours	30–39 hours	40 or more
Men	5	65	30
Women	20	69	11

Figure 21.9 Working hours per week in Denmark.

Managers and administrators	46.4
Professional and technical	44.3
Clerical and secretarial	39.6
Craft and related	44.3
Personal and protective services	42.5
Sales	42.3
Plant and machine operative	45.1
All occupations	43.8

Figure 21.10 Hours per week worked by occupational groups in the UK, 1999.

	Formal sector workers		Informal sector workers	
	Men	Women	Men	Women
Unpaid work	14	31	14	24
Paid work	53	56	23	21
Total	67	87	37	45

Figure 21.11 Time spent in paid and unpaid work in Bangladesh in 1995, in hours per week.

Summary

You have learned that:

- The expansion of the Chinese economy is likely to have a major impact upon the global economy during the early part of the twenty-first century.
- Some of the expansion will have positive effects on China and on other places, but others will be negative.
- Changing communications technology is altering the ways in which many people work, with some working at home, or independently.
- Working hours in MEDCs increasingly fit in with employers' ideas of a 'flexible' workforce. Such hours are often long and do not result in higher GNP.
- The communications and employment revolutions have not necessarily closed the 'gender gap', where women are paid less than men for longer or more unsocial hours.

References and further reading

United Nations Development Programme, *Human Development Report*, published annually. The best ones are:

1998 – which dealt with consumerism
1999 – which dealt with globalisation
2000 – which dealt with human rights

World Bank, *Word Bank Atlas 2000*

Web sites

The expansion of the Chinese economy is dealt with best by the *Financial Times* web page: http://news.ft.com/news/worldnews/asiapacific

Resolving the development gap

This section has shown how the development gap is widening between rich and poor, and how increasingly the global economy is controlled by large trade blocs or by TNCs. This chapter shows how the gap could be narrowed by a number of strategies such as debt rescheduling or abolition.

Resolving the debt crisis

The debt crisis concerns the amount of borrowing that a country holds, in relation to its ability to repay. The problem lies chiefly within the poorest LEDCs. It is referred to as the 'debt crisis' because LEDCs are unable to meet repayments. It is not a problem confined to LEDCs; in 1990, the external debt of the USA equalled the entire debt of LEDCs (US $1.34 trillion). By 2000, the combined debt of the 40 most-indebted nations alone (Figure 22.1) had reached US $212.6 billion.

Now there is increasing call for debt payments to be written off. Riots in Seattle in the USA in 1999 resulted in damage to commercial property (Figure 22.2) as those angered by the government's refusal to cancel debt protested on the streets. Because banks loaned the money, they are keen to see it returned for commercial reasons. Thus governments are likely to have to pay compensation. The UK government made £1 billion available in 2000 to cancel debt interest payments from those countries worst affected by the crisis.

Country	Total debt (US$ billion)	Country	Total debt (US$ billion)
Angola	12.2	Malawi	2.4
Benin	1.6	Mali	3.2
Bolivia	6.1	Mauritania	2.6
Burkina Faso	1.4	Mozambique	8.2
Burundi	1.1	Myanmar (Burma)	5.7
Cameroon	9.8	Nicaragua	6.0
Central African Republic	0.9	Niger	1.6
Chad	1.1	Rwanda	1.2
Congo Democratic Republic	13.0	São Tomé and Príncipe	0.2
Congo Republic	5.1	Senegal	3.9
Ethiopia	10.3	Sierra Leone	1.2
Ghana	5.9	Somalia	2.6
Guinea	3.4	Sudan	16.8
Guinea-Bissau	0.9	Tanzania	7.6
Guyana	1.6	Togo	1.4
Honduras	5.0	Uganda	3.9
Ivory Coast	14.8	Vietnam	22.3
Kenya	7.0	Yemen	4.1
Lao PDR	2.4	Zambia	6.9
Liberia	2.1		
Madagascar	4.4	**Total**	**212.6**

Figure 22.1 The most indebted nations.

Figure 22.2 Seattle in 1999 as those angered by global debt protested on the streets.

Structural Adjustment Programmes (SAPs) and debt rescheduling

The term 'structural adjustment' is used to describe a set of policies imposed in the 1980s by the International Monetary Fund (IMF) and the World Bank upon countries with severe debt as a condition for receiving new (or re-scheduling old) loans. LEDC governments are forced to reduce expenditure in order to prevent further borrowing to pay off their debts.

The World Bank and IMF argue that SAPs are necessary to bring debt-ridden countries out of crisis into economic recovery and growth. Economic growth driven by private sector foreign investment is seen as the key to development. These agencies argue that the resulting national wealth will eventually 'trickle down' or spread throughout the economy to the poor.

SAPs are designed to:

- reschedule a country's loans in order to make them more realistic
- improve investment potential from overseas by getting rid of trade and investment regulations
- boost foreign exchange earnings by promoting exports
- reduce government deficits through cuts in spending.

The other view of SAPs is shown in Figure 22.3. Although SAPs differ from country to country, they typically include:

- a shift from food crops for domestic consumption to the production of cash crops or commodities for export (for example vegetables for export from Kenya to the UK)
- abolition of food and agricultural subsidies to reduce government expenditure
- cuts in social programmes such as health and education
- privatisation of government enterprises in order to cut government expenditure.

Why have SAPs been criticised?

Some say that SAPs make debt economies efficient and competitive. But there is another side. SAPs force cuts in spending on education and the poor. Five countries - the USA, Japan, Germany, France, and the UK control 40% of votes in the IMF and World Bank - and many argue that these countries protect their own interests. When SAPs force privatisation of state businesses, many assets are purchased by large TNCs in these five countries.

Environmentally, SAPs require greater export volumes to pay off debts. The most important exports of LEDCs include timber, oil and gas, minerals, and cash crops, which causes deforestation, land degradation, desertification, soil erosion, increased production of greenhouse gases, and air and water pollution. Even then, some countries remain unable to pay debts or compete in global markets.

1 What do you see as the strengths and weaknesses of SAPs?

2 How would you convince a doubtful politician of the arguments for cancelling debts from the poorest LEDCs?

3 In recent years, the World Bank has become sensitive to criticisms of the effects it has had in the past upon issues in LEDCs. What suggestions could be made about altering the structure of the World Bank or its policies concerning SAPs?

Top-down development – the Mekong basin

This case study looks at a major project to dam the basin of the Mekong, one of South-East Asia's most important rivers and the world's twelfth longest. The river flows for 4200km from its source in China through Myanmar (formerly Burma), Lao People's Democratic Republic (PDR) for which it forms the border, Cambodia and Thailand to the delta in southern Vietnam (Figure 22.5). Its importance varies with each of the countries through which it passes. The scheme involves the construction of several dams, some of which have already been built and have met with much controversy from within the countries through which the Mekong passes (Figure 22.5). Finance is from the Asia Development Bank in conjunction with the governments of each of the countries. Although much effort has been made to

Figure 22.3 Virtuous reality.

Two approaches to economic development

'Top-down' development

The central model for the major part of the world's economy is capitalism. Most countries assume that individuals create wealth. Those with capital, willing to risk investment, are known as 'entrepreneurs'; they create wealth by investing in products or services which are sold. Economic expansion leads to greater employment, and wealth 'trickles down' to other members of society. Theorists such as Milton Friedman developed this model in the 1960s. Much economic development is founded on this model through loans and aid. MEDCs, particularly the USA, Japan and the EU countries, adhere to it strongly. They believe that the purpose of investment is to encourage economic development to take place where it is best able to do so, and that the people who know best where to invest are the entrepreneurs.

Budget items	Core to periphery 'trickle down'	Periphery to core 'bottom up'
Subsidies	6% of GDP	18% of GDP
Public sector wages	2.4% of GDP	4% of GDP
Social spending	8% of government budget budget	56% of government budget
Capital spending	16% of government budget	6% of government budget
Total government spending	26% of GDP (all Less Developed Countries)	29% of GDP
Budget deficits	4.8% (excluding India & China)	5.1%

Figure 22.4 Two approaches to ineqaulities.

Those who criticise the traditional 'trickle-down' model believe that those who are poorest remain the poorest unless action is taken. They claim that wealth does not 'trickle down', but relocates. A company or individual with capital to invest will search globally for a location in which highest returns are available. In the 1980s, much capital from the UK found its way not into the poorer peripheries of the UK, Europe or LEDCs, but into the NICs of South-East Asia, where expansion led to the creation of a new economic core (see page 213).

'Bottom-up' development

'Bottom-up' approaches reverse much of the 'top-down' approach, and are based on the assumption that those who know best about development are local people with skills and knowledge. What they lack is investment to help them develop. This approach involves working alongside disadvantaged people, rather than telling them what they should do – a criticism often made of 'trickle-down' approaches. It involves using local initiative and giving power to local people to plan and make decisions. The purpose of investment is to improve the lives of the disadvantaged and encourage economic development where it is needed. The work of NGOs is typical of this approach and includes projects carried out by development agencies and charities such as Christian Aid, Oxfam and ActionAid.

address issues raised by the project, it is still imposed on people from above, hence it is a 'top-down' model. Like most top-down schemes, it is a capital-intensive project with contrasting benefits.

The potential economic benefits of the dam building scheme are enormous. However, there is opposition to the scheme within and between the countries involved. One of the issues is that of silt. Rivers transport and deposit sediment which naturally creates problems when dams are built, particularly for those below the dam.

- Silt carried by the river collects behind the dam walls. The reservoir eventually silts up as there is no economic way of dredging out sediment.
- Water emerging from dams carries little or no sediment. This increases river energy which results in accelerated channel erosion downstream and prevents silt from reaching agricultural areas. Farmers therefore lose the means by which soils are replenished each year.
- Regulation of water flow behind the dams will reduce the flood level downstream. Farmers depending upon the flood for rice planting will suffer, and soils in the Mekong delta will gradually become more saline.
- Farmers whose land is submerged by the new dams lose their best-quality soils. With large numbers of people relocating and much farmland submerged, new land must be found. This is likely to lead to deforestation, which will result in increased soil erosion rates and more rapid siltation of the reservoir.

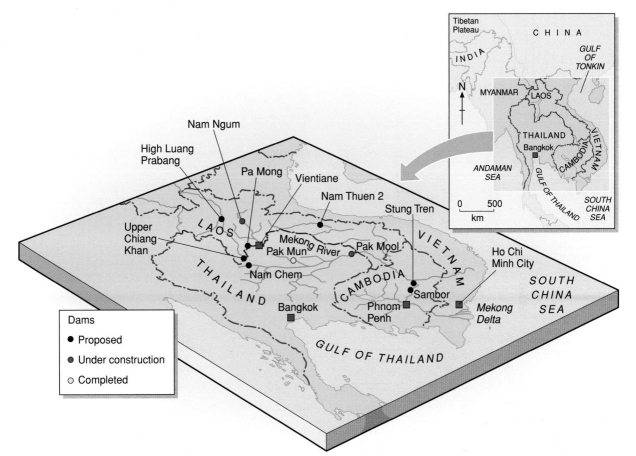

Figure 22.5 The location of the Mekong River in South-East Asia and the proposals to dam the river.

Country	Significance of the Mekong	Country	Significance of the Mekong
China	Roughly half the length of the Mekong passes through China. The upper basin is mountainous and inaccessible, but the southern part is one of the poorest areas of China and the government would like to dam the river to produce HEP for economic development. To do so would interrupt the flow of water downstream. This is consistent with China's policy of damming major rivers, for example the Yangtze.	Thailand	Only 36 per cent of Thailand's territory is within the Mekong basin, but the area is Thailand's poorest. Thailand would like to use the water to power industrial development. Rural–urban migration is a major problem in Thailand, as Bangkok dominates the country's economy. The Thai government would like to invest in rural areas to offer economic opportunities and stem the flow of migrants to the cities. This could include the building of dams, though any dams upstream would affect this.
Myanmar (formerly Burma)	Least affected by the flow of the Mekong, Myanmar contains several tributaries but none from upstream that would be affected by China's proposals. There are no major plans to build dams as yet, but any that might be built would have an impact on the flow downstream.	Cambodia	Nearly all of Cambodia is in the Mekong basin. It depends upon the flow of the river for the annual flooding of the Tonle Sap lake area (Figure 22.8) which deposits silt locally in which farmers plant rice. The poverty of the country's energy sources has resulted in rapid depletion of timber for firewood; an energy scheme to develop HEP would be welcomed. However, the displacement of people away from fertile land would be a problem here as elsewhere in the Mekong basin.
Lao PDR	One of the world's poorest countries, 90 per cent of the population of Lao PDR is dependent upon water from the Mekong and on agriculture that derives from it. Most water comes from tributaries of the Mekong within Lao, so upstream development affects it very little. However, Lao is constructing a dam for HEP, flood control, tourism and fisheries at Nam Ngum (Figure 22.5) which is likely to affect downstream flow.	Vietnam	At Phnom Penh, the Mekong forks into two distributaries to form the Mekong Delta. Triangular in shape, the delta forms a fertile area of 50 000km^2 that supports 40 per cent of the population (Figure 22.7). Annual floods deposit silt in which rice is grown and flush out salts that accumulate in soils during periods of low river flow in the dry season. Any damming of the Mekong upstream would reduce river flow in the monsoon and increase soil salinity.

Figure 22.6 The countries through which the Mekong River passes.

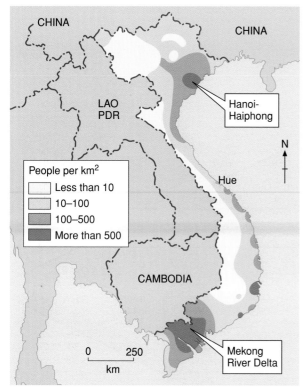

Figure 22.7 Population distribution in Vietnam, showing the importance of the Mekong.

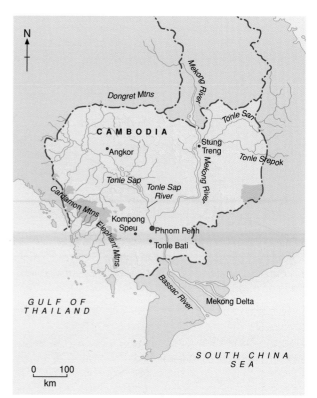

Figure 22.8 Tonle Sap and the lower Mekong basin.

1 Of the six countries in Figure 22.6, which would you say has the greatest ability to affect all the other countries? Why?

2 Which countries seem to want most from the scheme? Which want least? Construct a conflict matrix to show whether each country's objectives are feasible without conflict, and why.

3 The governments of each country are trying to work together. Decide in groups how key conflicts might be managed.

4 Should the scheme be allowed to go ahead?

Bottom-up approaches to development

Vietnam is one of the world's poorest countries, although it has made rapid progress in terms of human welfare. Women are poorer than men and hold lower status than men in Vietnamese society. They form 52 per cent of the workforce, and nearly three-quarters live in rural areas. Credit is traditionally limited for women; banks do not locate in the poorest and most remote areas in which those most in need of assistance live. The poorest women borrow from private moneylenders whose interest rates alone may be between 7 and 20 per cent per month.

CIDSE, a group of Catholic development agencies, began a development plan in Vietnam in the 1970s. In 1992, it began a credit and savings programme targeted at the poorest people in Ho Chi Minh City, which has since spread. Its objectives are:
• providing affordable credit to the poor through income-generating activities, as an alternative to moneylenders
• helping to tackle high unemployment rates
• helping to organise people into self-supporting groups.

It focuses upon small loans to poor women who support each other in groups. By 1996, it had loaned over US $250 000 to 6700 people across the country. Most importantly, the repayment rates exceed 95 per cent.

In 1993, CIDSE's Credit and Savings project reached Phan Thi Sao's area. One of the members came to explain it to her and to encourage her to join. Sao liked the programme because it encouraged people to save as well as to borrow. In June 1993, she received 400 000d [dong – the Vietnamese currency] as her first loan. She used some of this to buy a glass cabinet and cigarettes to sell with fruit. She used the rest to pay her children's school fees. Selling cigarettes, she could earn 10 000d to 11 000d per day. Her husband tried to earn about 15 000d each day. So their daily earnings increased to about 25 000d. She saved 5000d for repaying loans; the rest was spent on family needs. Every month she could save 80 000d for herself. After the first loan, she could afford to buy a bicycle for two children to ride to school. The balance of about 100 000d was used by her husband to repair and maintain his cyclo [bicycle taxi] and eventually to repay the loan.

The second loan came and, because of her good repayment, her loan was increased to 600 000d. She began another income-generating activity – ball sewing. In the evening after finishing the business in the afternoon, all family members ball-sewed. Every day they could finish two balls and they could get 7000d more. Every month they could save about 200 000d more. From this, she bought a fan for her children and new clothes for the family, costing about 200 000d.

Figure 22.9 The story of Phan Thi Sao.

1 Identify the benefits from Phan Thi Sao's loan. How far does this represent good value for money?

2 What are the key differences between this approach and top-down approaches?

3 How far do you think that CIDSE's work represents a good model for development?

Figure 22.10 Income into Phan Thi Sao's family **a** before the loan, **b** after the loan.

a

Monthly income of the family	
Husband: 13 000d/day x 30 days	390 000d
Wife: 7000d/day x 30 days	210 000d
Total	**600 000d**

Monthly expenditure of the family	
Rice: 45kg (2000d x 45)	90 000d
Food: three meals (8000d/day x 30 days)	240 000d
Salt, sugar, wood, glutamate	60 000d
Monthly house rental	45 000d
School fees (two daughters)	20 000d
Cyclo rent: 2000d x 30 days	60 000d
Water, electricity	30 000d
Other	30 000d
Total	**575 000d**
Balance	**25 000d**

b

Monthly income of the family	
Husband: 15 000d/day x 30 days	450 000d
Wife: 10 000d/day x 30 days	300 000d
Total	**750 000d**

Monthly expenditure of the family	
Rice	90 000d
Food: 10 000d/day x 30 days	300 000d
Salt, sugar, wood, glutamate	60 000d
Monthly house rental	45 000d
School fees	20 000d
Electricity, water	35 000d
Repayment: 5000d/day x 30 days	150 000d
Other	30 000d
Total	**730 000d**
Balance	**20 000d**

Summary

You have learned that:

- The debt crisis is a major factor in maintaining the development gap and in stifling further economic and social development in the poorest countries.
- Structural Adjustment Plans have largely served to further the interests of MEDCs rather than LEDCs, through loan rescheduling and privatisation of government property.
- 'Top-down' and 'bottom-up' models of development represent different viewpoints on how development should take place and whose needs are greatest. Top-down development schemes tend to be capital-intensive projects that bring conflicting benefits. Bottom-up development tends to focus more upon the poorest people.

References and further reading

Robert Chambers, *Challenging the Professionals*, IT Publications, London (1993)

Bob Digby and Graham Yates, *Global and Regional Disparities*, Heinemann Global Futures Pack B (1997)

Victoria Johnson *et al*, *Listening to smaller voices*, ActionAid, Chard (1995)

New Internationalist, March 1999 and May 1999

Colm Regan, *Armed with confidence*, CIDSE CLV programme (1996)

UNICEF *Viet Nam: Children and Women* (1994)

Web sites

ActionAid page on the internet:
http://www.oneworld.org/ActionAid

Films

Cyclo – a Vietnamese film about a young man earning a living on a cyclo and some of the issues of living in the poorest parts of urban Vietnam

The changing global economy: summary

Enquiry questions	Key ideas and concepts	Guidance and possible examples
The global economy What are the main global economic groupings? What links exist between the groupings? What are the factors encouraging a global economy?	• Definitions and characteristics of MEDC/NIC/LEDC. Concept of First, Second and Third Worlds. Development of trade blocs. • The current pattern of economic wealth. The concept of the North-South divide and the development gap. • The impact of uneven distribution of wealth on flows of trade, technology, food resources, investment, aid and people. • Concept of global interdependence. • Definition of globalisation. Role of transport, the information and communications revolution.	• Chapter 16 The North–South divide and the development gap. Defining development as a continuum, with its key characteristics. The influence of colonialism and evolution of trade blocs (e.g. EU and NAFTA) in creating the Third World. The rise of NICs such as those in South-East Asia. • Chapter 17 The banana trade – LEDC dependence on primary products and the hold that TNCs have on them. Flows of trade take food products such as bananas to MEDCs. Global interdependence – who wins and who loses from trade flows. Trade organisations (e.g. the WTO) that benefit MEDCs and their effects upon people and the environment. The emergence of Fairtrade as a model for the future.
Globalisation and changing economic activity What changes are taking place in the character and location of the global economy? Who are the key players in changing the location of economic activity? What are the implications of the changes in economic activity?	• The global shift and relocation of industry. • The changes within sectors – the decline of manufacturing relative to the rise of the service industry. Relate to theory – Clarke model. • The role of TNCs. Reasons for development. Implications of TNCs for global organisation of production and employment. • The role of governments in provision of incentives for inward investment. • The impact of globalisation and the global shift on countries at different stages of development.	• Chapter 18 Growth and changing economic activity in Taiwan. Reasons for growth and its impact on people, the economy and the environment. • Chapter 19 Study of TNC operations and impact. Mattel and its growth and development – mergers, consolidation and conglomeration. Global consumption patterns in MEDCs and how LEDCs supply goods for these. Emergence of green consumerism (e.g. non-pollutant products) and social consciences in issues such as child labour. • Chapter 20 The change from manufacturing to service over time. How the changing global economy has affected one region – the West Midlands. The changing nature of the car industry and its impact on employment.
Economic futures **Either** How might the global economy change in the future? **Or** How might the development gap be addressed?	• The expanding global economy; spatial distribution of new markets, products and services. The impact of new technologies on lifestyles. • Trade patterns, alliances and reforms. • Aid versus loans; the reassessment of Third World debt.	• Chapter 21 a) Economic expansion in China – the next tiger? b) The changing nature of work; flexible working and telecommunications in one country. Relocation to rural areas and flexible or independent working. Geographical issues related to the workplace (e.g. rising hours for some v. the semi-permanent unemployed; age and gender issues) • Chapter 22 Ways of addressing the debt crisis. Structural adjustment or debt abolition? The case for debt write-offs. Top-down v. bottom-up approaches to development in one country – the role of NGOs in approaching poverty (e.g. CIDSE).

Index

Page numbers in *italics* refer to Theory or Technique boxes